POLITICS AND LITERATURE
IN THE AGE OF SWIFT

Jonathan Swift was the most influential political commentator of
his time, in both England and Ireland. His writings are a major
source for historians of the eighteenth century, as well as including
some of the greatest works of satire in verse and prose. This volume
presents wide-ranging new perspectives on Swift's literary and political achievement in its English and Irish contexts, bringing together
some of the most energetic current scholarship on the subject in both
historical and literary studies. The essays consider Swift's attitude
to Dissenters, his relationship with Walpole, and his place in, and
understanding of, the political demography of colonial Ireland.
They also examine Swift's poems and pamphlets, and his hoaxes
and satires, showing his extraordinary versatility in a wide variety of
genres. There is a special emphasis on his political and personal
poetry, sometimes undeservedly overshadowed by the towering stature of his better-known prose masterpieces, *A Tale of a Tub* and
Gulliver's Travels. Full of original insights, this volume offers a rich
and important new treatment of Swift's central role in eighteenth-
century political and literary culture.

CLAUDE RAWSON is the Maynard Mack Professor of English at
Yale University. One of the most distinguished eighteenth-century
scholars working today, he has published widely on Swift, Fielding,
Boswell and many other authors and topics. He is Founding General
Editor of *The Cambridge History of Literary Criticism* and General
Editor of *The Cambridge Edition of the Works of Jonathan Swift*.

POLITICS AND LITERATURE IN THE AGE OF SWIFT: ENGLISH AND IRISH PERSPECTIVES

EDITED BY

CLAUDE RAWSON

CAMBRIDGE
UNIVERSITY PRESS

CAMBRIDGE UNIVERSITY PRESS
Cambridge, New York, Melbourne, Madrid, Cape Town, Singapore,
São Paulo, Delhi, Dubai, Tokyo

Cambridge University Press
The Edinburgh Building, Cambridge CB2 8RU, UK

Published in the United States of America by Cambridge University Press, New York

www.cambridge.org
Information on this title: www.cambridge.org/9780521190152

First published 2010

Printed in the United Kingdom at the University Press, Cambridge

A catalogue record for this publication is available from the British Library

Library of Congress Cataloging-in-Publication Data
Politics and literature in the age of Swift : English and Irish perspectives /
edited by Claude Rawson.
p.   cm.
Includes bibliographical references and index.
ISBN 978-0-521-19015-2 (Hardback)
1. Swift, Jonathan, 1667–1745–Political and social views.   2. Politics and literature–
England–History–18th century.   3. Politics and literature–Ireland–History–18th century.
I. Rawson, Claude Julien.   II. Title.
PR3728.P6P65 2010
828′.509–dc22

2010003267

ISBN 978-0-521-19015-2 Hardback

Contents

List of illustrations   *page* vii
List of contributors   ix
Preface   xi
List of abbreviations   xiii

PART I   THE POLITICAL SWIFT I (ENGLAND)

1   Jonathan Swift's political confession   3
    Ian Higgins

2   Situating Swift's politics in 1701   31
    Mark Goldie

3   Swift and Walpole   52
    Paul Langford

PART II   THE WRITER AND HIS WORLD

4   Burying the fanatic Partridge: Swift's Holy Week hoax   81
    Valerie Rumbold

5   Swift and the art of political publication: hints
    and title pages, 1711–1714   116
    James McLaverty

6   Swift's poetics of friendship   140
    Helen Deutsch

7   'now deaf 1740'
    Entrapment, foreboding, and exorcism in late Swift   162
    David Womersley

v

8   Savage indignation revisited: Swift, Yeats, and the 'cry'
    of liberty   185
    Claude Rawson

PART III   THE POLITICAL SWIFT 2 (IRELAND)

9   'Paltry underlings of state'? The character and aspirations
    of the 'Castle' party, 1715–1732   221
    D. W. Hayton

10 Old English, New English and ancient Irish: Swift
    and the Irish past   255
    S. J. Connolly

11 Jonathan Swift and the Irish colonial project   270
    Robert Mahony

Index   290

Illustrations

1 *A hue and cry after Dismal.* Reproduction courtesy of
the Syndics of Cambridge University Library.   *page* 122

2 *It's out at last: or, French correspondence clear as the sun.*   126

3 *Some advice humbly offer'd to the members of the October
Club.* Title page of the second edition: NLS, L.C.3339(6).
Reproduction courtesy of the Trustees of the National
Library of Scotland.   128

4 *The new way of selling places at court.* Title-page: CUL,
7540.d.45 (8). Reproduction courtesy of the Syndics
of Cambridge University Library.   130

5 *Some reasons to prove, that no person is obliged by his
principles, as a Whig, to oppose Her Majesty or her present
ministry.* Title-page. Reproduction courtesy of the Syndics
of Cambridge University Library.   131

6 *The importance of the Guardian considered.* Title page.
Reproduction courtesy of the Syndics of Cambridge
University Library.   133

7 *The conduct of the Allies.* Title page of the fourth edition.
Reproduction courtesy of the Syndics of Cambridge
University Library.   135

8 Annotated page from Swift's own copy of *Miscellanies*,
by kind permission of the Master and Fellows of Trinity
College, Cambridge.   164

9 Swift's epitaph in St Patrick's Cathedral, Dublin.   186

Contributors

s.j. CONNOLLY is Professor of Irish History at Queen's University, Belfast. His most recent books are *Contested Island: Ireland 1460–1630* (2007) and *Divided Kingdom: Ireland 1630–1800* (2008). He was General Editor of the *Oxford Companion to Irish History* (1998) and is also Joint Editor of the journal *Irish Economic and Social History*.

HELEN DEUTSCH is Professor of English at UCLA, and the author of *Resemblance and Disgrace: Alexander Pope and the Deformation of Culture* (1996) and *Loving Dr Johnson* (2008). She is currently working on two related projects: a collection of essays on eighteenth-century lyric form and a book on the literary afterlife of Jonathan Swift.

MARK GOLDIE is Reader in British Intellectual History at the University of Cambridge, and a Fellow of Churchill College. He has published extensively in the field of political, religious, and intellectual history in the period 1650–1750, including editing or co-editing two volumes in the Cambridge History of Political Thought series and various of Locke's political writings.

D. W. HAYTON is Professor of Early Modern Irish and British History and Head of the School of History and Anthropology at Queen's University, Belfast. He has published widely on the political history of Ireland and Britain in the early eighteenth century. He wrote the Introductory Survey for the 1690–1715 volumes of the *History of Parliament* (Cambridge University Press, 2002), and a collection of his papers on Irish political history appeared in 2004, entitled *Ruling Ireland, 1685–1742: Politics, Politicians and Parties*. He was elected a member of the Royal Irish Academy in 2008.

DR IAN HIGGINS is Reader in English at the Australian National University. He is the author of *Swift's Politics: A Study in Disaffection* (1994) and *Jonathan Swift* (2004), and of many articles on Swift and his contexts. He is an editor (with Claude Rawson) of *Gulliver's Travels* (2005) and is one of the general editors of the Cambridge Edition of the Works of Jonathan Swift.

PAUL LANGFORD, FBA, is Professor of Modern History in Oxford University, and Rector of Lincoln College, Oxford. He is General Editor of *The Writings and Speeches of Edmund Burke*, 1981–, eight volumes completed, and is Chairman of the History of Parliament Editorial Board. He is author of numerous books and articles, largely on Britain in the eighteenth century. They include *The Excise Crisis: Society and Politics in the Age of Walpole* (1975); *Public Life and the Propertied Englishman, 1689–1769* (1991); *A Polite and Commercial People: England 1727–1783* (1989); and *Englishness Identified: Manners and Character, 1650–1850* (2000).

ROBERT MAHONY is the author of *Jonathan Swift: The Irish Identity* (1995) and numerous articles on Swift's Irish writings. He retired as Professor of English from The Catholic University of America in 2008, where he also founded the Center for Irish Studies.

JAMES MCLAVERTY is Emeritus Professor of Textual Criticism at Keele University. He is the author of *Pope, Print, and Meaning* (2001) and textual adviser to the Cambridge Edition of the Works of Jonathan Swift.

CLAUDE RAWSON is the Maynard Mack Professor of English at Yale University, and a general editor of the Cambridge Edition of the Works of Jonathan Swift. His books include *Gulliver and the Gentle Reader: Studies in Swift and our Time* (1973); *Satire and Sentiment 1660–1830* (Cambridge University Press, 1994); and *God, Gulliver, and Genocide: Barbarism and the European Imagination, 1492–1945* (2001).

VALERIE RUMBOLD is Reader in English Literature at the University of Birmingham. She is the author of *Women's Place in Pope's World* (1989), and editor of *Alexander Pope: The Dunciad in Four Books* (1999) and of volume III of *The Poems of Alexander Pope*, containing the *Dunciad* in its 1728 and 1729 versions (2007). She is currently preparing a volume for the Cambridge Edition of the Works of Jonathan Swift, to include the Bickerstaff papers, *Polite Conversation* and *Directions to Servants*.

DAVID WOMERSLEY is the Thomas Warton Professor of English Literature at the University of Oxford and a Fellow of St Catherine's College. His recent publications include *Gibbon and the Watchmen of the Holy City: The Historian and his Reputation, 1776–1815* (2002) and an edition of James Boswell's *Life of Johnson* (2008). His edition of *Gulliver's Travels* in the Cambridge Edition of the Works of Jonathan Swift is in press.

Preface

This volume seeks to present a wide-ranging perspective on Swift's literary and political achievement in its English and Irish contexts. It brings together some of the most energetic scholarship in the subject in both historical and literary studies. The first and third sections deal directly with political ideas, events and relationships in England and Ireland. These include the large questions of Swift's attitude to Dissenters, his relationship with Walpole, and his place in, and understanding of, the political demography of colonial Ireland, as well as the important particularised topics of the Kentish Petition and Conolly's speakership of the Irish House of Commons.

The middle section, on 'The writer and his world', shows Swift in a more direct writerly mode. This includes the hoaxing, which is one of Swift's unsung gifts, culminating in *Gulliver's Travels* but beginning in a richly political April Fool's caper in 1708. It also includes the typographical strategies Swift exploited in his political pamphleteering of 1711–14, examined in a particularly fine example of the application of bibliographical studies to literary understanding. The largest part of this section concerns the poems, a deliberate emphasis designed to draw attention to Swift's distinction as a poet, still somewhat occluded by that of his friend Pope, and also by Swift's own towering reputation as the greatest of prose satirists. Swift's achievement as a poet has perhaps been more wholeheartedly celebrated by poets (from Byron and Yeats to Eliot, Auden, and Geoffrey Hill) than by critics, although critical and academic recognition in recent decades has been considerable. The poems studied here belong to the 1720s and 1730s, his greatest period both as a poet and as an activist in Irish politics. The third section begins with a close study of the 'Castle' party in the Irish Parliament, which often came within the range of Swift's fire in the writings of this period.

In planning this volume, I have avoided topics specifically dedicated to familiar major works already much discussed in their own right. *A Tale of a Tub, Gulliver's Travels,* and *A Modest Proposal* have been left to find their natural place within the various political and literary contexts provided by the individual contributors. The volume is closely associated with the Cambridge Edition of the Works of Jonathan Swift. Many of the contributors are editors or general editors, or serve on the advisory board. The volume could not have been undertaken without the support of Linda Bree, Publisher, Literature at Cambridge University Press, and Robert C. Ritchie, Director of Research at the Huntington Library, whose distinguished institution provided a setting for a conference, on 14–15 March 2008, at which early versions of these papers were delivered. I also owe thanks to all the contributors for their exemplary cooperation. The final preparation of this volume owes everything to the dedication and expertise of my assistant, Cynthia Ingram.

Abbreviations

Complete Poems	*Complete Poems*. Edited by Pat Rogers. Harmondsworth: Penguin, and New Haven: Yale, 1983.
Correspondence	*Correspondence*. Edited by David Woolley, 4 vols. Frankfurt: Peter Lang, 1999–2007.
Ehrenpreis	Irvin Ehrenpreis. *Swift: The Man, His Works, and the Age*. Vol. I: *Mr. Swift and His Contemporaries*. London: Methuen, 1962. Vol. II: *Dr. Swift*. London: Methuen, 1967. Vol. III: *Dean Swift*. London: Methuen, 1983.
JSt.	*Journal to Stella*. Edited by Harold Williams, 2 vols. Oxford: Clarendon Press, 1948.
ODNB	*Oxford Dictionary of National Biography*. Edited by H. C. G. Matthew *et al.*, 60 vols. Oxford University Press 2004. Online version at www.oxforddnb.com.
Poems	*Poems*. Edited by Harold Williams, 3 vols. 2nd edn. Oxford: Clarendon Press, 1958.
PW	*Prose Writings*. Edited by Herbert Davis *et al.*, 16 vols. Oxford: Blackwell, 1939–74.

PART I

The political Swift I (England)

CHAPTER I

Jonathan Swift's political confession

Ian Higgins

Jonathan Swift claimed a place for himself in the history of political thought. In April 1726 Swift was in London. He had an unproductive private meeting with King George's first minister, Sir Robert Walpole, on 'the affairs of Ireland'. After the meeting Swift reported that he could not reconcile Walpole's opinions on Ireland with 'the notions I had of Liberty'.[1] Writing to a Whig official in Dublin Castle later that summer, Swift declared that he was weary of being among Whig ministers 'who are all Rank Toryes in Government, and worse than Whigs in Church: whereas I was the first Man who taught and practiced the direct contrary Principle'.[2] The subject of this chapter is Swift as rank Tory in Church affairs and worse than Whig in affairs of state. It considers Swift's political self-portrait in relation to his Irish biography. The chapter examines his polemical reading and invective on the subject of Scots Presbyterianism, and the inflection this Church Tory gives to whiggish political language. This essay sees religious confession as central to the political extremism of Swift's reactive and insurgent writing. Swift's contemporaries did not divorce the priest from the political satirist, and this essay attends seriously to the anticlerical Whig Anthony Collins's imputation of Swift's place in a royalist and High Church polemical tradition of violent ironical invective.

Walpole's apparently imperious treatment of Swift at their private meeting prompted Swift to meditate revenge. In February 1727 he told his Hanoverian court contact, Henrietta Howard, to tell Walpole 'that if he does not use me better next Summer than he did the last, I will study revenge, and it shall be *vengeance Ecclesiastique*'.[3] Swift's *vengeance Ecclesiastique* perhaps recalls Bartolomeo Platina, whose *Vitae Pontificum* took vengeance on Pope Paul II for imprisoning him and depriving him of his offices.[4] Swift executed his threat in 'An Account of the Court and Empire of Japan' (written in 1728), a thinly disguised allegory satirizing George I and Walpole. The Hanoverian King 'although of the royal family, was a distant relation', and he is said to have caused the Jacobite

3

rebellion of 1715 by his proscription of the Tories. The character assassination of Walpole in the work focuses on his systemic bribery and corruption which would turn George II into Walpole's client.[5] This dangerously specific satire on the Hanoverian–Walpolean regime is incomplete and was unpublished in Swift's lifetime. This essay will address another aspect of Swift's *vengeance Ecclesiastique*: his shortest way with the Dissenters and its sometimes radical 'whig' political expression.

READING WITH MENACES

At the trial, in 1641, of Thomas Wentworth, first Earl of Strafford, lord lieutenant of Ireland and Charles I's chief councillor, the prosecution and defence contested the interpretation of almost every aspect of his controversial career. The 'pathos of Strafford's final trial and execution has also prompted historians to investigate the validity of the charges against him and to ask just what it was that Strafford died for'.[6] 'The Earl of Strafford the Day that he made his own Defence at his Tryall' appears in Swift's list *'Of those who have made great* FIGURES *in some particular Action or Circumstance of their Lives'* in his 'Of Mean and Great Figures'.[7] Swift knew what Strafford had died for. That 'illustrious Earl', Swift wrote in a letter of 1735, 'who dyed to preserve The Church, his King and the old Constitution, so shattered and crazy almost ever since'.[8] Wentworth's brand of ecclesiastical imperialism in Ireland during his time as lord deputy no doubt endeared him to Swift. With the support of Charles I and Archbishop Laud he had set about re-endowing the established but impoverished Church of Ireland and sought to bring it into line with Laudian reforms. He attempted to root out nonconformity in Ulster by pressuring the Scots Presbyterians settled there to conform to the established episcopal Church of Ireland or to remove back to Scotland. The Ulster Scots sympathized with the Scottish Covenanters. Wentworth imposed the notorious 'black oath' on them in 1639 requiring Ulster Scots to abjure the covenant.[9]

The 'Great Figure' Strafford made in his last days and martyrdom so impressed Swift that Strafford may be a background presence in some famous lines Swift wrote about himself in 'Verses on the Death of Dr. Swift, D. S. P. D.'. Although Strafford had expressed his willingness to sacrifice himself for King Charles, when the King gave his assent to the bill of attainder Strafford is reported to have said: 'Put not your trust in princes.'[10] Swift read the account of Strafford's trial in his copy of Edward Hyde, Earl of Clarendon's *The History of the Rebellion and Civil Wars in*

England. Swift admired Strafford's 'Great magnanimity' in persuading the King not to delay the order for his execution, but Swift was certainly critical of Charles I's 'weakness' in capitulating to the demands of his parliament, and he comments that the word of a king was 'Never to be relied upon'.[11] It is said of Swift in the 'Verses': 'He followed David's lesson just, / "In princes never put thy trust".'[12] Swift's 'Fair LIBERTY was all his cry; / For her he stood prepared to die; / For her he boldly stood alone; / For her he oft exposed his own' may recall lines from a passage in John Denham's *Coopers Hill*, in which Strafford's and Charles I's martyrdoms are commemorated: 'Fair liberty pursu'd, and meant a Prey / To lawless power, here turn'd, and stood at bay.'[13]

Swift annotated the prosecution's allegations at Strafford's trial with attentive animus in the margins of his copy of Clarendon's *History.* Clarendon wrote that the prosecution 'alleged "That at his coming from Ireland the Earl had said in council there; That if ever he returned to that sword again, he would not leave a Scottishman in that kingdom"'. Swift writes in the margin: 'And it was a good resolution.' Clarendon reports that it was alleged that when Strafford was back in England and the Lord Mayor and some aldermen of London did not give the satisfaction expected about the loan of moneys to the crown, Strafford said that he should '"tell the King, That it would never be well till he hanged up a Lord Mayor of London in the City to terrify the rest"'. Swift's marginal comment is: 'At worst, only a rash expression'.[14] Indeed, it was an expression Swift liked to use himself, as for example in his *A Short View of the State of Ireland* (written in 1727): 'I have often wished, that a Law were enacted to hang up half a Dozen *Bankers* every Year; and thereby interpose at least some short Delay, to the further Ruin of *Ireland.*'[15] Such resolutions and rash expressions, a rhetoric of extirpations and hangings, were a signature of Swift's polemic and invective satire against Whigs and Dissenters, according to Swift's contemporary Whig readers, for whom, as one Irish Whig put it in 1727, Swift was *'a Divine that scatters Fire-brands, Arrows, and Death'.*[16]

At one point in *The History of the Rebellion* Clarendon defines his terms: 'The Presbyterians, by whom I mean the Scots, formed all their counsels by the inclinations, and affections of the people.' 'Hellish Scotch dogs', writes Swift on the margin.[17] Swift's notorious Scotophobia, as Christopher Fox has called it, has its roots in religious confession and political allegiance as much as ethnicity.[18] The flagitious Scots, in Swift's venomous annotation in Clarendon and elsewhere, are overwhelmingly perfidious Presbyterians. The Scots are a cipher for Presbytery and Genevan Calvinist republicanism. Swift did make some exceptions in his treatment of the Scots. Swift's world may not have a dozen John Arbuthnots in it, but there were some good Scots in Swift's polemical reading of history. The royalist leader, the Marquess of Montrose, was one, or rather, as Swift wrote in his copy of Clarendon's *History*, 'the only man in Scotland who had ever one grain of virtue; and was therefore abhorred, and murdered publicly by his hellish countrymen'. Montrose was 'A perfect hero; wholly un-Scotified'. Swift followed Clarendon's account of Montrose's royalist military actions. Clarendon wrote that Montrose 'had in one battle killed fifteen hundred of one family, of the Campbells, of the blood and name of Argyle'. Swift adds in the margin: 'Not half enough of that execrable breed'. Against Clarendon's account of the sentence passed on Montrose in 1650, 'That he was ... to be carried to Edinburgh Cross, and there to be hanged upon a gallows thirty foot high, for the space of three hours', Swift wrote: 'Oh! if the whole nation, to a man, were just so treated! begin with Argyle, and next with the fanatic dogs who teased him with their kirk scurrilities.'[19]

This violent rhetoric was not confined to the private adversarial annotation in the margins of books of history and polemic that Swift read. In the first edition of *A Letter from a Member of the House of Commons in Ireland to a Member of the House of Commons in England Concerning the Sacramental Test* (published in December 1708), the polemical work that announced Swift's break with the Whig party, there is a passage, excised from later editions, in which Swift rounds on the leader of the Irish Whigs, the Irish MP Alan Brodrick, at this time perceived to be a principal supporter of the attempt to repeal the Sacramental Test in Ireland. Brodrick's real design, according to Swift, was the abolition of episcopal church government in Ireland. After an anecdote about how Brodrick, in parliament time, had shaken Bishop Thomas Lindsay 'by his Lawn Sleeve' and told the Bishop 'in a threatening Manner, *That he hoped to live to see the Day, when there should not be one of his Order in the Kingdom*', Swift wrote, in the first edition:

Now, because that Gentleman is ambitious to be thought one of our Patriots, I can put him upon a much better way of serving his Countrey, which is to take some Course that himself and his *whole worthy Family* may be *Hang'd* tomorrow Morning; and if this had been done (How long is it since my Lord *Capel's* Government?) about Fifteen Years ago, our miserable *Betrayed* Kingdom had been some Millions the better.[20]

Swift believes that the consequence for Ireland of a repeal of the Test would be that Scots Presbyterianism would become the national religion. Swift writes that the Scots in Ireland regard the established church as worse than popery, and they have 'come over full fraught with that Spirit which taught them to abolish Episcopacy at home'.[21]

Swift's violent animus against Scots Presbyterians and their Whig abettors expressed itself in rhetorical short ways with both. But there were also literal Swiftian menaces. Swift sought short ways with Whigs and Dissenters with the assistance of Henry St John when he worked for Queen Anne's Tory government. On 21 September 1711 Swift reports to Stella that the 'pamphleteers begin to be very busy against the ministry: I have begged Mr. secretary to make examples of one or two of them; and he assures me he will.' The space between rhetoric and actual physical threat is closed when, on 10 October 1711, a Whig writer who wittily reflected on Swift as 'an ambitious Tantivy' – the word 'tantivy' was a nickname for High Churchmen but it also meant 'swift' – is, at Swift's instigation, taken up by the secretary of state: 'he shall have a squeeze extraordinary . . . I'll *Tantivy* him with a vengeance.' On 16 October Swift confides to Stella that the victim of his *vengeance Ecclesiastique* is the French Protestant Whig journalist Abel Boyer: 'One Boyer, a French dog, has abused me in a pamphlet, and I have got him up in a messenger's hands: the secretary promises me to swinge him . . . I must make that rogue an example for warning to others.'[22]

SENTIMENTS OF A CHURCH-OF-IRELAND MAN

Much has been written about Swift's opposition to the Dissenters. The sources of his dislike have been traced to his family history, his early experiences as a priest in Antrim, and to his reading of history. His particular animus against Protestant Dissent and apparent lack of interest in promoting Protestant unity against the threat from popery would seem to identify him with Toryism in Ireland. However, Swift's polemical writing and political statements reflect a strong degree of idiosyncrasy and independence, as do the marginal annotations he made in books he read. Swift's Whig political profession but High Church religious confession are an apparent instance of this idiosyncrasy. In unpublished memoirs written in 1714, Swift wrote that it was at the beginning of Queen Anne's reign (when the terms Whig and Tory began to be employed in Ireland)[23] that:

I first began to trouble myself with the difference between the principles of Whig and Tory . . . having been long conversant with the Greek and Roman authors, and therefore a lover of liberty, I found myself much inclined to be what they

called a Whig in politics; and that, besides, I thought it impossible, upon any
other principle, to defend or submit to the Revolution: But, as to religion,
I confessed myself to be an High-churchman, and that I did not conceive how
any one, who wore the habit of a clergyman, could be otherwise.[24]

   Swift presents himself as a High Church Whig. The High Church part
is uncontroversial. The necessity of episcopacy and the view of it as an
apostolic institution are at the heart of his High Church ecclesiology. For
Swift the Church of England, and of Ireland, was the true Catholic
Church, and the claims of the rival confessions of Roman Catholicism
and Presbyterianism were invalid and subversive. Swift supported the
exclusion of papists and Dissenters – the overwhelming majority of the
Irish population – from civil, military, and ecclesiastical offices and
power. Whatever Swift's real political views were and however the political content of his unpublished imaginative writings might be interpreted,
this High Churchman's employment history in the 1690s certainly
suggests that at the start of his career Swift had a Whig political reputation.
He was secretary to Sir William Temple, a Williamite. He was recommended to Baron Capel, a strong Whig with a record of appointing and
promoting like-minded supporters who was made lord deputy of Ireland
in 1695, and Swift was advanced under Capel to his first living in the
Church of Ireland, in an Antrim parish. Swift later became chaplain to
the Earl of Berkeley, another Whig.
   Swift's claim to a hybrid High Church Whig political identity was not
implausible in Ireland. Swift, and later historians, have contended that no
conflict existed in Ireland between high churchmanship and the espousal
of Revolution principles.[25] Anglican Whigs in Ireland, as well as Tories,
could display considerable hostility against Dissent, especially against
Ulster Presbyterianism. Anglican Whigs were opposed to the relaxation
of the existing civil penalties imposed on Protestant Dissenters, and they
opposed English Whig government attempts to repeal or weaken the
Sacramental Test in relation to Protestant Dissenters.[26] Swift's ecclesiastical superior Archbishop William King has been claimed to be a
Church Tory and State Whig, as has Swift.[27] Since the revolutionary
political alternative to the Williamite settlement, Jacobitism, was overwhelmingly Roman Catholic in Ireland, Jacobitism there was beyond the
pale for most Irish Protestants, although, that said, there were a small
number of Protestant Jacobites in Ireland, some of whom Swift counted
among his friends.[28] Even high-flying Irish Tories can look whiggish. The
Irish High Churchman Francis Higgins, the Irish Sacheverell, described

James II as 'that Unhappy, Deluded, and Bigotted Prince' and William III as 'our *Gideon*', the 'Happy Instrument to us for Good', restoring and preserving 'our Civil and Religious Rights'. Higgins's Toryism is a matter of nuances and emphases, of innuendo and inflection. Higgins adds riders to his approval of the Williamite settlement, warning of a 'set of Men' threatening the 'Establishment in Church and State, under the pretences of greater Liberty of Conscience, and a more perfect and thorough Reformation' and of the 'very Fundamentals' being struck at since the Revolution.[29] This is Swift's idiom when he writes that those who had destroyed the monarchy and church in Charles I's time had called out 'for a *thorow Reformation*' and 'after the late King's coming to the Throne, there was a restless Cry from Men of *the same Principles*, for a *thorow Revolution*'. In his 'Sermon upon the Martyrdom of King Charles I' of 1726, Swift says that 'since the late Revolution, men have sate much looser in the true fundamentals both of religion and government'.[30]

Swift's High Church confession seems to have been a problem for his Whig reputation, because although he solicited further preferment it did not materialize from the Whig side of politics. Archbishop William King in Dublin, writing to Swift in London in February 1709, was not persuaded that Swift really was a Whig: 'But pray by what artifice did you contrive to pass for a Whig? As I am an honest man, I courted the greatest Whigs I knew, and could not gain the reputation of being counted one.'[31] By 1710 Swift had gravitated to Robert Harley, whose High Church clerical allies included Francis Atterbury and Thomas Lindsay. Among Swift's lost works is a pamphlet Letter supposedly addressed to the Irish Tory Bishop Thomas Lindsay in 1708. A manuscript pamphlet that may be this work will appear in the Cambridge Edition of the Works of Jonathan Swift. The hitherto unprinted work of 1708 is an answer to an anonymous pamphlet calling for the abolition of the Sacramental Test in Britain, supporting Scots Presbyterians, and denouncing Jacobite-episcopalians in Scotland and their High Church sympathizers. Swift, if it is he, defends the Test Act and discerns in the anti-Test pamphlet the old Solemn League and Covenant project to disestablish prelacy in England and introduce Presbyterian church government throughout Britain and Ireland. Swift gives acute attention to the Presbyterians' plea of merit in the Revolution and to the claim that it is in the civil interest of Great Britain to have a united Protestant interest. Swift points to the collusion of papists and Dissenters against the established episcopal church, and the support of Dissenters for James II's liberty of conscience by edict, and notes that radical Scots Covenanters in the North of Ireland refused to abjure the Catholic Pretender. The real principles of the Dissenters are the same as in 1641, presbytery and republicanism, and the main design is the abolition of episcopacy, as has happened whenever they gain civil power.[32] The unpublished manuscript defending the Sacramental Test in 1708 is in its politics a companion piece to the published *Letter Concerning the Sacramental Test.*

In 1710 Swift was recruited to write for the new Tory government. But preferment from the Tories was also long in coming. He tells Esther Johnson in February 1711: 'They call me nothing but Jonathan; and I said, I believed they would leave me Jonathan as they found me.'[33] Queen Anne would not permit Swift to kiss her hand. It is an honour that Lemuel Gulliver receives from Queens in the courts he visits, and Swift's syntax is rather emphatic about it: 'Her Imperial Majesty [of Lilliput] was pleased to smile very graciously upon me, and gave me out of the Window her Hand to kiss.' In Brobdingnag the 'Gracious Princess held out her little Finger', which Gulliver embraces in his arms, putting 'the Tip of it, with the utmost Respect, to my Lip'. But, as we know, things get even better for Gulliver, for he is taken up in the Queen's 'own Hand' or placed by the Queen 'upon her Hand'.[34] Swift's eventual preferment as Dean of St Patrick's came not from the hands of the Queen, but was in the gift of James Butler, second Duke of Ormond. In May 1714 the Duchess of Ormond's chaplain, Arthur Charleton, tells Swift 'at present we have disposed you in the first list of Rank Tories'.[35] There is evidence in the surviving correspondence of Irish High Churchmen that the new Dean of St Patrick's was still remembered as a 'vehement Whig',[36] and hostile Whig commentators after 1714 said that Swift had travelled from Whig to Tory and Jacobite and had offered to change sides and return to the Whigs.[37] But in Hanoverian England and Ireland Swift was certainly reputed to be a Jacobite. When the Whig Joshua, Lord Viscount Allen, accused 'some body without a name' of being 'a Tory, a Jacobite, an enemy to King George, and a libeller of the government', it was a 'character, the Dean said that many people thought, was applied to him'.[38]

Swift's High Church views not only contributed to his break from the Whig party, but they refract the meaning of what appear to be Whig revolution principles on the page. Swift's position statement of 1708 on religion and government, *The Sentiments of a Church-of-England Man,* first published in 1711, seems the classic expression of Swift as a High Church Whig. It is usually read in the contexts of English politics, as Swift's response to the allegiance controversy of 1689. In attempting to answer nonjuring objections to the transfer of the crown from James II to William and Mary in 1689, Swift advances the conservative conformist line of least resistance: the English nation in 1689 supposed the throne to be vacant, resistance was not involved for most of James II's subjects at the Revolution. But Swift does go further in this work. He claims that James's departure had left the body of the people free to fill the vacancy or indeed choose whatever government they or their representatives wanted, all of which reads like Lockean Whig revolution principles. However, it is probably apposite to note that the idea of James's departure as a dissolution of government would in fact reflect the Sentiments of a Church-of-*Ireland* Man. Comparable things were being said by some Irish Tory clerics, such as Archbishop of Tuam John Vesey, Bishop Edward Wetenhall, and Swift's acquaintance John Winder.[39] In England this language is radical whiggery, part of an argument for popular revolution. In Ireland it is an Anglican response to an actual breakdown of government caused not by popular resistance but by James's abandonment of the Anglican community of allegiance.[40] However, without quite saying so literally, Swift clearly believes in the *Sentiments* that there *is* a natural right to resist and depose a tyrannical king.[41] In 1708 a Whiggish political language of resistance and dynastic revolution may have had a double edge. The High Churchman may well have had post-Revolution events in his sights.

Swift writes in his 'Sentiments on Religion' that the Church-of-England Man 'hath a true Veneration' for episcopacy and therefore thinks 'the Abolishment of that Order among us, would prove a mighty Scandal, and Corruption to our Faith, and manifestly dangerous to our Monarchy; nay, he would defend it by Arms against all the Powers on Earth, except our own Legislature; in which Case, he would submit as to a general Calamity, a Dearth, or a Pestilence'. In the 'Sentiments on Government' the High Churchman says it is certainly the right opinion that under no pretence at all is it lawful to resist the unlimited power of the sovereign legislature, but he puts the case that lawful kings acting tyrannically can reasonably be resisted and driven out.[42] This Whig revolution principle has a different inflection if Swift is alluding to post-Revolution events. What were Swift's views on the subject's duty when episcopacy was abolished in Scotland under William III? (Prelacy was abolished in Scotland in July 1689 and an act passed on 7 June 1690 replacing church government by bishops with Presbyterian government in the Scottish Kirk.) The answer seems to be that Swift the High Churchman privately approved the Jacobite counter-revolution there, as his annotations in a copy of the Whig Bishop Gilbert Burnet's *History of His Own Time* appear to suggest. Against Burnet's account of how the Presbyterians rabbled the episcopal clergy at the time of the Revolution, Swift wrote: 'To reward them for which, King William abolished Episcopacy.' Burnet describes how 'the Earl of *Dundee*' possessed the episcopalians 'with such an opinion of another speedy Revolution, that would be brought about in favour of King *James*, that they resolved to adhere firmly to his Interests'. Swift wrote: 'He was the best man in Scotland.' Burnet reported that a Jacobite party now gave out that William's invasion was 'only a disguised and designed usurpation'. Swift: 'All this is certainly true.'[43] As the Irish Jacobite High Churchman Charles Leslie noted ironically in 1692 of William King's Whig vindication of the Revolution in *The State of the Protestants of Ireland* (1691): 'The same Argument will justifie what *Dundee* and the *High-landers* have done in *Scotland* against the Present Government: and it will justifie the *Episcopal* Party there, if they should take Arms every day, in opposition to the present Settlement of that Kingdom.'[44]

The abolition of episcopacy in Scotland and the alleged identical design of Dissenters in England and Ireland should they gain power produced menacing political sentiments in one of the most sensational High Church works in the first decade of the eighteenth century, *The Memorial of the Church of England, Humbly Offer'd to the Consideration of all True Lovers of Our Church and Constitution*. This work of 1705, probably by James Drake, was claimed to be another Whig hoax, like Defoe's *The Shortest-Way With the Dissenters*, designed to expose High Church extremism.[45] It was not a hoax, and the pamphlet deeply dismayed the Godolphin ministry trying to pursue a policy of moderation, and it was eventually burnt by the common hangman. The *Memorial* threatens the government with popular revolt: 'The Principles of the Ch[ur]ch of *E*[ngland] will dispose Men to bear a great deal; but he's a Madman that tries how much. For when Men are very much provok'd, Nature is very apt to Rebel against Principle, and then the Odds are vast on Nature's side.'[46]

Swift's language in the *Sentiments* of 1708 on resisting a tyrannical executive is similar to that in the *Memorial* of 1705. Swift writes: 'it is certain, that Princes have it in their Power to keep a Majority on their Side by any tolerable Administration; till provoked by continual Oppressions, no Man indeed can then answer where the Madness of the People will stop.'[47] In published writings elsewhere Swift wrote that 'Episcopacy ... held by the Church to be a Divine and Apostolical

Institution' is 'a fundamental Point of Religion', and that the bishops and clergy will not be content to give it up.[48] He valorized military activism in defence of episcopacy in Scotland. Swift was the ghost writer of the *Memoirs of Captain John Creichton*, published in 1731. In the *Memoirs* Creichton is an Irishman who fights in Scotland in support of the Scots episcopal church against what is depicted as a brutal and rebellious Scots Presbyterianism in the 1670s and 1680s. About one-third of the book is devoted to Creichton's loyal conduct in fighting with the Jacobite hero Viscount Dundee against William of Orange and the Scots Presbyterian Revolution interest.[49] Being a Rank Tory in the Church and worse than Whig in the State produced a Jacobitical revolution principle. Swift was 'worse' than a Whig perhaps because he does not just justify a right of revolution in the people in certain extreme circumstances but approves tyrannicide and political assassination, as his correspondence and imaginative satires attest.[50]

Swift was not alone in his extremism. Even the high-flying pulpit celebrity Luke Milbourne, proponent of an unreconstructed royalist political theology of divine right monarchism and absolute non-resistance, introduced a notorious caveat in a 30 January sermon of 1714. He observed that:

It has, indeed, been accounted a glorious Action to destroy a *Tyrant*, and if he be an Usurper of another Man's Right, I know not why it may not be esteem'd so now; but every *Lawful Prince* who acts *Tyrannically in some Particulars*, is not therefore to be presently denominated a Tyrant, nor is He immediately to be forcibly resisted, rebell'd against, or depos'd as such.

However, to have killed 'a *Cromwell*, might have been Meritorious in the Eyes of Many'.[51] Milbourne's sermons on the anniversary of the martyrdom of Charles I present the overturning of 'Church Government by Bishops' as a catastrophe for reformed Christianity, which was perpetrated under the tyranny of the rebels and usurpers during the Civil Wars and Commonwealth. Milbourne was understood to be saying that William III was a tyrant and could be acted against as such. The rabbling and murder of episcopalian priests, the abolition of episcopacy, and the Glencoe massacre showed that King William had failed 'to *maintain* the Liberties of Scotland'.[52] Swift never subscribed to Filmerian tenets of divine hereditary right, as did High Churchmen such as Luke Milbourne and Charles Leslie. His view expressed in the *Sentiments* of 1708 and elsewhere that sovereignty was absolute but that in the English constitution it was placed in the legislature of monarch in parliament aligns him with the reconstructed Tory positions advanced in the first decade of the eighteenth century by Humphrey Mackworth, Ofspring Blackall, and William Higden, and by Henry Sacheverell's Tory defence team at his trial. But Swift's High Church religious confession and his 'whiggish' views on resistance, paradoxically, re-align him with the High Church Tory extremists.

High Church religious confession also fuelled Swift's anticolonial writing; his Irish patriotism is often its political face. Swift's assertions of Irish legislative independence within the multi-kingdom monarchy and his complaints against British economic policy have a provenance in his ecclesiology. It is in the political rhetoric of *A Letter from a Member of the House of Commons in Ireland to a Member of the House of Commons in England, Concerning the Sacramental Test* of 1708 opposing Whig attempts to remove the Test in Ireland that we find anticipations of M. B. Drapier. Swift writes that the Test in Ireland is 'a Matter purely national'. The Whig attempt to repeal the Test by an act of parliament in England would be 'binding a Nation by Laws, to which they do not consent'. The British parliament's projected abolition of the Test in Ireland is being done for English Whig political interests and would be destructive of the established Church.[53] In writing against the English Whig government as M. B. Drapier, Swift invoked radical Whig ideologues: 'the Writings of [Viscount Molesworth], Mr. *Locke*, Mr. *Molineaux*, Colonel *Sidney*, and other dangerous Authors'.[54] But his assertion of Ireland's rights under the English crown had impeccable High Church and royalist antecedents among the settler population of late seventeenth-century Ireland. The first Earl of Orrery, for instance, hoped that the passage of the Cattle Acts would be prevented by Charles II, that a parliamentary 'act in England' shall not be admitted 'to bind Ireland'.[55]

Swift's hostility to British policies restricting Irish trade and manufacturing also has a confessional dimension, because the position of the Presbyterian Scots seems to have been strengthened by British legislation. The passing of the Woollen Act was seen to have advantaged the Ulster linen industry. As Swift wrote in the 1726 letter to the Earl of Peterborough about the grievances of Ireland which the post-Union parliament under Walpole would not address: 'the desperate condition of trade' was such 'that the whole country, except the Scotch plantation in the north, is a scene of misery and desolation'.[56] Prominent among the 'grievances' of Ireland listed by Swift which 'have been all brought upon that kingdom since the Revolution' was the intrusion of English interlopers into the Church of Ireland.[57] King George's English-born, Low Church Whig bishops, Swift is reported to have said, were 'a parcel of highwaymen' who in 'gowns and cassocks here pretend to pass for bishops'.[58] When one English Whig ecclesiastical appointment, Dr. Thomas Sawbridge, the Dean of Ferns, was arraigned in 1730 for rape, Swift told the Tory Earl of Oxford: 'There is a fellow here from England one Sawbridge, he was last term indited for a Rape. The Plea he intended was his being drunk when he forced the woman; but he bought her off; He is a Dean and I name him to your Lordship, because I am confident you will hear of his being a Bishop.'[59]

Swift's famous denunciation of colonialism at the end of *Gulliver's Travels* may well be a parodic repudiation of the pro-imperial discourse of an English Whig, Low Church bishop. Bishop White Kennett was a prominent propagandist promoting England's progress in the propagation of the Gospel in the colonies. In his ecclesiastical-imperial discourse Roman Catholic Spanish conquests in America were denounced and contrasted with Protestant English imperial enterprise which received hyperbolic praise. In a typical performance, Kennett explained that the Spaniards in South America 'used all the Engines of Terror, Force and Cruelty; in such a barbarous Manner, that their own Authors have made grievous Complaints of them'. However,

> when the *Northern* Parts of *America* were afterward discovered by the *English*, and some little Colonies were there settled; it did soon appear, that the Spirit of the Reformed Protestant Religion was very different from that of the Roman Church. For here, no one Instance was given of hunting poor Souls into a forc'd Conversion, or of putting any one to Death, or to any manner of Torture, for the Sake and Name of Religion.[60]

Swift's satire on the colonial project in Part IV, Chapter 12 of *Gulliver's Travels* alludes to Spanish atrocities, but subjects this kind of imperial discourse praising England to withering irony. Gulliver doubts 'whether our Conquests in the Countries I treat of, would be as easy as those of *Ferdinando Cortez* over the naked *Americans*'. A cavalry charge of 20,000 Houyhnhnms, Gulliver opines, would crush 'an *European* Army' – '*European*' rather than 'English' or 'British', because Swift implies that King George relied on a foreign mercenary standing army.[61] Gulliver's account of how 'a new Dominion' is founded by a 'Crew of Pyrates' with 'a free Licence given to all Acts of Inhumanity and Lust; the Earth reeking with the Blood of its Inhabitants' and that the 'execrable Crew of Butchers employed in so pious an Expedition, is a *modern Colony* sent to convert and civilize an idolatrous and barbarous People' precisely points to England. The notorious Buccaneer Captain Henry Morgan and his crew, who were licensed as privateers, had burned and sacked Panama and slaughtered the Panamanians. Morgan became lieutenant governor of Jamaica.[62] The bonehead Gulliver, unaware that he has just implicated England in this denunciation of colonialism, goes on, White Kennett-like, to praise 'the *British* Nation' as 'an Example to the whole World' for their way 'in planting Colonies; their liberal Endowments for the Advancement of Religion and Learning; their Choice of devout and able Pastors to propagate *Christianity*'. Swift would not have been surprised to learn, if he did not already know, that Dean Sawbridge had been an East India Company chaplain at the English Factory in Bombay.[63] Gulliver's hyperbolic praise of British colonial Christianity is a devastating Swiftian sarcasm against colonialism which also unmasks the rhetoric of Whiggish ecclesiastical-imperialism.

Swift's anticolonial rhetoric in his imaginative satire and in polemic such as *The Drapier's Letters* is more radical than his actual ontology. Swift's High Church Anglican confession meant that in Ireland he emphatically supported an exclusive and narrow Church-of-Ireland hegemony. Swift regarded Anglican Ireland as an equal part of the multi-kingdom monarchy with the right to legislative independence, and as having legal and political dominance over the Catholic 'native Irish', whom he regarded as a conquered people,[64] and over the Presbyterian Ulster Scots, who were to remain excluded from national offices. Swift also, of course, welcomed Irish conformity to English ways when, in 1704, under the second Duke of Ormond, the Sacramental Test was introduced in Ireland.

It is Swift's Irish political confession that provides a context for understanding a different colonial aspect of *Gulliver's Travels*, the Houyhnhnm treatment of the Yahoos in the fable of Part IV. At the Council of the Houyhnhnms it is debated 'Whether the *Yahoos* should be exterminated from the Face of the Earth'. The extirpation of the Yahoos is presented as Houyhnhnm pastoral care. The ruling Council considers the Yahoos a subversive threat to the island plantation economy. The '*Yahoos* were the most filthy, noisome, and deformed Animal which Nature ever produced' and 'the most restive and indocible, mischievous and malicious'. They have to be 'continually watched'.[65] When Gulliver arrives in Houyhnhnmland he fears being regarded as a cattle-killer or cattle-maimer.[66] This is precisely how the Houyhnhnm Council sees the '*Yahoo*' Gulliver, alleging that 'because I had some Rudiments of Reason, added to the natural Pravity of those Animals, it was to be feared, I might be able to seduce them into the woody and mountainous Parts of the Country, and bring them in Troops by Night to destroy the *Houyhnhnms* Cattle'.[67] The Yahoos are said not to be native to the country; they came to Houyhnhnmland from over the sea. There had been killing times in Houyhnhnmland in the past when the Yahoos had been hunted down.[68] Among the various possible meanings of the Yahoos it has been contended that they signify the 'savage' native Irish, and particularly perhaps Irish houghers.[69] But they can also be seen to be associated with the Scots Irish. Swift's imagery for the Scots Irish is also used for the Yahoos. In his virulent attack on the Anglo-Scots Union of 1707, for example, Swift depicts a personified Scotland as 'very ill-shaped; she hath bad Features, and a worse Complexion; she hath a stinking Breath, and twenty ill Smells about her besides'. A 'Presbyterian of the most rank and virulent Kind', she encourages 'a Company of Rogues and Thieves, and Pickpockets' to rob England's 'Hen-roosts, steal his Corn and Cattle, and do him all manner of Mischief' and has 'been known to come at the Head of these Rascals'.[70] The Scots are vassals who live in mountainous regions in the Scythian allegory at the conclusion of Swift's *Examiner* of 14 December 1710. The first Yahoos settled in the mountains, and they are treated as slaves by the Houyhnhnms.[71] In the *Tale of a Tub* volume of 1704 a barbaric Scythian ancestry is imputed to fanatic writers, sectarian preachers, and the puritan Roundheads. The covenanting Presbyterian Scots are likened to savage Scythians in Charles Leslie's *Rehearsal* of 1704.[72] The frequent references in Edmund Spenser, for example, to the 'Irish Scots' as Scythians who had arrived in the northern parts of Ireland was an origin myth that the Irish High Churchmen Swift and Leslie found satirically appealing because of its stress on the savage Scots-Irish connection.[73] Swift thought the Scots were worse than the Irish, but the Scots Irish were worst of all.[74] The barbaric, savage Yahoos may be a fictional image of the Scythian-sectarian-Scots Irish. The Houyhnhnms want to extirpate the Yahoos from the island and Gulliver, the gentle Yahoo, is expelled from Houyhnhnmland. Like an Ulster Scot forcibly uprooted by Wentworth, Gulliver takes to the sea, heading East and then North-East.[75]

SWIFT AND THE HIGH CHURCH POLEMICAL CANON

In his last work, *A Discourse Concerning Ridicule and Irony in Writing*, published in 1729, the anticlerical Whig friend of John Locke, Anthony Collins, traced a tradition of 'ironical, satirical, and polemical Divines',

from 'the *Laudean* Party' which carried on a 'Paper War with innumer-
able Pamphlets' designed to '*ridicule* the *Puritans*' to the more recent
High Church 'Discourses, and Tracts against the Nonconformists,
Whigs, Low-Church-men and Latitudinarians'. Collins identified this
High Church literary canon: 'the *Berkenheads*, the *Heylins*, the *Ryves's*,
the *Needhams*, the *Lestranges*, the *Nalsons*, the *Lesleys*, the *Oldesworths* ...
the *Eachards*, the *Tom Browns*, and *Swifts* ... the ... *Souths*, *Sherlocks*,
Atterburys, and *Sacheverels*'.[76] Literary scholars tend to dismiss Collins's
views as jaundiced by Whig bias and personal enmity. Quoting this
particular list of authors in which Swift is placed, one scholar has
commented that 'Collins may well have learned from Swift the power
of a nice, unflattering list'.[77] Swift certainly doctored Collins's lists when
he could. In *A Discourse of Free-Thinking* of 1713, Collins had said that
'such zealous Divines as our S[ACHEVEREL]Ls, our AT[TERBUR]Ys,
our SM[ALRID]GEs, our ST[UB]BSs, our HIGGINSs, our M[ILBOU]RNs,
and our SW[I]FTs' should be sent to the far East on a missionary
enterprise. Swift's satiric parody *Mr Collins's Discourse of Freethinking
Put into plain English, by way of Abstract for the Use of the Poor* (1713)
rewrites Collins's sentence as 'such Divines as Dr. *Atterbury*, Dr. *Smalridge*,
Dr. *Swift*, Dr. *Sacheverell*, and some others'.[78]

   Whether it is unflattering or not, Collins's 1729 list is almost occult
in associating Swift with writers of invective against Presbyterians and
Dissenters with whom Swift had elective affinities. Of the Laudian and
later Restoration polemicists Collins mentions, Swift possessed and had
read Charles I's chaplain Peter Heylyn's *Aërius Redivivus: or The History of
the Presbyterians* (second edition 1672), and pardoned its bias, writing in
1728 that 'It is written with some vehemence, very pardonable in one who
had been an observer and sufferer, in *England*, under that diabolical
fanatic sect which then destroyed church and state.' According to Swift,
'His partiality appears chiefly in setting the actions of the Calvinists in
the strongest light, without equally dwelling on those of the other side;
which, however, to say the truth, was not his proper business.' Heylyn's
extremism did earn some criticism from Swift, however. Heylyn accords
the space of just one page in Book 9 of his polemical History to the
treatment of the Protestants in France in the late sixteenth century.
He speaks of 'that course which unavoidable necessity had compelled'
the King of France to take of reconciling himself to the Church of Rome,
concluding that 'the *Hugonots* in *France*' 'can lay the blame on nothing
but their own Ingratitude, their Disobedience to their King, and the
Genevian Principles that were rooted in them, which made them enemies

to the Power and Guidance of all Soveraign Princes'. Swift comments: 'And yet he might have spent some more words on the inhuman massacre of *Paris* and other parts of *France*, which no provocation (and yet the King had the greatest possible) could excuse, or much extenuate.'[79]

Heylyn's fellow Laudian, the cavalier newsbook writer and satirist John Berkenhead, is a major figure in the development of propagandist idioms, modes, and genres. As editor of *Mercurius Aulicus*, a royalist journal with official backing, Berkenhead assumed a manner of bold assurance, lofty disdain, and affected indifference toward opponents that anticipate Swift's Olympian tone in the *Examiner*, and he mastered techniques of impersonation and insinuation in order to burlesque enemies and alarm moderate opinion, which was very much Swift's approach in his party writing.[80] Swift's satire of Enthusiasm in 'A Digression concerning the Original, *the Use, and Improvement of* Madness *in a Commonwealth*' in *A Tale of a Tub*, where he writes of 'a peculiar *String* in the Harmony of Human Understanding, which in several individuals is exactly of the same Tuning' which when struck 'those of the same Pitch ... will by a secret necessary Sympathy strike exactly at the same time', almost seems a palimpsest of Berkenhead's satiric use of the image in presenting the 'sympathy' of the House of Commons and the city of London 'as two strings set to the same tune ... if you touch one, the other by consent renders the same sound'.[81] Berkenhead's Laudian commitment to episcopacy and emphasis on outward conformity rather than doctrinal matters would be characteristic of Swift in politico-religious disputes.[82]

Swift knew Bruno Ryves's royalist journalism of 1643–4. His newsbook, *Mercurius Rusticus: or, The Countries Complaint of The Barbarous Outrages Begun in the Year 1642, by the Sectaries of this late flourishing Kingdom*, detailed the murders, plunderings, and other outrages suffered by the King's subjects, and the sacrileges committed upon the cathedral churches of England by parliamentarian troops. It was Swift's main source for information about his royalist grandfather, the cavalier clergyman whose memory he venerated, and of the Swift family's sufferings, which had forced Swift's father and uncles to emigrate to Ireland.[83] Ryves, who became Dean of Windsor after the Restoration, is a polemical-historical source for the anti-Presbyterian tracts Swift wrote on Whig attempts to repeal the Test Act.

Swift owned the indefatigable Tory polemicist Roger L'Estrange's *The Dissenters Sayings* (1681).[84] L'Estrange is satirized along with the Catholic convert John Dryden in *A Tale of a Tub* and *The Battle of the Books*. Swift had ideological reasons for linking and mocking these high-profile writers as mercenary, opportunistic hacks. Both L'Estrange and Dryden had been accused of supporting Cromwell before the Restoration, and after James II's accession they both supported James II's Declaration of Indulgence. They were pilloried together as James II's tools in contemporary satire, and Swift no doubt regarded them as time-serving apostates who had sided with Cromwell and later James II against the church and the confessional Anglican state.[85] However, L'Estrange's writings against Dissent provided Swift with much polemical pith for his satire linking Peter (popery) and Jack (Dissent) in *A Tale of a Tub*. There are other anticipations of Swift in L'Estrange's *Observator*, including the use, in a satirical political context, of the cannibal trope of eating and boiling children.[86]

Among the other names on Collins's list, the Restoration Church of England clergyman John Nalson was a prolific polemical writer against Presbyterianism and the sects, and a vividly vitriolic work such as *Foxes and Firebrands, or, A Specimen of the Danger and Harmony of Popery and Separation*, printed for Benjamin Tooke in 1680, is part of the arsenal upon which Swift drew in his satire on the agreement between Jack and Peter in *A Tale of a Tub*. Swift's indebtedness to Charles Leslie's pamphleteering, especially against Scots Presbyterians, Quakers, and the Socinians, is a subject in itself.[87] Swift's apologia for Charles Leslie in his pseudonymous satirical polemic against the Scots Whig Bishop Gilbert Burnet, *A Preface to the B[isho]p of S[a]r[u]m's Introduction To the Third Volume of the History of the Reformation of the Church of England* (1713), remembers Leslie's Scottish father, John Leslie, the royalist Church of Ireland Bishop of Raphoe. An ally of Wentworth and Laud, Bishop Leslie prosecuted Scots covenanters in his diocese, supported the imposition of the 'black oath', and was known as 'the Fighting Bishop'. His castle was a stronghold against the Irish Catholics in the uprising of 1641, and against the Parliamentarian and later the Commonwealth forces in the 1640s and early 1650s. He died just short of his hundredth birthday.[88] Swift wrote that Charles Leslie 'is the Son of a great and excellent Prelate, who, upon several Accounts, was one of the most extraordinary Men of his Age'.[89] The Jacobite William Oldisworth was Swift's successor as author of the *Examiner*. Swift's debts to the writings of the Tory High Churchmen Robert South and Francis Atterbury, to the Tory satirist Tom Brown, and to John Eachard's *The Grounds and Occasions of the Contempt of the Clergy and Religion Enquired into* (1670) have been noted in the literary scholarship on Swift. One of Swift's first recorded explosive outbursts against Dissenters, in a letter of 1704 ('Pox on the Dissenters and

Independents, I would as soon trouble my head to write against a louse or a flea') is perhaps an echo of a witty passage in Eachard on topics of academic disputation: 'perhaps the business is only, which is the noblest Creature a Flea or a Louse'.[90] A case can certainly be made that Collins has accurately listed Swift in a royalist and High Church literary history.

In December 1702 Daniel Defoe intruded a hoax entry into this High Church polemical tradition, an ironic abstract of contemporary avatars of this long tradition of invective against Dissenters. It is indicative of Swift's extremism that Defoe's *Shortest-Way with the Dissenters* turns out to be a proleptic imitation of Swift's violent rhetoric against Whigs and Dissenters. Swift alluded obliquely to Defoe's publishing sensation and did his best to control the damage done by this exposure of High Church extremism by dismissing as hyperbole Defoe's claims that High Church rhetoric elided into actual violence against persons.[91] Part of Defoe's punishment for publishing *The Shortest-Way with the Dissenters*, to stand three times in the pillory, was turned by Defoe into a public relations triumph. He produced *A Hymn to the Pillory* for the occasion and contemporary accounts say that he was showered with flowers rather than with refuse and rotten eggs. He afterwards used his famous appearance for self-publicity and publishing promotional purposes. Swift's satiric allusion to Defoe in *A Letter Concerning The Sacramental Test* of 1708 returns Defoe to anonymity. Swift strips the famous pillory episode of all grandeur with a parenthesis. Swift refers to the papers of insipid wretches that are part of the 'Coffee-house Furniture': 'One of these Authors (the Fellow that was *pilloryed*, I have forgot his Name) is indeed so grave, sententious, dogmatical a Rogue, that there is no enduring him.' This *'Presbyterian'* author is unnamed, and the famous fate about which Defoe had made so much noise is rendered unseemly and unspeakable, hushed up in an insouciant parenthetical aside.[92] Defoe's *The Shortest-Way With the Dissenters*, however, may well have been a creative influence on Swift, and it is among the possible prototypes for Swift's parody *Mr Collins's Discourse of Freethinking, Put into Plain English, by Way of Abstract for the Use of the Poor* (1713). Defoe said that in *The Shortest-Way* he had put into 'plain English' the 'plain design' of the High Churchmen.[93] Swift's analogous project in parodying Collins was to make plain or 'abstract' the atheism of freethinkers and identify it as the Whig party's religious policy.

Swift's polemic against Whigs and Dissenters, and especially against Scots Presbyterians in Ireland, seems sometimes to be taking him beyond the Pale. In one late ironic work Swift, personating a Catholic petitioner, persuasively presents the Catholics in Ireland as more deserving of toleration than the Protestant Dissenters from the established church.[94] In an unpublished paper containing a diatribe against an impious anti-episcopal Erastian Reformation, Swift remarks that it is to the scandalous way that the Reformation was carried out that 'we owe all the just reproaches that Roman Catholics have cast upon us ever since'.[95] The Irish Catholic Jacobite exile, Chevalier Charles Wogan, in a remarkable epistle to Swift in 1733, wrote that 'We are all brethren in fact.' He told Swift that 'Laud and Strafford' had made Swift's church 'one of the most firm and amiable societies in the universe, free from tyranny, inaccessible to heresy', whereas now 'all her hierarchy is in heterodox hands . . . Presbytery is become episcopal; and she is reduced, in regard of her authority and livings, to be only presbyterian.' Swift found this agreeable reading and in his reply wrote: 'I can assure you, that those wretches here, who call themselves a Parliament, abhor the clergy of our church more than those of yours, and have made an universal association to defraud us of our undoubted dues.'[96] Swift's poetic invective *The Legion Club* would be his notorious *vengeance Ecclesiastique* against them. The 'Age of Swift' attests to the first of Swift's *Thoughts on Various Subjects* printed in 1711: 'We have just Religion enough to make us *hate*, but not enough to make us *love* one another.'[97]

NOTES

1 *Correspondence*, II, 642.
2 Ibid., 650.
3 Ibid., III, 70.
4 Swift's library contained an edition of the *Historia B. Platinae de vitis pontificum Romanorum. AD.N. Iesu Christo usque ad Paulum II . . .* (Cologne, 1611), see Dirk F. Passmann and Heinz J. Vienken, *The Library and Reading of Jonathan Swift: A Bio-Bibliographical Handbook, Part I, Swift's Library in Four Volumes* (Frankfurt am Main: Peter Lang, 2003), Part I, vol. III, pp. 1625–8 (hereafter *Library*).
5 *PW*, V, 99–107 (99); *Correspondence*, II, 646, n. 5.
6 J. F. Merritt, 'Introduction: The Historical Reputation of Thomas Wentworth', in *The Political World of Thomas Wentworth, Earl of Strafford, 1621–1641*, ed. J. F. Merritt (Cambridge University Press, 1996), p. 2.
7 *PW*, V, 84.
8 *Correspondence*, IV, 77; Hermann Real, 'A New Letter from Swift: His Answer to the Earl of Strafford, 29 March 1735, Recovered', *Swift Studies*, 18 (2003), 20–5. Swift owned the Jacobite Thomas Carte's *Life of Ormonde*, which has a positive treatment of Strafford, see *Library*, Part I, vol. I, pp. 351–4; Merritt, 'Introduction', p. 12.

9 On Wentworth's administration in Ireland and the established church, see especially Ronald G. Asch, 'Wentworth, Thomas, first earl of Strafford (1593–1641), lord lieutenant of Ireland', *ODNB*, LVIII, 146–57; John Morrill, 'A British Patriarchy? Ecclesiastical Imperialism under the Early Stuarts', in *Religion, Culture and Society in Early Modern Britain*, ed. Anthony Fletcher and Peter Roberts (Cambridge University Press, 1994), pp. 209–37 (esp. pp. 222–31); M. Perceval-Maxwell, 'Strafford, the Ulster-Scots and the Covenanters', *Irish Historical Studies*, 18, no. 72 (1973), 524–51.

10 C. V. Wedgwood, *Thomas Wentworth First Earl of Strafford 1593–1641: A Revaluation* (London: Jonathan Cape, 1961), p. 380; Asch, 'Wentworth', *ODNB*.

11 See *Library*, Part I, vol. II, pp. 942–3.

12 'Verses on the Death of Dr Swift, D. S. P. D', ll. 345–6, *Complete Poems*, p. 494.

13 Ibid., ll. 351–4; John Denham, *Coopers Hill* (1668), ll. 325–6, in *Expans'd Hieroglyphicks: A Critical Edition of Sir John Denham's Coopers Hill*, ed. Brendan O Hehir (Berkeley and Los Angeles: University of California Press, 1969), p. 159.

14 *Library*, Part I, vol. II, 942.

15 *PW*, XII, 11.

16 The pro-government writer (and later Attorney General for Jamaica) Matthew Concanen, quoted in the *Grub Street Journal*, no. 38 (24 September 1730), p. 1, in *The Grub-Street Journal, 1730–33*, ed. Bertrand A. Goldgar, 4 vols. (vol. I: 1730) (London: Pickering & Chatto, 2002). Swift satirizes Concanen as the Grub Street poet who has reached deepest in 'the low sublime', see 'On Poetry: A Rhapsody' (1733), ll. 386, 413–14, *Complete Poems*, pp. 531–2.

17 *Library*, Part I, vol. II, 950.

18 Christopher Fox, 'Swift's Scotophobia', *Bullán*, 6 (2002), 43–65.

19 *Library*, Part I, vol. II, 953, 952, 953.

20 *PW*, II, 117, 283.

21 Ibid., 116.

22 *JSt.*, I, 365; II, 381, 384–5. Boyer was charged with seditious libel, but was discharged as a result of intercession at the highest level, from his sometime patron, Robert Harley, Earl of Oxford, see G. C. Gibbs, 'Boyer, Abel (1667?–1729), lexicographer and journalist', *ODNB*, VII, 61–4.

23 Henry Maxwell to James Stanhope, 25 March 1705; Henry Maxwell to James Stanhope, 6 December 1713 [recte January 1714], in D. W. Hayton, 'Henry Maxwell, M.P., Author of *An Essay upon an Union of Ireland with England* (1703)', *Eighteenth-Century Ireland*, 22 (2007), 28–63 (56, 58); Patrick Kelly, 'Ireland and the Glorious Revolution: From Kingdom to Colony', in *The Revolutions of 1688*, ed. Robert Beddard (Oxford: Clarendon Press, 1991), pp. 163–90 (p. 184). Charles Leslie claimed that 'the distinction of High and Low Church' was invented by Whigs and Dissenters at this time, see R. J. Leslie, *Life and Writings of Charles Leslie, M.A. Nonjuring Divine* (London, 1885), pp. 295–6.

24 'Memoirs, Relating to That Change which happened in the Queen's Ministry in the Year 1710', *PW*, VIII, 120.

25 *PW*, II, 283: 'the highest Tories we had with us [in Ireland], would make tolerable Whigs [in England]'; Joseph Richardson, 'Archbishop William King (1650–1729): "Church Tory and State Whig"?', *Eighteenth-Century Ireland*, 15 (2000), 54–76 (55). In England the phenomenon of clerical High Church Whiggism emerges in particular regions later in the Hanoverian period, see, for example, Jeffrey S. Chamberlain, *Accommodating High Churchmen: The Clergy of Sussex, 1700–1745* (Urbana/Chicago: University of Illinois Press, 1997).

26 Hayton, 'Henry Maxwell, M.P., Author of *An Essay upon an Union of Ireland with England* (1703)', 32, 33. For the party-political situation, see D. W. Hayton, *Ruling Ireland, 1685–1742: Politics, Politicians and Parties* (Woodbridge: The Boydell Press, 2004), esp. ch. 2 'Anglo-Irish politics, 1692–1704: the rise of party', pp. 35–105. See also Patrick McNally, 'The Hanoverian Accession and the Tory Party in Ireland', *Parliamentary History*, 14 (1995), 263–83 (264–5, 282–3).

27 On Archbishop King's political views: Philip O'Regan, *Archbishop William King of Dublin (1650–1729) and the Constitution in Church and State* (Dublin: Four Courts Press, 2000); S. J. Connolly, 'The Glorious Revolution in Irish Protestant Political Thinking', in *Political Ideas in Eighteenth-Century Ireland*, ed. S. J. Connolly (Dublin: Four Courts Press, 2000), pp. 33–8; Richardson, 'Archbishop William King (1650–1729): "Church Tory and State Whig"?', 54–76; Robert Eccleshall, 'The Political Ideas of Anglican Ireland in the 1690s', in *Political Discourse in Seventeenth- and Eighteenth-Century Ireland*, ed. D. George Boyce, Robert Eccleshall, and Vincent Geoghegan (Houndmills, Basingstoke: Palgrave, 2001), pp. 62–80; Christopher J. Fauske, ed., *Archbishop William King and the Anglican Irish Context, 1688–1729* (Dublin: Four Courts Press, 2004); Hayton, *Ruling Ireland*. For Swift, see Clive Probyn's entry on 'Jonathan Swift' in the *ODNB*, LIII, 465–79.

28 For assessments on Irish Protestant Jacobitism: Hayton, *Ruling Ireland*, p. 22; Thomas Doyle, 'Jacobitism, Catholicism and the Irish Protestant Elite, 1700–1710', *Eighteenth-Century Ireland*, 12 (1997), 29–59; Éamonn Ó Ciardha, *Ireland and the Jacobite Cause, 1685–1766: A Fatal Attachment* (Dublin: Four Courts Press, 2004 [2001]), esp. pp. 163–81; Ian Campbell Ross, 'Was Berkeley a Jacobite? *Passive Obedience* Revisited', *Eighteenth-Century Ireland*, 20 (2005), 17–30 (Berkeley's work was aimed at Trinity College students who had a reputation for Jacobitism). Swift's private conversations in 1711 with Ormond, and with the Jacobite Lady Eleanor Oglethorpe, about a 'remedy' for the succession crisis suggest discussion of the Jacobite option, see *JSt.*, II, 437; Hector McDonnell, *The Wild Geese of the Antrim MacDonnells* (Dublin: Irish Academic Press, 1996), p. 70. Irish Protestants were among the leaders of Jacobite conspiracy in England, among them the second Duke of Ormond, James Barry, fourth Earl of Barrymore, and the fourth and fifth Earls of Orrery.

29 *A Sermon Preach'd Before Their Excellencies the Lord Justices, at Christ Church, Dublin; on Tuesday the 28 th of August* ... (Dublin, 1705), pp. 12, 13, 20–1; *A Sermon Preach'd at The Royal Chappel at White-Hall; on Ash Wednesday, Feb. 26, 1706/7* (London, 1707), p. 7. Compare Swift's *Ode to the King On His Irish Expedition and the Success of his Arms in General* (1691) praising William III as a hero doing good, and gaining victory in a war of kings with James II and Louis XIV. In the pacification of the nation after William's conquest the poet hopes that the nation has been secured not just from popery but from the Presbyterian Scots (*Complete Poems*, pp. 43–6).

30 *PW*, III, 47; IX, 224.

31 *Correspondence*, I, 233.

32 'Of the Sacramental Test', Victoria and Albert Museum, National Art Library, Forster MS 536 (Pressmark F. 48.G.6. 7/11). 10 ms pages. Swift is answering *A Letter from A Gentleman in Scotland to his Friend in England, Against the Sacramental Test* ... (London, 1708), which has been wrongly attributed to Charles Leslie. The misattribution is corrected in F. J. M. Blom, 'The Publications of Charles Leslie', *Edinburgh Bibliographical Society Transactions*, vol. VI, Part I (1990), 10–36 (33). In Swift's writings against the Scots Presbyterians we see vividly why the thesis advanced by Linda Colley in *Britons: Forging the Nation, 1707–1837* (New Haven: Yale University Press, 1992) that a shared Protestantism united Britain against a Catholic Other required qualification. For the situation in Scotland, see Colin Kidd, 'Conditional Britons: The Scots Covenanting Tradition and the Eighteenth-Century British State', *English Historical Review*, vol. CXVII, 474 (Nov. 2002), 1147–76, and his *Subverting Scotland's Past: Scottish Whig Historians and the Creation of an Anglo-British Identity, 1689–c.1830* (Cambridge University Press, 1993); Clare Jackson, *Restoration Scotland, 1660–1690: Royalist Politics, Religion and Ideas* (Woodbridge: The Boydell Press, 2003). Cf. Fox, 'Swift's Scotophobia', 57.

33 *JSt.*, I, 193–4.

34 *Gulliver's Travels*, I. iv. 47; II. iii. 101, 102–3, 107.

35 The Rev. Arthur Charleton to Swift [22 May 1714], *Correspondence*, I, 605.

36 Ehrenpreis, II, 634; Louis A. Landa, *Swift and the Church of Ireland* (Oxford: Clarendon Press, 1954, rpt 1965), p. 73.

37 Leonard Welsted's *Characters of the Times; or, an Impartial Account of the Writings, Characters, Education, &c. of several Noblemen and Gentlemen, libell'd in a Preface to a late Miscellany Publish'd by P[o]pe and S[wi]ft* (London, 1728) says that Swift was 'a very strenuous Advocate for the *Whig* Cause' who disappointed in his ambitions 'turn'd all of a sudden a Tarmegant *Tory*; as he has offer'd several Times since, to turn *Whig* again' (pp. 44–5). Pope 'flew to *S[wi]ft*, and went *Pell-Mell* with him into the *Jacobite* Party' (p. 46). The Dean of St Patrick's was thus perceived to have had a similar political trajectory to another Church of Ireland Tory, Thomas Lindsay. Lord Egmont noted of the Lord Primate of Ireland, Dr Thomas Lindsay, that he had been 'at first chaplain to my Ld. Capel when Ld.

Deputy. he set out in the World a Whig, then turn'd high Church-man and
at last died a Jacobite', see British Library, Egmont Papers, Additional MS
47025, fol. 118. See Hayton, *Ruling Ireland*, p. 143 and note 38, and his *ODNB*
entry on Lindsay (XXXIII, 900–1). Swift had supported Lindsay's promotion
to Archbishop of Armagh and Primate of All Ireland in 1714. They collabo-
rated in attempts to place Tories on the Irish episcopal bench and in
positions of influence, see Ehrenpreis, II, 718; III, 41, 53–6, 346.

38 'The Substance of What was said by the Dean of St. Patrick's to the Lord
    Mayor and some of the Aldermen, when his Lordship came to present the
    said Dean with his Freedom in a Gold Box', *PW*, XII, 145.

39 Robert Eccleshall, 'Anglican Political Thought in the Century after the
    Revolution of 1688', in *Political Thought in Ireland Since the Seventeenth
    Century*, ed. D. George Boyce, Robert Eccleshall, and Vincent Geoghegan
    (London and New York: Routledge, 1993), pp. 36–72 (esp. pp. 50–6).

40 *PW*, II, 20–1. On the allegiance controversy in England: Mark Goldie, 'The
    Revolution of 1689 and the Structure of Political Argument: An Essay and an
    Annotated Bibliography of Pamphlets on the Allegiance Controversy',
    Bulletin of Research in the Humanities, 83 (1980), 473–564; Goldie, 'The
    Political Thought of the Anglican Revolution', in *The Revolutions of 1688*,
    ed. Robert Beddard (Oxford: Clarendon Press, 1991), pp. 102–36.
    On Anglican political thought and the Revolution in Ireland, see Robert
    Eccleshall, 'Anglican Political Thought', pp. 36–72; Kelly, 'Ireland and the
    Glorious Revolution: From Kingdom to Colony', pp. 163–90; Hayton, *Ruling
    Ireland*, ch. 1 'Two revolutions: Jacobite and Williamite', pp. 8–34.

41 *PW*, II, 20–3.

42 Ibid., 5, 16, 22.

43 Ibid., V, 290; *Bishop Burnet's History of His Own Time*, 2 vols. (Dublin, 1724,
    1734), vol. II, p. 14.

44 [Charles Leslie], *An Answer to a Book Intituled, The State of the Protestants in
    Ireland Under the Late King James's Government* ... (London, 1692), p. 46.
    From the time of the Revolution, Whig Jacobites had assailed the Revolution
    Settlement and arraigned the Williamite and later the Hanoverian regimes on
    Whig principles, see Mark Goldie and Clare Jackson, 'Williamite Tyranny
    and the Whig Jacobites', in *Redefining William III: The Impact of the
    King-Stadholder in International Context*, ed. Esther Mijers and David
    Onnekink (Aldershot: Ashgate, 2007), pp. 177–99.

45 *The Rehearsal*, nos. 99–102 (27 April–8 May 1706); see L. S. Horsley,
    'Contemporary Reactions to Defoe's *Shortest Way with the Dissenters*', *Studies
    in English Literature 1500–1900*, 16 (1976), 407–20 (417).

46 [James Drake], *The Memorial of the Church of England, Humbly Offer'd to the
    Consideration of all True Lovers of Our Church and Constitution* (London,
    1705), p. 12. For the proceedings in Scotland as a template for what the
    Dissenters design if they gain power in England, see esp. pp. 4, 7, 9, 30. The
    work was variously ascribed to Francis Atterbury, Charles Leslie, William
    Pittis, Humphrey Mackworth, and James Drake, see J. A. Downie, *Robert*

Harley and the Press: Propaganda and Public Opinion in the Age of Swift and Defoe (Cambridge University Press, 1979), pp. 80–100.

47 *PW*, II, 22.

48 Ibid., XII, 256.

49 Ibid., V, 120–81; Ralph Stewart, 'Swift and the Authorship of Creichton's *Memoirs*', *The Scottish Historical Review*, 72, no. 193 (April 1993), 80–9.

50 Ian Higgins, 'Killing No Murder: Jonathan Swift and Polemical Tradition', in *Swift's Travels: Eighteenth-Century Satire and Its Legacy*, ed. Nicholas Hudson and Aaron Santesso (Cambridge University Press, 2008), pp. 39–54.

51 *The Traytors Reward . . . in a Sermon Preach'd on the Thirtieth of January, 1713/ 14 . . .* (London, 1714), p. 18, in *The Royal Martyr Lamented, In Fourteen Sermons, Preach'd on the Thirtieth of January* (London, [1724]).

52 *The Royal Martyr Lamented, In Fourteen Sermons, Preach'd on the Thirtieth of January . . . by Luke Milbourne* (London, [1724]), see especially Sermon II, *The utter Extirpation of Tyrants and their Families. Preach'd 1707/8*, p. 5 and Sermon VIII, *The Traytor's Reward*, preface; White Kennett, *The Wisdom of Looking Backward* (London, 1715); *High Church Politicks: Or The Abuse of the 30th of January Consider'd. With Remarks on Mr. Luke Milbourne's Railing Sermons, and on the Observation of that Day* (London, 1710). For an extended discussion of Milbourne, see Andrew Lacey, *The Cult of King Charles The Martyr* (Woodbridge: The Boydell Press, 2003), pp. 197–205.

53 *PW*, II, 109–25 (112). See also: D. George Boyce, 'The Road to Wood's Halfpence and Beyond: William King, Jonathan Swift and the Defence of the National Church, 1689–1724', in *Political Discourse in Seventeenth- and Eighteenth-Century Ireland*, ed. D. George Boyce, Robert Eccleshall, and Vincent Geoghegan (Houndmills, Basingstoke: Palgrave, 2001), pp. 81–107; John Kerrigan, *Archipelagic English: Literature, History, and Politics 1603–1707* (Oxford University Press, 2008), pp. 362–76 (esp. p. 367).

54 *PW*, X, 86.

55 Raymond Gillespie, 'The Irish Protestants and James II, 1688–90', *Irish Historical Studies*, 28, no. 110 (1992), 124–33 (126).

56 *Correspondence*, II, 643–4; Kerrigan, *Archipelagic English*, p. 367.

57 *Correspondence*, II, 645, 643.

58 Ehrenpreis, III, 168.

59 *Correspondence*, III, 322; Ehrenpreis, III, 674–7.

60 [White Kennett], *An Account of the Society for Propagating the Gospel in Foreign Parts, Established by the Royal Charter of King William III . . .* (London, 1706), pp. 2–3. For White Kennett's activism in this area, see Rowan Strong, *Anglicanism and the British Empire c.1700–1850* (Oxford University Press, 2007), pp. 78–9. White Kennett may have been the model for Corusodes in Swift's *Intelligencer* no. 7 of 22–5 June 1728, see Jonathan Swift and Thomas Sheridan, *The Intelligencer*, ed. James Woolley (Oxford: Clarendon Press, 1992), pp. 93–100 (pp. 93–4).

61 *Gulliver's Travels*, IV. xii. 293.

62 Ibid., IV. xii. 294; Clement Hawes, 'Gulliver's Travels: Colonial Modernity Satirized', in Jonathan Swift, Gulliver's Travels and Other Writings, ed. Clement Hawes (Boston and New York: Houghton Mifflin, 2004), p. 26; Nuala Zahedieh, 'Morgan, Sir Henry (c.1635–1688)', ODNB, XXXIX, 121–8.

63 Gulliver's Travels, IV. xii. 294; Ehrenpreis, III, 675.

64 The first grievance listed by Swift in his letter to the Earl of Peterborough about his meeting with Walpole is 'That all persons born in Ireland are called and treated as Irishmen, although their fathers and grand-fathers were born in England; and their predecessors having been conquerors of Ireland, it is humbly conceived they [i.e. the ethnically English] ought to be on as good a foot as any subjects of Britain, according to the practice of all other nations, and particularly of the Greeks and Romans' (Correspondence, II, 643).

65 Gulliver's Travels, IV. ix. 271.

66 Ibid., IV. i. 224.

67 Ibid., IV. x. 279.

68 Ibid., IV. ix. 271–2.

69 For a summary of received views, see Jonathan Swift, Gulliver's Travels, ed. Claude Rawson and Ian Higgins (Oxford University Press, 2005), pp. 341–2.

70 'The Story of the Injured Lady' in PW, IX, 3–4.

71 Ibid., III, 40; Gulliver's Travels, IV. ix. 272.

72 PW, I, 61, 94, 175–6, 178; The Rehearsal, 30 December 1704.

73 See especially Edmund Spenser, A View of the State of Ireland, ed. Andrew Hadfield and Willy Maley from the first printed edition (1633) (Oxford: Blackwell, 1997), p. 45. On the Scythian–Irish connection, see Andrew Hadfield, 'Briton and Scythian: Tudor representations of Irish Origins', Irish Historical Studies, 28, no. 112 (1993), 390–408.

74 PW, XII, 306.

75 Gulliver's Travels, IV. xi. 284, 285.

76 Anthony Collins, A Discourse Concerning Ridicule and Irony in Writing (1729), introd. Edward A. Bloom and Lillian D. Bloom, The Augustan Reprint Society, no. 142 (Los Angeles: William Andrews Clark Memorial Library, 1970), pp. 28, 41, 26–8.

77 Michael DePorte, 'Contemplating Collins: Freethinking in Swift', in Reading Swift: Papers from The Third Münster Symposium on Jonathan Swift, ed. Hermann J. Real and Helgard Stöver-Leidig (Munich: Wilhelm Fink Verlag, 1998), pp. 103–15 (p. 106).

78 A Discourse of Free-Thinking, Occasion'd by The Rise and Growth of a Sect call'd Free-Thinkers (London, 1713), p. 43; PW, IV, 31.

79 Library, Part I, vol. II, 854; Peter Heylyn, Aërius Redivivus: or The History of the Presbyterians . . . 2nd edn (London, 1672), Book IX, p. 333. See also Swift's annotations on the English translation of the Italian historian Enrico Caterino Davila's Historie of the Civill Warres of France (London, 1647), in Hermann J. Real and Heinz J. Vienken, '"A Pretty Mixture": Books from Swift's Library at Abbotsford House', Bulletin of The John Rylands University Library of Manchester, 67 (1984–5), 522–43, and Library, Part I, vol. I, 500–8.

80 See P. W. Thomas, *Sir John Berkenhead 1617–1679: A Royalist Career in Politics and Polemics* (Oxford: Clarendon Press, 1969), esp. pp. 30–5, 97.

81 *PW*, I, 106; *A Letter from Mercurius Civicus to Mercurius Rusticus* (1643), in *Somers Tracts*, 2nd edn, ed. Walter Scott, 13 vols. (London, 1809–15), IV, pp. 580–98 (p. 592); Thomas, *Sir John Berkenhead*, p. 112.

82 Thomas, *Sir John Berkenhead*, pp. 80–1, 230–1.

83 *Mercurius Rusticus*, the fourth edition, corrected (London, 1723), Section VIII, pp. 82–8. See Hermann J. Real, 'The Dean's Grandfather, Thomas Swift (1595–1658): Forgotten Evidence', *Swift Studies*, 8 (1993), 84–93; Christopher Fox, 'Getting Gotheridge: Notes on Swift's Grandfather and a New Letter from Thomas Swift', *Swift Studies*, 20 (2005), 10–29. See also Joad Raymond, 'Ryves [Reeve], Bruno [Bruen] (c.1596–1677)', *ODNB*, XLVIII, 506–8.

84 *Library*, Part I, vol. II, 1069–70.

85 See for example the verse attacks on Dryden's conversion which linked L'Estrange and Dryden in *Poems on Affairs of State, vol. IV: 1685–1688*, ed. Galbraith M. Crump (New Haven and London: Yale University Press, 1968), pp. 73–90. See also Mark Goldie, 'Roger L'Estrange's *Observator* and the Exorcism of the Plot', in *Roger L'Estrange and the Making of Restoration Culture*, ed. Anne Dunan-Page and Beth Lynch (Aldershot: Ashgate, 2008), pp. 67–88.

86 See Goldie, 'Roger L'Estrange's *Observator*', p. 77.

87 For an overview, see Ian Higgins, 'Jonathan Swift and Charles Leslie', in *Loyalty and Identity: Jacobites at Home and Abroad*, ed. Paul Monod, Murray Pittock, and Daniel Szechi (Houndmills, Basingstoke: Palgrave, Macmillan, 2010), pp. 149–66.

88 See Ciaran Diamond, 'Leslie, John (1571–1671)', *ODNB*, XXXIII, 455–6.

89 *PW*, IV, 79.

90 Swift to the Rev. William Tisdall, 3 February 1703–4, *Correspondence*, I, 151; John Eachard, *The Grounds & Occasions of the Contempt of the Clergy and Religion Enquired into. In a Letter written to R. L.* (London, 1670), p. 31. See also Marcus Walsh, 'Samuel Johnson on Poetic Lice and Fleas', *N&Q*, 36, no. 4 (1989), 470.

91 See Higgins, 'Killing No Murder: Jonathan Swift and Polemical Tradition', pp. 46–50.

92 *PW*, II, 113. '*Daniel Defoe*' was added in a note at the bottom of the page later when the *Letter* was printed in Swift's collected *Works* of 1735.

93 *A Brief Explanation of a Late Pamphlet, Entitled, The Shortest Way with the Dissenters*, in Daniel Defoe, *The True-Born Englishman and Other Writings*, ed. P. N. Furbank and W. R. Owens (Harmondsworth: Penguin, 1997), p. 147. The possible affinities are noted, for example, in Miriam Leranbaum, '"An Irony Not Unusual": Defoe's *Shortest Way with the Dissenters*', *Huntington Library Quarterly*, 37 (1974), 227–50 (243).

94 *Reasons Humbly Offered to the Parliament of Ireland, for Repealing the Sacramental Test in Favour of the Catholicks* (written in 1733), *PW*, XII, 283–95.

95 'Concerning That Universal Hatred, Which Prevails Against The Clergy' (dated 1736), *PW*, XIII, 123–6 (125).

96 Charles Wogan to Swift, 27 February 1732–3, *Correspondence*, III, 591 and *Miscellaneous Pieces, In Prose and Verse. By the Rev. Dr. Jonathan Swift, Dean of St. Patrick's, Dublin* (London: Printed for C. Dilly, 1789, an unabridged text), p. 63; Swift to Charles Wogan 1735[–6], *Correspondence*, IV, 273.

97 *PW*, I, 241.

CHAPTER 2

Situating Swift's politics in 1701

Mark Goldie

SWIFT'S 'DISCOURSE OF ATHENS AND ROME' IN CONTEXT

The year 1701 saw a unique conjunction of the careers of Jonathan Swift, Daniel Defoe, and John Locke. In that year Swift published his first political tract, *A Discourse of the Contests and Dissensions between the Nobles and the Commons in Athens and Rome*. The aim of this chapter is to establish the unorthodoxy of its author's stance within the domain of Revolution Whiggery. By examining the polemical context, the political doctrines available to Swift to endorse or reject can be identified. Despite the classical theme of his tract, it reacted to a Lockean stratagem, in a year in which Locke's *Two Treatises of Government*, hitherto an obscure work, started to enter the mainstream of English political discourse. In 1701, while the Whigs adopted a populist political position that was Lockean in form, I suggest that Swift, though a Whig supporter at this juncture, deliberately avoided and inverted that populism. While Defoe and the Whig leader, Lord Somers, proved broadly Lockean, Swift did not. In showing that Swift refused to defer to the dominant Whig discourse, we can clarify his early political identity.

Swift, Defoe, and Locke were, at this juncture, supporters of the Junto Whigs, the most prominent figure among whom was John, Baron Somers, until recently Lord Chancellor. The Junto or Court Whigs had dominated William III's government in the late 1690s, but they were now out of power and confronted by a hostile Tory majority in the House of Commons. In the spring of 1701 the Tories impeached Somers and three other Junto lords, supplying the occasion for Swift's allegory, written to vindicate the Junto from their clamorous enemies. In its *dramatis personae*, the *Discourse* was transparent. Somers appears as Aristides, whom Swift describes as the 'Chancellor of Athens', 'a person of the strictest justice', who did 'mighty service [to] his country', but who, upon 'a slight and false accusation ... was banished by ostracism'.[1] Under the gossamer disguise of a narrative of partisan conflict in the ancient polities, Swift convicts the Tories of cynical opportunism, mendacious ingratitude, and treacherous ochlocracy.

Scholarship on Swift's politics has tended to examine the *Discourse* diachronically, within the frame of its author's career-long tergiversatory dialogue with Whiggism and Toryism, plundering works that were written over three decades for intimations of a fundamental Whiggism or an essential Toryism.[2] In this genealogical approach, the *Discourse* is compared with, *inter alia, Further Thoughts on Religion, A Tale of a Tub, The Sentiments of a Church of England Man, The Examiner, The Public Spirit of the Whigs, Gulliver's Travels*, and *Drapier's Letters*. By contrast, the method adopted here is synchronic, the *Discourse* considered in relation to Whig and Tory arguments at the moment of its composition.

The impeachment of the Junto lords occurred at a time when William III and the Whigs were deeply anxious about Louis XIV's aspiration toward a 'universal empire' over the European continent and were pressing for a renewal of the war against France that had been suspended by the Treaty of Ryswick in 1697. Outvoted in the Commons by war-weary Tories, the Whigs launched a campaign of popular agitation, cranking up the printing presses and the dramaturgy of popular outcry to bring pressure to bear on parliament. In consequence of the extraordinary affair of the Kentish petition, foreign policy quickly had repercussions in the domestic political arena, for, as we shall see, the affair provoked a controversy over the nature of representation within the English constitution. The press war of 1701 set in train the ideological contests of Queen Anne's reign.[3]

Hitherto, Swift had scarcely appeared in print. At the turn of the new century, his principal avocation was literary homage to Sir William Temple, who died in 1699, and whom he had served as secretary at Moor Park in Surrey. He prepared editions of Temple's *Miscellanea* and *Letters*, which carried brief prefaces of his own. On the stocks was his satire, *A Tale of the Tub*, which he would publish in 1704 with a dedication to Somers. From Temple, Swift imbibed a Williamite Whiggism which was committed to the Revolution, but also to a geopolitical perspective on its significance, proclaiming William's transformation of English foreign policy as the cynosure of a Europe liberated from 'popery and arbitrary power'. Swift also inherited Temple's classicism, and his *Discourse* drew inspiration from the latter's essay 'Of Popular Discontents', which regularly alluded to the factiousness of the ancient polities.[4] Having accepted the vicarage of Laracor in Ireland in 1700, it was on a brief visit to England in the following spring and summer, at the height of the Kentish furore, that Swift speedily penned the *Discourse*, which appeared in October and was 'greedily bought and read'.[5]

Swift, Defoe, and Somers published in 1701; Locke did not. Yet it is clear from Locke's correspondence that he was absorbed in reading what was published, kept abreast of newspaper reports, followed proceedings in parliament, backed the war party, and denounced the Tories for their craven appeasement of the European dictator.[6] It is also evident that Locke's colleagues were engaged on the Junto side, his parliamentary allies helping to orchestrate the press campaign.[7] More importantly, his *Two Treatises of Government* was invoked in the debate that arose from the Kentish petition. Scholars have shown that the *Two Treatises*, which had been published anonymously in 1689 and was only rumoured to be authored by Locke, was not well-known in the decade following its publication and was rarely mentioned in print.[8] It was the affair of the Kentish petition that established Locke's book as canonical, albeit chiefly through the diatribes of its Tory enemies, who detected its partisan deployment by the Junto Whigs. Within another dozen years, Swift himself would note the stature attained by the *Two Treatises* when he referred to 'writer[s] upon government from Plato to Mr. Locke'.[9]

THE PEOPLE'S RIGHT TO PETITION

On 29 April 1701 the freeholders of Kent gathered at Maidstone and agreed a petition, which was presented to the House of Commons on 8 May. It warned of the French threat and called upon the House to vote war taxation. One phrase proved explosive: the House, the petition urged, ought 'to have regard to the voice of the people'.[10] The Tories reacted fiercely, conscious that a statute of 1661 had outlawed 'tumultuous petitioning', passed in reaction against the besieging of parliament by City and Leveller petitioners during the Civil War. The House duly condemned the Kentish petition as 'scandalous and seditious, and tending to destroy the constitution of parliaments', and jailed the five gentlemen who had presented it.[11] When, however, the petitioners were released at parliament's prorogation in June, the Whigs ensured that they were rapturously applauded as national heroes. A great feast was held, a commemorative medal struck, and their images engraved for public sale.[12]

Amidst this furore, the terms of post-Revolution political argument were dramatically reconfigured. In defending the 'voice of the people', the

Whigs augmented the doctrine of the right of resistance against tyrannical monarchs, through which they legitimated the Revolution, by canvassing the accountability of parliaments to the people. Revolutionary activism was thereby transmuted into constitutional populism. In the new political landscape, the danger was perceived to reside less in overmighty princes than in overweening parliaments. Having, historically, defended parliaments against kings, the Whigs now adopted the mantle of defenders of the people against parliaments. For their part, the Tories, in repudiating the men of Kent, put aside the politics of divine right monarchy and now upheld the supremacy of parliament against the anarchy of the mob. There was, in all this, a high degree of contingent opportunism, the Junto Whigs suddenly rediscovering a populism which many thought they had abandoned while in power in the 1690s, while the Tories, still saddled with Whig taunts against divine right absolutism, rushed to embrace the honour of parliament.

In the Whig position lay the germ of radical programmes that would emerge in parliamentary reform movements after 1760 and reappear in the First Amendment of the American Constitution, which outlaws 'abridging ... the right of the people ... to petition'. These later voices are epitomised in Catherine Macaulay's insistence on MPs 'obeying every mandate of constituents'.[13] Yet there is no need to be proleptic, for the Whig stance had roots in seventeenth-century claims on behalf of rights of petitioning, addressing, and instructing MPs that had erupted in 1640 and again in 1680.[14]

Locke's *Two Treatises* was implicated in this controversy. It was invoked in the most penetrating Whig pamphlet published in defence of the 'voice of the people', John Somers's *Jura Populi Anglicani,* and its premisses were shared by the most notorious Whig productions in prose and verse, those by Defoe. At this moment, the repertoire of the *Two Treatises* was expanded. No longer only a defence of the revolutionary dissolution of government, nor narrowly a tutorial on the follies of Filmerism, it became an essay on the relationship between the people and their elected representatives. It is not anachronistic to envisage here a doctrine of 'democratic' accountability, if our usage of 'democracy' is precise. Locke and the Whigs were not universal suffrage democrats; an extended franchise was not the issue. Rather, the Whigs advocated a position that was democratic in the sense of what was owed to the constituent 'people', and their devices for rendering an assembly adequately representative of popular demands were, as contemporaries observed, echoes of classical Greek conceptions of democracy. The enforced accountability of MPs to their constituents could be construed as a surrogate for the direct democracy that had existed in ancient polities. Athens became a common point of reference in 1701, and Swift was scarcely eccentric in turning to the ancients in his *Discourse*.

Pamphleteers distinguished between the people 'collective' and the people 'representative', the former being the whole body of the people, either in a pre-governmental 'state of nature' or in an Athenian-style citizen assembly (a direct and not a representative democracy). By contrast, the people 'representative' was the populace embodied in elected representatives, characteristic of the 'Gothic' system that pertained in the large modern polities of the post-classical world. The Tories contended that the Whigs were utopian ancients who failed to recognise the impracticability of Greek solutions for modern polities. That the Greek precedent was on their minds is exemplified in a remark made by one author: 'Athens was a perfect democracy, and it was certainly the right of the collective body of the people there, to cast their government into what form they pleased.'[15] In his *Discourse*, Swift similarly contrasts 'a people represented' – the modern system – as opposed to 'the commons collective', 'as it was of old'. Likewise, he remarked that Athens had a 'senate' of 400, which although it 'seems to have been a body representative of the people ... the people collective reserved a share of power to themselves'.[16]

JOHN SOMERS AND THE PEOPLE'S DELEGATES

Swift, Defoe, and Locke were not the only significant contestants in the paper war. Two other prominent authors can be identified: Somers himself on the Whig side, and Sir Humphrey Mackworth for the Tories. Somers's *Jura Populi Anglicani* was a key work in the Whigs' new populist stance.[17] It indicts the Tories, asserting that their reluctance for war fuels French ambition, that they are shot through with Jacobitism, and that their loyalty to the Revolution is doubtful. The Tories thus inherit their pre-Revolution propensity to sell England's interests to French 'popery and slavery'. The tract's principal theme, however, is that the Commons's treatment of the Kentish petitioners was tyrannical, 'a notorious infringement of the liberties of the people', 'an intolerable sort of slavery', and 'a lawless and arbitrary act'.[18] Somers's hectic recapitulations of such claims characterise the hyperbolical language of liberty deployed on such signal occasions when the arrest of individuals could be polemically magnified as symbolic of the fate of every Englishman's freedom. From

John Lilburne in the 1640s to John Wilkes in the 1760s, the wrongful arrest of a citizen by order of the Commons was dramatised as heralding despotism.

Despite their Commons' majority, Somers regarded the Tories as merely a 'faction', since the 'honest party' and 'the whole people without doors' (excepting only Jacobites and papists) opposed them. Though elected, the Commons might act despotically, in which case it ceases to have the character of the people's 'representative'. Somers turns to a Lockean formula: 'It is very evident that the representatives of the people are those to whom, when they [the people] entered into society, they resigned up that power which they had in the state of nature, to punish offences against the law of nature.' In other words, if those to whom the people resign their power should thereafter betray their trust, then the foundation of obedience is broken. MPs 'have a trust reposed in them, which if they should manifestly betray, the people . . . must have a right to help and preserve themselves'.[19] Here Somers hovers on the brink of the Lockean dissolution of government and the right of resistance.

Yet Somers's purpose was not to revive revolutionary politics, but to assert a doctrine of delegacy. Members of parliament should obey their electors' instructions and be their mouthpieces; they should hold themselves mandated and bound, and not at liberty to form independent views. Such a view was, however, contrary to the orthodoxy that each MP was elected to exercise his own judgement, as captured in a remark repeated in every edition from 1669 to 1755 of Edward Chamberlayne's handbook, *Angliae Notitiae*, which described an MP as having a 'power absolute to consent or dissent without ever acquainting those that sent him'.[20] This was the doctrine that Edmund Burke would famously uphold in his speech to the Bristol electors in 1774: an MP is to use his own discretion, for constituents cannot anticipate arguments arising in parliamentary debate; parliament is a deliberative body and not a congress of mandated delegates. 'Authoritative instructions, mandates issued, which the member is bound blindly and implicitly to obey, to vote, and to argue for, though contrary to the clearest conviction of his judgement and conscience, these are things . . . which arise from a fundamental mistake of the whole order and tenor of our constitution.'[21] Burke's principle belonged to a broader doctrine of 'virtual representation', by which every commoner, whether enfranchised or not, was represented, and was indeed held to be 'virtually' present in parliament.

Somers's doctrine of delegacy contradicted this English orthodoxy. His tract identifies two instruments of delegacy: petition and instruction.

He revived the right of commoners to petition the House, recalling the mass Whig petitioning campaign against Charles II and boasting that the City of London's 'monster' petition of 1680 was 'a roll of above 100 yards in length', so many were the thousands of signatories.[22] It was on this topic that Somers explicitly cited Locke's *Two Treatises*:

'Tis certain that nothing can be more agreeable to nature, and a plainer dictate of reason, than that those who apprehend themselves aggrieved be allowed a liberty to approach those by petition who know their grievances, or perhaps are the authors of them, and consequently able to redress them. When men entered first into society, and gave up that right which they had to secure themselves in the state of nature, 'tis manifest that they did it for the preservation of property, which is the end of government ... If men entered into society to preserve [property], and therefore are so entitled to it, that (as a very learned and ingenious author tells us*) 'the supreme power cannot take from any man any part of his property without his own consent'.[23]

Against the asterisk, the marginal note reads: 'The author of two Treatises of Government, pag. 277'. For Somers, the Lockean principle that we cannot rationally consent to surrender to government that which we installed government to preserve entailed an irrevocable right of petitioning.

Petitioning was a close neighbour of another practice: the sending of instructions to prospective MPs, which implied that MPs were bound by the electorate's prescriptions. The Whigs used this device in 1679–81 and again in the autumn election of 1701, when around twenty constituencies are known to have served instructions. The Buckingham electors, for example, 'exhort, charge, and require' their MPs to pursue measures 'for pulling down the exorbitant power of France'. These instructions were collected in *The Elector's Right Asserted*, the preface to which repeatedly describes MPs as 'delegates', and denies that MPs have a free voice or free vote. It is false, the anonymous prefacer argues, to claim that 'as soon as ever the members are chosen, they were then left to the absolute freedom of their own wills, to act without control', for thereby our 'servants' would become our 'masters'. An MP should 'represent' in the strict sense of being a 'delegate and substitute' for the will of his electors.[24] The practice of giving instructions at elections continued periodically thereafter. It was defended in 1733 by Viscount Bolingbroke, who called MPs 'attorneys of the people',[25] but repudiated by David Hume, who thought instructions led to 'a pure republic'.[26] In the orthodox view, which Hume here expresses, the only remedy was to dismiss an MP at the next election – which is why Rousseau insisted that the English were only free at election time.[27]

It is anachronistic to presume that democratic populism must be characterised by demands for a universal franchise. That is the democracy of the moderns, and Somers was an ancient, whose calls for mandation and delegacy functioned as surrogates for Athenian direct democracy. His *Jura Populi Anglicani* contains a scintillating historical tour that ranges from Greek polities to modern republics, those states which 'transact all things ... by delegates'. Such was formerly the practice of the Achaians, Samnites, and Tuscans, and today of the Dutch, Swiss, Grisons, Venetians, and Lucchesi.[28] His tract was as indebted to Algernon Sidney as to Locke in its wide-ranging appeal to classical and Gothic example, and it melded a jurisprudential Lockean language of natural rights with a classical language of public virtue. Somers invoked, for example, the 'Lacedemonian matron' who 'renounced her own son, when he fled from battle, and forgot the services which he owed his country'.[29] Such eclecticism was commonplace in Whig rhetoric: Locke and the Spartan matron marched in step. Here was a Greek ideal of democratic accountability, underpinned by Lockean consent theory.

DANIEL DEFOE AND THE PEOPLE'S ORIGINAL POWER

A week after the Kentish men were arrested, an incandescent Daniel Defoe presented his stunningly forthright *Legion's Memorial* to the Commons, wherein he spoke on behalf of the 'people of England': 'your masters'. Defoe commanded the Speaker to deliver his memorial to the House, for 'it is required by them who have both a right to require, and power to compel, *viz.* the people'. Defoe registered the 'undoubted right of the people' to petition their representatives, and he warned that were the people to deem parliament oppressive, they possessed a right of extra-parliamentary redress.[30]

Defoe was scaling the heights of a notoriety recently attained when his poem *The True-Born Englishman* (1700) sold 80,000 copies. He now turned to produce his most sustained delineations of his political ideas, in prose form in *The Original Power of the Collective Body of the People of England*, which appeared at the close of 1701, and, in verse, his epic poem *Jure Divino*, which he began shortly afterwards, though it was not published until 1706.

Defoe loudly advertised the new Whig populism. The main thrust of his *Original Power* is a critique of Tories who rested their case on the supreme authority of parliament, for the 'parliamentary branch of power is no more infallible than the kingly'. Since Members of the Commons are the people's 'trustees', the 'last resort' is the people, 'not in the representatives, but in their original the represented'. Defoe's aim was therefore the 'declaring the rights of the people of England, not representatively but collectively considered'. The people, 'who are the original of all delegated power, have an undoubted right to defend their lives, liberties, property, religion and laws'. Eulogies to 'the beauty of our constitution' were of little import if parliament becomes oppressive, and Defoe proceeds to assert the rights of petitioning and instructing. Here again we find the language of consent, trust, and delegacy, the distinction between the people representative and collective, and an insistence on popular accountability.[31]

The extent of Defoe's debt to Locke is a large question, not to be pursued here.[32] An eclectic author, Defoe read widely, absorbed rapidly, and rarely paused to construe learned texts with exactitude, still less to advertise discipleship. In his journal, the *Review*, he cited Locke with approval, in tandem with Sidney, if only to insist that he did his own thinking. 'I know what Mr. Locke, Sidney and others have said ... and I must confess, I never thought their systems fully answered: but I am arguing by my own light, not other men's.'[33] Somers chose to deploy Locke explicitly, Defoe did not; and nothing in the Whigs' 'Athenian turn' required sourcing in Locke's *Two Treatises*. In situating Swift's *Discourse*, what matters is that Whiggery's most sonorous voices enunciated a democratic doctrine of the answerability of parliament to its constituents.

THE TORIES AND THE MIXED POLITY

For Revolution Tories, the crisis of 1701 presented an opportunity to wean Toryism from the incubus of Stuart absolutism. In this context, the most significant tract was Sir Humphrey Mackworth's *Vindication of the Rights of the Commons of England*. In August 1701 Locke's publisher sent him a copy, judging it a 'silly book, which is cried up by the Tories'.[34] Since Mackworth's overarching theme was the supremacy of parliament, his position was quite unlike anything the Tories would have endorsed in the 1680s.[35]

What is striking is Mackworth's adoption of the classical trinitarian conception of the constitution as a beneficent mixture of the three possible forms of polity: monarchy, aristocracy, and democracy. He opens by applauding the 'excellency of the government of England, by king, lords, and commons', and the 'just balance of the constitution'. Although there exists an 'absolute, supreme, and legislative authority', it lies conjointly 'in three distinct persons or bodies', which provide 'mutual checks' to each other.[36] Such a conception had been anathema to Stuart absolutists, for whom the crown had been sovereign and parliament subordinate, and who deplored the notion of the 'mixed' polity. They had insisted that it was a dangerous mistake to reconfigure the three estates, which, properly, comprised the lords spiritual, lords temporal, and commons, as king, lords, and commons, for the king was not an estate and not co-equal. Such an error, they contended, made possible a spurious conceptual marriage between the classical mixed polity and the feudal estates, a cardinal misconception propagated by the enemies of the Stuarts. Ideas of the mixed polity had sustained Parliamentarian claims during the 1640s and those of the Whigs in the 1680s. Although Charles I had, in a conciliatory moment, notoriously and all too eloquently endorsed precisely this doctrine, in his *Answer to the Nineteen Propositions*, issued on the eve of the Civil War in 1642, Restoration Tories had repeatedly repudiated the king's 'error'.[37] Accordingly, it was a momentous reversal that Mackworth now accepted this doctrine; indeed, he duly cited Charles I's *Answer* with approval.[38]

Mackworth's strategy, in the *Vindication* as well as in later tracts, was to occupy the high ground of parliamentary supremacy in order to indict Whig claims concerning an autonomous popular authority. Constitutional safety lies, he argues, in checks and balances among the three elements that comprise parliament, and not in an anarchic appeal to the people beyond. In Hobbesian mood, he holds that there had been an absolute revocation of right by the people in establishing their political institutions, so that there remains no residuum 'out of doors'. 'All the power [of] ... the people ... is delegated to ... their representatives in Parliament.' Mackworth's focus is, however, less the juridical revocation of right than its implications for representation. 'The people' simply do not subsist outside the Commons: 'the House of Commons are truly said to be the whole people of England in epitome, contracted into a small body', so that 'whatever is done by the elected is ... done by the electors'. This is the principle of virtual representation, and Mackworth uses precisely this term: the voice of the House 'is virtually the voice of every particular subject'. He proceeds to reject the right to give instructions to MPs, since proceedings in the Commons are by 'mutual debates' and 'a general consultation of all the wise representatives of parliament' in circumstances where individual citizens are unlikely to 'understand the true state and condition of the kingdom'. In outlining this deliberative principle, Mackworth adumbrated what was to become eighteenth-century orthodoxy: the Burkean position.[39]

Mackworth's was not an isolated voice, as several other writers endorsed his repositioning of Toryism. Charles Davenant's essay, 'The Danger of Appealing to the People from their Representatives in Parliament', attacked Somers's *Jura Populi Anglicani* and echoed Mackworth's *Vindication* in upholding the harmony of the three estates, and in holding it dangerous to 'set up a fourth estate, consisting of the people, with distinct rights'. If the people are deemed the 'last resort', then, Davenant protests, 'we are a democracy'. The people have wholly 'devolved' their power to their representatives; 'to appeal from their representatives to the multitude, is setting the axe to the very root of the constitution'. Davenant proceeds to reject the applicability of the Whigs' Athenian utopianism to a modern Gothic age. It is 'the wisdom of the Gothic models, to contract multitudes into a small number, by which they may be represented'. The Whigs' hankering for a Greek solution is nonsensical in a large modern state in which the Gothic system of representation obviates Greek democracy.[40]

James Drake echoed an aspect of Mackworth's argument that recollected the Hobbesian notion of an irrevocable transfer of popular authority. He avers that since the people have delegated their powers absolutely to parliament, 'upon whom all their rights and powers are devolved', the Whigs were erroneous in asserting the 'reserved power' of the 'collective body' of the people. Drake observes that the Whigs' present purpose in claiming 'all power to be originally in the people' was simply to 'argue against the power of the House'. The phrase 'the consent of the people' is thus a factitious pawn of 'mercenary noise and clamour'.[41] Elsewhere, Drake succinctly abridged this claim: the Whigs set up the 'gaderene mob' against 'the most august ... senate in the universe'.[42] Mackworth's position was also shared by the Tory clergy. On Restoration Day, 29 May 1701, a rising star of the Church, Francis Atterbury, preached before the Commons. The English constitution, he proclaimed, is 'wisely moulded out of all the different forms and kinds of civil government', contains 'all the advantages of those several forms, without sharing deeply in any of their great inconveniences', and 'whose several parts have a proper check upon each other'. In preaching thus, he echoed Charles I's *Answer to the Nineteen Propositions*.[43]

SWIFT AND ARISTOCRATIC WHIGGISM

It is now possible to situate Swift's *Discourse* within this conceptual terrain. In an autobiographical essay written around 1714, Swift tells us that the *Discourse* was his first serious reflection on politics: 'It was then

I first began to trouble myself with the difference between the principles of Whig and Tory.' He remarked that 'having been long conversant with the Greek and Roman authors, and therefore a lover of liberty, I found myself much inclined to be what they called a Whig in politics; and that, besides, I thought it impossible, upon any other principle, to defend the Revolution'.[44] On the face of it, Swift avers an uncomplicated Whiggery, yet, quite apart from his subsequent conversion to the Queen Anne Tories, his *Discourse* was far from endorsing the Somers–Defoe position.

The *Discourse* remains a perplexing work, since it supports the Whigs in unexpected ways, and Swift's use of allegory encourages indeterminacy of meaning. The tract certainly backed the Junto, so manifestly that both Somers and Gilbert Burnet were suspected to be its author; and, once Swift's authorship became known, he was courted by the Junto leadership, Lords Halifax and Sunderland alongside Somers.[45] Yet its main line of argument runs counter to the populist Whiggism outlined above. Quite the contrary, Swift appropriates from the Tories their own charge of dangerous populacy. The tract reads as if Swift was unaware of the Junto party line, yet he must quite deliberately have inverted its arguments in returning the accusation of democracy against the Tories. The *Discourse* opens on neutral ground and offers elements of the Whig position, but ultimately sheers away from it.

Few in 1701 would have disagreed with Swift's opening shibboleths. The best form of government is trinitarian, a balance of the 'one, the few, the many'. This, he contends, is both a Greek truth and a Gothic institution, and is, in turn, grounded in nature and reason. Athens, Sparta, and Rome erected their constitutions upon this tripartite principle. The archetypal forms of monarchy, aristocracy, and democracy can, in England, 'be fairly translated as, king, lords, and commons'. Mixed polities sustain liberty, and the balance is essential, 'an eternal rule in politics among every free people'. Tyranny occurs when any element disrupts the balance, and is not, properly speaking, the seizure of power by a single person, but rather 'the breaking of the balance by whatever hand'.[46] Thus far Swift was nonpartisan, for although such doctrines were now trumpeted by the Tories, they were not precepts from which Whigs dissented, albeit their current emphasis was on the constituent power of the people that underlay the mixed constitution.[47]

Swift then moves into conceptual territory which the Whigs had, for the moment, made their own by lambasting the overmighty House of Commons. He expounds the notion that tyranny may be perpetrated as readily by parliaments as by monarchs: an assembly is 'as capable of enslaving the nation' as a king.[48] Yet, although the *Discourse* provides a sustained and barely disguised attack on the Tory Commons, Swift refuses to appeal over its head to the collective body of the people. Far from it, because danger also lies in an overmighty people, as the Tories themselves maintained. Swift's key claim is that the Tory Commons is, by its own account, the plenary embodiment of the people. In other words, Swift accepts the Tory premise that the people are virtually present in their representatives, and then taunts the Tories with anarchic populism for brandishing the supremacy of that House of Commons and exercising supremacy in despotical ways. If the Commons claims to be 'the people', and if the Commons arbitrarily destroys great statesmen through the demagogic instrument of impeachment, then it is they who are tyrannic democrats. This is the theme that Swift elaborates at great length by narrating the cyclical waxing of popular power in Greece and Rome and its disastrous consequences. He repeatedly uses the phrase the '*dominatio plebis*, the tyranny of the people'.[49]

Far from appealing to the constituent power of the people, Swift upholds the principle of aristocracy. In deploring the impeachment of noblemen, he regards such episodes as archetypal instances of the destructive folly of the plebeians in tearing down patricians, through a grisly theatre of gratuitous mock justice, popular revenge, and the cruel punishment of ostracism. In rehearsing the principle of the mixed and balanced constitution, Swift celebrates the aristocracy as the proper balance or fulcrum that lies between monarch and commons.[50] The corruption of the ancient constitutions of Greece and Rome arose through plebeian usurpation and aristocratic humiliation. The Tory Commons is likened to the Decemviri, the Ephori, the Tribunes, and the demagogues of Argos. 'The orators of the people at Argos (whether you will style them in modern phrase, great speakers in the House, or only in general, representatives of the people collective) stirred up the commons against the nobles; of whom 1600 were murdered.' Likewise, the tribunes of the people at Rome attacked the optimates, 'accusing to the people whatever noble they pleased'. Swift relates the patriotic achievements of, and ungrateful injustices inflicted on, great statesmen, men 'honoured and lamented by their country, as the preservers of it', who 'have had the veneration of all ages since paid justly to their memories', men wrongly 'impeached for high crimes and misdemeanours'. He recounts the virtuous services and undeserved fates of Aristides, Miltiades, Themistocles, Pericles, Alcibiades, and Phocion. By the 'rash, jealous, and inconstant humour of the people' these men were destroyed, to the downfall of the commonwealth of Athens.[51]

Swift's regard for patrician rule could scarcely have been further removed from Defoe's demotic celebration of the multitude or Somers's exposition of democratic delegacy.

A key theme for Swift is the propensity of ambitious and discontented patricians cynically to betray their own class by demagogic mobilisation of the mob against their enemies. Thus the Tory leadership is likened to the Gracchi, 'advancing the power of the people' by eliminating their fellow nobles, and, too often, the people have been dupes of these alienated patricians. The tribunes at Rome, ostensibly the people's guardians, 'grossly imposed on' the people, 'to serve the turns and occasions of revengeful or ambitious men'. The Gracchi set a model for Marius, Pompey, and Caesar, who pulled down patrician power in the name of the people, until the commons had so 'trampled on the senate, there was no government left but a *dominatio plebis*'. The constitution and the liberties of Rome were ruined by the breaking of 'the balance between the patricians and plebeians'.[52]

Throughout Swift's indictment, there are, nevertheless, occasional instances of deference to the virtue of the collective body of the people. This emerges when he charges the Tories with electoral fraud. There is 'right still in the whole body', the Whig majority at large, rather than in the Tories' slim Commons' majority, misconstrued by them as 'the people' and acquired by the arts of manipulation.[53] Yet Swift's dominant theme remains profoundly anti-populist, as he repeatedly vilifies the mob, the rabble, 'popular clamours', the 'depths of popularity', the 'madness of the people'. In ochlocracy lies the ruination of liberty.[54] Swift stood for patrician libertarianism, not vernacular populism.

CHARLES LESLIE READS SWIFT'S 'DISCOURSE'

The eccentricity of Swift's position in the *Discourse* is accurately captured in a remarkable Tory tract of 1703, Charles Leslie's *New Association of the Modern Whigs and Fanatics*, in which Leslie offers a critical review of Whig pamphleteering over the previous two years. Here, uniquely, Swift, Defoe, and Locke are juxtaposed, for Leslie singles out the *Discourse*, *Legion's Memorial*, and the *Two Treatises*, together with Somers's *Jura Populi Anglicani*, intertwining them as belonging to the same cause. He determinedly misreads the *Discourse*, construing it as a populist tract, intent as he is on accusing all Whigs of demagoguery. On closer inspection, however, Leslie recognises that the *Discourse* will not fit this template, and this enables him to charge the Whigs with intellectual incoherence. Leslie was unaware that the *Discourse* had been written by Swift and thought it Somers's work, for he describes its author as 'the cock of the party', the 'manager'.[55]

Leslie was an Irish Jacobite, memorably described by John Tutchin as 'High Church, Nonjuring, bog-trotting, lying Leslie'.[56] He disguised his Jacobitism to appeal to broad Tory sentiment and became one of the most successful controversialists of Queen Anne's reign. His numerous polemics encompassed every target in the fearful mind of High Churchmen: latitudinarians, Dissenters, Quakers, Socinians, deists, and, not least, the whole edifice of Whig and 'republican' political theory. In his journal, *The Rehearsal*, launched in 1704, Leslie presented himself as an unreconstructed advocate of patriarchal monarchy and defender of Filmer. In discussing the concept of representation in *The New Association*, however, Leslie was willing to keep company with Sir Humphrey Mackworth's new model Toryism. A rumbustious and hectic piece, *The New Association* comprises plenty of short paragraphs and exclamation marks, designed for quick reading by dyspeptic Tory gentlemen and clergy.

One target is Locke. Leslie sneers at 'the great L—k in his Two Discourses of Government'. This was the first time that Locke had been called 'great', as author of the *Two Treatises*. Whereas the *Two Treatises* was still scarcely mentioned in 1700, it had now become canonical: the affair of the Kentish petition was the making of Lockean politics. Leslie identifies Locke as a democrat, even a franchise democrat, eliding the Lockean principle which 'makes the consent of every individual necessary' with the 'impossible ... nonsense' that 'everyone must ... vote for his representative'.[57] In taking this to be 'necessary to their scheme', in the plural, Leslie situates Locke within the wider Whig programme. Strikingly, Leslie sees Locke as a kind of Greek democrat, whose naivety prevented him from recognising that, in modern polities, universal consent is doubly disavowed, both by the necessity of having representatives, and by restricting the franchise to the propertied. Although Locke had not intended to refer to representation or to particular constitutions when he fashioned the concept of universal consent as the foundation of legitimate polities, Leslie conflates Lockean consent with representation, a connection prompted by the controversies of 1701. Leslie also refers to 'Legion', that is, to Defoe's *Legion's Memorial,* and to the 'new crop of devils, who are entered into the herd of swine; we heard them lately grunt from Kent'. Leslie detects in the Kentish petition the doctrine that the Commons was not the plenary embodiment of the people, was not sovereign, and was answerable to a popular supremacy.[58]

In riposte, Leslie rescues the honour of parliament and recapitulates the Tory doctrine of virtual representation. 'Is not a House of Commons ... virtually the people, and the whole power of the people lodged with them? Here they [the Whigs] begin to boggle! For there have been Houses of Commons that have not pleased them. And we have seen them set up Legion against the Commons.' When baulked, the Whigs dismiss the Commons as tyrannical usurpers, just as the senates of Rome, Sparta, and Athens had been slighted by the Decemviri, Ephori, and the Four Hundred. Here Leslie quotes selectively from Swift's *Discourse*, extracting remarks that point in a populist direction. For Leslie, the *Discourse* places 'the people' above the Commons and is guilty of bandying that dangerous slogan, *vox populi, vox dei*. 'The great patron of liberty', as he terms the author of the *Discourse*, 'says, that the saying, *vox populi, vox dei*, ought to be understood of the universal bent and current of a people; not of the bare majority of a few representatives; which is often procured by little arts, and great industry and application.' Thus provoked by the *Discourse* – or his reading of it – Leslie unleashes taunts and invective. How is the 'universal bent' of the people to be known, if not through evidence of the election of representatives to the Commons? The Whig answer is, 'from a mob or legion ... this is *vox populi*', but such a notion is both 'senseless' and 'nauseous'.[59]

Nonetheless, Leslie could scarcely avoid finding other themes in Swift's *Discourse*. He notes the *Discourse*'s appeal to the nobility and its worries about the mob's licentiousness and the ease with which the populace is misled. Such features suggest to Leslie that both the *Discourse* and the Whigs are riddled with inconsistency, and feebly fearful of their own Pandora's box; hence the author of the *Discourse* is 'forced to tack about, and overturn every stone he had laid in his foundation'. In reality, the Whigs speak only for a 'people' of their own construing, are contemptuous of a people who choose to vote Tory, and are terrified of a people not under their control. For Leslie, the Whig invocation of the people is opportunistic and dangerous, and Swift's *Discourse* allows him to convict the Whigs of muddle and hypocrisy.[60]

Leslie further protests that the Whig language of 'the people' is fraudulent. Such an entity has no reality: it is a rhetorical construct, the artifice of cynical politicians and publicists. The 'people' is not a universal but a particular, a faction; it is a sonorous, manufactured weapon. 'Every party and faction call themselves the people', and the Whigs 'usurp the name of the people to themselves'. By manipulating the idea of 'the people', a faction can bring to bear the wrath of the mob against whosoever is the faction's chosen target, whom they proclaim 'the public enemy of the people'. The Whigs are not democrats but demagogues, a crew of fallen noblemen in combination with hired scribes and a manipulated mob. Leslie was, of course, supplying a mirror image of Swift's own claims.[61]

Like other Tories, Leslie constantly labels the Whigs 'commonwealthmen' and 'republicans', and instinctively seeks to connect them with Civil War rebels and regicides. Specifically, the Whigs are 'republicans' if they reject not only high doctrines of divine right monarchy, but also the mixed polity and the supremacy of the triune parliament. For, by asserting the reserve power of the collective body of the people, they thereby erase parliament. The sovereignty of the people is, in the last resort, incompatible with a mixed polity that accords equal place to the crown and nobility.

SWIFT'S IDENTITY IN 1701

In Leslie's swingeing attack on the Whigs, the chief function of Swift's *Discourse* was to enable him to convict them of incoherence. This was perceptive, for while Swift ran his colours up the Junto's mast, his *Discourse* could not satisfactorily be colligated with the stance shared by Somers, Defoe, and Locke. Accordingly, the Whiggism of the *Discourse* was decidedly distinctive. The tract was partisan, but advertised its author's refusal to endorse the Junto's polemical position. It has been said of the *Discourse* that it was only incidentally Whig, that its commitment was covertly Tory and that 'the accident of its occasion made [Swift] look more like a Whig than he ever was'.[62] This seems persuasive, albeit apt to presume a perennial or essential Swiftian political identity. The *Discourse* entirely avoided the new populist reading of Locke, so noisily trumpeted by the Junto's pamphleteers throughout that summer of 1701. Swift preferred to place his trust in Aristides' statesmanship and to hold that liberty is best secured by aristocratic virtue.[63]

NOTES

1 Jonathan Swift, *A Discourse of the Contests and Dissentions* [sic] *Between the Nobles and the Commons in Athens and Rome*, ed. Frank H. Ellis (Oxford, 1967); quotation at p. 94. This is the standard edition. The *Discourse* is also reprinted in *PW*, I, 193–236.
2 The principal works on Swift's politics are: J. A. Downie, *Jonathan Swift: Political Writer* (London, 1984); Downie, 'Swift's Politics', in Hermann J. Real and Heinz J. Vienken, eds., *Proceedings of the First Munster Symposium*

on Jonathan Swift (Munich, 1985); Ian Higgins, *Swift's Politics: A Study in Disaffection* (Cambridge, 1994); F. P. Lock, *Swift's Tory Politics* (London, 1983); David Oakleaf, *A Political Biography of Jonathan Swift* (London, 2008). Higgins and Lock insist on Swift's Tory identity, Downie his Whiggish. See Downie's review of Higgins: 'Swift and Jacobitism', *English Literary History*, 64 (1997), 887–901. See also: Kenneth Craven, *Jonathan Swift and the Millennium of Madness* (Leiden, 1992); Michael DePorte, 'Avenging Naboth: Swift and Monarchy', *Philological Quarterly*, 69 (1990), 419–33; Irvin Ehrenpreis, 'Swift on Liberty', *Journal of the History of Ideas*, 13 (1952), 131–46; Daniel Eilon, *Faction's Fictions: Ideological Closure in Swift's Satire* (Newark, NJ, 1991); Isaac Kramnick, *Bolingbroke and his Circle: The Politics of Nostalgia in the Age of Walpole* (Cambridge, MA, 1968), pp. 206–13; Edward Rosenheim, 'The Text and Context of Swift's *Contests and Dissensions*', *Modern Philology*, 66 (1968), 59–74.

3 For the historical context see J. A. Downie, *Robert Harley and the Press: Propaganda and Public Opinion in the Age of Swift and Defoe* (Cambridge, 1979), ch. 2; Henry Horwitz, *Parliament, Policy, and Politics in the Reign of William III* (Manchester, 1977), ch. 12; Mark Knights, *Representation and Misrepresentation in Later Stuart Britain* (Oxford, 2005), pp. 130–4, 195–202, 239; Craig Rose, *England in the 1690s* (Oxford, 1999), ch. 4; and Ellis's Introduction to Swift, *Discourse*. For the ideological context see Philip Ayres, *Classical Culture and the Idea of Rome in Eighteenth-Century England* (Cambridge, 1997); Mark Goldie, 'The English System of Liberty', in Mark Goldie and Robert Wokler, eds., *The Cambridge History of Eighteenth-Century Political Thought* (Cambridge, 2006); J. P. Kenyon, *Revolution Principles: The Politics of Party, 1689–1720* (Cambridge, 1977). For some implications of the Kentish petition see P. A. Hamburger, 'Revolution and Judicial Review: Chief Justice Holt's Opinion in *City of London* v. *Wood*', *Columbia Law Review*, 94 (1994), pp. 2091–153.

4 Published in *Miscellanea, Part the Third* (1701).

5 *PW*, VIII, 119.

6 E. S. de Beer, ed., *The Correspondence of John Locke*, 8 vols. (Oxford, 1976–89), VII, letters 2851, 2853, 2855–6, 2860–1, 2865, 2870, 2874, 2886–7, 2919, 2940, 2942–3, 2947, 2990, 3061.

7 Downie, *Harley and the Press*, ch. 2.

8 John Dunn, 'The Politics of Locke in England and America in the Eighteenth Century', in J. W. Yolton, ed., *John Locke: Problems and Perspectives* (Cambridge, 1969); J. G. A. Pocock, *The Machiavellian Moment: Florentine Political Thought and the Atlantic Republican Tradition* (Princeton, 1975), ch. 13. For a more sanguine view of Locke's early impact see 'Introduction', in Mark Goldie, ed., *The Reception of Locke's Politics*, 6 vols. (London, 1999), I, pp. xvii–lxxi. Also M. M. Goldsmith, '"Our Great Oracle, Mr. Lock": Locke's Political Theory in the Early Eighteenth Century', *Eighteenth-Century Life*, 16 (1992), 60–75; James Moore, 'Theological Politics: A Study of the Reception of Locke's *Two Treatises of Government* in England and Scotland

in the Early Eighteenth Century', in M. P. Thompson, ed., *John Locke and Immanuel Kant* (Berlin, 1991); M. P. Thompson, 'The Reception of Locke's *Two Treatises of Government, 1690–1705*', *Political Studies*, 24 (1976), 184–91.

9 Swift, *The Public Spirit of the Whigs* (1714): *PW*, VIII, 43. It is not known when Swift read Locke's *Two Treatises*. For other occasional references to Locke see *PW* II, 80, 85, 97; X, 86–7.

10 Defoe reprinted the petition in *The History of the Kentish Petition* (1701): *The Political and Economic Writings of Daniel Defoe*, eds. W. R. Owens and P. N. Furbank, 8 vols. (London, 2000), II, pp. 52–3.

11 *Journal of the House of Commons*, XIII, p. 518.

12 The engraving is reproduced in Swift, *Discourse*, Fig. 2.

13 Catherine Macaulay, *An Address to the People of England* (1775), p. 18.

14 Paul Kelly, 'Constituents' Instructions to Members of Parliament in the Eighteenth Century', in Clyve Jones, ed., *Party and Management in Parliament, 1660–1784* (Leicester, 1984); Derek Hirst, *The Representative of the People?: Voters and Voting in England under the Early Stuarts* (Cambridge, 1975), pp. 161–6; Kathleen Wilson, *The Sense of the People: Politics, Culture, and Imperialism in England, 1715–1785* (Cambridge, 1995), pp. 125–6, 133–4.

15 James Drake, *The Source of our Present Fears Discover'd* (1703), p. 48.

16 Swift, *Discourse*, pp. 92, 123; cf. pp. 84, 87, 112.

17 The tract is generally attributed to Somers, on whom see William L. Sachse, *Lord Somers* (Manchester, 1975); Robert M. Adams, 'In Search of Baron Somers', in Perez Zagorin, ed., *Culture and Politics from Puritanism to the Enlightenment* (Berkeley, 1980).

18 John Somers, *Jura Populi Anglicani, or the Subject's Right of Petitioning* (1701), pp. iii, v, 18, 29; cf. p. 24.

19 Ibid., pp. v–vi, 51. Cf. John Locke, *Two Treatises of Government*, II, paras. 87, 89, 149, 221.

20 Quoted in Betty Kemp, *King and Commons, 1660–1832* (London, 1957), p. 43.

21 *The Political Philosophy of Edmund Burke*, ed. Iain Hampsher-Monk (London, 1987), p. 110.

22 Somers, *Jura Populi*, pp. 33–5, 38.

23 Ibid., p. 30; Locke, *Two Treatises*, II, para. 138.

24 *The Elector's Right Asserted* (1701), pp. 1–4; Narcissus Luttrell, *A Brief Historical Relation*, 6 vols. (Oxford, 1857), V, p. 119; W. A. Speck, *Tory and Whig: The Struggle in the Constituencies, 1701–1715* (London, 1970), pp. 29–30.

25 Quoted in Wilson, *Sense of the People*, p. 134.

26 David Hume, *Political Essays*, ed. Knud Haakonssen (Cambridge, 2005), p. 19.

27 Rousseau, *The Social Contract* (1762), bk 3, ch. 15, 'Deputies or Representatives'.

28 Somers, *Jura Populi*, p. 51.

29 Ibid., p. vi.

30 Defoe, *Political and Economic Writings*, II, pp. 39–46; see also *The History of the Kentish Petition*, at pp. 47–66.

31 Defoe, *The Original Power of the Collective Body of the People*, in *Political and Economic Writings*, II, pp. 99–128, quotations at pp. 107, 111–12, 115–16, 119. *Legion's Memorial* and the *Original Power* are also reprinted in Defoe, *The True-Born Englishman and Other Writings*, eds. P. N. Furbank and W. R. Owens (Harmondsworth, 1997), pp. 72–109; the latter in Goldie, *Reception of Locke's Politics*, I, pp. 329–53.

32 For Defoe's Lockeanism see Paula R. Backscheider, *Daniel Defoe: His Life* (Baltimore, 1989), pp. 76, 162, 168–72; Backscheider, 'The Verse Essay, John Locke, and Defoe's *Jure Divino*', *ELH: English Literary History*, 55 (1988), 99–124; for a contrary view: Katherine Clark, *Daniel Defoe: The Whole Frame of Nature, Time, and Providence* (Basingstoke, 2007).

33 Defoe, *Review*, III, no. 108 (10 Sept. 1706).

34 Locke, *Correspondence*, VII, no. 2990.

35 On Mackworth see J. A. W. Gunn, *Beyond Liberty and Property: The Process of Self-Recognition in Eighteenth-Century Political Thought* (Kingston and Montreal, 1983), ch. 4; Clayton Roberts, *The Growth of Responsible Government in Stuart England* (Cambridge, 1966), ch. 8.

36 Humphrey Mackworth, *A Vindication of the Rights of the Commons* (1701), epistle dedicatory, pp. 2, 5.

37 See Mark Goldie, 'John Locke and Anglican Royalism', *Political Studies*, 31 (1983), 61–85.

38 Mackworth, *Vindication*, p. 9.

39 Mackworth, *Free Parliaments* (1704), p. 9; Mackworth, *Vindication*, pp. 32, 38–9. See also: Mackworth, *The Principles of a Member of the Black List* (1702).

40 Charles Davenant, *Essays upon Peace at Home and War Abroad* (1704), in Charles Whitworth, ed., *The Political and Commercial Works of Charles Davenant*, 5 vols. (1771), IV, pp. 292–4.

41 James Drake, *A History of the Last Parliament* (1702), pp. 96, 129, 131–2. When hauled before the House of Lords for this tract, James cited *Jura Populi Anglicani* in evidence.

42 James Drake, *The Legionites Plot* (1702), pp. 5, 8. See also John Humfrey, *Letters to Parliament-Men* (1701).

43 Francis Atterbury, *A Sermon Preached Before the House of Commons* (1701), p. 19.

44 Swift, *PW*, VIII, 119–20.

45 Ibid., 119.

46 Swift, *Discourse*, pp. 83–5, 87. So pronounced was Swift's Polybian exposition of the trinitarian doctrine that it became a significant source in Revolutionary America: C. Bradley Thompson, 'John Adams's Machiavellian Moment', *Review of Politics*, 57 (1995), 389–417. See also M. M. Goldsmith, 'Public Virtue and Private Vices: Bernard Mandeville and English Political Ideologies in the Early Eighteenth Century', *Eighteenth-Century Studies*, 9 (1976), 488–9.

47 Mixed monarchy is compatible with democratic foundations, although, as Tories pointed out, it is liable to be threatened by such foundations. See the remarks of Charles Leslie discussed below.

48 Swift, *Discourse*, p. 88.

49 Ibid., pp. 87, 97, 106, 108.

50 Swift was not alone on the Whig side in invoking the aristocracy as the 'balance' of the constitution: see *A Vindication of the Rights and Prerogatives of the Right Honourable the House of Lords* (1701).

51 Swift, *Discourse*, pp. 87, 94, 97, 103; cf. p. 112.

52 Ibid., pp. 102, 107, 108, 110.

53 Ibid., p. 114. Tory electoral manipulation amounts, for Swift, to 'servile flatteries of the people'; so hostile was he to demagoguery that he apparently countenances bribery of electors, commonplace avarice being safer than eloquent frenzy: *Discourse*, pp. 126–7.

54 Ibid., pp. 115, 120.

55 Charles Leslie, *The New Association, Part II* (1703), Supplement, pp. 12, 14. Drake attributes the *Discourse* to Burnet: *Source of our Present Fears*, p. 48.

56 John Tutchin, *The Observator*, IV, p. 81.

57 Leslie, *New Association, Part II*, Supplement, p. 4. For Leslie as a critic of Locke see Gunn, *Beyond Liberty and Property*, ch. 4; Kenyon, *Revolution Principles*, ch. 7; Moore, 'Theological Politics'; Gordon Schochet, *Patriarchalism in Political Thought* (Oxford, 1975), ch. 11.

58 Leslie, *New Association, Part II*, p. 36.

59 Ibid., pp. 27–8; Supplement, p. 10; Swift, *Discourse*, p. 114.

60 Leslie, *New Association, Part II*, p. 28; Supplement, pp. 10–13. For another assessment of Swift's *Discourse* as a defence of aristocracy and hence out of kilter with the Junto position see Drake, *Source of our Present Fears*.

61 Leslie, *New Association* (1702), p. 14; *Part II*, Supplement, p. 5.

62 Lock, *Swift's Tory Politics*, p. 179; cf. Higgins, *Swift's Politics*, p. 4.

63 For commenting on earlier versions of this chapter I am indebted to Clare Jackson.

CHAPTER 3

Swift and Walpole

Paul Langford

On Wednesday 27 April 1726, at 8 o'clock in the morning, Jonathan Swift and Sir Robert Walpole met, probably in the Prime Minister's house in Arlington Street, Piccadilly. The meeting lasted somewhat more than an hour. Apparently it was the only such, one to one. Other contacts were of a different kind. In the previous week Swift had been invited to a dinner party in Chelsea, selected by Walpole to provide fellow guests whom he would have appreciated. A year later there was a further, accidental encounter between the two in an unidentified social gathering, amounting to no more than a 'civil Compliment' on Walpole's part. It seems that only on these three occasions did Swift and Walpole find themselves in the same room.[1]

None the less, scholars have made Walpole the arch-antagonist of Swift's later career.[2] The oft-quoted remark made by Swift to Pope, in 1725, that he was 'no more angry with [Walpole] Th[a]n I was with the Kite that last week flew away with one of my Chickins and yet I was pleas'd when one of my Servants shot him two days after' hardly sounds indifferent.[3] The fact is that during the last two decades of his active life he had Walpole much in his mind, as his correspondence and other writings reveal. And any man who named his longstanding housekeeper Sir Robert Walpole and did the same when her daughter succeeded her in 1735, in both cases expecting friends and acquaintants to follow his practice, was unlikely to dismiss Walpole from his thoughts for long.

Robert Walpole and Jonathan Swift were more or less contemporaries. Walpole was nine years younger than Swift. They both died in 1745. Neither had been intended for a political career. Walpole was destined for the cloth, after Eton and King's College, Cambridge. Characteristically he later speculated that he might have become Archbishop of Canterbury. In the event he was saved from the Church, or the Church was saved from him, when his elder brother died in 1698. He built his formidable political career as much on talent and industry as his family connections.

He was the first and also (with the exception of the Elder Pitt) the only eighteenth-century Prime Minister who could not boast an ennobled father.

Swift was hardly to be compared to a landed gentleman like Walpole, but his father had been a lawyer in Ireland, his grandfather a parson in England. Despite his relative poverty, his association with the Temple family put him in touch with the political world of the 1690s. It was his ordination in 1694 rather than his rank that restricted his role. Other impecunious Trinity College men of letters, for example Richard Steele and Edmund Burke, found their way to political prominence. In any event the bug of politics bit Swift and never really left him.

Swift's direct engagement with English politics was owed to the Tory 'revolution' of 1710 (his terminology) which brought him into close contact with its leading beneficiaries, Robert Harley and Henry St John. Despite his Whig background, he quickly became the foremost publicist of the new regime. Walpole might have been seen in 1710 as a natural target. As a junior war minister he had made his mark. In the Sacheverell impeachment which had so disastrously backfired on the Whigs, he was its leading prosecutor and perhaps the only one to gain reputation by it. In the lower House he was a resourceful and knowledgeable speaker.

Swift was not restrained in his assault on key members of the previous ministry. Godolphin was the subject of a bitterly personal lampoon in October 1710.[4] As the author of *The Examiner* between November 1710 and June 1711, Swift mercilessly berated Wharton, foul defiler of the altar, and Marlborough and his wife, corrupt architects of their family's aggrandisement.[5] Walpole appears only once and then by way of quotation from St John who, in September 1710, had urged *The Examiner*, before Swift took it over, to make Walpole blush for shame after the Sacheverell débâcle.[6] Swift merely noted that he had shown no signs of remorse.[7]

Swift's devastating tract *The Conduct of the Allies* (27 November 1711) swept away the foundations of 'a War of the *General* and the *Ministry*' (as he called it).[8] Despite Walpole's close relationship with both Godolphin and Marlborough he was not mentioned. In December 1711 Nottingham was severely handled by Swift as the Tory renegade whose speech in the Lords threatened to bring down the Government by defeating its peace proposals in the upper House.[9] Walpole made an identical motion in the lower House, and was shortly afterwards expelled from the Commons for corrupt handling of a forage contract when Secretary at War. Walpole apparently went out of his way to identify Swift as Nottingham's arch enemy. 'I heard at Court, that Walpole (a great Whig member) said, that I and my whimsical club writ it at

one of our meetings, and that I should pay for it.'[10] Yet Swift had nothing
to say in public on the subject of Walpole's motion. Only in *The History
of the Four Last Years of the Queen*, not published until 1758, did Swift
retrospectively refer to Walpole's motion in the Commons as a simple
matter of fact, without comment.[11] Moreover, when Walpole regained his
seat in the Parliament of 1713–15, he played a prominent part in defending
Steele against both the Government and Swift. Walpole's closest
colleague, James Stanhope, appears twice in *The Publick Spirit of the
Whigs*, as do others, including managers of Sacheverell's trial, Nicholas
Lechmere, Sir Peter King, and Sir Thomas Parker.[12] Walpole is ignored.

If Swift did not acknowledge Walpole, Walpole certainly acknowledged Swift. In his *A Short History of the Late Parliament*, Walpole
referred to Swift's *Conduct of the Allies* as a 'new lesson'.[13] It was not
wholly sarcasm. The opposition was taken by surprise by Swift's concentration on the burdens of the war effort and the cynicism of Britain's allies
in exploiting its military success. In the Commons, on 22 April 1714,
Walpole attacked the Ministry's 'Account how far the Peace is complete
between her Majesty's Allies and France and Spain; and what is yet
wanting to make the same universal; as also what Obstructions her
Majesty has met with in her Endeavours to make the same universal
and complete'.[14] Who was or were responsible for the 'Account' is not
known, but Walpole suggested the involvement of Swift when he referred
to 'the style of some late Pamphleteers'. His colleague Aislabie specifically
referred to Swift's defence of Tory mistreatment of the Catalans in *The
Publick Spirit of the Whigs*. Peter Wentworth's report of this debate on
22 April fits well with Swift's later references to both the speakers and the
subject.[15] He took some pride in 1724 in reporting that Walpole had made
'a Speech directly against me, by Name, in the House of Commons, as I was
told a very few Minutes after, in the Court of *Requests*, by more than fifty
Members'.[16] In his 'The Author upon Himself', perhaps written in July 1714
but not published until 1735, he also coupled Walpole and Aislabie as
identifying him for revealing the full extent of the Peace negotiations.[17]

Swift's subsequent writings in defence of Toryism made only a single
reference to Walpole. This occurs in *The History of the Four Last Years of the
Queen*, drafted in 1713 but unpublished until 1758. It appears to have been an
insertion, probably added when Swift was revising the text in the mid-1720s.

He was a Person much caressed by the Opposers of the Queen and Ministry,
having been first drawn into their Party by his Indifference to any Principles; and
afterwards kept steddy by the loss of his Place. His bold, forward Countenance,

altogether a Stranger to that Infirmity which makes Men bashfull, joined to a Readyness at speaking in Publick, hath justly entitled him among those of his Faction to be a Sort of Leader of the Second Form; and must excuse me for being so particular about one who is otherwise altogether obscure.[18]

The magisterial Sir Harold Williams missed the significance of this passage.

Williams established the version of the *History* now at Windsor in the Royal Archive and also reported Swift's later amendments.[19] He dwelled heavily on a passage which accused the Whigs of packing the House of Lords with their 'Clients or Proselytes' in order to justify Harley's creation of twelve Tory peers to force through the Peace. Swift appeared to have considered striking out what under the subsequent Hanoverian regime would have been particularly offensive. The passage was accordingly excised in the 1758 and subsequent editions, and was rightly reinstated in Davis's edition of Swift's *Prose Works*.[20] Williams thought this amendment the only one of material significance in the revised text. 'No other excision, addition, or correction, either in length or importance, is comparable to this.'[21] In fact the passage concerning Walpole was twenty-three lines of printed text, only six lines shorter than the 'Clients or Proselytes' paragraph. It also matters because it is apparently the only judgemental remark about Walpole by Swift in any of his extant writings purporting to have been penned before the death of Queen Anne. Like some other revisions in the manuscript it makes little sense if recorded in the composition of 1713. It looks much more like a gratuitous swipe at Walpole before the Hanoverian Accession made possible a regime of dunces. In reality Walpole was a respected and popular Whig leader in and out of the House of Commons. He was also regarded by the Tories as a dangerous opponent.

When Swift's *History* was finally published in 1758 the characters that he drew of Marlborough, Godolphin, Sunderland, Wharton, Cowper, Nottingham, and Walpole aroused much interest and some controversy. Burke included them in the first volume of the *Annual Register*. He commented that the characters 'may serve as a striking example of the melancholy effects of prejudice, and party zeal; a zeal, which whilst it corrupts the heart, vitiates the understanding itself, and could mislead a writer of so penetrating a genius as Doctor Swift, to imagine that posterity would accept satire in the place of history'.[22] Burke took the opportunity nonetheless to draw out the strengths of his compatriot's political writing. Others were less generous. The author of a response to Swift's *History*

noted 'the venomed malevolence of Swift's rhapsodical Tory-book' and
pointed to the hypocrisy of Swift in his treatment of Walpole. 'Since the
accession of the present illustrious family, Swift often threw himself in the
way of this obscure man, whom he would have made an angel of light had
he seconded his ambitious views.'[23]

Why was Walpole ignored in Swift's political writings between 1710
and 1715? One possibility is that Swift, in his own judgement, or in that of
his leaders, believed that Walpole was not beyond redemption as a
moderate Whig capable of allying with moderate Tories. He had, after
all, thrown in his lot with Godolphin and Marlborough in 1705, at a time
when Junto Whigs were still suspicious of them. Some Whigs remained
doubtful of Walpole's dependability. On the verge of the fall of the Whig
ministry in 1710 Sir Richard Temple, of a tougher Buckinghamshire cast
than Norfolk Whigs, told him candidly: 'Wee whiggs here are quite of
another make, and those that ought to judge the best, think you have
drawn this upon yourselves, by your complyance from time to time.'[24]
Harley evidently agreed with them. Although he removed Walpole from
his Secretaryship at War in September 1710, he permitted him to remain
in the profitable office of Treasurer of the Navy until June 1711 in the hope
that he could still be won over. When he eventually expelled Walpole
from the Commons in January 1712, it was to prevent him participating in
the crucial debates on peace negotiations. Even then he seems not to have
ruled out a coalition of moderates. He attended a meeting of Whigs
in March 1713, perhaps including Walpole. As late as July 1714 his rival
St John was putting out feelers, though in the event Walpole was absent in
Norfolk.[25] Alienating an up-and-coming politician was taking a risk. On
the other hand Swift may simply have underrated Walpole. If so, it was a
mistake, though not one that Swift, with characteristic stubbornness, ever
admitted.

From 1714, when Swift returned to Dublin, to 1724, when he published
the first of the *Drapier's Letters*, he was almost silent on the subject of
British politics, though he continued to work on the tracts which he had
been preparing in the last years of the Queen's reign. It was William
Wood's infamous project to introduce a new copper currency in Ireland
that made it possible to portray the Dean and the Prime Minister as
antagonists, though Swift was not the initiator of the controversy that set
Ireland in flames. Nor indeed was Walpole the originator of the project.
Swift was certainly convinced that he had penetrated the Prime Minister's
hide, writing in March 1725 'that Mr. W[alpole] thinks himself personally
offended'.[26] If Walpole was personally offended it was perhaps by

A Serious Poem upon William Wood, issued in Dublin on 17 September 1724 and in the London press in October. It includes Walpole as a dragon called Brass whose belly had two sows in it, presumably the Duchess of Kendal and the Countess of Darlington, the King's mistresses, the former at least implicated in the South Sea Bubble and Wood's patent.[27] The fourth and most audacious of the *Drapier's Letters*, which Carteret had little alternative but to prosecute for its seditious reflections on King and ministers, probably gave the greater offence. The only minister named was Walpole, who promised to '*ram them* [the notorious halfpennies] *down our Throats*', to force us to '*take these Half pence or eat our Brogues*', and to '*make us swallow his Coyn in Fire-Balls*'.[28] These quotations were doubtless Wood's rather than Walpole's, though it was not beyond Swift to have invented or at least exaggerated them himself. In any event, ironic panegyric was the most effective means of deriding a minister of state without sedition. 'What Vile Words are these to put into the Mouth of a great Counsellor, in high Trust with his Majesty, and looked upon as a prime minister.'[29] Walpole could not be anything but hostile to Wood's project thanks to 'this one invincible Argument, that he has the Universal Opinion of being a Wise Man, an able Minister, and in all his Proceedings pursuing the *True Interest* of the *King* his Master: And that, as his *Integrity* is above all Corruption, so is his *Fortune* above all *Temptation*'. In consequence the Irish would 'be left to possess our *Brogues* and *Potatoes* in Peace, as Remote from Thunder as we are from Jupiter'.[30]

Walpole eventually cancelled Wood's patent, reimbursing Wood at the expense of the Irish taxpayer, but Swift had no intention of being remote from Jupiter. Whether he saw himself as Irish ambassador at large or whether he meant to relaunch himself in English life is not clear, though his trip to London in 1726 was compatible with either or both. Swift's re-entry into the literary and political world of England in March 1726 was a considerable success, not least at Leicester House, where he was naïve enough to be flattered by the Princess of Wales, and her husband's mistress, Mrs. Howard. The famous interview with Walpole on 27 April was less satisfactory. Ostensibly the discussion centred on Swift's plea for a new deal on behalf of Ireland.[31] If Swift thought that Walpole was another Harley in the making, he was quickly disabused. Walpole expressed little interest in Ireland. The misunderstanding and negligence which largely characterised his treatment of it plainly struck Swift in their interview. Historians of Ireland tend to share his view.[32] Moreover Walpole had even less interest for Swift. By July Swift was writing, 'I am weary of being among Ministers whom I cannot govern.'[33] On the 20th he wrote

'I have absolutely broke with the first Minister.'[34] It can hardly be coincidence that Gulliver took his first steps in public life soon afterwards, when Swift, posing as one Richard Sympson, wrote to the publisher Benjamin Motte on 8 August.

However divided Swiftian scholarship is on the subject of *Gulliver's Travels* as political satire, so far as Walpole is concerned there is a core of specific incidents that associate him closely with Flimnap, Treasurer of Lilliput, not least because Edmund Curll's publication of a key to the text tended to establish them.[35] They include:

1) the art of rope dancing before the Emperor, described by Sir Charles Firth as symbolising 'Robert Walpole's dexterity in parliamentary tactics and political intrigues'[36]

2) the royal cushion which preserved Flimnap from breaking his neck (more pointedly described by Curll as the King's cushion), signifying the Duchess of Kendal's favour which restored Walpole and his brother-in-law Townshend to grace (I.i)[37]

3) the story of the coloured strings, blue, red, and green (originally purple, yellow, and white) to avoid risk, which suggested reward for exceptional leaping and creeping before the Emperor – they represented the knightly Orders of the Garter, the Bath, and the Thistle, one of which (Bath) Walpole revived, and two of which he awarded to himself, the Bath in 1725, the Garter in 1726 (I.i)[38]

4) Flimnap's claim that 'he was forced to take up Money at a great Discount; that Exchequer Bills would not circulate under nine *per Cent*, below Par', which implied Walpole's financial mismanagement, probably in 1726 (I.iv)[39]

5) the informers employed by the Treasurer, Clustril and Drunlo (I.vi), who were plausibly matched by Arthur Case to Walpole's informers, Andrew Pancier and the Reverend Philip Neynoe, who figured in his success in bringing Atterbury to trial[40]

6) the report that 'the Treasurer took a Fancy to be jealous of his Wife' (I.vi), which drew attention to reports of Walpole's disintegrating marriage.[41]

If nothing else Flimnap confirmed Walpole in the public mind as the senior partner in the family firm of Walpole and Townshend. Defenders of Walpole denied resemblances but in the process fell into the trap of conceding its underlying plausibility. Their panegyrics merely provoked further derision: 'the wise director of the publick Affairs; he is the Delight of his Royal Master, and the Darling of the People'.[42] Illustrations were deployed to sharpen the resemblance with Walpole. *Lemuel Gulliver's Travels Into Several Remote Nations of the World. Compendiously methodized, for publick Benefit* included a frontispiece captioned 'Above, the Lilliputian Scene survey, Beneath, see Flimnap, by his Wand, bear sway.'[43] It was all too easy to fill out Flimnap to add further touches to Walpole's portrayal. A scatological history of Lilliput included an entire chapter on Gulliver's peering through a bedroom window of Flimnap's country house to view the Treasurer's wife disrobed and joined in bed by her aristocratic lover.[44] Walpole's marital and extra-marital behaviour played a larger part in public distaste than is generally recognised.

Walpole had left for his annual autumn break in Norfolk a few days before the publication of *Gulliver* at the end of October, but he is unlikely to have been unaware of it for long. By late November Swift was claiming to have had reports of Walpole's condescending irritation with him: 'Sr Rt Walpole says he has the length of my Head.'[45] *Gulliver* coincided with the emergence of a formidable opposition coalition, orchestrated by Bolingbroke and Pulteney. The most vitriolic personal attack was Bolingbroke's *The Occasional Writer*, published in three successive letters during January and February 1727. They exposed the Premier as cynical, corrupt, and above all a third-rate exponent of Grub Street journalism. Walpole, perhaps unwisely, allowed himself to complain in the House of Commons on 7 March that Bolingbroke's onslaught 'was contrived out of the greatest personal enmity to him that perhaps was ever known'.[46]

When Swift returned to London in April 1727 he was breathing fire and studying revenge.[47] By May he was writing to Dublin that he was the victim of Walpole's 'Beasts and Blockheads for his Pen-men, whom he pays in ready Guineas very liberally. I am in high Displeasure with him and his Partisans.'[48] Lord Hervey, who was certainly not one of the latter, had composed a telling *Answer to the Occasional Writer* and in the process linked Bolingbroke with Swift, reminding both of their venal partnership in the last years of Queen Anne.[49] Swift's proposed riposte merely repeated what Bolingbroke had already said to more effect. Its most effective sally was developed from a hint by Bolingbroke himself, dwelling on the way that Walpole's pervasive influence revealed his 'character transferr'd into the administration'.[50] Swift developed it thus:

I think it very unnecessary to give the character of a great minister in the fullness of his power, because it is a thing that naturally doth itself, and is obvious to the eyes of all mankind; for his personal qualities are all derived into the most minute parts of his administration ... Every twinge of the gout or gravel will be felt in their consequences by the community: As the thief-catcher, upon viewing a house broke open, could immediately distinguish, from the manner of the workmanship, by what hand it was done.[51]

The interest of the piece is that it was Swift's first systematic critique of Walpole as Prime Minister. In the event it was not published (until 1765), perhaps because Bolingbroke seems to have had doubts about it, perhaps because it was overtaken by events. The death of George I raised high hopes that Walpole would be removed from power. Swift was among those hopeful enough to kiss the new King and Queen's hands on their accession. In the event Walpole was preferred to a coalition of alienated Whigs and proscribed Tories.

Swift never returned to England after 1727. Nor, however, did he lose his animus towards Walpole. A number of his writings were directed against Walpole and his works, though few of them reached the public at the time. His 'Account of the Court and Empire of Japan', written in 1728 but not published until 1765, was his clearest and fullest account of the enemy to date: disgraced in the senate, skilled in senatorial forms, dextrous in purchasing votes, corruptly accumulating vast sums of money laid out in paintings, buildings, and estates, and enriching his friends and relations:

He had the best among all false appearances of courage, which was a most unlimited assurance, whereby he would swagger the boldest men into a dread of his power, but had not the smallest portion of magnanimity, growing jealous, and disgracing every man, who was known to bear the least civility to those he disliked. He had some small smattering in books, but no manner of politeness; nor, in his whole life, was ever known to advance any one person, upon the score of wit, learning, or abilities for business. The whole system of his ministry was corruption.

The climax was an imagined speech which Walpole made before George II and his Council, frankly avowing that the Hanoverian Succession depended on corrupting Parliaments, electors, and foreign courts with the taxes which he had artfully designed at the expense of the nation's debts.[52] The *Craftsman* regularly published allegories and analogies of this kind, but rarely with such pointedness.

For the greater part Swift pursued Walpole in verse rather than prose.[53] Little of it was published when its topicality might have taken effect. Several political poems were included in George Faulkner's edition of Swift's *Works* in 1735. 'On Mr. Pulteney being Put Out of the Council', prophesying Walpole's fall, was written in 1731, when it would certainly have been noticed.[54] 'To Mr. Gay', rather misleadingly titled by the time Swift had finished with it also in 1731, included a new analysis of Walpole's retention of power on the accession of George II:

> And, such was then the temper of the times,
> He owed his preservation to his crimes.
> The candidates observed his dirty paws,
> Nor found it difficult to guess the cause:
> But when they smelt such foul corruptions round him;
> Away they fled, and left him as they found him.
> Thus, when a greedy sloven once has thrown
> His snot into the mess; ''tis all his own.'[55]

By 1735 these satires had lost their sting; moreover, Walpole had survived the excise crisis and won yet another general election. The most unpublishable of Swift's political poems was 'Directions for a Birthday Song', said to be of 1729. It mocked Walpole as George II's Maecenas. But the central theme was the royal family, its ill-favoured young princes, its laughable German origins, above all the absurdities and weaknesses of the King and Queen. It would certainly have provoked a prosecution; George II was five years dead before it made a public appearance in 1765.[56]

One satire that Swift did publish as soon as written, *A Libel on Dr. Delany, and a Certain Great Lord* in February 1730, had Walpole figuring as the enemy of Ireland.[57] It is hard to believe that Walpole was unaware of it, if only because Pope, infuriated by Swift's praise of his refusing 'to lick a rascal statesman's spittle',[58] wrote to the Prime Minister's Secretary to deny his knowledge of it, let alone guilt.[59] Swift's fourteen-line 'Character of Sir Robert Walpole' was also published, without date, as a broadsheet. It also found its way into a miscellany of anti-Walpolian propaganda in 1733.[60] It ended 'Tho' I name not the Wretch, you know who I mean – 'Tis the Cur-Dog of Britain and Spaniel of Spain.' Swift relished associating dogs with Walpole, but the only evidence that it is his derives from a MS draft (not in his hand) among letters received from Swift by Mrs. Howard. A particularly interesting piece is 'The Progress of Patriotism: A Tale', published in the *Craftsman* and then in the *Intelligencer* of Swift and Sheridan. It is well-informed about Walpole's Chelsea home and a tellingly comic account of a patriot's seduction there by the Prime Minister and his friends. Modern editors have understandably rejected it on the grounds that Swift repeatedly disowned it to his friends. Even so, Swift was not incapable of false denial, perhaps especially of something published in a journal undeniably associated with him.[61]

Swift came close enough to prosecution, nonetheless. In 1733 two of several poems that he had entrusted to his protégé, Matthew Pilkington, having obtained for him the post of chaplain to the Lord Mayor of London, Swift's friend John Barber, were published for Pilkington's benefit in London. *An Epistle to a Lady* and *On Poetry: A Rapsody* included insinuations aimed at Walpole and more dangerously at the royal family. The prosecution was dropped only in 1735. There is a not very convincing story that Walpole planned action against Swift himself but retreated when warned that a force of 10,000 men would be needed to bring the Drapier to London.[62] It is doubtful whether Walpole thought in terms of legal prosecution to defend his own reputation. When he did act, for example to promote the stage censorship legislation in 1737, it was to protect the Hanoverian dynasty, not himself.

Swift had reason to fear Walpole's machinery of state. He could hardly expect mercy if his sedition was traced to him. Nor was he neglected by defenders of government. Among the men of 'desperate Fortunes, or worse Characters' who made up the patriot opposition Swift featured alongside Pulteney and Bolingbroke as 'an Irish Dean, who, though one a happy Genius, and some Learning, was such a debauched immoral Man, that whatever was known to come from him was of no Weight with the People'.[63] Whether Walpole really did trouble himself about Swift is debatable. It is perfectly possible that Swift invented stories of Walpole's antagonism to magnify his own significance. His complaints about Walpole's quarrel with Gay were plainly more about his own grudge against Walpole.[64] Similarly he blamed Walpole for his alleged mistreatment by the King and Queen, claiming simultaneously that he had never given Walpole cause to be offended or provoked.[65]

Swift's attitude to Walpole had much in it of disdain, as if he was barely worthy of combat, as Godolphin, Marlborough, Nottingham, and Wharton had once been. Yet Walpole was a colossus, and the lasting impact that he had on British politics far exceeded that of the Tory administration that Swift had done so much to advocate and defend. An alternative possibility is that Swift had sufficient sense of his own increasing remoteness from Walpole's world of politics to refrain from attempting an attack on it. As early as January 1721 he admitted the indiscretion of 'attempting subjects where those talents are necessary, which perhaps I may have lost with my youth'.[66] He may have had that in mind in 1733 when there seemed a real possibility that Walpole's excise crisis would finally bring him down. At the time he was heavily engaged against the threat of legislation repealing the Irish Test which could in some measure be traced to ministers in London. Friends in England were surprised that instead of helping to bring a Prime Minister in the cause of English liberty, he had 'dwindled into an Irish Sollicitour'.[67]

In retrospect it was perhaps fortunate that Swift did not commit himself to a major onslaught against the Walpole regime that could compare with the *Conduct of the Allies* and the *Drapier's Letters*. Swift's political judgement had critics even when he was sure that his knowledge was sufficient to sustain it. One of Swift's fundamental misunderstandings had to do with the nature of Courts, though it was a subject in which he took considerable pride. His claim in 1727 to 'have known Courts these 36 years' seems somewhat excessive.[68] In fact it was only during Harley's ministry of 1710–14 that he can be said truly to have entered on Court life, which, as he noted in March 1712, took the place of earlier coffee-house days.[69] Even then, it is extraordinary that he should be so close to the heart-beat of Harley's Government without ever being presented to the Queen herself. Despite Harley's promise of an introduction in the early days of their relationship, he never expressed surprise or dismay at his distance from the Queen. He can hardly have been unaware of the impact of his controversial writings, even if it took him time fully to grasp the damage they did. Contemporaries close to the Court had no doubts, and their assessment passed into the received wisdom on the subject.

The Court during the last years of the last Stuart monarch's life was highly unpredictable, not only because the Queen's health was variable, but also because her peculiar combination of volatility and stubbornness proved unreadable by those who served her. Moreover, regardless of Harley's failure to maintain his control, the tortuous politics of the last days of his Government combined with the likelihood of a succession crisis to make the Court exceptionally important. Not that Swift was more perceptive than either Harley or St John. He certainly overestimated the influence of the Somerset family in the winter of 1711–12. What matters more was his exaggeration of the dominating power exerted by favourites.[70] His notion that Walpole's rise had depended solely on the Duchess of Kendal is a classic instance. Yet he made the same mistake when he resumed his interest in the Court in the mid-1720s. The notion that George II and his Queen preferred Walpole's experience, management skills, and proven commitment to the Hanoverian Succession came as a genuine shock to Swift. His own conclusion that Walpole had simply offered bribery, corruption, and an enhanced royal civil list was oversimplified, reflecting his ignorance of Walpole's pragmatic reputation for shrewd direction of policy both at home and abroad. Just as he had overestimated the Queen's favourites, the Duchess of Marlborough, the Duchess of Somerset and Lady Masham, so he overestimated the power of Mrs. Howard. Bolingbroke and others shared his dismay at the turn of events in 1727, but none of them so bitterly and unfairly as he resented the role of the royal mistress. Nor did they share his unremitting pursuit of Mrs. Howard for what he took to be 'good for nothing but to be a rank Courtier'.[71]

When Swift turned from the Court to other institutions, he turned first to the House of Lords. He saw English governance as rooted in a Gothic monarchy saved by a vigorous aristocracy from the absolutism that had emerged in other European states. Unfortunately the Civil Wars of the 1640s had rendered the nobility powerless. The Restoration gave it a chance of renewal, but the Whig project under William III and Anne definitively commercialised and demoralised the aristocracy. Leaders they might remain, but where they led was perdition. Their wars resulted in ever-increasing taxes, an uncontrollable National Debt, and corruption on a scale that prevented the English constitution from righting itself or renewing its subjects' vigour and vitality.

When Harley found himself unable to govern the House of Lords, he attributed it to two decades of venal peerage creations manipulated by the Whig Junto. Swift had no hesitation in justifying the creation of twelve new peerages to rebalance the party composition of the upper House and secure its support for the Peace of Utrecht. But in the light of another Whig hegemony in 1714 Harley's radical reform proved a temporary hiatus in the decline of the nobility. Under Hanoverian rule, Swift saw the same degradation that had marked the 1690s and 1700s. In April 1724 he wrote to Charles Ford in London, 'Pray bring over with you a printed List of the House of Lords, for I long mightily to see the Names of so many new ones in this happy Reign.'[72] His suspicion of George I's new creations was justified by quantity. By 1724 eighteen new peerages had been created since the Hanoverian Accession. Queen Anne had added only three in her reign as a whole, apart from the twelve whose creation had been notoriously forced on her.

The King of Brobdingnag questioned Gulliver closely on the subject: 'What Qualifications were necessary in those who are to be created new Lords: Whether the Humour of the Prince, a Sum of Money to a Court-Lady, or a Prime Minister; or a Design of strengthening a Party opposite to the publick Interest, ever happened to be Motives in those Advancements' (II. vi)'[73] As it happened, George II proved more conservative than his ruling predecessors. In the fifteen years of his reign up to the fall of

Walpole, he added only twelve new peers. Walpole's narrow majority depended on the bishops and the Scottish peers; he could hardly be described as swamping the old English peerage with new creations. Nor does Swift seem to have noticed that in 1718 it was Walpole who had foiled the attempt of his Whig colleagues in government to perpetuate a Whig oligarchy in the Lords.

The Commons was crucial to Walpole's success. His resourcefulness in debate, his sensitivity to the mood of the House, his management of the Court and Treasury party as it became known, and above all his appeal to the many independent Whigs who had little interest in office all made his tenure of the Premiership the defining template of the eighteenth-century political system. Both Harley and St John had regarded the lower House as the ladder to the upper and thereby pre-eminence in Court and Cabinet. Each of them took a peerage as soon as possible, respectively in 1711 and 1712. Walpole looked at it the other way around. Control of the Commons made him pre-eminent in Court and Cabinet. Despite numerous rumours in the early 1720s that he would take a peerage, he did so only on his fall in 1742. In the meantime he was capable of enjoying to the full the advantages to which he had access, honours, offices, perquisites, and wealth, but not a peerage.

By 1737 Swift recognised that Walpole's 'government of Parliament' was indispensable, itself an interesting way of putting it. He 'might have been a Duke many years ago, if it had been possible to govern the Parlmt without him'.[74] Like many of his generation and like his political friends, he could not imagine that Parliament might be developing a degree of government in its own right. Swift found it hard to think of the Commons emerging as the dominant presence in the post-1688 constitution. His ideal House of Commons was indeed remarkably like a junior House of Lords, a concept that Lord Shelburne revived half a century later.[75] The lower House was meant to exhibit the independence and property of the country gentry; their values and manners would imitate those of the upper House. His tract, *Some Free Thoughts upon the present State of Affairs*, written in the summer of 1714 but unpublished until 1741, portrayed Tory dissensions during the last days of Queen Anne in terms of the Court and the House of Lords. He apparently regarded the Commons as a disruptive but by no means the driving force in politics.[76]

Swift seems not to have attended a debate in St Stephen's. In *An Enquiry into the Behaviour of the Queen's Last Ministry*, commenced in 1715 but published only in 1765, he praised St John's oratory to the skies, yet never heard it: 'His Talent of Speaking in publick, for which he was so very much celebrated, I know nothing of except from the Informations of Others.'[77] When he spoke of Harley's debating skill in the Commons he admitted depending on others to confirm it: 'I have heard that he spoke but seldom in Parliament, and then rather with Art than Eloquence.'[78] Although he drafted for Harley's ministry major statements in the lower House, he had no evident sense of its atmosphere and ambience. When he visited Westminster it was principally to lobby on behalf of Irish interests in the Court of Requests. Yet it was Swift's *Conduct of the Allies* that provided the blueprint for the Commons in the 1711–12 session. Walpole conceded the point in his *Short History of the Late Parliament*: 'this was to be found the whole Scheme of the Proceeding of that Session.' In fact Walpole went into some detail to explain the relationship between Swift's arguments, the ministry's agenda enacted in the Commons, and the resulting adoption not only of the Peace but his own expulsion for alleged corruption.[79] Swift was certainly not shy of revealing his indirect role in Parliament.[80] In June 1714 Arbuthnot reminded him 'you know parliamentary manadgement is the forte'.[81] Yet it was not a term that Swift readily acknowledged. When he used the word 'management' in politics, it signified a manoeuvre or démarche. The newer concept of government through the management of the Commons, of which both Harley and Walpole were outstanding exponents, seems to have escaped him.

Gulliver's account of English government has a cursory reference to the House of Commons. He assured the King of Brobdingnag that the principal gentlemen 'were freely picked and culled out by the People themselves' (II.vi), the King shrewdly countering by asking 'whether a Stranger with a strong Purse might not influence the vulgar Voters to chuse him before their own Landlord' (II.vi).[82] Swift's Harringtonian notion was that the landowners of England could only be restored to their proper role by depriving Court and City of their corrupt influence. He thought he had seen all too clearly when working for the Harley ministry that it had no choice but to reward those who helped the Court. He recalled to Gay that in this time 'all Employm[en]ts went to Parl[ia]ment mens Friends who had been usefull in Elections'.[83]

His unpublished notes for a new scheme of governance, drawn up c.1728, assumed that there were 10,000 landowners in England, of whom 1,000 were Members of Parliament, jurors, and other governors of localities, all of them corruptly influenced. Reform required that the other 9,000 men of honesty should abolish the influence of the Crown and corporate institutions, the Bank, the East India interest, the South Sea Company. The people would then be left to restore the constitution.

This was what had happened in 1710. 'This excellent assembly', 'that illustrious assembly' had restored the honour of Parliament.[84] Such a crude and partisan characterisation of the electoral system was hardly adequate.

Some of Swift's settled principles were beginning to look anachronistic in the new dynamics of the twenties and thirties. He had expressed with compelling clarity a standard Tory presumption that moneyed men were destroying the landed interest – 'a new Estate and Property sprung up in the hands of Mortgagees'. The greater the Government's borrowing, the more it was forced to mortgage taxation for many years ahead. And most alarmingly its inability fully to fund war expenditure forced it to borrow short-term at a high discount, unleashing yet further financial projects in the form of lotteries or annuities. Whig finance was to blame, until in 1710 Harley sought to stabilise this system of 'general mortgage'.[85] Whig propagandists deified the value of credit, making possible not only commercial growth, but also a new kind of public virtue. Swift's response in *The Conduct of the Allies* was telling. 'I have often reflected on that mistaken Notion of Credit, so boasted of by the Advocates of the late Ministry: Was not all that Credit built upon Funds, raised by the Landed Men, whom they so much hate and despise?'[86]

Rescuing a rationale for Swift's political evolution and treating it as a comment on Walpolian corruption has little to commend it. Swift's own consistency was hardly impressive, especially in the brief period when his fortunes were closely tied to those of government. In the 1690s he strongly supported place bills designed to exclude ministers of the Crown from the House of Commons, and was to do so again in the 1730s.[87] Harley's use of the House of Lords to kill off the place bill of 1712 had his full approval, not least because the power of the Queen and her ministers would be curbed. In his *History of the Four Last Years of the Queen* Swift recorded his view that the royal prerogative had been 'sufficiently humbled within Twenty Years past'. It was, however, deleted from the text that he revised after the Hanoverian Accession.[88] Evidently, further humbling the prerogative delegated to Walpole was highly desirable. Swift seems to have been blind to his own hypocrisy in this respect. In 1730 Walpole used the upper House to reject a bill which would have prevented MPs from holding pensions under the Crown rather than defeating it in the lower House where members would find it embarrassing to face their electors after voting against a popular cause. Swift confidently told Bolingbroke: 'I believe in your time you would never, as a Minister, have suffer'd an Act to pass through the H. of C-s, only because you were sure of a majority in the H. of L-s to throw it out; because it would be unpopular, and conse-quently a loss of reputation.'[89] Not only Harley but St John had followed exactly the same tactics against the place bill of 1712.

In electoral matters Swift's nostrums tended to reflect the party politics that he favoured according to the times. In *A Discourse of the Contests and Dissensions*, 1701, he explicitly advocated the use of bribery in elections as necessary, having in mind the Whig success in the preceding general election, on the grounds that 'it will be safer to trust our Property and Constitution in the hands of such, who have pay'd for their Elections, than of those who have obtained them by servile Flatteries of the People'. When he championed the Tories for putting principle before corruption in the general election of 1710, he found it convenient to cancel the passage in the republished edition of 1711.[90] As for ministerial use of patronage his blistering denunciations of Walpole would have been more defensible if he had not been closely involved in Harley's ministry. Such hypocrisy was to be accepted from most politicians, but Bolingbroke and Pulteney were somewhat more cautious in the way they manoeuvred around their own activities. Bolingbroke's political writings were elaborately structured to explain the specific vices of Walpolian politics. Pulteney went out of his way to portray himself as a patriot above office and disdainful of patronage for purposes of management.

Reading the letters of Swift, Bolingbroke, Bathurst, and Gay in 1780, Horace Walpole, who referred to 'the malignant Swift', declaimed: 'Oh, my father! Twenty years of peace, and credit, and happiness, and liberty, were punishments to rascals who weighed everything in the scales of self!'[91] Horace was far from impartial, but he had a point. In fact some opponents of Walpole, notably the elder Pitt, later admitted the wisdom of his policies. Moreover, in many ways Walpole rather resembled Harley, not least in his moderation, his emphasis on peace, his commitment to sound finance, and his preference for avoiding religious controversy. If Harley had been in Walpole's place it is unlikely that Swift would have found his measures objectionable. The 'Republican Principles' that he identified in *The Conduct of the Allies* as typical of Whiggery in the 1690s and 1700s, and had come to detest by the time he penned *The History of the Four Last Years of the Queen* could hardly be described as characteristic of Walpole's regime.[92] After all, by 1726, Swift was describing Walpole and his colleagues as 'Rank Toryes in Government'.[93] He made an exception for Walpole's Whiggish 'carelessness of the Church of England', but even this was a fair way removed from the hard-line Whig policies of Stanhope and Sunderland, which implied the repeal of the Test Acts both in Britain and Ireland, and radical intervention in the universities. When Charles Ford wrote to Swift in June 1736 that 'the act for repealing the Test would have passed, if Sir Robert Walpole had not seen the necessity of his speaking, which he did in the most artful manner he had ever done in his life',[94] Swift's grudging response was presumably his remark that he wished 'every Minister of State could do so much for the Service of the Publick'.[95] Walpole's thinking had more to do with the political prudence of stabilising the relationship of Church and State. Even so, allowing for Harley's commitment to the Church, the outcome in the 1720s and 1730s would probably have been much the same.

By the mid-1730s what was left of Swift's political thinking was reduced to portraying Walpole as the enemy of a limited monarchy near to collapse under the pressure of 'the present luxury, infidelity, and a million of corruptions'.[96] 'Let me suppose a chief minister from a scanty fortune, almost eaten up with debts, acquiring by all methods a monstrous overgrown estate, why he will still go on to endeavour making his master absolute, and thereby in the power of seizing all his possessions at his pleasure, and hanging or banishing him into the bargain.' A prudent regard for his own self-preservation would surely make such a minister 'go farther, and endeavour to be king myself'.[97] This was a theme that Swift had often invoked. Walpole was in this respect another Cromwell or Marlborough bent on using a standing army to make himself a dictator. Neither Swift nor his patriot friends in England could concede that the Walpole regime, for all its leader's cynicism, was more in the nature of a balanced polity than a descent into corrupt absolutism. Oiling the wheels of government was not the same as turning it into an unstoppable leviathan of state. There was no insincerity about Walpole's repeated insistence on his accountability to Parliament and his recognition of the importance of independent opinion within the Commons.

There is a story that Swift purchased a luxurious coach by way of celebrating Walpole's fall from power in 1742. Whether he was capable of reflecting on its significance seems doubtful. If he had expectations, they were certainly disappointed. Walpole escaped with his neck and his fortune safe, effectively making the impeachment of a chief minister a thing of the past. Bolingbroke had given up any hope of power, Pulteney had virtually destroyed any prospect of power, and even Carteret enjoyed power for only a brief period. The abolition of party was at best postponed for a further generation, and then only superficially. Walpole's alleged machinery of corruption was left largely untouched without inhibiting the growth of parliamentary sovereignty and without unleashing a tyrannical absolutism.

It is hard to glimpse anything that Swift might have accurately prophesied about Walpole's long tenure of power and legacy, with perhaps one exception. On more than one occasion he had argued that the most successful ministers of state had to have something of the commonplace about them. In his *An Enquiry into the Behaviour of the Queen's Last Ministry*, he remarked 'that a small Infusion of the Alderman was necessary to those who are employed in publick Affairs'.[98] In 1719 he developed the argument for Bolingbroke. Great geniuses, he thought, hardly ever enjoyed 'long service in the ministry'. Somers was the only exception, whose mean extraction had:

taught him the regularity of an alderman, or a gentleman-usher ... Have you not observed, that there is a lower kind of discretion and regularity, which seldom fails of raising men to the highest stations, in the court, the church, and the law? It must be so: For Providence, which designed the world should be governed by many heads, made it a business within the reach of common understandings; while one great genius is hardly found among ten millions ... I plainly see, that fellows of low intellectuals, when they are gotten at the head of affairs, can sally into the highest exorbitances, with much more safety, than a man of great talents can make the least step out of the way.[99]

It seems likely that this had as much to do with Walpole as with Somers. Whether it was fair to Walpole is another matter.

'Appendix (See n. 39 below)'

Flimnap 'was forced to take up Money at a great Discount; that Exchequer Bills would not circulate under nine *per Cent*, below Par' (I.vi).[100]

1 Walpole was First Lord of the Treasury from 1715 to 1717, and then from 1721 to 1742. During his tenure he faced a number of financial crises, including his management of the Fifteen, the South Sea crisis, and the Atterbury Plot. None of these fitted the phrase, not least because they were emergencies which tended to result in substantial support for government, at any rate where Whig financiers were concerned. The principal instance that did fit the phrase arose from what seemed a revolution in international relations in 1725–6. In May 1725 Spain and Austria came together in the Alliance of Vienna, an unpredictable coalition threatening to destabilise the Peace of Utrecht in 1714. The response in September 1725 was the Alliance of

Hanover, based primarily on Britain, France, and the United Provinces. By January 1726, when Parliament convened, Walpole was coming increasingly under pressure from fears of war. His concern was to postpone rearming until absolutely necessary and to reassure the City and the Commons that he could maintain government borrowing at current interest rates. In advance of the new parliamentary session he was making it known that there would be no war, and that the annual malt tax and land tax would remain unchanged since 1724.[101] Many observers doubted whether he would succeed in either respect.

2 In August 1725 the London stock market had peaked, South Sea stock at 122, Bank at 138.[102] By January 1726 they had lost fourteen points. It was reported that Walpole had warned Jews against selling stock with a view to leaving England; English laws were capable of keeping them within the country.[103] Dutch holders of stock were also selling. On 29 January Walpole went out of his way in the Commons to complain of stockbrokers deliberately sinking stock. He insisted none the less that the following year's supply would continue to be funded at 3 per cent interest.[104] The East India Company and South Sea Company were already threatening to raise interest rates to 5 per cent to support their own position. The lottery approved in 1726 in order to meet earlier commitments ended by being largely undertaken by the Bank. By March South Sea stock was barely above 100. Fear of war plainly dominated the markets. Within five years of the South Sea bubble Walpole was facing a considerable challenge.

3 On 1 February the Tory William Shippen responded to the Prime Minister's criticism of stock jobbers by openly claiming that Walpole himself was deliberately lowering stocks in order to buy them with a view to profit when conditions improved. Walpole's ire was understandable. The debate was not publicly reported, but it was inevitably passed by word of mouth, not least by MPs themselves. William Stratford, Canon of Christ Church Oxford, longstanding friend of the Harley family, recorded Shippen's accusation in a letter to the second Earl of Oxford.[105] Swift was in England by mid-March, planning to visit Stratford in Oxford en route from Chester to London. Shippen's accusation must surely have reached Swift, whether from Stratford or one of his opposition friends, probably Pulteney or Bolingbroke. After his meeting with Walpole in April, it would be hardly surprising if he took the opportunity of *Gulliver's Travels* to bring up to date the Prime Minister's difficulties. By mid-May Bank

stock was below 120, South Sea Stock below 100. Swift can hardly have been unaware of the pressure experienced by the First Lord of the Treasury.

4 Walpole survived the session of 1726. The naval armaments required to blockade Spain in the West Indies and Russia in the Baltic were announced late in the session on a vote of credit that postponed additional taxation until the following session. This had plainly been his intention from the beginning, unless he had in mind procrastination to resolve the impasse between the two Alliances. Considering that only two months elapsed between the opening of Parliament in January and the King's message requiring additional forces in March, the latter seemed unlikely. With Parliament prorogued, the finance markets remained steady, without regaining any of the losses sustained during the previous months.

5 Swift spoke to his friends of breaking with Walpole for good in late July. A month later he submitted the final text of *Gulliver's Travels* to the publisher, Motte. Flimnap's 'discounting' fitted well with the events of 1726. Walpole had narrowly averted a crisis but was to face a far more damaging one in the following months unless the descent into open warfare was averted.

6 What is more perplexing about Swift's attribution to Flimnap is the second clause of the sentence: 'that Exchequer Bills would not circulate under nine *per Cent*, below Par. (I.vi)'. Exchequer Bills had a long history and were to have a much longer one. They were in theory issued by the Treasury itself. Their purpose was to raise cash for supply requirements according to necessity from session to session. The normal expectation was that they would be redeemed in due course, depending on the incidence of taxation duly collected. During the Walpole years the use of Exchequer Bills had become a relatively efficient and reliable way of providing government with short-term finance. Increasingly they depended on the Bank of England, which usually guaranteed the issue of Exchequer Bills, employing them as a circulating medium comparable to currency bills. Regularly at the end of a parliamentary session, the Treasury negotiated with the Bank or other parties to start the process conventionally known by the 1720s as the 'Bank Circulation'.

7 Exchequer Bills were rarely at a discount. A small discount had arisen during the War of the Spanish Succession in 1711, but, as Swift himself recorded, Harley had succeeded in raising Exchequer Bills to par with specie,[106] prohibiting the Bank from discounting of 3 per cent, and

stopping the depredations of those who dealt in remittances of money to the army.[107] Whether Swift fully understood the operation of government borrowing is debatable. His friend Erasmus Lewis, Under-Secretary of State during Harley's ministry, corrected his account of Harley's reforms, though broadly supporting Swift's approval.[108] In any event, since Harley's day Walpole had made further improvements to the use of Exchequer Bills.[109] They were usually at a premium because the purchasers of Exchequer Bills were rarely 'called' for cash to their full liability. The common practice was to fund the Exchequer Bills from the land and malt taxes, the most predictable of all taxes. By the time the Bills were redeemed, their owners customarily made a handsome profit. Discounting Exchequer Bills at 9 per cent below par would have been an extraordinary eventuality.

8 Walpole's financial strategy for the session of 1726 was to fund earlier commitments which threatened to weaken the Government's reliability. His object was to redeem earlier Exchequer Bills by borrowing on a lottery that provided lenders with the security of their return and the possibility of profits deriving from winning tickets. No doubt he had in mind the issue of further short-term paper securities to underwrite the rearming likely to take place between the sessions of 1726 and 1727. In the event Walpole had trouble ensuring the success of the lottery, and it was left to the Bank to supply the missing cash. More importantly, thanks partly to the vote of credit approved in March, a new annual issue of Exchequer Bills was needed as part of war preparations. This process had hardly got going when Swift sent the manuscript of *Gulliver's Travels* to Motte. The Bank 'Circulation' did not begin until July. Throughout the following year it operated at a handsome premium. Swift's reference to 9 per cent discounts hardly fits these aspects of financial operations in 1726.

9 There is, however, another possibility. Exchequer Bills had a precise significance, but they were easily confused with other short-term borrowing devices employed by government departments other than the Treasury. One of these was the practice of issuing what were called army debentures.[110] They had a long and not altogether reputable history. They were, however, crucial to the War Office when it called for immediate cash in the event of unpredicted, additional expenditure. Their redemption was not guaranteed, and there were doubts about their legal status in that respect. The result was that they were sometimes heavily discounted, usually winding up in the hands of City speculators. The revival of army debentures during the

war crisis of 1726 resulted in some striking discounts. Swift's stay in England happened to coincide with their reissue. They quickly fell from par in early January to 8 per cent below par at the end of the month. They rose two points to 6 per cent below par and remained there until May. In June they fell again to 8 per cent below par and to 9 and even 10 per cent through July. Throughout the summer and autum they never rose above 5 per cent below par, and continued to sink to 9 per cent from time to time. The implication was that Walpole had either lost control of his borrowing or was engaging in the corrupt practices identified earlier by Shippen. Swift would have been unwise to refer specifically to army debentures in print. Flimnap's discounted fictitious Exchequer Bills offered a safer way of challenging the integrity of the Prime Minister without being liable to charges of libel or sedition.

10 Considering Swift's relationship with Pulteney, it is noteworthy that Pulteney was taking a considerable interest in the army debentures. More interesting still was the Prime Minister's decision in 1727 to devote the growing surplus on the sinking fund to redeem army debentures. Walpole himself later admitted that knowledgeable speculators might have prophesied this use of the sinking fund. In the early months of 1727 purchasing of army debentures quickly raised their value to par. Holders who had retained earlier issues were to make spectacular profits once redemption had been secured by statute. Pulteney was to make much use of this episode to indict Walpole as deliberately enriching himself and his friends. In the bitter tirade that led to his duel with Lord Hervey, Pulteney made clear his belief that Walpole had set out to make the maximum use of his personal investment as well as that of his friends.[111] In 1741 he proposed it as a major charge in a future impeachment of Walpole, though the Prime Minister strongly denied any part in discounting or using the sinking fund to benefit the holders of the army debentures.[112] Swift never went on to have Flimnap impeached, but the clue to his discounting might have been remarkably prophetic.

NOTES

1 Swift to the Earl of Peterborough, [28 April 1726], *Correspondence*, II, 642;
   Swift to Lady Elizabeth Germain, [8] January 1733, ibid., III, 574; *Complete
   Poems*, p. 851, note to 'Verses on the Death of Dr. Swift', line 192. George
   Faulkner revealed the third encounter in his 1739 edition of the 'Verses'.

2 Bertrand Goldgar, *Walpole and the Wits: The Relation of Politics to Literature, 1722–1742* (Lincoln, Nebr., 1976), p. 36; F. P. Lock, *Swift's Tory Politics* (London, 1983), p. 162.

3 Swift to Pope, 26 November 1725, *Correspondence*, II, 623.

4 *The Virtues of Sid Hamet the Magicians's Rod*, published in October 1710; *Complete Poems*, pp. 109–12.

5 *PW*, III, 27–9, 57, 68–9, 19–24.

6 [Henry St John], *A Letter to The Examiner* ([London], 1710), p. 4.

7 *PW*, III, 86.

8 The Cambridge Edition of the Works of Jonathan Swift: B. A. Goldgar and I. Gadd (eds.), *English Political Writings 1711–1714: The Conduct of the Allies and Other Works*, (No. 8), (Cambridge, 2008), p. 83.

9 *An Excellent New Song, Being the Intended Speech of a Famous Orator against Peace*, *Complete Poems*, pp. 117–19.

10 18 December 1711, *JSt.*, II, 442.

11 *PW*, VII, 18.

12 Goldgar and Gadd, *English Political Writings*, pp. 253, 258, 260.

13 [Robert Walpole], *A Short History of the Late Parliament*, 2nd edn (London, 1713), p. 8.

14 The 'Account' was delivered to the Commons on 14 April 1714 and printed in *House of Commons Journals*, xvii. 567–72.

15 Peter Wentworth to his brother the Earl of Strafford, 23 April 1714, *The Wentworth Papers, 1705–1739*, ed. J. J. Cartwright (London, 1882), pp. 376–7.

16 H. Davis (ed.), *The Drapier's Letters to the People of Ireland against receiving Wood's Halfpence by Jonathan Swift* (Oxford, 1935), p. 127 (Letter VI, To Lord Chancellor Middleton, published in 1735). Davis seems to associate this remark with December 1711–January 1712, pp. 307–8.

17 *Complete Poems*, pp. 164, 670.

18 *PW*, VII, 65.

19 Harold Williams, *Jonathan Swift and the 'Four Last Years of the Queen'* (London, 1935).

20 *PW*, VII, 18–19.

21 Williams, *Jonathan Swift and the 'Four Last Years of the Queen'*, p. 83.

22 *The Annual Register, or a view of history, politicks and literature, of the year 1758* (London, 1759), pp. 256–62.

23 *A Whig's Remarks on the Tory History of the Four Last Years of Queen Anne By Dr. Jonathan Swift* (London, 1758), pp. iv, 44–5.

24 William Coxe, *Memoirs of the Life and Administration of Sir Robert Walpole, Earl of Orford* (3 vols., London, 1798), II, p. 27.

25 B. Rand (ed.), *Berkeley and Percival: The Correspondence of George Berkeley afterwards Bishop of Cloyne and Sir John Percival afterwards Earl of Egmont* (Cambridge, 1914), p. 113; Erasmus Lewis to Swift, 29 July 1714, *Correspondence*, II, 33.

26 Swift to Charles Ford, 11 March 1725, *Correspondence*, II, 547.

27 *Complete Poems*, p. 275.

28 Davis, *The Drapier's Letters*, pp. 80, 85 (Letter IV, To the Whole People of Ireland, October 1724).

29 Ibid., p. 85.

30 Ibid., pp. 86–7.

31 Swift to Peterborough, [28 April 1726], *Correspondence*, II, 642.

32 D. W. Hayton, *Ruling Ireland, 1685–1742: Politics, Politicians and Parties* (Woodbridge, Suffolk, 2004), chap. 8.

33 Swift to Thomas Tickell, 7 July 1726, *Correspondence*, II, 649–50.

34 Swift to James Stopford, 20 July 1726, Ibid., II, 659–60.

35 *A key, being observations and explanatory notes, upon the travels of Lemuel Gulliver. By Signor Corolini, a noble Venetian now residing in London* (London, 1726).

36 J. P. W. Rogers (ed.), 'Swift, Walpole, and the Rope-Dancers', *Papers on Language and Literature*, 8(1972), 159–71; *PW*, XI, 22–3; C. H. Firth, *The Political Significance of 'Gulliver's Travels'* (Proceedings of the British Academy, 1919, vol. IX), pp. 8–9.

37 *PW*, XI, 23.

38 Ibid.

39 Ibid., 48. See Appendix to this chapter, p. 70.

40 Ibid., 49; A. E. Case, *Four Essays on 'Gulliver's Travels'* (Princeton, 1945), p. 80. Walpole's ruthless use of Neynoe, who ended by committing suicide, is described in G. V. Bennett, *The Tory Crisis in Church and State 1688–1730* (Oxford, 1975), pp. 238–71 passim.

41 *PW*, XI, 49.

42 *A Letter from a clergyman to his friend, with an account of the travels of Capt. Lemuel Gulliver, and a character of the author* (London, 1726), p. 17.

43 London, 1726.

44 *Memoirs of the Court of Lilliput, written by Captain Gulliver* (London, 1727), pp. 77–89.

45 Swift to Mrs. Howard, [1]7 November 1726, *Correspondence*, III, 55.

46 A. N. Newman (ed.), *The Parliamentary Diary of Sir Edward Knatchbull, 1722–1730*, Camden 3rd ser., xciv. 67.

47 Swift to Mrs. Howard, 1 February 1727, *Correspondence*, III, 70.

48 Swift to Rev. Thomas Sheridan, 13 May 1727, ibid., II, 84.

49 *An Answer to the Occasional Writer, NO II*, 2nd edn (London, 1727), p. 9.

50 Bolingbroke to Swift, 18 May 1727, *Correspondence*, III, 89.

51 'A Letter to the Writer of the Occasional Paper', *PW*, V, 97.

52 Ibid., 99–107.

53 An exception was 'The Answer of the Right Honourable William Pulteney, Esq; to the Right Honourable Sir Robert Walpole', dated 15 October 1730 but not published until 1768. It dealt well with Walpole's treatment of opponents as Jacobites. Whether Swift was the author is uncertain. *PW*, V, 111–19.

54 *Complete Poems*, pp. 471–2.

55 Ibid., pp. 466–70, lines 155–62.

56 Ibid., pp. 388–95.

57 Ibid., pp. 404–9.

58 Ibid., line 82.

59 Pope to William Fortescue, 20 February [1730], George Sherburn, *The Correspondence of Alexander Pope* (5 vols., Oxford, 1956), III, p. 91.

60 *Robin's Panegyrick. Or, the Norfolk Miscellany. Part III* (London, [1733]), p. 140.

61 *The Country Journal: or, The Craftsman*, 3 August 1728; J. Woolley (ed.), *Jonathan Swift and Thomas Sheridan: The Intelligencer* (Oxford, 1982), pp. 147–55.

62 *Complete Poems*, pp. 514–36; [Thomas Sheridan], *The Life of the Rev. Dr. Jonathan Swift, Dean of St. Patrick's, Dublin* (London, 1784), pp. 277–8.

63 *Remarks on the R-p-n of the H- of C-ns to the K-g; and His M-j's A-s-r. Address'd to all True Britons* (London, [1728]), pp. 28–9.

64 Swift to Mrs. Howard, 21 November 1730; Swift to Pope, 20 July 1731; Swift to Lady Suffolk, 26 October 1731; Swift to Lady Elizabeth Germain, 8 January 1733; *Correspondence*, III, 342–3, 412–13, 438, 574–5.

65 Swift to Lady Suffolk, [27 July 1731]; Swift to Gay and Duchess of Queensberry, 3 October 1732; ibid., 415–16, 543.

66 Swift to Pope, 10 January 1721, ibid., II, 362.

67 Bathurst to Swift, [29 March 1733]; Charles Ford to Swift, 14 April 1733; ibid., III, 626–7.

68 Swift to Gay and Pope, 23 November 1727, ibid., 141.

69 *JSt*, II, 522.

70 J. A. Downie, *Jonathan Swift Political Writer* (London, 1984), p. 162.

71 Swift to Gay and the Duchess of Queensberry, 29 June 1731, *Correspondence*, III, 403.

72 Swift to Charles Ford, 2 April 1724, ibid., II, 494.

73 *PW*, XI, 113.

74 Swift to Lord Orrery, [26–31 March 1737], *Correspondence*, IV, 141.

75 Denis O'Bryen, *A Defence of the Right Honourable the Earl of Shelburne* (London, 1782), pp. 53–4.

76 Goldgar and Gadd. *English Political Writings*, pp. 297–8.

77 *PW*, VIII, 134.

78 Ibid., 136.

79 Walpole, *A Short History*, pp. 8, 25.

80 *PW*, VII, 79–80.

81 John Arbuthnot to Swift, 26 June 1714, *Correspondence*, I, 624.

82 *PW*, XI, 112–13.

83 Swift to Gay, 8 January 1723, *Correspondence*, I, 442.

84 'Notes for a Proposal for Virtue', *PW*, XIV, 14–15; *The Examiner*, 29 March 1711, *PW*, III, 119–20.

85 *PW*, VII, 70–1.

86 Goldgar and Gadd, *English Political Writings*, p. 97.

87 Downie, *Jonathan Swift Political Writer*, p. 40.

88 *PW*, VII, 96, 236.
89 Swift to Bolingbroke, 21 March 1730, *Correspondence*, III, 294.
90 *PW*, I, 301–2.
91 W. S. Lewis (ed.), *The Yale Edition of Horace Walpole's Correspondence* (48 vols., New Haven, 1937–83), XXV, pp. 6–8, Walpole to Horace Mann, 13 January 1780.
92 *PW*, VII, 21.
93 Swift to Thomas Tickell, 7 July 1726, *Correspondence*, II, 650.
94 Charles Ford to Swift, 3 June 1736, ibid., IV, 311.
95 Swift to Charles Ford, 22 June 1736, ibid., 316.
96 Swift to Pulteney, 8 March 1735, ibid., 66.
97 Swift to Pulteney, 12 May 1735, ibid., 107.
98 *PW*, VIII, 139.
99 Swift to Bolingbroke, 19 December 1719, *Correspondence*, II, 315–16.
100 *PW*, XI, 48.
101 W. Stratford letters to the Earl of Oxford, 13 January 1726, *HMC Portland* (London, 1901), VII, p. 416.
102 These and subsequent figures derive from newspapers in the Burney Collection in the British Library and Nichols Newspapers in the Bodleian Library.
103 25 January 1726, *HMC Portland*, VII, p. 417.
104 3 February 1726, ibid., p. 420.
105 3 February 1726, ibid.
106 *The Examiner*, 7 June 1711, *PW*, III, 168.
107 *PW*, VII, 75–6.
108 Lewis to Swift, 8 April 1738, *Correspondence*, IV, 513.
109 P. G. M. Dickson, *The Financial Revolution in* England (London, 1967), pp. 379–87.
110 Ibid., pp. 394–6.
111 W. Pulteney, *A Proper Reply to a Late Scurrilous Libel* (London, 1731), p. 21.
112 R. Chandler, *The History and Proceedings of the House of Commons from the Restoration to the Present Time* (London, 1742), XII, p. 112.

PART II

The writer and his world

Burying the fanatic Partridge: Swift's Holy Week hoax

Valerie Rumbold

Thanks to Swift's *Predictions for the Year 1708*, the astrologer John Partridge is primarily known for something that never actually happened, namely the death that Swift's fictitious Isaac Bickerstaff predicted for him on 29 March 1708. The event, like Partridge himself, comes to us already crossed out: the death is remembered as a glorious non-event, and Partridge as a man supposedly dead who wouldn't lie down. But as one of the characters in *Polite Conversation* might have said (but didn't), there are more ways to kill a dog than hanging, and in the case of the offensive Partridge, Swift experimented with modes of execution well beyond the obvious.[1]

To approach the Bickerstaff papers as, in effect, an experiment in cruel and unusual punishment runs counter to some of the older traditions in the critical reception of this favourite among Swift's early works. Swift's timing, as George Mayhew pointed out in convincing detail, suits the general scheme of an April Fools' Day jest and might on the face of it suggest that the Bickerstaff hoax was simply a more developed version of the practical jokes that Swift enjoyed setting up for 1 April, in effect a ritualised expression of his motto 'Vive la bagatelle' (in the following year, for example, he would lure book-lovers out on a fool's errand by advertising a non-existent sale of rare books).[2] In addition William Burns has convincingly suggested that Swift may have had 'Black Monday' in mind (an eclipse on Monday 29 March 1652 for which astrologers issued prophecies whose non-fulfilment became a major debating point for sceptics).[3] The Bickerstaff papers have often been enjoyed as the most genial and light-hearted of Swift's satirical works, and their singling out of Partridge was indeed often attributed simply to his prominence among the producers of astrological predictions deplored by enlightened opinion, just as Swift's success was for a long time estimated by Partridge's apparent failure to produce an almanac for several years afterwards. More recent work has revised several of these assumptions and opened the way for a broader interpretation: it is now clear that Partridge's failure to issue almanacs for 1710, 1711, 1712 and 1713 was the result of a commercial dispute unconnected with the hoax; recent understandings of the role of astrology and of almanacs in the culture of the time are more nuanced and less simply dismissive; and, most importantly of all, it has been increasingly recognised that Swift's singling out of Partridge responds specifically to the challenge that his enormously popular almanacs constituted to traditional Anglican views on the relation of church and state.[4]

Partridge's was a radical Whig protestantism defined by its hatred of popery and adulation of William III, ever keen to denounce supposedly popish corruption in the established church.[5] For Swift, as he would later explain in a sermon, the implications of such a position were clear and ominous:

But the followers of those who beheaded the Martyr [Charles I], have not yet renounced their principles; and, till they do, they may be justly suspected: Neither will the bare name of Protestants set them right. For, surely, Christ requires more from us than a profession of hating Popery, which a Turk or an Atheist may do as well as a Protestant.[6]

Had there been no rebellion to exile the princes, he continued, there need have been no Revolution and no need for William, whose innovations had solved the problem of popery at the cost of exacerbating the problem of dissent:

The children of the murdered Prince were forced to fly, for the safety of their lives, to foreign countries; where one of them, at least, I mean King James II. was seduced to Popery; which ended in the loss of his kingdoms, the misery and desolation of this country, and a long and expensive war abroad. Our deliverance was owing to the valour and conduct of the late King; and, therefore, we ought to remember him with gratitude, but not mingled with blasphemy or idolatry. It was happy that his interests and ours were the same: And God gave him greater success than our sins deserved. But, as a house thrown down by a storm is seldom rebuilt, without some change in the foundations, so it hath happened, that, since the late Revolution, men have sate much looser in the true fundamentals both of religion and government, and factions have been more violent, treacherous, and malicious than ever, men running naturally from one extreme into another; and, for private ends, taking up those very opinions professed by the leaders in that rebellion, which carried the blessed Martyr to the scaffold.[7]

In defence of the established church's middle way between popery and fanaticism, church and monarch were for Swift mutual guarantors: a weakening in either, or of the union between them, meant freedom for Partridge, but oppression for Swift. In 1707–8 he had been specifically forced to confront the spectre of such oppression on his embassy to London to negotiate the remission for the Church of Ireland of the First Fruits and Twentieth Parts: the price set by the Whig administration was repeal of the Test Act in Ireland, for Swift a recipe for the ruin of the Church of Ireland at the hands of protestant nonconformists.[8]

Partridge, moreover, was offering very specific provocations in 1707–8, and the *Merlinus Liberatus* for 1708 (which appeared, like all almanacs, late in the previous year) is profitably read in relation to the Bickerstaff papers.[9] Considered in this light, two aspects of Swift's response stand out as particularly innovative. The first is his handling of politics: unlike some earlier parodists, Swift lards his mock predictions with politically tendentious material, but at the same time adopts an elitist disdain that refuses to accord Partridge's claims the dignity of point-by-point refutation; in this way, and in marked contrast with Partridge's habitual antagonist George Parker, he effectually sidelines Partridge as a political commentator and sets the pattern for his later representation in Steele's *Tatler* and beyond.[10] (Thus, as Eddy long ago suggested, the Bickerstaff papers might be seen as fulfilling – and with peculiarly apt artfulness – Parker's expressed desire that 'some able Polite Pen of the Church of England' would deal with Partridge.)[11] The second aspect of Swift's innovation, however, partakes of the kind of defence of the church, already familiar from *A Tale of a Tub*, that verges on blasphemy in its defence of sacred mysteries. The Church of England, this chapter will argue, had already taken official (but arguably counterproductive) action to suppress the most offensive contents of Partridge's *Merlinus Liberatus* for 1708; in this context the aptness of the riposte by which Swift goes one better and cancels Partridge himself adds a new dimension to the hoax.[12] At the same time Swift's cancelling of Partridge also enacts a kind of Christological parody, for in 1708 the day of Partridge's predicted death was Monday in Holy Week, and 1 April was Maundy Thursday. Swift's favourite celebration of All Fools was thus overlaid onto the most solemn week of the Anglican calendar. This was a coincidence that Partridge's almanac, in common with the other almanacs for the year, made abundantly plain, but Swift would transmute it from mere coincidence into a satirical indictment of Partridge's offence, as he would have seen it, against Christianity itself. Swift's hoax turns Partridge into a kind of antichrist who, far from dying and rising again, is doomed to the perpetual limbo of a dead man who won't lie down.

POLITICAL PREDICTIONS

Partridge's characteristic product was the kind of almanac called, in the trade, 'blanks', that is, an almanac whose calendar section (set out with a facing pair of pages for each month) had a blank column on the right-hand side of the right-hand page. Originally these had been left blank so that purchasers could write in their own memoranda, but by Partridge's time most of the space was filled with printed dates and comments. Partridge, like many other almanac makers, used this column for carefully qualified prognostication of likely occurrences; educated readers, predisposed to dismiss astrology as a spurious claim to magical foreknowledge, were increasingly likely to see this as calculated prevarication. In addition, Partridge mingled his hints of things to come with characteristically inflammatory religious and political commentary that supplemented the already copious polemic in his prefatory verses and supplementary prose sections.

Partridge's radical Whig polemic constituted a major irritant, at least to readers of conservative views on church and state. The style of his pronouncements could only increase the irritation, for he practised a characteristic rhetorical balancing by which he gave with one hand only to take away with the other, affecting to cloak partisan agendas in the garb of simple prudence. For example, in his *Merlinus Liberatus* for 1708 Partridge speaks in the blank column for February of a possible peace, yet prevaricates not only about whether it will actually come about, but also about whether it should even be attempted:

Fresh Endeavours and Resolutions about Peace, and the Method and Ways to attain it; and to that end Agents, Envoys and Ambassadors are dispatcht to several Courts to sollicit both in Publick and Private in order to effect it. Application made to the QUEEN of *England* also to that end, God direct Her Council in this great Work, I had rather have no Peace than not to have a durable one; it is a hard Case to Treat and Agree with one that hath neither Conscience nor Honesty.[13]

He then begins his column for March with a breezy nod to all eventualities: 'If Peace is not yet Concluded, there will be occasion for spilling more Humane Blood'; and in June he is still executing his characteristic one step forward and two steps back: 'But after all, things will do well, and there is such a thing as a General Peace at hand, but not on a sudden.'[14]

Swift does not create a parody almanac with calendar tables, nor even a set of predictions linked to astrological charts or to systematic divisions of the year (as Tom Brown had done in his more playful and less political parody, 'A Comical View of the Transactions … in … London and Westminster', which he ascribed to 'Silvester Partridge'),[15] but adopts a discursive framework that allows him to allude to astrological discourse without the clutter and distraction of producing a parody almanac as such (it has indeed been suggested that he may have taken a hint from a selection of some of Partridge's most famous prophecies that had been reprinted in 1689 without astrological data or tables).[16] He is careful to begin by establishing Bickerstaff as an ostensibly impartial critic of astrological prediction: Bickerstaff pairs Partridge with his Tory rival Gadbury, expressing the surprise and disdain he feels 'when I observe Gentlemen in the Country, rich enough to serve the Nation in Parliament, poring in *Partridge's* Almanack, to find out the Events of the Year at Home and Abroad; nor dare to propose a Hunting Match, till *Gadbury* or he have fixt the Weather'.[17] He is also impartially dismissive in lumping together the self-serving political controversies of rival imposters with their dubious cures for disreputable diseases:

To mention no more of their impertinent Predictions; What have we to do with their Advertisements about *Pills and Drinks for the Venereal Disease*, or their mutual Quarrels in Verse and Prose of *Whig* and *Tory*, wherewith the Stars have little to do.[18]

A similar note is sounded in his general indictment of the vague and qualified terms in which almanacs couch their prognostications: 'for their Observations and Predictions, they are such as will equally suit any Age or Country in the World'.

All this gives Bickerstaff an advantageous position from which to launch his own predictions, and behind his carefully established screen of impartiality Swift now lays a politically strategic train of references. As preamble he makes Bickerstaff claim (in a move that is one of many signs of Swift's detailed familiarity with the topics and rhetoric of astrological controversy) that he has already successfully foretold two major disasters of the 1707 campaign in the War of the Spanish Succession, namely the Toulon campaign, which culminated in the wreck of the fleet and the drowning of Admiral Sir Cloudsley Shovell, and the defeat at Almanza. Thus encouraged, he now invites his readers to inspect the various almanacs for 1708: 'I find them all in the usual Strain, and I beg the Reader will compare their Manner with mine', and he stresses once more that he lays 'the whole Credit of my Art upon the Truth of these Predictions'.[19] He then introduces, along with the kind of vague and utterly predictable material typical of almanacs, a sequence of predicted deaths that would have proved, if fulfilled, even more significant to the outcome of the war than Toulon and Almanza, practically wiping out the House of Bourbon and its support base.[20] By the year's end, he predicts the deaths of the French king, Louis XIV; his minister of war and finance, Chamillard; his son, the Dauphin; and his great-grandson, the infant Prince of the Asturias, heir to Philip V of Spain; which leaves his other grandson, the Duke of Burgundy, to take the throne of France. In addition, the Cardinal Archbishop of Paris and Philip V's key advisor, Cardinal Portocarrero, both die, along with the Pope who had acquiesced in Philip's succession.[21] The pope is to be 'succeeded by a Cardinal of the *Imperial* Faction' (i.e. the Hapsburgs); while the King of Sweden also 'declares for the Emperor'. Yet, having predicted a near-total rout of the Bourbon interest, Bickerstaff pointedly abstains from interpretation. Concluding his predictions with the prophecy that 'the young *French* King sends Overtures for a Treaty of Peace', Bickerstaff piously remarks, 'which, because it is a matter of State that concerns us here at home, I shall speak no further of it' (ostentatiously parading, in implied contrast with Partridge's alarmist commentaries, the exemplary discretion of a loyal subject).[22]

At one level, by these politically momentous prophecies Swift has simply carried to the point of absurdity a habit of hinting at the demise of European enemies for which Partridge had become notorious. At a deeper level, however, it is striking what a clean sweep Bickerstaff makes of the Allies' enemies, and yet how he leaves one key Bourbon representative in place, namely Louis XIV's grandson, Philip V of Spain. Philip admittedly ends the year stripped of much of his support, but he has not been deposed from the Spanish throne. Yet Philip was precisely the person who had to be removed if the proviso of 'no peace without Spain' was ever to be fulfilled: this was to prove the sticking point in peace negotiations with Louis in 1708–9; and the treaty concluded at Utrecht in 1713 would in the end (after further complications in the prospective succession) leave Philip still in possession, once he had renounced his place in the succession to the throne of France.[23] Swift in effect plays out in his *Predictions* a scenario that, though exaggerated, is not entirely unlike the one for which he would later emerge as propagandist, when, increasingly disillusioned with the Whigs' lack of commitment to the established church in Ireland, he in 1710 threw in his lot with Harley and the Tories. It is clear enough that Partridge is being baited in the *Predictions* with the prophecy of his own death, but he is arguably also being teased by the political implications of the *Predictions* as a whole.

In having Bickerstaff preface these deaths of the eminent with what he declares to be the mere 'trifle' of Partridge's own death Swift may also be focusing his attack by a specific allusion to Partridge's recently published work, namely the account of apparitions portending imminent death that he had included in the discursive section (following the calendar) of his 1708 *Merlinus Liberatus*; for what is Bickerstaff if not a phantom sent to warn Partridge that he is soon to die?[24] That prophecy, along with those of the deaths of foreign dignitaries more obviously eminent (if less immediately familiar to the mass of Partridge's popular audience) might initially seem open to incontrovertible disproof, once the dates were past and the persons evidently still alive;[25] but Partridge would notoriously find that such disproof was not so straightforward (and Davis noted that even in Partridge's own practice, attempts to discredit rival astrologers by challenging them to the accurate drawing of nativities characteristically foundered in a babble of claims and counterclaims).[26] Partridge had, however, once in his life made an unforgettable prediction of downfall and death that he later claimed had come true, and N. F. Lowe has convincingly suggested that it is to this that Swift alludes in his own prediction of Partridge's death.[27] Under James II Partridge had fled to the Netherlands, where he issued his astrological no-popery polemics under the name of John Wildfowl, and in 1687, in *Mene Tekel*, he hinted not only that there would be a revolution in 1688, but also that James II would die. (Even here, though, the onus was on readers to apply his planetary prognostications to specifics: Partridge hints at dangers to 'great men in this Quarter, and perhaps a *King* or *Prince* too'; he sets out a table of personal astrological data; he discusses the danger that the year's planetary dispositions might constitute to a person of a particular age; but he holds back all along from pointing out in so many words that all this applies to King James.)[28] But whatever merit he might later claim for having foretold the Revolution, on the point of James's actual death he was wrong, and his retrospective self-justification is so interesting in relation to Swift's hoax that it is worth quoting in full:

I find some peevish People are apt to exclaim against Astrology, *because the* late King *did not dye in* October *or* November 1688, *pretending that I had said in Print he would then die, but I would very fain have them show it to me where I have so said: Indeed I did think he would have died, and yet his not dying is no Injury to Astrology, unless amongst those that are malicious and something worse: However I shall say but two things in the case,*

1 *To those that understand* Astrology ... *what I predicted was fully verified, for it happened within a Month of the time mentioned; and now the thing is over, I will defy them to give me any reason for it, that shall have the same Effect in another Nativity, or something like it: Let them outdo it if they can.*

2 *To those that know nothing of* Astrology, *there is no blame to be laid on the Art, nor indeed I cannot see how they can blame me; for the Effect is so like* Death, *that it doth as well for the Deliverance of the* Nation, *and I hope they cannot say but it happened at the same time I had predicted it to. It is indeed a* Civil Death, *and to him I think worse than* Death.*[29]

Swift seems to glance in general at this prediction by making Bickerstaff rest his own commitment to astrology on an improbably alleged prediction of the Revolution by the astronomer Edmund Halley:

I was once of the Opinion with those who despise all Predictions from the Stars, till in the Year 1686, a Man of Quality shew'd me written in his *Album,* That the most learned Astronomer Captain *H.* assur'd him, He would never believe any thing of the Stars influence, if there were not a great Revolution in *England* in the Year 1688.[30]

It was, however, Partridge's insinuation that James II would actually die in 1688, and his subsequent attempt at self-justification, that offered Bickerstaff a more specific opportunity to repay him in his own coin; for by invoking the doctrine of the king's two bodies, Partridge had furnished the hint by which he too would in his turn be disgraced with civil death. Henceforth Partridge also has his own two bodies, the public one of which, constructed in print, is notoriously dead, while, as with James II in exile, the other, a mere body stripped of significance, refuses to lie down and be quiet. For so vitriolic an anti-Jacobite, a more infuriating parallel could hardly be imagined.

COBLER, STARMONGER, AND QUACK

By giving his attack on Partridge the title *Predictions for the Year 1708,* Swift places the emphasis of his hoax firmly on prediction, explicitly sidestepping the usual astrological cautions about the interaction between free will and planetary dispositions.[31] Partridge, indeed, had explicitly disowned any such publications on his return to England after the Revolution:

This therefore I will tell you once for all, That I never did write any thing by the name of Prophecy, *nor never will; and therefore you may be sure if any such thing shall be published at any time under the Notion of* Prophecy, *or any other Title in a single Sheet in my Name, it is not mine; but an Abuse upon me, and a Cheat upon you, done and managed by some of the little People that cheat by Retail.*[32]

Swift's is in effect a variation on the small-format fraud that Partridge had envisaged, and as such it omits altogether not only the astrological basis of the predictions, but also the many useful elements (the obligatory calendar pages, with their usual supplements of phases of the moon, tide tables, lists of kings and queens etc.) that made almanacs, in the days before pocket diaries, an indispensable aid to personal organisation. Whereas these useful items were frequently itemised on the titles of almanacs, Swift uses the title of his *Predictions* purely to focus his general charge against almanacs: '*Written to prevent the People of* England *from being further impos'd on by vulgar Almanack-makers*'. All almanac-makers but Bickerstaff are thus indicted of imposition; they are 'mean illiterate Traders between us and the Stars'. By contrast, the reader is to understand, the 'large and rational Defence of this Art' that Bickerstaff promises for the future (marking a clear distance between Swift's sceptical connoisseurship in the genre and Bickerstaff's typically astrologer-like idealism about the potential of a reformed practice) will be neither mean, nor illiterate, nor based in strategies of commercial profit. As he will declare at the end of his pamphlet, 'My Fortune has plac'd me above the little Regards of Scribbling for a few Pence, which I neither value nor want.'[33]

Bickerstaff in fact deploys throughout the *Predictions* a thoroughly conventional elite emphasis on rank and independence as criteria of political competence, criteria by which the average almanac-maker is inescapably convicted of incompetence and presumption, and of leading the people of England into dangerous error. In a very different and much more threatening political context, but working from very similar assumptions, Swift would later warn his congregation in his sermon *On False Witness*:

Let me advise you to have nothing at all to do with that which is commonly called Politicks, or the Government of the World; in the Nature of which it is certain you are utterly ignorant; and when your Opinion is wrong, although it proceeds from Ignorance, it shall be an Accusation against you.[34]

In line with this doctrine, Bickerstaff refuses in the *Predictions* to dignify Partridge's political assertions with an answer, a strategy that would in the longer term play a vital part in reducing Partridge in the eyes of posterity to a mere failed astrologer.

It was a strategy that Swift would continue in *The Accomplishment of the First of Mr. Bickerstaff's Predictions* (1708), complementing it this time, as

Phiddian remarks, by distancing himself somewhat from the tone of a pretender to astrological science: 'He exudes impartiality, wisdom, and polite skepticism in a manner prophetically reminiscent of Mr. Spectator.'[35] This avoidance of direct engagement with Partridge's politics is further sustained in Swift's *Elegy on Mr. Partridge* (1708), with its famous concluding *Epitaph*, and in *A Vindication of Isaac Bickerstaff* (1709): it contrasts markedly with the point-by–point refutation typical of Partridge's controversies with rival astrologers, as evidenced in his notoriously bitter feud with the high-church loyalist George Parker.[36] The view of Partridge that would descend to posterity is given its definitive form in the *Epitaph*, where he is reduced to the status of '*A* Cobler, Starmonger, *and* Quack', and even in death is less to be pitied than his hapless clients: '*Weep all you Customers that use* / *His* Pills, *his* Almanacks, *or* Shoes.'[37]

Swift's reductive account of Partridge in the *Epitaph*, not as a political commentator or would-be student of the heavens, but as a tradesman in shoes, patent medicines and predictions (with 'Starmonger' suggesting that the stars are just one more commodity to be bought and sold) resonates interestingly with the 1701 poem 'The Humble Petition of Frances Harris'.[38] In that poem, when the victim of theft reveals her plight, the bystanders' thoughts turn first to the traditional recourse of the poor in such emergencies: 'they would have had me gone to the Cunning Man'. But Mrs. Harris, with a woundingly backhanded compliment, turns instead to her trusted friend Swift: 'No, said I, 'tis the same Thing, the *Chaplain* will be here anon.'[39] On being asked 'can you cast a *Nativity*, when a Body's plunder'd?', Swift gives himself a retort of comic indignation, protesting that 'I was never taken for a Conjuror before, I'd have you to know.'[40] Just how offensive the term could be, even in the mouth of a self-proclaimed astrologer, can be judged from Partridge's own usage: in 1708 he expressed his professional contempt for 'a Conjuror near Aldgate-Church' who claimed he could make a bad wife good, despite having 'a B—h of a Wife himself, and cannot cure her'; and in 1708, the author of *Mr. Partridge's Answer to Esquire Bickerstaff's Strange and Wonderful Predictions for the Year 1708* retorts 'O rare Conjurer!' against Bickerstaff himself. (Bickerstaff, meanwhile, had laid down the challenge that 'I will allow … any … of the Fraternity, to be not only Astrologers, but Conjurers too, if I do not produce a hundred Instances in all their Almanacks, to convince any reasonable Man, that they do not so much as understand common Grammar and Syntax.')[41] Beneath the humour of the 'Humble Petition', Swift's play with the terms 'Cunning Man' and 'Conjurer' suggests a fundamental unease about the potential levelling of his priestly authority, in the popular mind, with what he takes to be merely fraudulent claims to penetrate the secrets of nature. By labelling Partridge 'A Cobler, Starmonger, *and* Quack' Swift brushes aside astrology's by now residual claims to the disinterested study of nature and levels it with shoemaking and quack medicine as just one more expedient by which an uneducated man can make a living at the expense of the poor and credulous.

Partridge had no difficulty in identifying the political quarter from which the Bickerstaff hoax came, although in writing to his friend Isaac Manley, the Postmaster-General for Ireland, he did not initially settle on the correct individual:

I don't doubt but you are Imposed on in Ireland also by a pack of Rogues about my being dead, the principall Author of it is one in Newgate Lately in the Pillory for [a] Libell against the State, there is no such Man as Isaack Bickerstaff, it is a sham Name, but his true Name is Pettie, he is always Either in a Cellar, a Garret or a Jaile, and therefore you may by that Judge what kind of Reputation this fellow hath to be Credited in the world.[42]

William Pittis, though not in fact the author of the *Predictions*, was notoriously a high-church pamphleteer, and this identification suggests that Partridge at least was in no doubt that Bickerstaff's intervention was primarily political.

Another testimony to the political dimension of the hoax's reception was *Mr. Partridge's Answer* (a response that, if not written by Partridge himself, is very much in his style), which regales the public with a politically explicit point-by-point critique very much in the manner of Partridge's characteristic onslaughts on rival astrologers.[43] This response takes up precisely the kinds of detailed political interpretation that Bickerstaff loftily declines to engage with in Partridge's texts. The *Answer* cites and attacks Bickerstaff point by point, vilifying him as disloyal to the cause of protestant England: he is accused of insinuating that battles will end badly for the Allies ('otherwise what harm will the particulars do the Government, which he seems affraid to offend'); and his prediction of an unspecified commander's death is condemned as 'another Jacobite S[h]uffle, as if this would be one of the Confederates, or why would not such a positive and infallible Fortune-teller as this, [have] discovered who he belong'd to?'[44] Bickerstaff is also accused of unseemly joy at the coronation of the new French king:

Having killed the *Dauphine*, and Old *Lewis* the preceeding Month, he makes the Duke of *Burgundy* a King in this: At which time he hears Bells and Guns, and sees the Blazing of a 1000 Bonefires. The Conjuror sure is in a mighty Rapture, at the News of the *French* King's Coronation, that he can hear nothing but Joy and Transport, here's Loyalty in Perfection.

Yet in *Mr. Partridge's Answer*, just as Bickerstaff had refused to engage with Partridge's detailed agenda, so this performance of Partridge's characteristic rhetoric and ideology evades the most challenging implications of Bickerstaff's scenario for the coming year, with its effective demolition of the Bourbon threat; instead it trots out default gibes against presumed disloyalty while taking for granted the necessity of continuing the war. For this Partridge, it makes no difference that the new French king would be so much younger and less experienced than the old, nor that he would have lost most of his international support: whatever the shift in the balance of power, for this incarnation of die-hard anti-popery Whiggery, it is easier to condemn Bickerstaff's prediction of bells and bonfires at the accession of a French king than to entertain possibilities for a negotiated peace. *Mr. Partridge's Answer*, whatever its authorship, fully lives up to the reputation for obsessive and aggressive bigotry that had originally singled Partridge out as Swift's target. It also suggests a resistance to moving beyond old certainties that is arguably ill placed to deal with radically changed circumstances.

In contrast with *Mr. Partridge's Answer*, it is striking that even when Bickerstaff does, in *A Vindication of Isaac Bickerstaff, Esq.*, glance briefly at the kinds of politics that Partridge had made his own, the topics are fleetingly and ironically handled, and in no way amount to an engagement with Partridge on his own terms: dismissing reports that the Cardinal Archbishop of Paris had not in fact died, Bickerstaff retorts, 'But how far a *French* Man, a *Papist*, and an *Enemy* is to be believed, in his own Cause, against an *English Protestant*, who is *true to the Government*, I shall leave to the candid and impartial Reader.'[45] Bickerstaff neatly appropriates to himself the patriotic virtues that Partridge had made his own, while ironically leaving the undead protestant astrologer in the same limbo as the undead popish archbishop. Later readers of the Bickerstaff papers who have taken Partridge purely at Swift's strategic devaluation miss the fun that arises from the contrast between the ineffectual figure conjured by Bickerstaff and the fire-breathing controversialist familar to contemporary almanac readers, a commentator who, however beloved by no-popery zealots among his vast and largely uneducated readership, was by this time testing the patience not only of high-church Tories, but also of Whigs more pragmatically attuned to current political realities.

ECCLESIASTICAL CENSORSHIP

Although there was in general no pre-publication censorship after the expiry of the Printing Act in 1695, there was an important exception in the case of almanacs. The Stationers' Company, which derived significant income from its monopoly on almanacs, continued to submit them for ecclesiastical approval; and the task of vetting them seems to have fallen to archiepiscopal chaplains.[46] Partridge was an old hand at this game, having played cat-and-mouse with the censor for many years before the expiry of the Act; but in 1708, as Capp notes, significant parts of his text were suppressed. This is particularly noteworthy, since *Merlinus Liberatus* for 1708 is precisely the Partridge item most directly relevant to the Bickerstaff papers. The action taken by the ecclesiastical censor is plain from its mutilated pages: two sections have been replaced by lines of blank rules, with no attempt to respace or conceal the changes.[47] This was arguably a counterproductive intervention, since the highly visible evidence of interference not only provided Partridge's supporters with a focus for resentment, but also posed readers of all dispositions the intriguing riddle of reconstruction: what could Partridge have written that was so much worse than his past offences that it had been blanked out? Swift, knowing not only Partridge's familiar agenda, but also the particular opportunities given him by the current events of the year, would have had no difficulty whatsoever in imagining suitably inflammatory text to fill in the blanks.

The great political topic for the 1708 almanacs was the 1707 Act of Union between England and Scotland; and in addition there was continuing interest in campaigns and possible peace negotiations in the War of the Spanish Succession. The first censored passage in Partridge's 1708 *Merlinus Liberatus*, which follows preliminary advertisements for his patent medicines and tables of useful dates, occurs in a prefatory poem entitled 'On the Glorious Union of the Two Kingdoms. By way of Introduction'. The poem begins, under the title, with nine lines of blank rules, after which thirty-six surviving lines of verse take up the story:

> This drew the Screen, all Men of each Degree,
> The *Lame* they walk'd, the *Blind* began to see;
> All-pitying Heaven too, unites the rest,
> To save the *QUEEN* from *Bears* and worser *Beasts*.
> When Heaven works, what's undertook must be,
> *The how* we know not but th'Effect we see.
> Thus Heaven's hidden Hand the Method taught,

> The *QUEEN* gave Order, *God and Nature wrought.*
> Perplext with Enemies, yet manag'd well,
> Beset with Dangers, carry'd on by Skill.
> All Things agreed, agreed to make it great,
> The Glorious *Union* is by this compleat.[48]

When Partridge returns to the Queen near the end of his poem it is solely to focus on the Union:

> But this great Work shall the *QUEEN*s Merit raise
> On Pillars founded for *Eternal Praise*
> Two Kingdoms join'd will add to *Britain's* Fame,
> A single Title to a double Name.
> And Times *Long Arm* shall hand it down, and tell
> Those yet unborn how great the Thing, how well

And here, having reached the foot of the page, the verse stops short, without full stop or grammatical resolution.

An instructive contrast is offered by *The Ladies Diary: or, The Womens Almanack* for the same year, 1708. This bears an elaborate portrait of the Queen on its title page, and around the image are arranged ten lines of verse:

> Hail *ANNA*, best of Queens, in you Combine
> The brightest Glories of your Royal Line.
> They taught their *Britons* to o'ercome in *Fight*,
> You teach us both to *CONQUER* and *UNITE.*
> Oh Harmony! Like what they know above,
> Where all is *UNION*, and Eternal *LOVE.*
> Heaven did for *ANNE* the Glorious Work Ordain,
> To Crown the Blessings of Her Wondrous Reign:
> Posterity Her Pious Care shall bless,
> While Men love Freedom and are pleas'd with Peace.

Here the Union is taken as a further instance of the Queen's already established merit (a considerable advance on Partridge's grudging praise), and she is also presented as the culmination of her Stuart 'Royal Line' (a commendation unthinkable for Partridge). Indeed, Partridge may well have courted suppression by couching comparisons of Anne to her Stuart forebears in terms so insulting as to be judged unprintable. This is, of course, mere speculation, but speculation is precisely what censorship of this kind invites. The blanked page displays established power, but it also prompts even the most loyal reader to imagine enormities.

The blanked-out lines also presumably blamed Tories and churchmen for opposing the Union, since the first lines that the purchasers were actually allowed to read suggest that progress was only possible once metaphorical lameness and blindness had been dealt with. Indeed, later in his poem Partridge goes on to say:

> What *Wars* and *Feuds*, what *Murders* have been done
> By *Artful* and *Religious Knaves* begun.
> 'Twas their being parted made the Borders bleed,
> But holy Island did it, not the *Tweed.*
> Henceforth no more Disputes about this Point,
> If *George* or *Andrew* is the greater Saint;
> Nor yet which *Nation* of the Two is *best,*
> Or who with most *Religion* most is *Blest.*

Despite the apparent even-handedness, his regular readers would be in no doubt on which side of the religious divide the problem had lain: it could hardly be a nation with a presbyterian established church. For Swift, in contrast, the Union not only compromised the English constitution, but also rewarded Scots dissent at the expense of Irish loyalty. He would write in *The Story of the Injured Lady* that Scotland 'is of a different Religion, being a Presbyterian of the most rank and virulent Kind, and consequently having an inveterate Hatred to the Church'.[49] In *Verses said to be Written on the Union* he would lament that 'The Queen has lately lost a Part / Of her entirely-*English* Heart' and end with the warning that 'tossing Faction will o'erwhelm / Our crazy double-bottom'd Realm'.[50] He for one would have had no difficulty in ventriloquising the offensiveness of the cancelled portion of the prefatory poem to the 1708 *Merlinus Liberatus.*

Following the mutilated poem on the Union come the usual calendar pages, the core of the almanac. Each month occupies a complete opening, headed by twelve lines of verse spread six by six across the heads of the two pages; and by February Partridge is again in trouble with the censor. On the left-hand page of the February opening, reflecting on mankind's moral corruption, he opines:

> First Pride began, and then Revenge took place,
> Hence Persecution, and 'tis still the Case;
> And tho' there was no Weapon, Sword, nor Spear,
> ----------   ----------   ----------
>   ----------   ----------
> ----------   ----------   ----------[51]

The allusions here are hard to identify in any detail, but it seems clear that present persecution is being deduced from Satanic pride, possibly by way of the sin of Cain, the first murderer, against Abel, his righteous victim. Given the usual tracks in which Partridge's rhetoric of persecution ran, the cancelled lines had very probably applied the notions of pride, revenge and persecution to the high-church party. Again, as readers recalled Partridge's accustomed topics and agendas in quest of the likely contents of the suppressed passages, they were unavoidably drawn into complicity in a politics that the church had arguably rendered only the more potent by its efforts to suppress it.

Markedly contrasting with the 1708 *Merlinus Liberatus* are the almanacs for that year offered by Partridge's long-term antagonist, George Parker, and by Job Gadbury, a cousin of the recently deceased originator of a noted royalist and high-church (if not crypto-catholic) almanac.[52] *Parker's Ephemeris* for 1708 begins with a forthright and detailed refutation of Partridge's predictions.[53] His prefatory poem in praise of the Stuart line blames religious fiends for murdering Charles I, caricatures the dissenting interest and couples it with popery as an obstacle to uniting the nation. He also supplements his calendar by explaining the development of Holy Days since the Reformation and gives a list for each month. Gadbury, for his part, gives a positive view of the state of the nation under Queen Anne, assuring his readers in his infilled blank column for November 1708 that 'We of *Great Britain* are in as hopeful a Condition, could we but see it, and be thankful, as any Nation in *Europe*; and our Persons, Estates and Liberties, are safe and secure under a most Gracious Queen.' Like Parker, he gives prominence to the times and seasons of the liturgical year, and dedicates the headings of his calendar pages to this topic; so while in February Partridge is incurring censorship by talk of persecution, Gadbury is explaining that 'the Purification of the Blessed Virgin . . . is also called *Candlemass*; because, among the *Romans*, it is observed with a great many Lights in their Churches all the day long, in Honour of our Saviour, that was the true Light of the World'.[54] An equally revealing contrast is provided by the six lines of verse that Gadbury places at the foot of his table of kings and queens of England:

> See here a Race of *England*'s Glorious Kings,
> All which have done or suffer'd mighty things,
> So left the Throne whereon Just *Anna*'s set,
> To out-do all that ever reigned yet.
> May *Anna*'s Glories scale the Azure Sky,
> And make her Name to reach Eternity.[55]

And at the foot of the verses Gadbury sets the loyal motto *Omnis Potestas a Deo est* ('All power is from God'). Partridge, in contrast, gives a very different but equally predictable verse:

Monarchs like Rivers, small at first appear,
Increase in Strength and Power Year by Year;
But when well grown, they think of walking out,
And justle their weak Neighbours round about.
See *France* for this, who like a *Tyrant* rules,
Advis'd by Knaves, how to Enslave his Fools.[56]

Partridge insists that Louis's tyranny is simply what monarchy naturally grows into, given time: the longer a monarch reigns, the longer a little evil has in order to grow into a great one. Even when, at the end of his annual calendar, he does include a prayer for the Queen, it is carefully directed against his particular enemies: 'God preserve and bless Queen *ANNE*, and defend her from all her Enemies Temporal and Spiritual, Jack and Tack.'[57] The Queen confronts not merely temporal enemies (e.g. Louis XIV), but also spiritual enemies (notably, as Partridge afficionados would know, the high-church party). The summary phrase for her enemies, moreover, is 'Jack and Tack', i.e. Jacobites and Irish catholics. For Swift, in contrast, the Whig and dissenting interests that Partridge constructs as normative are the real focus of danger.

PARTRIDGE AS PARODIC ANTICHRIST

Mayhew long ago accustomed us to think of the Bickerstaff hoax as an April fool, and so it clearly is.[58] But although he noted the overlap of the festival of All Fools in 1708 with the most sacred penitential season of the Christian year, he treated the calendrical coincidence rather as a problem that Swift deftly sidestepped than as an opportunity that he embraced.[59] Mayhew suggested that although Swift may have been the author of the anonymous *An Answer to Bickerstaff*, which, if published, would have alerted readers to the fact that the original *Predictions* had been by the author of the *Tale of a Tub*, he may have withheld it from publication for fear of compromising his candidacy for English ecclesiastical appointments, as well as his sensitive role as Ireland's solicitor for the First Fruits: to have disclosed his authorship would have been to identify himself with an April Fool hoax in a year when 1 April was also Maundy Thursday.[60] Yet although Mayhew's attention to possible offence among the devout and to Swift's need to protect himself from it is characteristically shrewd, it is worth exploring the possibility that this overlaying of the secular and liturgical calendars may have looked, to the author of the *Tale*, more like an opportunity than a problem.

Given the centrality of religion to Partridge's accumulated offences, there is a ghastly appropriateness in making his humiliation take the form of a parody of the sacred events commemorated over Holy Week and Easter. Some sense of the sacredness of the season is given, for instance, by *Parker's Ephemeris*, which makes special mention of Palm Sunday, Maundy Thursday, Good Friday and Easter Day as focuses of observance (and notes the monarch's ritual washing of feet on Maundy Thursday, even specifying the use of the antiphon 'A new commandment', with its emphasis on the monarch's devout imitation of Christ).[61] Fuller assistance with devotions and meditations was offered by Swift's non-juring acquaintance Robert Nelson in *A Companion for the Festivals and Fasts of the Church of England* (1704). Although Nelson sets the bar characteristically high in terms of appropriate observance, he usefully indicates what the ordinary devout layperson, equipped only with the standard resources of the Book of Common Prayer (BCP), could practically aspire to, since (exceptionally for the BCP) each weekday of Holy Week is allocated its own collect, epistle and gospel:

[The Church of England] calls all her devout Members every day this Week to meditate upon our Lord's Sufferings; having collected in her *Offices* all those Portions of Scripture that relate to this tragical Subject; increasing their Humiliation, by the Consideration of our Saviour's: That with penitent Hearts, and firm Resolutions of dying likewise to Sin, they may attend their Saviour through the several Stages of his bitter Passion.[62]

Partridge too was, in a sense, to be put to death, but his claims not to be dead and never to have been dead would be stoutly denied. As he would not really die, he could hardly be resurrected and would always be remembered as the man who had to protest that he was not really dead. From this angle, the likely publication date for Swift's *Predictions* of 2 February, Candlemas Day, may also be significant, quite apart from its traditionally being, as Mayhew notes, the day on which unsold almanacs for the year were called in.[63] This feast of the Purification of the Virgin Mary (the focus given by the BCP), is the occasion of Simeon's acclamation of Jesus as 'a light to lighten the gentiles' (as noted in Gadbury's calendar heading for February) and would have been a liturgically apt moment for Swift to shine his own uncomfortably bright light on Partridge's almanacs, not only for their attacks on the temporal and spiritual foundations of the Church of England, but also for their reliance on a supposed science that the elite was increasingly inclined to dismiss as mere superstition.

Partridge's last full day of life, 28 March, was to have been Palm Sunday, enabling him (had he been so minded) to attend church and participate fully in the devotions set out for that day in the BCP. The following day, 29 March, the Monday before Easter, was the day appointed for his death. If we follow Mayhew's conjecture, the *Answer to Bickerstaff* that would have served, had it been published, as a print equivalent to the cry of 'April Fool!' would have been planned for release on 1 April, Maundy Thursday, when Queen Anne distributed the Royal Maundy in the Banqueting House in Whitehall. The following day, Good Friday, was the most sacred fast-day of the year, although Nelson hints that it was far from universally observed: "tis to be hoped that *Good-Friday* may retrieve the ancient Reverence that was paid to it, since Authority has so worthily required it to be observed as a day of Devotion, and sequestred from all Worldly Business'.[64] By Good Friday, however, Swift's fun with Partridge could be held, nominally at least, to have subsided (and this would still arguably have been the case even if the *Answer to Bickerstaff* had in fact been published on Maundy Thursday, instead of being withheld). On this timetable, a devout reader of Bickerstaff could, first, enjoy the joke, and, second, reflect as the week drew to its close on the edifying juxtaposition of the humiliated scourge of the church with the triumphant resurrection of its founder. On Easter Day, moreover, such a devout humorist might well have found a particular piquancy in the Easter Anthems: 'Christ being raised from the dead, dieth no more: death hath no more dominion over him.'[65] The case of Partridge, whose passion, through Bickerstaff's *Predictions*, had occupied the beginning of this Holy Week as Christ's the end, was instructively different: he hadn't really died, and yet death had established a permanent dominion over him. Indeed, when Partridge denied in his 1709 almanac that he was or ever had been dead, Bickerstaff would ridicule him in his *Vindication* for his implied 'Opinion, That a Man may be alive now, who was not alive a Twelvemonth ago': behind Bickerstaff's common-sense scepticism, Swift is arguably again invoking the uniquely sacred counter-example of Jesus Christ.[66]

'ETIAM MORTUUS LOQUITUR'

Partridge, to judge from his letter to Manley, had easily detected the high-church agenda behind the Bickerstaff persona and seems to have taken the attack very much in his stride. Whether or not he had anything to do with *Mr. Partridge's Answer to Esquire Bickerstaff's Strange and Wonderful*

Predictions for the Year 1708, he continued to prepare his *Merlinus Liberatus* for 1709 just as usual, adding to his usual title a final note 'to inform the World that I am Living, contrary to that base Paper said to be done by one *Bickerstaff*'. Otherwise the formula continues as before. His poem at the foot of the table of kings and queens, for instance, insinuates without stating a contractarian position on the institution of monarchy:

> When Virtuous Kings do on the Throne appear,
> They're for the Peoples good Intrusted there ...
> But when Luxurious and in Lewdness lost,
> They live like Drones upon the publick Cost.[67]

The introductory poem comprises a page and a half on the congenial topic of '*a Dialogue between a Red-hot* Jeroboam Tory, *and a* Jerusalem Whig, *about the Calves at* Dan *and* Bethel' (this time, apparently, not quite overstepping the censor's exasperation threshold). The calendar page for January is headed with a typical aspiration towards peace, coupled with an objection on principle to any peace likely to be proposed: '*Pax prae omnibus.* / Provided it be a good Penny-worth ... The *Jacks* and *High-Church* are for Peace. But why? to embroil the Nation and the publick Affairs, and to bring in Master *Perkin* and Popery. Brave Fellows.' For February, Partridge foresees that 'Publick Councils and Private Meetings' will be busy, 'And this thing of Peace seems to be the Subject that doth principally take up their time', and adds his customary rider, 'God grant a Blessing to their Endeavours, and send an Honourable Peace or none'. But the way in which he proceeds to develop his insinuations is perhaps surprising, since he departs from his routine allegation that peace is a popish Jacobite stratagem to blame 'Incendiaries' for blocking peace out of self-interest. Yet this is the point at which he reintroduces Bickerstaff, and it may be that he is suggesting that the apparent advocates of a Tory peace have deeper motives of personal advantage that may, once peace seems achievable, spur them on to undermine it by fraudulent newsmongering: 'There are now some Incendiaries employ'd and set on work by them that do not think it is for their Interest to have Wars at an end. Much lying News dispersed about the time; and also Scandalous Pamphlets. Perhaps we may have a second *Bickerstaff* appear.'[68] Following the calendar, Partridge prognosticates as usual for the four quarters of the year, discusses a sample nativity and takes up some recurrent issues in astrological theory. Only at the end of this material, and just before the medical and other advertisements that close the pamphlet, does he respond at any length to Bickerstaff:

You may remember there was a Paper published predicting my Death on the 29th of *March* at Night 1708, and after the day was past, the same Villain told the World I was dead, and how I died; and that he was with me at the time of my death. I thank God, by whose Mercy I have my Being, that I am still alive, and (excepting my Age) as well as ever I was in my Life, as I was also at that 29th of *March*. And that Paper was said to be done by one *Bickerstaffe*, Esq; But that was a sham Name, it was done by an *Impudent Lying Fellow*. But his Prediction did not prove true: What will he say to excuse that? For the Fool had considered the *Star of my Nativity* as he said. Why the Truth is, he will be hard put to it to find a *Salvo* for his Honour. It was a bold Touch, and he did not know but it might prove true.[69]

And with that, Partridge returns to his regular business of consultation by appealing to 'a Gentleman who hath writ two Letters to me' to send in his address so that Partridge 'may undeceive him, and set him right in the matter'.

After 1709, Partridge's contractual difficulties prevented him from publishing an almanac until late 1713, when he published his exultantly titled *Merlinus Redivivus* for 1714. This time he had several scores to settle, for in his absence from the market several opportunists had sought to fill the gap, and in a note at the end of his almanac he denounces 'all those Prophecies, Predictions, Almanacks, and other Pamphlets, that had my Name either true or shamm'd with the want of a Letter' as 'impudent Forgeries, by a Breed of Villains, and wholly without my Knowledg or Consent'.[70] In contrast with this rough and ready vilification of such 'beggarly Villains that have scarce Bread to eat without being Rogues', he devotes the first page of his almanac to an ironic dedication to Bickerstaff, whom he now boasts to have survived:

There seems to be a kind of fantastical Propriety, in a *Dead Man*'s Addressing himself to a Person not in Being. *Isaac Bickerstaffe* is no more ... like many an Old Man that is reported so by his Heirs, I have lived long enough to bury my Successor.[71]

As the letter proceeds, it becomes clear that Partridge's claim to 'have lived long enough to bury my Successor' refers to the fact that Bickerstaff's life, although continued after the original hoax in the pages of Steele's *Tatler*, had ended with the winding up of the paper in 1711. Partridge, while focusing principally on Bickerstaff in his *Tatler* incarnation, continues by making it clear that he now knows exactly who was behind the original hoax:

Now, Sir, my Intention in this Epistle, is to let you know, that I shall behave my self in my new Being with as much Moderation as possible, and that I have no longer any Quarrel with you, for the Accounts you inserted in your Writings

concerning my Death, being sensible that you were no less abused in that
Particular, than my self. The Person from whom you took up that Report,
I know, was your Name-sake, the Author of *Bickerstaffe's Predictions*, a notorious
Cheat.* And if you had been indeed as much an Astrologer, as you pretended, you
might have known that his Word was no more to be taken, than that of an *Irish*
Evidence, that not being the only *Tale of a Tub* he had vented. * *Vide* Dr. *Sw*—

Finally, he concludes with an appeal (with Steele and Addison most
obviously in mind) for the good offices of any future reviver of the
Bickerstaff persona:

I have nothing to add further, but only that when you think fit to return to Life
again, in whatever Shape, of a Censor, a Guardian, an Englishman, or any other
Figure, I shall hope you will do Justice to
  Your Revived Friend, and Servant,
  JOHN PARTRIDGE.

This is a suggestive moment, particularly when read in conjunction with
the promise of 'as much Moderation as possible': Partridge seems to
gesture towards possible accommodation with a Bickerstaff no longer
construed as high-church agitator, but as agent of polite Whig journalism.
Yet (as will be described below), this Bickerstaff too had adopted from
Swift, and deployed to major effect, some key strategies for marginalising
this embarrassing reminder of the radical Whig heritage.

  The 1714 almanac of the '*Revived*' Partridge has as its prefatory poem
'Scipio and Hanibal', a thinly veiled insinuation of his dissatisfaction with
the way in which the war was concluded: in allusion to Marlborough he
deplores 'The *Villany* of *Roman Gratitude*' to 'this great Conqueror, /
Who thus did end the Second *Punick* War'.[72] There is no place in this
almanac for eulogy of the Queen, but instead a continued emphasis,
through the rubrication in the blanks column of the calendar pages, on
his hopes for the succession. For May he records the birthday of 'the
Noble and Illustrious *GEORGE* the present Elector of HANNOVER . . .
whom GOD preserve, for the future Advantage of the Protestant Religion'; and he expresses the hope that 'by the good Grace and Mercy of
GOD we shall be better acquainted with that Family hereafter, which
hath given such visible Demonstrations of their Courage and Bravery in
the Wars against both the *French* and *Turks*'.[73] For October he reminds
'my Countrymen who are Lovers of the Noble Family of *HANNOVER*' of
the birthday of George's mother, Sophia, who would have been, at the time
of writing, next in line to the throne (although in the event she would
die on 8 June 1714, a fact which Partridge foresees as little as the death of

the Queen herself on 1 August – one is reminded of Bickerstaff's recollection of how 'poor K. *William* was pray'd for many Months after he was dead').[74] For November he recalls the birthday of the late King William and how he 'deliver'd us from Popery and *French* Slavery, with Arbitrary Power at the end of it'.[75] On the contrary side, he foresees for the spring agitation throughout Europe 'to promote Idolatry, Popery, and the Devil's Cause' and issues a warning to anyone tempted to remonstrate ('What not believe the Chevalier, when he speaks truth [?]'): 'Whenever you bring him in here, you pull in Popery and *French* Slavery, and away go Abbey-Lands to the Devil, *Rome* I mean; and then Fire and Faggot.'[76] The repetition of the phrase 'Popery and *French* Slavery', already used in his commemoration of King William, underlines the ingrained oppositional rhetoric with which he invokes the Hanoverian succession as England's best hope.

Partridge was understandably exultant over recent events when he set to work on his almanac for 1715, this time under yet another title formula. In *An Almanack for ... 1715* he is at last free from the irksome need to preserve nominal reverence for a Stuart monarch and can dedicate his almanac formally to George I.[77] Included in his offering to his potential protestant hero is some prime no-popery material, including a memorial of Samuel Johnson, chaplain to William Lord Russell, whipped from Newgate to Tyburn for 'writing an Address to the Protestant Soldiers in K. *James*'s Army, exhorting them to an Abhorrence of Popery', along with an advertisement for his recently published works.[78] At the foot of the calendar blank in which this reminder of popish Stuart oppression is displayed, Partridge concludes with a prayer for the new king that celebrates his satisfaction at finding himself once more on the winning side:

make him an Instrument of maintaining the Ballance of *Europe*, of securing and enlarging the Protestant Interest abroad, and of transmitting our Liberties both Civil and Religious to all Generations. In order to this, may all that have betray'd their Country, either in Peace or War, meet with their deserv'd Punishment!

Partridge, like the incoming king, wants to see those responsible for the Tory peace indicted for treason, and 1715 was indeed to prove the year of greatest danger for those of Swift's friends who had directed negotiations: Prior and Oxford were arrested, and Bolingbroke fled to France.[79]

Yet at this promising conjunction of affairs, it was finally Partridge's fate, on 24 June 1715, to die in fact. His almanac, like others whose marketability outlived their originators, continued to appear under the familiar name that constituted its 'brand' – a procedure that Bickerstaff had highlighted in his *Vindication*:

There is one Objection against Mr. *Partrige*'s Death, which I have sometimes met with, although indeed very slightly offered; That he still continues to write Almanacks. But this is no more than what is common to all of that Profession; *Gadbury, Poor Robin, Dove, Wing*, and several others, do yearly publish their Almanacks, although several of them have been dead since before the *Revolution.*[80]

The Partridge *Almanack* for 1716 takes care, however, to invoke the personal authority of the dead man by claiming to be made 'from a Copy written with the Doctor's own Hand'.[81] In 1717 the old *Merlinus Liberatus* title was restored, and a similar assurance was offered to 'the Protestant Reader' that the contents had been 'Printed from a Transcribed Copy, written with the Doctor's own Hand'; but what is most notable in this year is the use of a new motto on the title page, '*Etiam Mortuus Loqui-tur*'.[82] This is a quotation from Hebrews 11.4, 'he being dead yet speaketh', and it is hard not to read the epigraph as referring not only to the recent death of John Partridge, but also to the mock-death previously inflicted on him by Bickerstaff. Depending how much credence is given to the claim that Partridge had, in effect, written out tables and prognostications for two years ahead, it may even be that Partridge himself had chosen this epigraph as his last laugh against Bickerstaff.

The 'he' in this quotation is Abel, presented in Hebrews 11.4 as the original victim, and type of Christ:

By faith Abel offered unto God a more excellent sacrifice than Cain, by which he obtained witness that he was righteous, God testifying of his gifts: and by it he being dead yet speaketh.

By analogy, Partridge asserts a righteousness attested by God; and Swift is besmirched with the mark of Cain. The significance deepens as we read on, for Abel figures in Chapter 11 of Hebrews as the first in a long list of the heroes of faith:

These all died in faith, not having received the promises, but having seen them afar off, and were persuaded of *them*, and embraced *them*, and confessed that they were strangers and pilgrims on the earth.
    For they that say such things declare plainly that they seek a country.[83]

It is then the burden of the next chapter that readers should focus on the 'promise', now fulfilled in Jesus, and 'run with patience the race that is set before us, Looking unto Jesus the author and finisher of *our* faith'.[84]

If, as Hebrews 11.4 puts it, 'they that say such things declare plainly that they seek a country', then Partridge had been saying very plainly for a very long time what kind of country it was towards which he was urging his numerous and largely ill-educated readers: it was remarkably like the United Provinces of the Netherlands, where he had in the 1680s sought refuge from James II; and Swift, like other high-church observers, had been consistently alarmed at any such prospect.[85] Partridge's posthumous motto picks up an analogy that had been traded back and forth between establishment and dissent in the later seventeenth century, and places him as righteous Abel.[86] Abel, divinely vindicated against Cain his murderer, stands in Hebrews at the head of a line that culminates in Christ, whose vindication by God is testified in the resurrection. Whoever selected the motto, it can be read as an aggressively theological, if doomed, riposte to Swift's Holy Week hoax.

As the years passed, however, the reality was that Partridge's almanac would lose its distinctive political tone. In 1773, for example, *Merlinus Liberatus* was still being published as 'By John Partridge', with its '*Etiam Mortuus Loquitur*' motto, and was still counting the years from 'our Deliverance by *K. William* from Popery, and Arbitrary Government' and 'the Horrid, Popish, High-Church, Jacobite Plot'. But, despite the familiar title, this was a very different pamphlet. Its monthly poems are shorter, and the commentary is in general supportive of 'the church' and laudatory of the royal family. Anti-catholic venom remains, but times have changed and popery is no longer charged to the Church of England, nor to the ruling house. May's poem celebrates the Queen's birthday:

Let her free Soul and glorious Actions shew,
She's Enemy to Rome, and Tyrants too

The blank column in the calendar adds the pious hope, 'whom God long preserve for the good of the Protestant Religion in *Great Britain* in particular'.[87] There is now a comfortable distance about invoking, in September, 'the glorious City of *London* burnt by those vile Incendiaries the Papists', even though readers are still exhorted to 'Let it remain a Monument of Gratitude to God, of Caution to *England*, and Protestants in general, & Shame to *Rome*'.[88] Should conflict arise, as is feared for October, between church and people, then the almanac can only attribute it to fraud and malice, and put its weight firmly behind the church:

if the Crew can get their Ends no other way, they will be scandalizing the Clergy by lying Pamphlets, and false Reports in private, to animate, if possible, the People against them; but we hope the Church will continue in a flourishing

Condition, notwithstanding the Contrivances of the Moles to undermine her by Policy, and the Rats who fly in her Face by open Violence.[89]

Times have indeed changed, but it is hard to imagine Partridge himself ever settling into quite so tame a relation to established power. On the other hand, even before Partridge's death in 1715, his reputation as a vitriolic partisan had already been subjected to a highly effective campaign of depoliticisation. Taking its hint from the Bickerstaff hoax, this campaign would increasingly marginalise his political commentary and fix his image in the public mind as a figure of fun much closer to Swift's 'Cobler, Starmonger, *and* Quack'.

PARTRIDGE IN THE 'TATLER'

In 1709 Swift's Bickerstaff persona was taken up by Steele as supposed author of the *Tatler* (1709–11). Steele clearly realised the strategic value of Swift's focus on Partridge as a figure of fun rather than a political commentator and shifted his own references to Partridge ever further and further away from republican Whig ideology. Indeed, he seems to have grasped that the very recollection of ideological forebears such as Partridge was a threat to the politely modernising version of Whig culture that it was his business to promote (much as Addison would later realise in relation to Milton, although in that case republicanism would be drowned out by paeans to epic religious sublimity rather than by satire of plebeian pretensions to scientific authority); and while Steele had not yet, in the *Tatler*, entirely softened the sharper edges of his own Whig commitments, his satirical sidelining of Partridge marks a strategic step very much in the right direction.[90]

Steele takes up, with the Bickerstaff persona, the precedent set in the Partridge affair to 'print Bills of Mortality', which he presents as the *Tatler*'s key sanction against errors and delinquencies of style, morals and behaviour. Having summarised the state of play between himself and Partridge, Steele's Bickerstaff concludes:

I have in another Place, and in a Paper by it self, sufficiently convinc'd this Man that he is dead, and if he has any Shame, I don't doubt but that by this Time he owns it to all his Acquaintance: For tho' the Legs and Arms, and whole Body, of that Man may still appear and perform their animal Functions; yet since, as I have else where observ'd, his Art is gone, the Man is gone. I am, as I said, concern'd, that this little Matter should make so much Noise; but since I am engag'd, I take my self oblig'd in Honour to go on in my Lucubrations, and by the Help of these Arts of which I am Master, as well as my Skill in Astrological

Speculations, I shall, as I see Occasion, proceed to confute other dead Men, who pretend to be in Being, that they are actually deceased. I therefore give all Men fair Warning to mend their Manners, for I shall from Time to Time print Bills of Mortality; and I beg the Pardon of all such who shall be nam'd therein, if they who are good for Nothing shall find themselves in the Number of the Deceased.[91]

Thus the dead Partridge becomes the first of many to be sentenced to death by the imaginary entity who will soon invest himself with the formal dignity of Censor of Great Britain. That death sentence is recalled again soon afterwards when Bickerstaff, fearing that the prediction of deaths might be catching, warns that he himself '*cannot hold out with any tolerable Wit*' unless his readers send in letters for him to print and discuss.[92]

A sign of what is to come is an early reference to Partridge in *Tatler* No. 2 as 'Mr. Partridge the Conjuror', the supposed seller of what is claimed to be a bottle of magic water.[93] Like Swift, Steele mocks the patent medicines that were so important a component of Partridge's business, but as significant is the contemptuous term 'conjuror'. In No. 11 it is the doggerel verse that formed such a feature of his almanacs that is mocked, in conjunction with his notorious 'death': he is summed up as one 'who, Poetical as he was, could not understand his own Poetry; and Philomathical as he was, could not read his own Destiny'; but readers are not invited to disinter any of the potentially inflammatory topics typical of that poetry.[94] In No. 56 a reference to Partridge's 'Answer to an Horary Question, at what Hour of the Night to set a Fox-Trap' focuses on the lowly preoccupations of his clients.[95] In No. 67 Bickerstaff laments the refusal of those he has declared dead to lie down and be quiet, since 'Mr. Didapper', despite warnings of imminent death 'for wearing red-heel'd Shoes', 'appear'd yesterday with a new Pair of the same sort'; and Bickerstaff adds, with affected despair, that still 'Partridge walks about at Noon-day'.[96] In No. 73 Partridge's astrological pretensions are again invoked when a sharper assures a potential conspirator that the ruin of their intended victim is assured: 'Partridge has cast me his Nativity, and I find by certain Destiny, *his Oaks must be fell'd.*'[97] Meanwhile, Bickerstaff's declarations of death support a gibe against the law when a younger brother realises the potential for taking such deaths in a legally binding sense: '*Whereas … a young Gentleman … has taken my Discourses upon* John Partridge *and others in too literal a Sense, and is suing an elder Brother to an Ejectment; the aforesaid young Gentleman is hereby advised to drop his Action, no Man being esteem'd dead in Law, who eats and drinks, and receives his Rents.*'[98] In these years Partridge was having his own troubles with the law, quite independently of Swift's campaign, about his right to publish his almanac, which to the extent that 'Partridge' was the brand-name of an almanac, rendered it indeed a dead letter, and No. 96 takes occasion to print an indignant declaration by 'my departed Friend *John Partridge*' to the effect 'That he is still Living, in Health, and they are Knaves that reported it otherwise'.[99] Some time after the commencement of Bickerstaff's declarations of death in his role as Censor, the consequences of having so many unburied corpses lying around the city are taken up by the Company of Upholders (i.e. undertakers) in No. 99, where it is suggested, quite logically, that they should make a start by burying Partridge.[100]

An unusual reference to Partridge's politics does, however, occur in No. 118, where, in response to a civil letter from Partridge allegedly dated '*From the Banks of* Styx', Bickerstaff comments:

> The foregoing Letter was the more pleasing to me, because I perceive some little Symptoms in it of a Resuscitation; and having lately seen the Predictions of this Author, which are written in a true Protestant Spirit of Prophecy, and a particular Zeal against the *French* King, I have some Thoughts of sending for him from the Banks of *Styx*, and reinstating him in his own House, at the Sign of the *Globe* in *Salisbury-Street.*[101]

Readers are here invited to remember Partridge's former ranting in the protestant interest, but they are guided only as far as values that most of their compatriots can unite around, namely commitment to protestantism and enmity to the king of the nation with whom they are at war. Partridge as a figure is still undermined by the whimsical play with his supposed death, and Steele stops short of resuscitating his notorious insistence on the evils of monarchy as a system, or on the complicity of the high-church party with popish corruption. Even so, Steele works in a sly, though far less offensive, gibe at high-church theology, making Partridge ask for '*Mr. Dodwell's* Book against the Immortality of the Soul', a work by the non-juror Henry Dodwell, whose argument that the human soul, naturally mortal, could be rendered immortal only through the sacrament of baptism had seemed eccentric even to fellow non-jurors.[102] But such a doctrine, according to Partridge (that life-long scourge of the high-church party) would now, ironically, be 'of great Consolation to our whole Fraternity, who would be very glad to find that they are dead for good and all, and would in particular make me rest for ever'.[103] This wistful yearning for everlasting rest distances this attenuated Partridge still further from the fury of old-style Whig rabble-rousing, while still allowing the new-style Whig *Tatler* a politely sceptical quip at the expense of high-church metaphysics.

For the rest of the *Tatler*'s run, however, references to Partridge are increasingly sparse. In No. 124 a poor country visitor who aims to make his fortune in the lottery asks Bickerstaff to choose him a ticket because, 'finding my Friend Mr. *Partridge* dead and buried', he has concluded that Bickerstaff is 'the only Conjuror in Repute'.[104] Again, Partridge is presented as the favourite magician of the gullible rustic. He is mentioned once more in relation to the appearance of *Squire Bickerstaff Detected* in 1710 (which appeared as by Partridge, even though his almanacs had been suppressed), and this gives Bickerstaff the opportunity to issue an ironic warning to 'Beware of Counterfeits, for such are Abroad'.[105]

In January 1711 Steele laid down the Bickerstaff mask once and for all, and, though he conceded that he had been criticised for touching on 'Matters which concern both the Church and State', he defended himself by asserting 'That the Points I alluded to are such as concerned every Christian and Freeholder in *England*'.[106] Evidently he had not succeeded in persuading all his readers that his agenda was inoffensively apolitical, but to the extent that he had made that possibility more thinkable, he had been helped by refocusing Partridge as the quintessential practitioner of an astrological system no longer taken seriously by the elite. When, in the *Spectator*, Addison joined Steele in further marginalising the potentially divisive specifics of political discourse, readers were no longer invited even to recall the once famously deceased astrologer: all the partridges in the *Spectator* have feathers, and are there to be shot by the likes of Sir Roger de Coverley. Steele and Addison do not, for obvious reasons, revive the more theologically radical aspect of Bickerstaff's Holy Week hoax (a task taken up only by the selector of the posthumous motto '*Sic mortuus loquitur*'). Even so, in contrast with the crude blanks by which the ecclesiastical censor had originally tried to suppress the radical Partridge, the polite Whig periodical's terminal de-emphasis of his political significance does indeed confirm the effective death of the more significant of the astrologer's two bodies, marking the end point of a process in which Swift, for his own very different reasons, had shown the way.

NOTES

I am grateful to the participants in the 2008 Huntington symposium for their useful responses to a preliminary version of this chapter, and to Maureen Bell, Alexander Lindsay and James McLaverty for particular generosity in sharing their special expertise. During final revision I also benefited from discussion with John

McTague, who kindly gave permission for me to cite his unpublished work on the Bickerstaff hoax and its political contexts.

1 F. P. Wilson, *The Oxford Dictionary of English Proverbs*, 3rd edn (Oxford: Clarendon Press, 1970), 'ways'. Versions are attested from the late seventeenth century.

2 George Mayhew, 'Swift's Bickerstaff Hoax as an April Fools' Joke', *Modern Philology*, 61 (1964), 270–80; *PW*, IV, 267.

3 William Burns, '"The Terriblest Eclipse that Hath Been Seen in Our Days": Black Monday and the Debate on Astrology during the Interregnum', in Margaret Osler, ed., *Rethinking the Scientific Revolution* (Cambridge University Press, 2000), pp. 137–52 (p. 152, n. 66). As the calendar in any almanac would make clear, 29 March 1708 was also a Monday.

4 For Partridge's career and significance, see Bernard Capp, *Astrology and the Popular Press: English Almanacs 1500–1800* (London: Faber and Faber, 1979), pp. 49–50, 92, 94–9; and Patrick Curry, 'Partridge, John (1644–1715)', *ODNB* (www.oxforddnb.com/view/article/21484, accessed 7 Aug. 2008). Davis, in his Introduction to *Bickerstaff Papers and Pamphlets on the Church* (1966), identified 'the violence with which he had abused the clergy of the Church of England' as Swift's provocation, citing Partridge's almanacs for 1706 and 1707 (*PW*, II, x–xii). Ehrenpreis, II, 198 suggests that Swift may have come across Partridge, a native of East Sheen, much earlier in life, when he was working nearby for Sir William Temple: this possibility will be further explored by John McTague in his forthcoming D.Phil. thesis.

5 Contrast the views of William III summarised by Ian Higgins, in *Swift's Politics: A Study in Disaffection* (Cambridge University Press, 1994), pp. 45–52.

6 *PW*, IX, 228.

7 Ibid., 224.

8 Marcus Walsh, 'Swift and Religion', in Christopher Fox, ed., *The Cambridge Companion to Jonathan Swift* (Cambridge University Press, 2003), pp. 161–76 (p. 163); and in the same collection, Christopher Fox, 'Politics and History', pp. 31–47 (p. 33).

9 John Partridge, *Merlinus Liberatus: Being an Almanack for the Year of our Blessed Saviour's Incarnation 1708*. Mayhew, 'Swift's Bickerstaff Hoax', usefully details some resemblances between the general predictions in this almanac and Swift's *Predictions* (276–7). For the timing of almanac production, see Capp, *Astrology*, pp. 40–1, 59.

10 For earlier mock almanacs that featured 'nonsense, mild social satire and ridicule of the almanac's empty but solemn predictions', see Capp, *Astrology*, p. 33.

11 William Alfred Eddy, 'The Wits *vs.* John Partridge, Astrologer', *Studies in Philology*, 29 (1932), 29–40 (36), citing George Parker, *Merlini Liberati Errata* (1692), p. 20.

12 See p. 93 and n. 46 below.

13 Partridge, *Merlinus* (1708), sig. A6.

14 Ibid., sig. A7, B2.

15 *The Works of Mr. Thomas Brown, in Prose and Verse; serious, moral, and comical,* 2 vols. (1707), I, 43–73.

16 For the suggestion that Swift's *Predictions* 'both in tone and typography seem to have been modelled on the quarto pamphlet *Annus Mirabilis,* 1689', see *Correspondence,* I, 190. *Annus Mirabilis or Strange and Wonderful Predictions and Observations Gathered out of Mr. J. Partridges Almanack 1688. With some Remarks also, out of his Almanack 1687* was published in London in 1689: it was a selection from the prognostications bearing on the Revolution that Partridge had published abroad, selected after the event for their apparent accuracy. Despite a degree of resemblance in format, their anti-catholic rhetoric and emphasis on astrological detail set them at some distance from Swift's *Predictions,* which draw more widely on Partridge's professional and political controversies.

17 [Isaac Bickerstaff], *Predictions for the Year 1708,* by Jonathan Swift, p. 4. The copy cited is ESTC T124498, available via *Eighteenth Century Collections Online.*

18 Ibid., p. 3.

19 Ibid., p. 4.

20 Cp. Robert Phiddian, 'A Name to Conjure with: Games of Verification and Identity in the Bickerstaff Controversy', in Richard H. Rodino and Hermann J. Real, eds., *Reading Swift: Papers from the Second Münster Symposium on Jonathan Swift,* pp. 141–50 (p. 144).

21 [Bickerstaff], *Predictions,* p. 7.

22 Cp. Bickerstaff's caution that 'those in Power have wisely discourag'd Men from meddling in Publick Concerns, and I was resolv'd by no Means to give the least Offence' (ibid., p. 8); and for a similar deference to authority by Gadbury under James II, see Capp, *Astrology,* p. 50.

23 For 'no peace without Spain', see Bertrand A. Goldgar and Ian Gadd, eds., *Jonathan Swift: English Political Writings 1711–1714: The Conduct of the Allies and Other Works,* the Cambridge Edition of the Works of Jonathan Swift. (No. 8), (Cambridge University Press, 2008), p. 4. For failed peace negotiations in 1708–9, see Ehrenpreis, II, 317 and Anthony Levi, *Louis XIV* (Cambridge, MA: De Capo Press, 2004), pp. 264–5; for Philip's renunciation of his French claim, see Ehrenpreis, II, 562–3.

24 Partridge, *Merlinus* (1708), sig. C2–C2v. Mayhew, 'Swift's Bickerstaff Hoax', plausibly suggests that the 'raging Fever' of which Partridge is to die alludes to a mortal fever that Partridge had predicted for London in April (p. 277).

25 [Bickerstaff], *Predictions,* p. 3.

26 *PW,* II, xi.

27 N. F. Lowe, 'Why Swift Killed Partridge', *Swift Studies,* 6 (1991), 70–82.

28 John Partridge, *Mene Tekel: Being an Astrological Judgement on the Great and Wonderful Year 1688* (1688), sig. A5–5v.

29 John Partridge, *Mene Tekel Upharsin. The Second Part of Mene Tekel: Treating of the Year MDCLXXXIX* (1689), sig. A3–A3v.

30 [Bickerstaff], *Predictions*, p. 8. For Halley's actual character as an astronomer, see Alan Cook, 'Halley, Edmond (1656–1742)', *ODNB* (www.oxforddnb.com/view/article/12011, accessed 7 Nov. 2008).

31 Cp. the two paragraphs 'I must add one Word more . . . needless to repeat' ([Bickerstaff], *Predictions*, p. 4).

32 Partridge, *Mene Tekel Upharsin*, sig. A2v.

33 [Bickerstaff], *Predictions*, p. 8.

34 *PW*, IX, 186.

35 Phiddian, 'A Name', p. 145.

36 See for example the opening sections of *Parker's Ephemeris* (1708), and for an overview of the controversy, Bernard Capp, 'Parker, George (1654–1743)', *ODNB* (www.oxforddnb.com/view/article/21298, accessed 7 Aug. 2008).

37 *An Elegy on Mr.* Partrige, *the Almanack-maker, who Died on the 29th of this Instant* March, *1708*, *Poems*, I, 97–101.

38 For 'starmonger', see *OED*, 'star', *n.*^{1}, first citation from Ben Jonson.

39 *Poems*, I, 72 (lines 48–9).

40 Ibid. (lines 58, 60).

41 [Bickerstaff], *Predictions*, p. 2.

42 *Correspondence*, I, 189 (letter dated 24 April 1708).

43 As with many of the pamphlets associated with the Bickerstaff hoax, authorship is uncertain. Mayhew treated *Mr. Partridge's Answer* as John Partridge's genuine response ('Swift's Bickerstaff Hoax', 274–5), but it has more commonly been regarded as the work of an impersonator, notably in the postscript to the pseudo-Bickerstaffian *A Continuation of the Predictions* (1708), where it is attributed to Richard Ball, and in the title of the recently identified *Esquire Bickerstaff's Reply to Dr. Partridge's Pretended Answer* (London: J. Mophev, 1708) (not in ESTC, but described, with title photograph, in Maggs Bros. Catalogue 1393, where Ball is also discussed, pp. 194–204: ESTC N72338 is a Dublin reprint). There are moments in *Mr. Partridge's Answer* when the mask seems to slip and Partridge is referred to in the third person, but at the very least the polemical vigour of the critique catches important aspects of Partridge's manner and ideology.

44 *PW*, II, 205, 206.

45 *Vindication*, in ibid., 161.

46 Capp, *Astrology*, pp. 50, 240, and n. 175 (p. 398) and 8 (p. 434), the latter citing names of licensers who signed off extant copies of almanacs. The censored portions of *Merlinus Liberatus* for 1708 are found on sigs. A3v–A4 and A5v.

47 Although the general quality of printing is too poor to put it beyond doubt that the alterations were inserted into the forme after the type had been set, slight wobbliness in the relevant areas of the copies examined is at least consistent with that supposition. For such cheaply printed material, extensive resetting is unlikely to have seemed worthwhile.

48 Partridge, *Merlinus* (1708), sig. A4.

49 *PW*, IX, 4.

50 *Poems*, I, 96.

51 Partridge, *Merlinus* (1708), sig. A5v.

52 Job Gadbury, *Ephemeris: Or, A Diary Astronomical, Astrological, Meteoro-logical, for the Year of our Lord, 1708* (London, 1708), sig. B6. Patrick Curry, 'Gadbury, John (1627–1704)', *ODNB* (www.oxforddnb.com/view/article/10265, accessed 7 Aug. 2008).

53 *Parker's Ephemeris*, pp. 4–12.

54 Gadbury, *Ephemeris* (1708), sig. B5v.

55 Ibid., sig. 7v.

56 Partridge, *Merlinus* (1708), sig. A2v.

57 Ibid., sig. B8.

58 Mayhew, 'Swift's Bickerstaff Hoax'.

59 Ibid., 279.

60 Ibid., 273–4.

61 'A new commandment I give unto you, That ye love one another; as I have loved you, that ye also love one another', taken from Jesus's farewell discourse, following his washing of the disciples' feet and the sharing of the last supper (John 13.34).

62 *The Book of Common Prayer and Administration of the Sacraments, and other Rites and Ceremonies of the Church, according to the Use of the Church of England; together with the Psalter or Psalms of David, Pointed as they are to be Sung or Said in Churches* (London, 1702); Robert Nelson, *A Companion for the Festivals and Fasts of the Church of England, with Collects and Prayers for each Solemnity* (London, 1704), pp. 389–90.

63 Mayhew, 'Swift's Bickerstaff Hoax', 273, 278.

64 Nelson, *Companion*, p. 389.

65 BCP, Easter Anthems.

66 [Bickerstaff], *Vindication*, p. 6 in *PW*, II, 162.

67 Partridge, *Merlinus Liberatus* (1709), sig. A3r. (Not currently available via ECCO: the BL copy is included in PP2465, a bound-up set of the almanacs for 1709.)

68 Ibid., sig. A5r.

69 Ibid., sig. C7r–8r.

70 John Partridge, *Merlinus Redivivus: Being an Almanack for ... 1714*, sig. C8.

71 Ibid., sig. A1v.

72 Ibid., sig. A4.

73 Ibid., sig. B1.

74 [Bickerstaff], *Predictions*, p. 3.

75 Partridge, *Merlinus Redivivus*, sigs. B6, B7.

76 Ibid., sig. C6v.

77 John Partridge, *An Almanack for ... 1715* (1715), sig. A1v.

78 Ibid., sig. B8r; for the significance of the publication, see Melinda Zook, 'Johnson, Samuel (1649–1703)', *ODNB* (www.oxforddnb.com/view/article/14916, accessed 7 Aug. 2008).

79 Frances Mayhew Rippy, 'Prior, Matthew (1664–1721)', *ODNB* (www.oxforddnb.com/view/article/22814, accessed 7 Aug. 2008); H. T. Dickinson,

'St John, Henry, styled first Viscount Bolingbroke (1678–1751)', ibid. (www. oxforddnb.com/view/article/24496, accessed 7 Aug. 2008); W. A. Speck, 'Harley, Robert, first earl of Oxford and Mortimer (1661–1724)', ibid. (www.oxforddnb.com/view/article/12344, accessed 7 Aug. 2008).

80 *Vindication*, in *PW*, II, 163. For further examples of almanacs that outlived their originators, see Capp, *Astrology*, p. 43.

81 Sig. A1v. It is not clear at what point the compilation of 'Partridge' was taken over by Charles Ledbetter (whose relative detachment from the historical Partridge is indicated by his willingness to reprint Swift's verses against him), but the examples usually cited date from the 1730s and later (Capp, *Astrology*, p. 239 and n. 4 [p. 434]); J. Bryden, 'Leadbetter, Charles (1681–1744)', *ODNB* (www.oxforddnb.com/view/article/16233, accessed 28 Aug. 2008).

82 *Merlinus Liberatus* (1717), sig. A1v.

83 Hebrews, 11.13–14.

84 Ibid., 12.1–2.

85 Curry, 'John Partridge', *ODNB*.

86 Cp. the contrary applications of the brothers' story offered by the Quaker William Bayly's *Iacob is become a Flame and the House of Esau Stubble, or, the Battail betwixt Michael and the Dragon, in which the Seed of the Woman is Bruising the Serpents Head. And Cain the First Birth (the Persecutor) is found the vagabond, and Abel and Abraham (that wandred) the Freinds of God. … With a few words to the priests, Bishops, Episcopal-men, and professors of this last age, and a short warning to the rulers and inhabitants of the earth* [c. 1662], and by Henry Glover's sermon commemorating the execution of Charles I, *Cain and Abel Parallel'd with King Charles and his Murderers* (1664). I owe to John McTague the information that 'Cain and Abel' had also been cited by a government informer as the title of a polemical piece allegedly circulated by the exiles in the Netherlands against James II.

87 *Merlinus Liberatus* (1773), sig. A8v–B1r.

88 Ibid., sig. B5r.

89 Ibid., sig. B6r.

90 Cp. *Squire Bickerstaff Detected*, variously attributed to two Whigs, Rowe and Congreve, which in contrast retains Partridge's characteristic politics as part of its satire, making him address 'my dear Countrymen of these united Nations' as 'a *Briton* born, a Protestant Astrologer, a Man of Revolution Principles, and Asserter of the Liberty and Property of the People', and blame the campaign against him on papists and Jacobites: 'that *Culprit* aforesaid, is a *Popish* Emissary, has paid his Visits to St. *Germains*, and is now in the Measures of *Lewis* XIV'. See also the final number of the *Tatler* for Steele's recognition that he had given offence by taking up a party-political position (*The Tatler*, ed. Donald F. Bond, 3 vols. (Oxford: Clarendon Press, 1987), III, 364).

91 Bond, *Tatler*, I, 23. Bond speculates (22, n. 27) that Swift may even have composed this section.

92 Ibid., 62–3.

93 Ibid., 24, record of variants.
94 Ibid., 99.
95 Ibid., 394.
96 Ibid., 462.
97 Ibid., 504.
98 Ibid., 523.
99 Ibid., II, 96.
100 Ibid., 112–13.
101 Ibid., 201–2.
102 Henry Dodwell, *An Epistolary Discourse, Proving, from the Scriptures and the First Fathers, that the Soul is a Principle Naturally Mortal; but Immortalized Actually by the Pleasure of God. ... Wherein is Proved, That None have the Power of Giving this Divine Immortalizing Spirit, since the Apostles, but only the Bishops* (1706).
103 Bond, *Tatler*, II, 202.
104 Ibid., 232–3.
105 Ibid., III, 135.
106 Ibid., 364.

CHAPTER 5

Swift and the art of political publication: hints and title pages, 1711–1714

James McLaverty

In his essay on Swift in the *Lives of the Poets*, Johnson raises important questions about the nature and quality of Swift's literary artistry in his political writing in the period 1711 to 1714, questions that merit a response. He credits Swift with a major influence on English politics in the period, but he denies that his success was the reward of a fully developed art. In his summing up, he judges that 'In the reign of Queen Anne he turned the stream of popularity against the Whigs, and must be confessed to have dictated for a time the political opinions of the English nation.'[1] But the analysis of Swift's style that follows suggests a limited talent whose delight was in simplicity: 'This easy and safe conveyance of meaning it was Swift's desire to attain, and for having attained he deserves praise, though perhaps not the highest praise.'[2] The unperplexed and undecorated quality of Swift's writing, as Johnson saw it – it is not true, he says, that Swift has no metaphors, but his metaphors are merely necessary ones – leads to heavily qualified praise of individual works, notably *The Conduct of the Allies*. The success of the pamphlet in establishing the case for peace is recognized, but Johnson sees that success as stemming from the people's readiness to embrace a case that should have been obvious:

> *Whatever is received*, say the schools, *is received in proportion to the recipient.* The power of a political treatise depends much upon the disposition of the people; the nation was then combustible, and a spark set it on fire. It is boasted, that between November and January eleven thousand were sold; a great number at that time, when we were not yet a nation of readers. To its propagation certainly no agency of power or influence was wanting. It furnished arguments for conversation, speeches for debate, and materials for parliamentary resolutions.
>
> Yet, surely, whoever surveys this wonder-working pamphlet with cool perusal, will confess that its efficacy was supplied by the passions of its readers; that it operates by the mere weight of facts, with very little assistance from the hand that produced them.[3]

It is possible to concede the importance of the public response, and of the political case itself, without accepting this negative assessment of Swift's contribution, though it seems to represent Johnson's settled opinion, expressed once more, bluntly, in Boswell's *Life of Johnson*, where Johnson says that the *Conduct* is 'a performance of very little ability', explaining that Swift 'told what he had to tell distinctly enough, but that is all. He had to count to ten, and he has counted it right.'[4]

What Johnson's account of Swift's writing most obviously omits is the large-scale inventiveness that can endow a plain sentence with complexity: the fiction or pretence that creates a space for play, allows interaction between a variety of imitated voices, or draws on contexts in which plain speaking comes startlingly as a surprise. Our name for such large-scale inventiveness would probably be structural irony, emphasizing the opportunity for vocal play, but in his own discussions Swift's emphasis is on inventiveness, and the term he uses is 'hint'. What is necessary for successful satirical and political writing is a hint. From his time in London, when we know something of his intimate thoughts about writing through the *Journal to Stella*, through to his own imagined panegyric in *Verses on the Death of Doctor Swift*, published in 1739, the hint is central to Swift's thinking about literary creativity. It is the essential seed from which writing, especially political writing, will emerge. This particular meaning of 'hint', and its use by Swift and his circle, seems to be unrecognized by the *Oxford English Dictionary*, though perhaps it is related to the sense from 1621, 'something to lay hold of, a "handle"'. It is clearly related to the ordinary sense of hint, a suggestion made by someone else, but it goes beyond that. A literary hint is a prompt to creativity and a force shaping the outcome; it can be your own idea or it can be someone else's. A good literary hint needs to suggest both form and content. Indeed, for a hint to be worth its name it would have to fuse form and content: to see them together is to grasp the way to write. For Swift and his circle, it was also to grasp a way to publish, for literary form was closely, though not indissolubly, tied to forms of publication. Those in search of a hint did well to pay attention to the book trade, to look quizzically at the printed matter all around them, and to reflect on how some parody, some game, some hoax, some sottiserie, might provide the form in which a syntactically and metaphorically simple sentence would take on complexity.

Swift and Pope both use 'hint', as a noun and as a verb, in a quite modern way. Swift writes of Steele in the *Journal to Stella*, 'I had a hint given me, that I might save him in the other employment', while Pope in a famous line in his *Epistle to Dr Arbuthnot* writes that Atticus will 'Just hint a fault, and hesitate dislike'.[5] But they also use the noun in the specialized way I have been discussing. At the beginning of *The Dunciad*, Pope pictures Dulness looking into the seething mass of degenerate creativity that is Grub Street:

> Here she beholds the Chaos dark and deep,
> Where nameless Somethings in their causes sleep,
> 'Till genial Jacob, or a warm Third day,
> Call forth each mass, a Poem, or a Play:
> How hints, like spawn, scarce quick in embryo lie,
> How new-born nonsense first is taught to cry.[6]

In Grub Street this semi-inert fertility is to be regarded with loathing, but in one's own creativity it is treasured. Pope claims that a Grub Street hint requires the intervention of a bookseller, Jacob Tonson, or a theatre manager, to give it literary form, but, as I think is now generally recognized, the book trade had its role in shaping the work of the Scriblerians as well as their enemies.[7]

Swift was throughout his life notably fertile in hints and generous to his friends in making suggestions. Most famously, he gave the hint for *The Beggar's Opera*, ending a letter, 'What think you of a Newgate pastoral, among the whores and thieves there?'[8] And when he rescued Pope's *Dunciad* from the fire it was probably with the hint that the long-planned progress of Dulness could be combined with an attack on Pope's critic, Lewis Theobald.[9] In his early years of engagement in English politics, the *Journal to Stella* makes clear Swift's general excitement at his own inventiveness, which very much focused on his capacity to generate hints.[10] He often refers in the *Journal* to the hints that he is laying down or giving away, sometimes preparing to turn aggression into creativity: 'And I am come home rolling resentments in my mind, and framing schemes of revenge: full of which (having written down some hints) I go to bed';[11] 'I gave my lampoon to be printed. I have more mischief in my heart; and I think it shall go round with them all, as this hits, and I can find hints';[12] 'I studied at leisure, writ not above forty lines, some inventions of my own, and some hints.'[13] Often Swift is concerned with hints for the *Tatler*, either for himself or for Steele: 'I fancy you'll smoak me in the *Tatler* I am going to write; for I believe I have told you the hint';[14] 'We have scurvy *Tatlers* of late . . . I have one or two hints I design to send him';[15] 'You are mistaken in all your conjectures about the *Tatlers*. I have given him one or two hints';[16] 'No the *Tatler* of the *Shilling* was not mine, more than the hint, and two or three general heads for it';[17] 'To my knowledge he had several good hints to go upon; but he was so lazy and weary of the work, that he would not improve them.'[18] Later Swift found he had supplied hints for the *Spectator*: 'Yesterday it was made of a noble hint I gave him long ago for his *Tatlers*, about an Indian supposed to write his travels into England. I repent he ever had it . . . all the under-hints there are mine too.'[19] Harrison was also given hints for his *Tatler*,[20] and Manley for her Guiscard narrative[21] and *Comment on Hare's Sermon*.[22] The occasional *Examiner* read 'as if he had given some hints',[23] while he and Bolingbroke said they would 'now and then send hints' for that paper,[24] which he did.[25] As the *Journal to Stella* progresses, hints become less important, though when a letter appears vindicating Maccartney from the murder of Hamilton, Swift says, 'I must give some hints to have it answered'.[26]

If references to hints drop off in the *Journal to Stella*, Swift's pride in his capacity to generate them still shows up famously in *Verses on the Death of Doctor Swift*, when the 'impartial' assessor says of Swift that:

> To steal a Hint was never known,
> But what he writ was all his own. (317–18)

Modern editions point out that this passage closely resembles John Denham's 'On Mr. Abraham Cowley':

> To him no author was unknown,
> Yet what he wrote was all his own. (29–30).[27]

So that the claim to independence is deeply dependent; indeed, the final line is almost the same. I have at different times thought different things about this couplet: at first that it was an ironic joke at Swift's (or his panegyrist's) expense; then that it was a claim advanced soberly (the echo being a matter of chance); but now that Swift is playing with what a hint is. A hint is always taken from somewhere else; it is always picked up. To steal another's idea is wrong; to take it and adapt it (as Swift does with the La Rochefoucauld maxim that stimulates the *Verses* or with Denham's couplet in these lines) is a vital aspect of invention.

Swift's inventiveness is central to his achievement in political writing. Pope boldly begins the preface to his translation of the *Iliad* by saying, 'Homer is universally allowed to have had the greatest *Invention* of any writer whatever', and, though Swift may not rival Homer in what might be thought of as *ex nihilo* creativity, his ingenuity in manipulating and developing established materials is extraordinary. He was both hindered and helped by the limitations of the somewhat feeble genres that were open to him. As a prose writer, a political writer, and a satirist, the paths to distinction open to him were not so clear as they were for his friend Pope. For Pope, the poetic forms – the pastoral, the mock-epic, the verse essay, and the verse epistle – carried with them their evident disciplines. Swift, on the other hand, had the very large number of sub-genres of the political article and pamphlet open to him. He succeeds in enlivening them, but, taken both individually and as a bunch, they are short in surface attraction and distinctiveness. Among the more popular forms were these: the account; the advice to X, Y, or Z; the answer; the argument; the defence; the description; the dialogue; the discourse; the dissertation; the essay; the letter; the meditation; the memoir; the memorial; some observations; the petition; the prediction; the project; the proposal; several reasons; some reflections; a refutation; some remarks; the state of X, Y, or Z; the scheme; some thoughts; a vindication. Literary criticism has taken little care of these writings, paying scant attention to their kinds and to the distinctions between them, but on the whole their demands do not seem to be great, nor their rules strict. Swift was very aware of these genres and sub-genres (the index to the Teerink-Scouten bibliography is full of them), and he either uses them himself or responds to all those I have mentioned.[28] What is remarkable in Swift is his power, often, I shall suggest, by reference to book-trade conventions, to vivify these kinds, to make them memorable, and to add twists and turns and inventions of his own.

In exploring Swift's political writings between 1711 and 1714 I am deeply indebted to the editors of the recently published volume edited by Bertrand A. Goldgar and Ian Gadd in the Cambridge Edition of the Works of Jonathan Swift.[29] I had the privilege of working with them on the volume, and in what follows I draw heavily on their scholarship. In discussing them I shall give special attention to title pages. In this period the general expectation was that authors would have a role in creating their title pages. In his *New Introduction to Bibliography* Philip Gaskell says, 'the title page was set from copy, which might indicate roughly how it was to be set out', though he thinks the details might be left to the compositor.[30] The Chiswell papers in the Bodleian, containing licensed manuscripts and title pages in manuscript and type, confirm the potential for full authorial engagement in the process,[31] and Swift clearly regarded designing the title page as part of the author's responsibility. In expressing his contempt for Steele in *The Publick Spirit of the Whigs*, he offers a quasi-bibliographical analysis of the contents of *The Crisis*, before highlighting 'the Generosity of our Adversaries in encouraging a Writer, who cannot furnish out so much as a Title-Page with Propriety or common Sense'.[32]

Swift's ingenuity seems most characteristic in the middle of this period, with his reaction to the occupation of Dunkirk by British forces under the command of General Jack Hill on 8 July 1712. This occupation was of the first importance to Swift, and he responded to it in a series of pamphlets. The *Journal to Stella* reveals his anxiety that the French handover of Dunkirk, which was to signal agreement between Britain and France and the beginning of serious negotiations, would not take place. If Louis XIV's grandson Philip was to be recognized as Philip V of Spain, Harley's ministry said, Philip had to renounce the French throne. When that was done, Dunkirk would be handed over to the British as a pledge and a proper armistice would be declared. But the occupation was delayed, and Swift was 'very desponding' as a consequence.[33] After investing so much of his energy in recommending a peace, he was faced with the shocking prospect that peace would not be achieved. His anxiety is clear in a letter to Stella of 1 July 1712, where he says: 'I wish it were over . . . If we have Dunkirk once, all is safe'.[34] A week later, General Hill entered Dunkirk and all was safe. The occupation had its personal symbolism also because Jack Hill was Abigail Masham's brother, and a personal friend of Swift's, sending him a snuff box as a present.[35] Swift's response was not to think in terms of a celebratory ode, as he might have done in his youth, but of indulging in some Grub Street jesting. Grub Street was on his mind because it had come under threat from the government's Stamp Act, which taxed papers at a halfpenny a half-sheet, and he responded in the *Journal* by exclaiming on 18 January 1712, 'so farewel to Grub-street',[36] before finally declaring, 'Grubstreet is dead and gone' on 7 August that year.[37] Perhaps it was a sense of nostalgia, therefore, that sent him to Grub Street for inspiration to celebrate this momentous occupation. On 17 July he told Stella, 'Since Dunkirk has been in our Hands, Grubstreet has been very fruitfull: pdfr [Swift] has writt 5 or 6 Grubstreet papers this last week'.[38] The papers have been identified as two poems and the five prose broadsides, all published between 10 and 19 July: *A Dialogue upon Dunkirk, It's Out at Last, A Hue and Cry after Dismal, Dunkirk Still in the Hands of the French* (of which no copy has survived), and *A Letter from the Pretender*.[39] All four extant documents are ingenious and show Swift's ability to take, and develop, a hint.

The most amusing and typographically inventive of these pieces is *A Hue and Cry after Dismal* (see Figure 1). Strikingly, for this sort of spoof, it is beautifully printed, a complicated job, well executed. Gadd

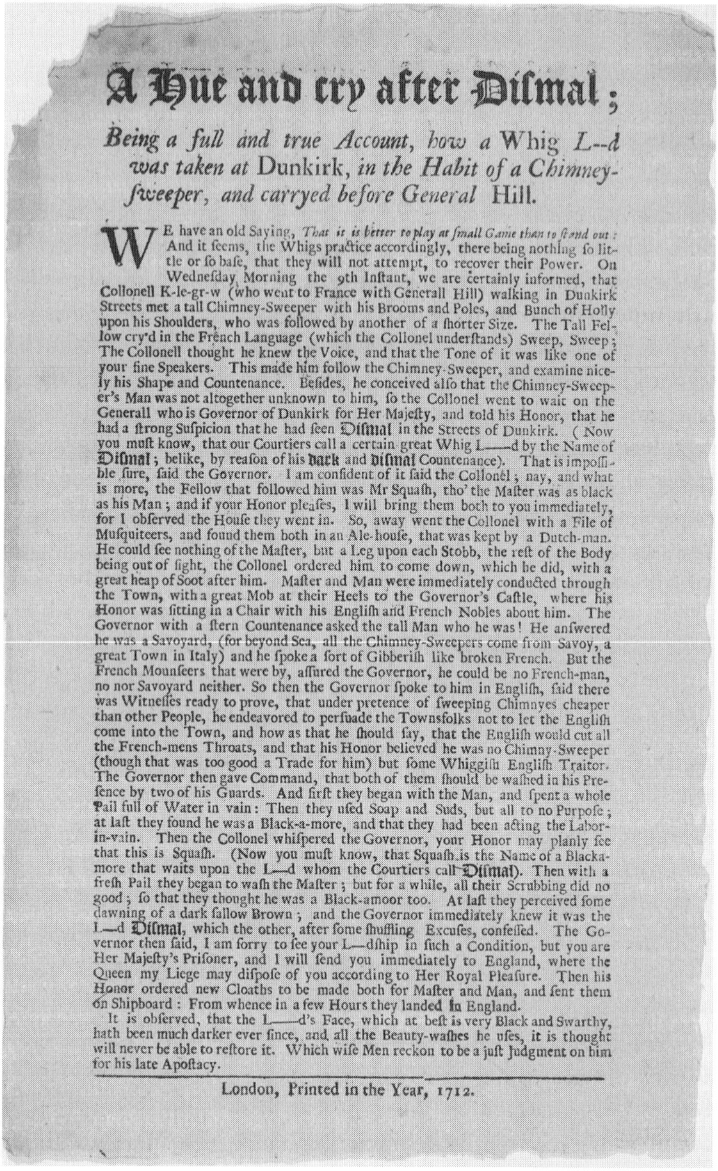

A Hue and cry after Dismal;

Being a full and true Account, how a Whig L--d
was taken at Dunkirk, *in the Habit of a Chimney-
sweeper, and carryed before General* Hill.

WE have an old Saying, *That it is better to play at small Game than to stand out:* And it seems, the Whigs practice accordingly, there being nothing so little or so base, that they will not attempt, to recover their Power. On Wednesday Morning the 9th Instant, we are certainly informed, that Collonell K-le-gr-w (who went to France with Generall Hill) walking in Dunkirk Streets met a tall Chimney-Sweeper with his Brooms and Poles, and Bunch of Holly upon his Shoulders, who was followed by another of a shorter Size. The Tall Fellow cry'd in the French Language (which the Collonel understands) Sweep, Sweep; The Collonell thought he knew the Voice, and that the Tone of it was like one of your fine Speakers. This made him follow the Chimney-Sweeper, and examine nicely his Shape and Countenance. Besides, he conceived also that the Chimney-Sweeper's Man was not altogether unknown to him, so the Collonel went to wait on the Generall who is Governor of Dunkirk for Her Majesty, and told his Honor, that he had a strong Suspicion that he had seen Dismal in the Streets of Dunkirk. (Now you must know, that our Courtiers call a certain great Whig L——d by the Name of Dismal; belike, by reason of his **back** and **dismal** Countenance). That is impossible sure, said the Governor. I am confident of it said the Collonel; nay, and what is more, the Fellow that followed him was Mr Squash, tho' the Master was as black as his Man; and if your Honor pleases, I will bring them both to you immediately, for I observed the House they went in. So, away went the Collonel with a File of Musquiteers, and found them both in an Ale-house, that was kept by a Dutch-man. He could see nothing of the Master, but a Leg upon each Stobb, the rest of the Body being out of sight, the Collonel ordered him to come down, which he did, with a great heap of Soot after him. Master and Man were immediately conducted through the Town, with a great Mob at their Heels to the Governor's Castle, where his Honor was sitting in a Chair with his English and French Nobles about him. The Governor with a stern Countenance asked the tall Man who he was! He answered he was a Savoyard, (for beyond Sea, all the Chimney-Sweepers come from Savoy, a great Town in Italy) and he spoke a sort of Gibberish like broken French. But the French Mounseers that were by, assured the Governor, he could be no French-man, no nor Savoyard neither. So then the Governor spoke to him in English, said there was Witnesses ready to prove, that under pretence of sweeping Chimnyes cheaper than other People, he endeavored to perswade the Townsfolks not to let the English come into the Town, and how as that he should say, that the English would cut all the French-mens Throats, and that his Honor believed he was no Chimny-Sweeper (though that was too good a Trade for him) but some Whiggish English Traitor. The Governor then gave Command, that both of them should be washed in his Presence by two of his Guards. And first they began with the Man, and spent a whole Pail full of Water in vain: Then they used Soap and Suds, but all to no Purpose; at last they found he was a Black-a-more, and that they had been acting the Labor-in-vain. Then the Collonel whispered the Governor, your Honor may plainly see that this is Squash. (Now you must know, that Squash is the Name of a Blacka-more that waits upon the L——d whom the Courtiers call Dismal). Then with a fresh Pail they began to wash the Master; but for a while, all their Scrubbing did no good; so that they thought he was a Black-amoor too. At last they perceived some dawning of a dark fallow Brown; and the Governor immediately knew it was the L——d Dismal, which the other, after some shuffling Excuses, confessed. The Governor then said, I am sorry to see your L——dship in such a Condition, but you are Her Majesty's Prisoner, and I will send you immediately to England, where the Queen my Liege may dispose of you according to Her Royal Pleasure. Then his Honor ordered new Cloaths to be made both for Master and Man, and sent them on Shipboard: From whence in a few Hours they landed in England.

It is observed, that the L——d's Face, which at best is very Black and Swarthy, hath been much darker ever since, and all the Beauty-washes he uses, it is thought will never be able to restore it. Which wise Men reckon to be a just Judgment on him for his late Apostacy.

London, Printed in the Year, 1712.

Figure 1. *A hue and cry after Dismal.*

suspects, and he is most probably right, that all Swift's political works of this period were undertaken by John Barber, the government printer, and distributed by his publisher, John Morphew. Perhaps sometimes the actual printing was farmed out to someone else, but I assume that, because both Swift and Barber were working for the government, Swift did not have to worry about finding a bookseller to act for him or the money to pay his costs. He was free to experiment, in collaboration with Barber, who was something like a personal friend.[40] A hue and cry is a formal or informal call for the capture of a criminal, in this case a proclamation. In the early nineteenth century it was part of the title of the *Police Gazette*. The hue and cry had been used before for political purposes. There was quite a flurry of them in the 1680s, for Titus Oates and Roger L'Estrange for example. There is even a *Hue and Cry after Daniel Foe* in 1711, and Swift's essay in the genre provoked an immediate response in a *Hue and Cry after Dr. Swift*. These pieces do not necessarily follow the form of an official notice: what is essential to them is the characterization of an opponent as criminal.

In this case Swift and Barber have created an elegant broadside imitation of a flyer or poster. The heading, in a very crisp black letter, or 'English' as contemporary printers would have called it, sets up the hoaxing quality of the publication.[41] It is a type that was used mainly for statute law, for official government declarations, for posters, for the edition number on title pages, and for the mastheads of newspapers, for example, the *London Gazette*, and it is still found on the *Daily Telegraph* and *Daily Mail* to this day. Its use in a hue and cry is obviously appropriate, but, more surprisingly, it also appears in several other of Swift's title pages of this period and in the poems. Although it tends to retain a connection with its legal functions, it also carries with it an air of the antique and the mysterious. Moxon, in his *Mechanick Exercises*, says of the compositor, 'English obsolete Words he Setts in the English Character',[42] and that practice seems to shape Swift's sense of the letter, though he extends its use so that it represents what is alien and strange. In his poems the whole of 'A Famous Prediction of Merlin' and of 'The W—ds-r Prophecy' are printed in black letter, the former so convincingly printed that Ames was fooled into including it in his *Typographical Antiquities* (1749). Black letter is also used flatteringly but to suggest the out of the ordinary in the 'Ode to the Athenian Society': 'Ye Great Unknown' (lines 60 and 188); 'Cruel Unknown' (242), 'Charges of a Smile' (253); it is used in 'The Virtues of Sid Hamet the Magician's Rod' to refer to the rod as an 'Heir-loom' (64), probably a glance at Godolphin's relationship with the Churchills; and it is also used in poems to highlight particular names. Notable among those names is 'Dismal', which appears in black letter in the first line of 'Toland's Invitation to Dismal', and in 'Peace and Dunkirk'.[43] In *A Hue and Cry*, black letter is used in the heading and, within the notice, for the name 'Dismal', and for the adjectives 'dark' and 'dismal', which are applied to the villain of the piece. 'Dismal' in Swift's headline is Daniel Finch, Earl of Nottingham. Finch had long belonged to the camp of Swift's enemies, for William Wotton, the critic of *Tale of a Tub*, transformed in the fourth edition of 1710 into its annotator, had been Finch's chaplain and had dedicated his *Reflections upon Ancient and Modern Learning* (1694) to him. The preface to *Tale of a Tub* ridicules him as a long-winded orator, but in December 1710 he had offended much more deeply by deserting the Tories and threatening the survival of the ministry by moving the address to the Queen saying that there could be no peace without Spain. If the condition of peace was that the Hapsburgs rather than the Bourbons had to rule Spain, there would be no peace. As Swift said to Stella, 'Lord Nottingham, a famous Tory and speech-maker, is gone over to the Whig side: they toast him daily, and lord Wharton says, It is *Dismal* (so they call him from his looks) will save England at last'.[44] If Nottingham was a saviour to the Whig Lord Wharton, to Swift he was an apostate and deserter. His opposition in the Lords had made necessary the drama of the Queen's appointment of twelve new peers. At the moment of occupying Dunkirk and securing peace, therefore, the idea of implicating the defeated Nottingham must have seemed irresistible. So in *A Hue and Cry* Swift plays on the nickname 'Dismal', a reference to Nottingham's 'dark and dismal Countenance', and introduces him to Dunkirk as an agent-provocateur chimney-sweep, apprehended at his dirty work:

On Wednesday Morning the 9th Instant, we are certainly informed, that Collonell K-le-gr-w (who went to France with Generall Hill) walking in Dunkirk Streets met a tall Chimney-Sweeper with his Brooms and Poles, and Bunch of Holly upon his Shoulders, who was followed by another of a shorter Size. The Tall Fellow cry'd in the French Language (which the Collonel understands) Sweep, Sweep; The Collonell thought he knew the Voice, and that the Tone of it was like one of your fine Speakers. This made him follow the Chimney-Sweeper, and examine nicely his Shape and Countenance.[45]

On interrogation, his true purpose is revealed:

So then the Governor spoke to him in English, said there was Witnesses ready to prove, that under pretence of sweeping Chimnyes cheaper than other People, he endeavored to persuade the Townsfolks not to let the English come into the Town, and how as that he should say, that the English would cut all the French-mens Throats, and that his Honor believed he was no Chimny-Sweeper (though that was too good a Trade for him) but some Whiggish English Traitor.[46]

The concluding phrase 'Whiggish English Traitor' is the judgement of the man Swift aims at. In Dunkirk, cleansed of his disguise, Nottingham can be seen for what he is, and the darkness of his countenance can be recognized by 'wise Men' to be 'a just Judgment on him for his late Apostacy'.[47]

The other so-called Grub Street pieces of this period show a similar ingenuity. *It's Out at Last* (see Figure 2) presents an absurdly naïve version of the Whig position. In this case, Swift has made up his own title and sub-title, both suggesting that a guilty secret has been revealed, but it had been known from November 1711 at the latest that the ministry wanted peace with France. This piece is a plain irony, with a suitably plain page. The writer of it is blind, not only to the previous negotiations, but to the possibility that they and the peace could be valued differently. The behaviour of the Tories is contrasted with that of Marlborough and the Whigs, who scorned to take towns 'without Powder and Bullets, Blood and Wounds'.[48] This contrasting 'treacherous Surrender of Dunkirk' through negotiation is for the writer merely evidence that the ministry has been corresponding with the French.[49] Swift's implication is 'Yes, it has, and with triumphant success.'

A Dialogue upon Dunkirk continues in even sharper form the idea that the Whigs are out of date, that history has overtaken their arguments. This time Swift uses a regular political and philosophical form, the dialogue, but he sets it up ingeniously. The key is in the date. The Whig and the Tory are arguing about the taking of Dunkirk, as can be seen from the beginning of the dialogue:

Whig.] Well, Mr. Tory, What do you think of the Expedition to *Dunkirk*? We were told the Town was to be Delivered a Week ago, the Troops Embark'd, and the new Governor just ready to take Horse. What! Has Old *Lewis* outwitted you? I observe your Faction are damnably down in the Mouth: If it ben't a Secret, prithee tell us where it sticks.[50]

Here all the anxieties expressed in the *Journal to Stella* are put in the mouth of a Whig opponent, but the piece is dated in its heading '*Sunday* Morning the 6th Instant', which means that the Whig's crowing is out of date and the ministry's success assured. General Hill sailed for Dunkirk on 6 July, arrived on the 7th, and took possession on the 8th, when

It's Out at Last:

O R,

French Correspondence

Clear as the S U N:

There is a Story goes of an old Prophetefs, that Prophefied always true to no purpofe; for her Fate was, never to be *believ'd*: The fame thing has happen'd, to a worthy Patriot and Member of the Houfe of *Commons*, who has openly in his Speeches declar'd that he was fure that the M——ftry *Corefponded* with *France*, and that in a little time there would appear manifeft Proofs of it; but fuch is the Stupidity or rather Malignancy of the *Tory*-Party, that they took no manner of notice of what this Eloquent Gentleman warn'd them of, in his pathetick Harangues, 'till now that they have a convincing Proof of it, with a witnefs, in this treacherous Surrender of *Dunkirk*.

It is judicioufly obferved by a learned Author, that the Fate of Princes and States is very hard; for Plots againft them are never believ'd 'till they are executed, and confequently without the poffibility of being prevented; for every-body will allow me, that what is already executed, is fo. I am afraid this will be foon verify'd upon this Nation, by the Clandeftine giving up of that Important Place.

I take it, that the Surrender of *Dunkirk* is fo plain a proof of our M——ftry's Correfponding with *France*, that I fhould pity any Man, as oppreffed with a ftrong Lethargy, fhould he doubt of it any more: I fay this as well to vindicate the Honour of that worthy Gentleman, as to awaken this infenfible droufy Nation, who cannot perceive that it is Day when the Sun fhines.

It was pleafantly faid by a *Swedifh* Poet,

Timeo Danos Dona ferentes.

I am afraid of the *Danes* when they bring Prefents.

Let us only confider the value of this Prefent of the *French* Monfieur; the many Millions it has coft him; the many more it has coft us: It is not only giving us a ftrong Fortification, but Fleets of Frigats and Privateers, and all Pretences afterwards to difturb our Trade in the Channel, and all this is ftill doubted when it is taken from him, and given to us: And can any Man imagine he does all this for nought? If any Man can fhow me that ever he did the like before, I will yield the point; but if no fuch Inftance can be given, it muft follow demonftratively, that he reckons the prefent M——ftry his Friends: for give me leave to fay, no Man would make fuch a valuable Prefent but to a Friend, and it were very unbecoming for any but a Friend to accept of it: Therefore I wifh the Pa——ent would make the M——ftry give an account if they came honeftly by it.

I have often ruminated in my Mind, of the Reafons that have induc'd the F——h Monfieur to make this Surrender; and I will give you my Conjectures in fhort. I think, in the firft place, it is not altogether improbable that he has Sold it now, as he Bought it before; and I wifh that may not be the chief Reafon of the Scarcity of Species at this time. 2*dly*, I believe he has done it out of pure fpight to the *Whigs*, whom he knows to be his irreconcileable Enemies; and I will be bold to fay, if he had been ftudying for it, he could not have ferv'd them a more malicious fpightful Trick. 3*dly*, Why may it not be a Token of Love to the *Tories*, and particularly to my Lady M——fham, for the great Service fhe has done him: and I am the more confirm'd in my Opinion, fince the Governor has been nam'd.

Let us now confider the Difference between the Old and the New M——ftry: They fcorn'd to accept of *Dunkirk* and a dozen more ftrong Towns of the *French* King, when they were offer'd; a plain and convincing Proof that they had no fecret Dealings with *France*. The D. of M——gh fcorn'd that modern Frenchify'd way of taking of Towns; he fcorn'd fo pitiful a Conqueft, without Powder and Bullets, Blood and Wounds. By the fame uncorrupt and generous Temper, they refus'd a Sum of Money which the F——h King offer'd them to help to drive the D. of *Anjou* out of *Spain*. It *fhall never be faid that* England *took* French *Money*, was the Saying of a Great and a Wife Minifter; a Saying which ought to be Engrav'd in Letters of Gold upon his Tomb-ftone. O the miferable Condition of the Nation, that has been forc'd to part with fo uncorrupt, fo wife, and fo truly an *Englifh* M——ry! Men that, for their own Ends, are carrying on private Bargains with our Enemies; in purfuance of which, they have not only accepted of *Dunkirk*, but would, without any manner of Hefitation, take *Toulon* and St. *Malo* too, if they were offer'd.

Thus I think it is plain, from what has been faid, that our M——ry are in a clofe Correfpondence with *France*; and, that the F——h Monfieur expects Juftice from them, not to fay fome little Faveur to boot. I wifh the Nation had open'd their Eyes before it was too late, and confider'd well before they had any Dealings with the Devil; for it is well known, that when once he has drawn them in to accept of the leaft Trifle as a Prefent, they are his for ever after.

L O N D O N : Printed in the Year M DCC XII.

Figure 2. *It's out at last: or, French correspondence clear as the sun.*

Nottingham the chimney-sweep was found. Indeed this triumphant broadside is linked to *A Hue and Cry* by the black letter 'Dismal' at the end of the dialogue, as Wharton and Nottingham are accused of having negotiated their pardons with the young Pretender's father.

The final Grub Street broadside, *A Letter from the Pretender to a Whig-Lord*, picks up this allegation against the ministry's opponents. The letter on a topic of current interest is a familiar form of political writing, but here Swift and Barber take it more literally, arranging the type to represent a document, with an extra-large signature from the Pretender at the end. The letter, which we are to guess is written to the Earl of Wharton (the number of dashes, though one is a full stop, is right), assumes a correspondence between the Whig lords and the Pretender. It begins, 'I thank you heartily for your Letters.' The body of the letter is concerned with the disposal of offices. Although individuals are referred to in code, it is still clear that the Duke of Marlborough is to have a commission for life, and that Dismal is to become Lord Privy Seal, a post for which he had been passed over in 1711. A careful calculation of payments is in keeping with the habits we find in many other of Swift's publications.

The letter formed the basis of several of Swift's publications in this period. The ingenuity with which he provides variations on the form is remarkable. *Some Advice Humbly Offer'd to the Members of the October Club, in a Letter from a Person of Honour* (1712); *A New Way of Selling Places at Court. In a Letter from a Small Courtier to a Great Stock-Jobber* (1712); *Some Reasons to Prove That No Person is obliged by his Principles as a Whig, to Oppose Her Majesty or her Ministry. In a Letter to a Whig-Lord* (1712); *The Importance of the Guardian Considered, in a Second Letter to the Bailiff of Stockbridge* (1713): all these letters point forward to Swift's most brilliantly conceived series, *The Drapier's Letters*, where he takes on the persona of the drapier in order to attack and defeat the government, varying the letters according to their addressees: the shopkeepers, tradesmen, farmers, and common people; Mr. Harding the printer; the Whole People of Ireland; and Viscount Molesworth.

It is notable that the letters of the period 1711–1714 have a double title, one to give the content and the other to give the form. In *Some Advice Humbly Offer'd to the Members of the October Club, in a letter from A Person of Honour*, the addressees needed particularly skilful handling (see Figure 3). The October Club was a large Tory grouping of some 140 members of Parliament who were pressing for the government to be more active in taking offices from Whigs and giving them to Tories. Swift, who

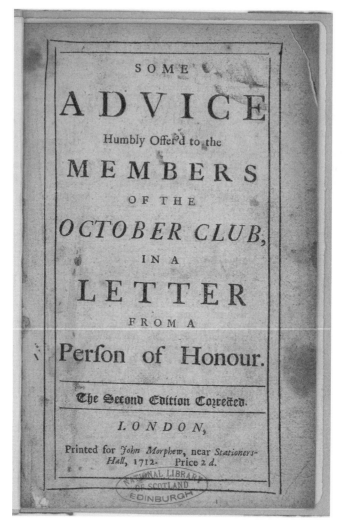

Figure 3. *Some advice humbly offer'd to the members of the October Club.*

was friendly with many of the members, nevertheless described it in hostile terms to Stella:

We are plagued here with an October Club, that is, a set of above a hundred parliament-men of the country, who drink October beer at home, and meet every evening at a tavern near the parliament, to consult affairs, and drive things on to extreams against the Whigs, to call the old ministry to account, and get off five or six heads. The ministry seem not to regard them, yet one of them in confidence told me, that there must be something thought on to settle things better.[51]

But if Swift was to conciliate this group and reconcile it to government policy, the greatest tact would be required. Hence the 'Humbly' in the title and the awkward claim to dignity for the author as a 'Person of Honour'. Swift had no honour as a member of Parliament or of the Privy Council; he had no title and no office. Only in a moral sense was Swift a man of honour. He begins with a directness that suggests complete honesty, though the sentiments are flattering: 'Gentlemen, Since the first Institution of your Society, I have always thought you capable of the greatest Things.' But in this letter, which is essentially a defence of Harley, it turns out not to be the writer's moral qualities so much as his closeness to the centre of power that matters:

This Letter is sent you, *Gentlemen*, from no mean Hand, nor from a Person uninformed . . . I may therefore assume so much to my self, as to desire you will depend upon it, that a short time will make manifest, how little the Defect you complain of, ought to lye at *that Door*, where your Enemies would be glad to see you place it.[52]

To be admitted to read this letter is a privilege; its author is dignified by his closeness to power rather than by honour.

Another letter from an insider, but one that might reflect rather ironically on *Advice to the October Club* is the one that constitutes *The New Way of Selling Places at Court* (see Figure 4). The title page is interesting. Although 'Court' is in as large a type and stands out well, the chief words on the title page are 'Selling Places'. They are in black letter and fill the whole line. This is a case where the words picked out are not only highlighted but rendered strange by their unusual typography. Professor Goldgar explains that Isaac Fielding had been selling places to interested parties, even though he had no power over them. Unfortunately for Fielding, his attempt to sell the Vice-Chamberlainship had come to the attention of the Vice-Chamberlain himself, who had no intention of surrendering his post. Swift associates the story with the selling of stocks and shares and confers on it the additional value of exonerating the ministry from the charges of corruption that behaviour like Fielding's might promote.

Some Reasons to Prove, That no Person is obliged by his Principles, as a Whig, To Oppose Her Majesty Or Her Present Ministry, also 1712 (see Figure 5), uses both the letter form and black letter in a different way again. This time the play in the title page is with the imagined addressee.

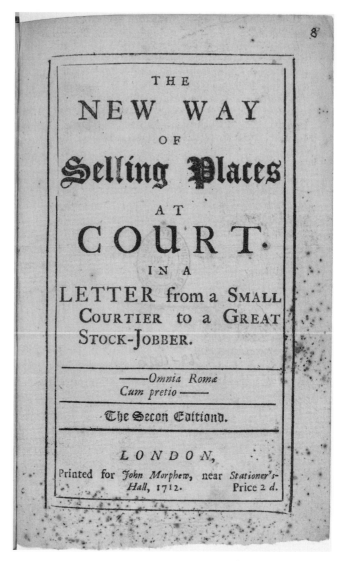

Figure 4. *The new way of selling places at court.*

The black letter section here ('In a Letter to a Whig-Lord') is clearly of subsidiary interest, but it highlights the oddity of the addressee and provokes curiosity as to exactly who the Whig Lord might be. Although the Whig Lord's identity is deliberately left open, Swift and other sympathizers with the ministry were trying to win over Whigs at this time, and

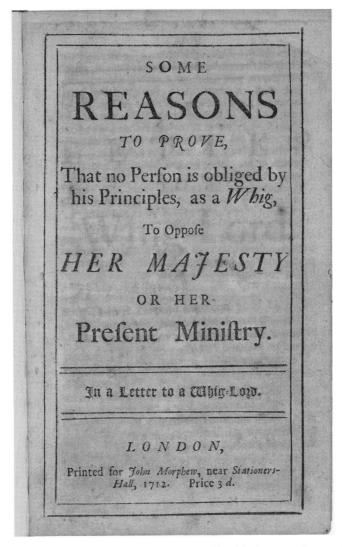

Figure 5. *Some reasons to prove, that no person is obliged by his principles, as a Whig, to oppose Her Majesty or her present ministry.*

his fundamental lack of sympathy with those being wooed is well caught in a letter to Stella of 29 December 1711:

I desired lord Radnor's brother, at Court to-day, to let my lord know I would call on him at six, which I did, and was arguing with him three hours to bring him over to us, and I spoke so closely, that I believe he will be tractable; but he is a scoundrel, and though I said I only talked for my love to him, I told a lie; for I did not care if he were hanged: but every one gained over is of consequence.[53]

There is a conflict throughout between the basic reasonableness of the pamphlet and the contempt for the Whigs that is always ready to erupt through it.

The remaining letter of this period, *The Importance of the Guardian Considered, in a Second Letter to the Bailliff of Stockbridge*, is different again: this is an imitation of someone else's letter. The reason Swift is writing to the Bailiff of Stockbridge is that Steele had written to him first. The letter is a response to, and a sarcastic retaliation on, two pieces by Steele. In his *Guardian* of 7 August 1713 Steele had complained that Dunkirk had not been demolished, as the agreement with the French said it was to be. For the Whigs it remained a threat as long as the French might regain it, and it held out the possibility of being the port from which a Jacobite rebellion might be launched. In the form of a letter from 'English Tory' to Nestor Ironside, Steele three times says that 'The British Nation expect the immediate Demolition' of Dunkirk. As Professor Goldgar tells us, the word 'expect' was seized upon by the Tories as a direct attack on the royal prerogative.[54] Steele felt the need to defend himself and did so on 23 September with *The Importance of Dunkirk Consider'd: In Defence of the Guardian of August the 7th, in a letter to the Bailiff of Stockbridge*, the borough that had made Steele its member of Parliament that summer. *The Importance of The Guardian Considered* (see Figure 6) is a direct riposte. What is delightful about this title page is the combination of the scorn of its main title – the *Guardian* isn't important at all – with the irony 'By a Friend of Mr. *St–le*', an irony that carries a personal weight. For Swift, to his own mind, had been a friend to Steele, long after the change of ministry, only to find his friendship rebuffed. Swift takes his addressee seriously, and grounds his reply in recognition of his provincial office:

> *You Mr.* Bailiff, *and at the same time the whole Burrough,* may please to take Notice, that *London*-Writers often put Titles to their Papers and Pamphlets which have little or no Reference to the main Design of the Work: So, for Instance, you will observe in reading, that the Letter called, *The Importance of Dunkirk*, is chiefly taken up in shewing you the *Importance* of Mr. *St—*; wherein it was indeed reasonable your Burrough should be informed, which had chosen him to Represent them.[55]

The relation between the titles, therefore, sets up the personal assault on Steele that constitutes a major part of the pamphlet. After a sideplay on

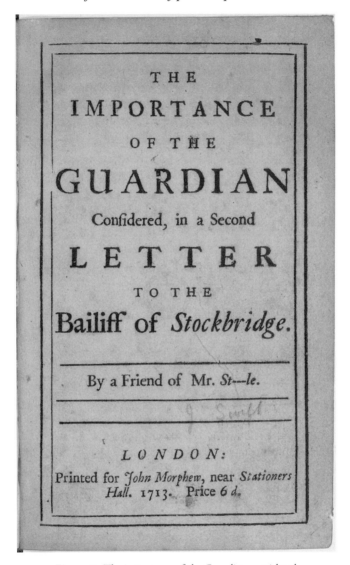

THE

IMPORTANCE

OF THE

GUARDIAN

Confidered, in a Second

LETTER

TO THE

Bailiff of *Stockbridge.*

By a Friend of Mr. *St---le.*

J. Swift

LONDON:

Printed for *John Morphew,* near *Stationers Hall.* 1713. Price 6 *d.*

Figure 6. *The importance of the Guardian considered.*

how Steele publishes himself writing to himself, the pamphlet develops into a commentary on *The Importance of Dunkirk.* This is an important Swiftian mode at this time. One of his publications is, of course, of the Barrier Treaty itself, with a preceding commentary, and additionally, as a critique of it, the alternative treaty that ministers had prepared but that was in the end ignored. In *The Importance of the Guardian* Swift is quoted in italics or summarized with marginal page notes to show the authenticity of the rebuttal. There is an acute awareness of how documents can be turned against themselves. There is a parallel with the way Wotton's *Observations on Tale of a Tub* had been taken, denatured, and turned into an explanatory commentary in Swift's own edition of *Tale of a Tub*. This time Swift is the commentator, but once more the original work is undermined.

We can see in these examples how a genre as seemingly straightforward as the letter can be developed in very different ways. *The Conduct of the Allies* represents a similar ingenious appropriation. This is the work of which Johnson said, 'He had to count to ten, and he has counted it right', but I think that is to underestimate the importance of the angle from which Swift approaches his material, the way he seizes on a sub-genre of political writing and turns it to his purpose. Once again, the title page (see Figure 7) is very revealing, especially its use of black letter, which makes the allies the main focus of the pamphlet, while insinuating that it is perhaps the conduct of the 'Late Ministry' that is really disturbing and mysterious. Other important pamphlets of the period assess 'conduct', but they are concerned with individuals. The most significant and controversial of these was perhaps John Friend's *Account of the Earl of Peterborow's Conduct in Spain* (1707), a pamphlet referred to in the *Journal to Stella*,[56] and the most recent *An Account of the Earl of Galway's Conduct in Spain and Portugal* (1711), a defence of a man Swift despised, which appeared while *The Conduct of the Allies* was being prepared.[57] In his pamphlet Swift takes a much broader view of responsibility – it is not individuals but nations and ministries that may be at fault – and of the meaning of the word 'conduct'. He is not concerned merely with the planning and organization of campaigns but with the moral, strategic, and financial behaviour of his participants. If we compare the argument of *The Conduct of the Allies* with that in Swift's first *Examiner* paper, which also presents a case against the war, we see that in the *Examiner* the change of ministry, the nature of the previous ministry, and the state of the nation come first.[58] In *The Conduct of the Allies*, the war itself and the supporting alliances are examined and condemned, and the curious behaviour of the 'Late Ministry', with accompanying personal and financial investment in the war, then becomes the necessary explanation of a sorry state of affairs. The bold and clear-sighted escape from personal and party critique is what is distinctive about Swift's art in this pamphlet. It is notable that

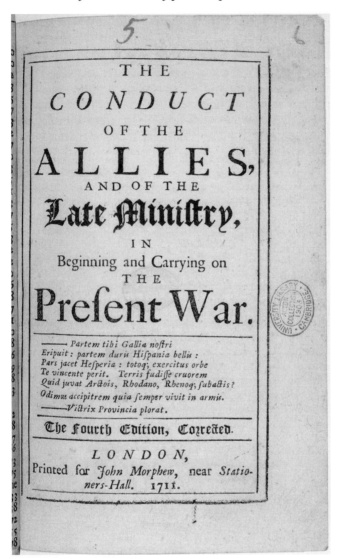

THE
CONDUCT
OF THE
ALLIES,
AND OF THE
Late Ministry,
IN
Beginning and Carrying on
THE
Present War.

——— *Partem tibi Gallia nostri*
Eripuit: partem duris Hispania bellis:
Pars jacet Hesperia: totoq; exercitus orbe
Te vincente perit. Terris fudisse cruorem
Quid juvat Arctois, Rhodano, Rhenoq; subactis?
Odimus accipitrem quia semper vivit in armis.
———*Victrix Provincia plorat.*

The Fourth Edition, Corrected.

LONDON,
Printed for *John Morphew,* near *Statio-*
ners-Hall. 1711.

Figure 7. *The conduct of the Allies.*

Trevelyan, in his still very readable history of Anne's reign, was shocked by Swift's willingness to attack the war itself.[59]

Swift's criticism of the allies and the ministry draws on two techniques that make his case seem an obvious one. One is counting, a device that he had drawn on in his bills of gratitude and ingratitude in the *Examiner* 17 and was to use to such devastating effect in the *Drapier's Letters* and in *Modest Proposal*. So many troops were promised but so few troops were sent; so much money was guaranteed but so little money paid. Again and again Swift's points are about the disproportion of the distribution of the war effort. And alongside these calculations goes a prose that emphasizes accumulation by its use of parallelism. Swift uses his punctuation, especially the colon, brilliantly in *The Conduct of the Allies* to suggest an overwhelming weight of evidence and an inescapable conclusion. His colons bind units together to create something that is more than a sentence but less than a paragraph, a sequence that demands assent. Take this example, where he has just completed the first part of his essay:

But if all this be true: If, according to what I have affirmed, we began this War contrary to Reason: If, as the other Party themselves, upon all Occasions, acknowledge, the Success we have had was more than we could reasonably expect: If, after all our Success, we have not made that use of it, which in Reason we ought to have done: If we have made weak and foolish Bargains with our Allies, suffered them tamely to break every Article, even in those Bargains to our Disadvantage, and allowed them to treat us with Insolence and Contempt, at the very Instant when We were gaining Towns, Provinces and Kingdoms for them, at the Price of our Ruin, and without any Prospect of Interest to our selves: If we have consumed all our Strength in attacking the Enemy on the strongest side, where (as the old Duke of *Schomberg* expressed it) *to engage with* France, *was to take a Bull by the Horns*; and left wholly unattempted, that part of the War, which could only enable us to continue or to end it. If all this, I say, be our Case, it is a very obvious Question to ask, by what Motives, or what Management, we are thus become the *Dupes* and *Bubbles* of *Europe*?[60]

The paragraph encapsulates the whole movement of the argument of *The Conduct*: the evidence leads overwhelmingly to a negative assessment of the war and the Whigs become the solution to a puzzle, rather than the immediate object of attack.

I have tried in this chapter to show that Swift's political writing depends for its success on the seizing of a hint: the bringing to bear on politics of some ingenuity of general conception, through the reappropriation of an established genre or sub-genre. This ingenuity has as one of its bases the close observation of the book trade, with all its quirks and solemnities, and involves the fusion of unlikely elements or the twisting of them from their usual course: *A Hue and Cry after Dismal* or *The Conduct of the Allies*. Such structures often display their character in their title pages, on which, as we have seen, considerable care was lavished.

In following his 'hints' Swift gives play to his irony without resort to the tropes and figures whose absence Johnson remarks. That Johnson himself grasped this aspect of Swift's art is evident from his closing evaluation in *Lives of the Poets*, which my discussion has sought to support:

It was said, in a Preface to one of the Irish editions, that Swift had never been known to take a single thought from any writer, ancient or modern. This is not literally true; but perhaps no writer can easily be found that has borrowed so little, or that in his excellences and all his defects has so well maintained his claim to be considered as original.[61]

NOTES

1 *The Lives of the Most Eminent English Poets; with Critical Observations on their Works*, ed. Roger Lonsdale, 4 vols. (Oxford: Clarendon Press, 2006), vol. III, p. 208, para. 110.
2 Ibid., p. 209, para. 114.
3 Ibid., p. 196, paras. 47–8.
4 James Boswell, *Life of Johnson*, ed. George Birkbeck Hill, rev. L. F. Powell, 6 vols. (Oxford: Clarendon Press, 1934), vol. II, p. 65.
5 *JSt.*, I, 68. Steele is especially associated with hints, in both senses; *The Twickenham Edition of the Works of Alexander Pope*, ed. John Butt *et al.*, 11 vols. (London and New Haven: Methuen, 1939–69), vol. IV, *Epistle to Arbuthnot*, line 204.
6 *The Poems of Alexander Pope*, vol. III, *The Dunciad*, ed. Valerie Rumbold (Harlow: Pearson-Longman, 2007), book I, lines 55–60.
7 See Peter Stallybrass and Allon White, *The Politics and Poetics of Transgression* (Ithaca: Cornell University Press, 1989) for an early statement of the case.
8 *Correspondence*, II, 178.
9 Maynard Mack, *Alexander Pope: A Life* (New Haven: Yale University Press; New York: W. W. Norton, 1985), p. 454.
10 The concern with hints seems particularly a feature of his discussion of political writing, though Swift was acutely aware of his originality in other respects. He was particularly proud, for example, to have written in his 'Description of a City Shower' something quite new, combining as it does observations of life in London with an imitation of Virgil's Georgics: 'They say 'tis the best thing I ever writ, and I think so too' (*JSt.*, I, 62).
11 *JSt.*, I, 13 (10 September 1710).
12 Ibid., 41 (4 October 1710).
13 Ibid., 78 (1 November 1710).
14 Ibid., 56 (13 October 1710).
15 Ibid., 79 (3 November 1710).
16 Ibid., 110 (30 November 1710).
17 Ibid., 124 (14 December 1710).

18 Ibid., 151 (2 January 1711).

19 Ibid., 254–5 (28 April 1711).

20 Ibid., 165 (15 January 1711).

21 Ibid., 244 (16 April 1711).

22 Ibid., II, 402 (3 November 1711).

23 Ibid., I, 296 (22 June 1711).

24 Ibid., II, 430 (5 December 1711).

25 Ibid., 603 (15 January 1713).

26 Ibid., 656–7 (7 April 1713).

27 See *Poems*, II, 565, and *Complete Poems*, p. 854.

28 H. Teerink, *A Bibliography of the Writings of Jonathan Swift*, 2nd edn, ed. Arthur H. Scouten (Philadelphia: University of Pennsylvania Press, 1963).

29 Jonathan Swift, *English Political Writings, 1711–1714*, ed. Bertrand A. Goldgar and Ian Gadd (Cambridge University Press, 2008).

30 *A New Introduction to Bibliography* (Oxford: Clarendon Press, 1974), p. 52.

31 Chiswell papers, MS Rawl. D730. I discuss the interesting case of William Wake in 'Questions of Entitlement: Some Eighteenth-Century Title Pages', in *The Margins of the Text*, ed. D. C. Greetham (Ann Arbor: University of Michigan Press, 1997), pp. 173–98 (pp. 179–80).

32 *English Political Writings, 1711–1714*, p. 247.

33 *Correspondence*, I, 126.

34 *JSt.*, II, 544.

35 *Correspondence*, I, 434.

36 Ibid., II, 466.

37 Ibid., 553.

38 Ibid., 548.

39 See David Woolley, 'The Canon of Swift's Prose Pamphleteering, 1710–1714, and The New Way of Selling Places at Court', *Swift Studies*, 3 (1989), 96–123.

40 See the account in *English Political Writings, 1711–1714*, pp. 327–33.

41 Philip Luckombe in *A Concise History of the Origin and Progress of Printing* (London: Adlard and Browne, 1770), pp. 238–9, gives a good account of black letter, or Gothic, or Old English. He explains that it was sometimes used with italic and roman (as it is by Swift) and that it was disliked by printers because it used up so much ink.

42 Joseph Moxon, *Mechanick Exercises on the Whole Art of Printing, (1683–4)*, ed. Herbert Davis and Harry Carter, 2nd edn (London: Oxford University Press, 1962), p. 218.

43 Black letter is to be found in *Poems*, I, 17, 21, 23, 24, 102–4, 134, 147–8, 162, 168–9; II, 369; III, 1058, 1078, and continues to represent the alien on, for example, the title pages of the first *Drapier's Letter* and *A Modest Proposal*.

44 *JSt.*, II, 430–1.

45 *English Political Writings, 1711–1714*, pp. 195–6.

46 Ibid., p. 197.

47 Ibid.

48 Ibid., p. 185.

49 Ibid., p. 183.
50 Ibid., p. 189.
51 *JSt.*, I, 194–5.
52 *English Political Writings, 1711–1714*, p. 112.
53 *JSt.*, II, 451–2.
54 *English Political Writings, 1711–1714*, p. 33.
55 Ibid., p. 220.
56 *JSt.*, I, 91.
57 It is possible the pamphlet defending Galway had a direct influence on the naming of *Conduct of the Allies*. When, on 7 November 1711, Swift says, 'Some friend of lord Galway has, by his directions, published a four-shilling book about his conduct in Spain; to defend him' (Williams, *JSt.*, II, 406), he must surely have this *Account* in mind, rather than the book Williams suggests, and Swift makes a significant reference to *Conduct of the Allies* on 10 November (*JSt.*, II, 408); it was substantially written by then, but not published until 27 November.
58 *Swift vs. Mainwaring: The Examiner and The Medley*, ed. Frank H. Ellis (Oxford: Clarendon Press, 1985), pp. 1–10.
59 George Macaulay Trevelyan, *England under Queen Anne*, 3 vols., reissue (London: Longmans Green, 1936), vol. III, p. 192.
60 *English Political Writings, 1711–1714*, pp. 81–2.
61 *Lives of the Poets*, vol. III, p. 214, para. 141.

CHAPTER 6

Swift's poetics of friendship

Helen Deutsch

And the people said unto Saul, Shall Jonathan die, who hath wrought this great salvation in Israel? God forbid: as the LORD liveth, there shall not one hair of his head fall to the ground; for he hath wrought with God this day. So the people rescued Jonathan, that he died not.

I Samuel 14:45

The sage presents himself as an enemy only to conceal his enmity. He shows his hostility so as not to hurt with his wickedness. And why does he take such pains? Out of friendship for mankind, philanthropic sociability. His pose ... consists – in the sheer difference between hot and cold, exalted anger and icy lucidity – *in feigning to be precisely what he is*, in telling the truth to conceal the truth and especially to neutralize its deadly effect, to protect others from it.

(Jacques Derrida, *The Politics of Friendship*)

My first epigraph points to a particular historical moment when Jonathan Swift, in an ironic drama he had written himself, emerged as the foremost friend of 'the whole people of Ireland', a collective his *Drapier's Letters* had summoned into being. When the recently appointed English viceroy, John, Lord Carteret, arrived in Ireland in 1724 to respond to the popular resistance provoked by the *Drapier's Letters*, he issued a proclamation demanding the arrest for sedition of the author 'of the "wicked and malicious" tract by M. B. Drapier'.[1] As John Traugott notes in his brilliant retelling of the story, Carteret's gesture was ironic: he knew very well that Swift and M. B. Drapier were one and the same, that the former would not be named, and that the latter could not be found. Swift responded to the proclamation by sending messengers out into Dublin to remind the people of the words from I Samuel 14:45. The passage, in Traugott's phrase, 'became a password repeated by rote throughout Dublin. A bold stroke, more ironic comedy to screw up the pitch of gaiety and solidarity, all but a direct challenge to majesty.'[2]

140

While this ironic moment of popular defiance of English authority is comic, in Traugott's view Swift's successful defeat of Wood's coinage must ultimately be seen as tragic, and this brings me to the second provenance of my epigraph, Traugott's essay itself, ' "Shall Jonathan Die?" Swift, Irony, and a Failed Revolution in Ireland'. The revolutionary potential of Swift's rhetoric in the *Drapier's Letters*, his ironic gestures toward an independent and self-governing Ireland, remained unfulfilled, relegated 'glimmering into the heavenly orbit of utopias'.[3] Politics, Traugott argues, was a game Swift knew he could not win, and his writing life was a dissonant mixture of utopic yearning and corrosive irony. Yet while Swift could not realize revolution in his own time, his work has a political afterlife. Evoking Parnell and Yeats as inheritors of Swift's inspiration, Traugott lingers on Swift's paradoxical endurance as an absence:

W. E. H. Lecky, the great Irish historian, wrote that Swift had created the political consciousness of the Irish people, to bear fruit in the next century; but when Lecky saw that Swift's teachings would mean the end of Anglo-Irish hegemony, he regretted his enthusiasm for them and repressed his chapter on Swift in his *Leaders of Public Opinion in Ireland*. A real revolution destroying the Anglo-Irish nation (so-called) did come, as Lecky feared; and we would have to communicate with Swift's ghost to know whether he thought his ironic sedition of 1724 was a success or failure.[4]

This act of censorship leaves the question of Swift's influence unanswered, evoking Edward Said's characterization of Swift's career as 'a literary one whose record exists in works that ought to have become political history but which linger on, like the Struldbruggs, as ineffectual remnants'.[5] But while Said sees Swift's corpus 'as a negative judgment passed on itself for not having succeeded as an event',[6] Traugott sees Swift's failure to change his own historical moment as the very source of his endurance. Irony's negativity is Swift's literary badge of honour, locating him in a genealogy that reaches back to Socrates.

The ironist can only make us 'know' what is not ... Yet, as Socrates alone knows what is not and can by his irony bring others to know it, this genius of his, it turns out, is an unsuspected golden treasure, a gift of freedom from delusion and the possibility of a new beginning. The apprentice ironist rids himself of the blather of received opinion that he once spoke as the dummy of the state's ventriloquism. Irony bestows upon him the subjectivity of personal life. He can hope to know himself. It is the beginning of consciousness.[7]

'It would be something like the truth to think of Swift's irony', Traugott concludes, 'as making possible a "revolution" in consciousness.'[8] This revolution can only be articulated ironically in scare quotes, but in dispelling delusion it offers the possibility of freedom of thought to generations of readers beyond the moment of the text's historical failure. Traugott answers his own question implicitly and ironically. Jonathan shall not die, because irony keeps him alive as friend to the reader.

Nowhere does Swift talk more easily to us than in his poetry, and in *Verses on the Death of Dr. Swift* the question of the enduring effectiveness of his writing emerges from the emptiness of polite conversation.[9] When Said describes the controversial self-eulogy that concludes the poem as an expression of Swift's 'extraordinarily proleptic sense of himself as a problem for the future',[10] and when Clive Probyn, correcting Said, evokes the power not of Swift himself but of his style of allegory 'to work in a forward direction, proleptically',[11] both are provoked by the negative excess of Swift's irony, by the sense of Swift and his writing as '*too much for his own time*'.[12] What would it mean to read 'the problem for the future' Swift poses, the intimacy he creates with his reader, as part of the history of friendship? How can we read Swift as a particular example of the '*contretemps*' that Jacques Derrida, in his meditation on the classical tradition of friendship that Swift knew well, evokes to describe the utopian ideal of friendship, an ideal riven at its origin by the phrase from Aristotle that haunts his book, 'O my friends, there is no friend'?[13]

For Derrida, as for Swift, friendship emerges from the experience of loss of an ideal and points beyond it, 'for to love friendship, it is not enough to know how to bear the other in mourning; one must love the future'.[14] We might say that Swift's poetry imagines the ideal friend proleptically in the future reader. At the threshold of life and death, of pagan and Christian ethical modes, of historical definitions of love and friendship, Swift's poetry builds a lasting monument from mortal flesh and transient historical particulars. It offers a vehicle for friendship between the living and the dead enabled by a revolution in consciousness.

To better understand what such friendship might mean, we should remember that the figure of Socrates that Traugott evokes to explain Swift's irony is drawn from Alcibiades' drunken recounting of his unsuccessful seduction of the philosopher in Plato's *Symposium*. Reversing the standard Platonic chiasmus of wise older lover and beautiful young beloved, Alcibiades describes Socrates as resembling the ugly satyr dolls that, when opened up, reveal beautiful golden gods, icons of virtue. But while his metaphors evoke a fantasy of an ideal achieved, in reality Alcibiades, despite his strenuous efforts to possess his beloved's wisdom, remains unsatisfied. Socrates gently reminds him that there might be nothing beneath his ugly exterior, no gold to be exchanged for beauty's brass. Similarly conflating the fragile world of the flesh with the elusive immortality of truth and virtue, the two poems I've chosen to represent Swift's private and public modes of friendship – 'Stella's Birthday (1727)' and *Verses on the Death of Dr. Swift* – engage the reader in just as elusive a pursuit, in a friendship that offers unrecognizable forms of love.

Swift's ironic elusiveness and self-confessed misanthropy seem to render him less a friend to the reader than a potential enemy. He famously articulated his equivocal relationship to humankind to Pope in 1725 as a couplet-like balance of general loathing and particular affection: 'principally I hate and detest that animal called man; although I heartily love John, Peter, Thomas, and so forth.'[15] We therefore approach him with caution, afraid of being exposed as the butt of his joke, *rationis incapax*. The colloquial immediacy of Swift's poetry evokes a dramatic presence, a feigning to be precisely what he is, so vital that when we read Swift's verses it seems as if this most artful of parodists is alive and talking to us. We read Swift's poetry in dangerously comfortable *tête à tête*.

'How can we become critically engaged with poetry that appears to require little intellectual effort for its comprehension?', asks Clive Probyn in an essay on the realism and raillery of Swift's poetry, a poetry he rightly characterizes as largely occasional, conversational, and demanding of 'predominantly *oral* attention', demanding, in other words, our own acts of vocal impersonation. 'Is there a critical vocabulary for private versified talk?'[16] In his 1718 poem 'To Mr. Delaney', verses he admits 'which might as well have been in Prose' (10), Swift instructs his young friend on the rules for this sort of familiar speech, the polite conversation he valued, subverted and parodied throughout his literary career:

> Our Conversation to refine
> True Humor must with Wit combine;
> From both, we learn to Railly well;
> Wherein French Writers most excell:
> Voiture in various Lights displays
> That Irony which turns to Praise;
> His Genius first found out the Rule
> For an obliging Ridicule:
> He flatters with peculiar Air
> The Brave, the Witty, and the Fair;
> And Fools would fancy he intends
> A Satyr where he most commends.   (29–40)

While fools mistake the elegant raillery between mutually admiring and witty friends for satire, for 'the pert Dunces of Mankind' (45), 'the Diff'rence lyes abstruse / 'Twixt Raillery and gross Abuse' (47–8).[17] 'Raillery', Swift opined, 'is the finest part of Conversation'; sociability is therefore witty war.[18] His 'very civilities', Thomas Sheridan wrote in his biography of Swift, 'bore the appearance of rudeness, and his finest compliments were conveyed under the disguise of satyr'.[19] If, as Richard Steele pronounced, 'equality is the life of conversation', Swift's poetry gives this truism the lie, freighting the colloquial ease meant for equals with a didactic irony that puts the listener in her place. As Probyn puts it, 'informality is a trick which can be learned by both friend and enemy'.[20] 'Laugh with all Men', Swift advised Thomas Sheridan, 'without trusting any.'[21]

Through their laughing intimacy, Swift's poems expose the equivocal nature of amity, a tension between particular loves and general antipathies that constitutes a crucial crux in friendship's history in the West. Alan Bray recovers the early modern English part of this history in *The Friend*, a book he considered a kind of historical supplement to Derrida's *Politics of Friendship*, offering an 'archaeology' of 'the ethics of friendship' in its detailed depiction of a traditional society solidified through volitional, publically sworn, spiritual, homosocial ties. These ties had 'the binding force of a betrothal', indeed were sacramental acts of marriage witnessed by the community, rendered legible in the public sphere through a complex corporeal rhetoric in which both an embrace and a letter in a friend's own hand were performative gifts.[22] Friendship's language could be interpreted cynically – one man's spiritual brother was another's sodomite, one man's *alter idem* was another's instrument – but in its ideal form it modelled a Christian society that transformed strangers from potential enemies into loving kin. The traditional society Bray uncovers was largely but not entirely effaced by an Enlightenment civil society newly rooted in the primary bond of heterosexual marriage,[23] and based on an ideal of obligatory universal benevolence in which friendship 'is understood to be essentially private – "just friends"'[24] and of a lesser order than conjugal heterosexual love. Dr. Johnson posed the ethical problem raised by the older model of friendship in playful conversation with the Quaker Mary Knowles when he remarked, 'All friendship is preferring the interest of a friend, to the neglect, or, perhaps, against the interest of others ... Now Christianity recommends universal benevolence, to consider all men as our brethren, which is contrary to the virtue of friendship, as described by the ancient philosophers. Surely, Madam, your sect must

approve of this; for you call all men *friends*.' Mrs. Knowles trumps
Johnson by arguing that 'our Saviour had twelve Apostles, but there was
one [John] whom he *loved*'.[25] This exchange highlights the tension in the
philosophy of friendship, figured here as the irreconcilable difference
between pagan singularity and Christian universality, which is the ethical
catalyst of both Bray's and Derrida's accounts. William Blake put the
paradox even more provocatively: 'He who loves his Enemies betrays his
Friends; / This surely is not what Jesus intends.'[26] And he proves himself
Swift's heir when he demands of his patron, Hayley, and thus of the
reader: 'Thy Friendship oft has made my heart to ake / Do be my enemy
for Friendships sake.'[27]

Verses on the Death of Dr. Swift, inspired by Rochefoucauld's bitter
maxim 'in the adversity of our best friends, we find something that doth
not displease us', is Swift's public oration on the enmity of friendship and
the emptiness of civility, epitomized most brutally by the ladies, 'whose
tender Hearts / have better learn'd to act their Parts' (225–6) at the card
game, as they unconsciously pun on the Last Judgement – 'The Dean is
dead, (*and what is Trumps?*)' ... 'He lov'd the Dean. (*I lead a Heart*)'
(228, 239).[28] In the much-debated seriously ironic conclusion to this
poem, Swift does for himself what only the rarest of friends, Laelius for
Scipio in Cicero's *De amicitia*, Montaigne for La Boetie in his essay on
friendship, can do for another: he delivers his own eulogy. But he does so
in marked contrast to that literary-philosophical tradition which celebrated the highest form of friendship, *amicitia*, as a union of two male
souls so complete that it triumphed over death. Cicero's Laelius describes
this rare bond as a mirror of mutuality:

He who looks upon a true friend, looks, as it were, upon a sort of image of
himself. Wherefore friends, though absent, are at hand; though in need, yet
abound; though weak, are strong; and – harder saying still – though dead, are
yet alive; so great is the esteem on the part of their friends, the tender recollection
and the deep longing that attends them. These things make the death of the
departed seem fortunate and the life of the survivors worthy of praise.[29]

This highly influential evocation of ideal friendship has particular affinities with the familiar letter's power to make absent friends present; it
informs the epistles of Saint Jerome, the 'ideal friendship token[s]' of
Erasmus's letters to his scholarly circle, indeed, the novels of Richardson,
to name only a few points of influence.[30] The exemplary familiar letter,
which in Virginia Woolf's memorable phrase 'owes its origin to the love
of friends',[31] becomes the textual reliquary for Laelius's sentiments, which

articulate the mourner's solitary melancholy as dyadic exemplarity, an intimacy that calls the community to witness.

The true friend, in Cicero's dense formulation, is the object of one's self-love, an *alter idem* ('another the same', or in Bacon's phrase 'another himself')[32] so worthy that one friend's death becomes a gift to the other. Small wonder that Montaigne opined, 'so many coincidences are needed to build up such a friendship that it is a lot if fortune can do it once in three centuries'.[33] Swift's verses on his own death emerge, by contrast, from the wreckage of that mundane world of instrumental friendship in which any friend can become an enemy, in which the only true friend is the passionately impartial speaker whose various ironic slips remind us – lines 317–18, 'To steal a Hint was never known / But what he writ was all his own', to give one example, are in fact borrowed from John Denham's *On Mr. Abraham Cowley* – that he is and is not Swift himself.[34] Playing no favourites, Swift writes verses on his own death as one 'quite indiff'rent in the Cause' (307), one who, unlike Montaigne, for whom 'the reader takes the place of the dead friend', would seem to demand no emotional response.[35]

Swift's intimate occasional poems to Esther Johnson, the woman he considered his most valuable friend, otherwise known as the Stella poems, are the closest he ever came to *amicitia*'s self-colloquy and to the ideal friendship that loves another as the same.[36] They are also, in Said's phrase, examples of 'the closest Swift ever came to demonstrating the peripheries at which conversation shades subtly into writing'.[37] The conversation these poems perform, it must be noted, is not the viciously degraded mode that Swift skewers throughout his career, but rather exchange 'designed to preserve the presence to each other of the conversants', the one form of society in which, however ephemerally, an ideal might be realized.[38] The Stella poems violently invert the empty world of civility skewered in *Verses on the Death of Dr. Swift*: 'in deliberate and pointed contrast' to the vapidity of polite society, notes Probyn, they are 'almost brutally self-analytic'.[39] Probyn's unintentional ambiguity here – it is Stella, Swift's other self, who is brutally analysed in these poems, whose pride, obstinacy, anger, and spite are publicly chastised – reveals that despite or perhaps because of such ruthless honesty, their frank speaking of truths that other friends might keep silent, they are also love poems of the queerest kind.

The only poem I've taught in twenty-five years that ever moved a student to tears was Swift's final poem to Stella. Apparently this reaction is more common than you would think. When I wrote to a colleague recently that I was working on the Stella poems, she responded by saying that when she introduced them to a group of Texas undergraduates, many responded with heartfelt personal outpourings about their own loved ones. I want to build on this observation by pointing to Margaret Anne Doody's assessment in her essay on 'Swift and Women': 'Swift's poems to Stella deserve credit as original love poems, a literary kind in which the eighteenth century is hardly rich. They are new inventions in the poetic language of love.'[40] They are also innovations in the philosophical literature of friendship.

By considering Swift's last poem to Stella, written in 1727 shortly before her death and in the midst of his own illness, in relation to a seemingly very different love poem, the conclusion to George Herbert's 1633 collection of devotional lyrics, *The Temple*, 'Love III', we can discern what might be original about Swift's poetry of friendship. By putting these two Anglican divines in conversation with one another (and I think it is safe but not necessary to assume that Swift read Herbert), I hope to render strange the powerful familiarity of Swift's last Stella poem by illuminating its debt to a religious, didactic mode of lyric on the one hand, and to a Christianized classical tradition of friendship on the other. Here the name 'Stella' can be our guide, pointing both in public and private directions, toward the starry resonance of Stella's real name, 'Esther', and toward a lyric tradition that also informs Herbert, epitomized by the courtly love sonnets of Philip Sidney.

My turn to Herbert was inspired by Helen Vendler's return to the poet in *Invisible Listeners: Lyric Intimacy in Herbert, Whitman, and Ashbery*. As her title might indicate, and as those familiar with her style of rigorously sensitive close reading might guess, Vendler is not interested in historicizing intimacy. She wants instead to outline a unique lyric mode in which the poet searches out and in the process rhetorically models an ideal form of intimate relation – Herbert's with God, Whitman's with a future reader, Ashbery's with the Renaissance painter Parmigianino. Her description of Herbert's project in *The Temple* illustrates the ethical thrust of her argument:

What is the attraction, to a poet of intimacy, of addressing or describing an invisible Friend? In actual worldly relations ... there occur countless obstacles to intimacy: age, circumstance, illness, overwork. An invisible addressee or listener, by contrast, makes the poem resemble one of those 'pure' problems posed by mathematics ... In the ether of the invisible, psychological models can be constructed unhindered by anything but the speaker's attitude toward that proposed relation, and so the conditions and hypotheses of such intimacy ... can be explored freely, and a heart-satisfying ethics of intimate relation can be suggested.[41]

We shall see shortly that it is exactly those quotidian obstacles to intimacy, in the form of ageing mortal bodies, in which Swift is interested. For now let's observe that Vendler is not the first to praise the colloquial familiarity Herbert's poetry establishes with a God imagined as a friend; the 'quintessential Herbertian tone', as she puts it, 'is one of intimate confiding'.[42] But so intent is she on abstracting and idealizing Herbert's addressee that Vendler not only elides but militantly legislates against the embodied dimensions of Herbert's divine audience, sublimating the 'Love' of 'Love III' into friendship unencumbered by flesh.

By contrast, in one of the most important and controversial readings of the poem, Michael Schoenfeldt has termed 'Love III' a 'kind of epithalamion, consummating, like Spenser's *Epithalamion* appended to the *Amoretti*, [*The Temple*'s] frustrating and difficult courtship'.[43] This consummation – which imagines the soul's final sacramental union with God as both erotic encounter and heavenly feast – 'is invested with a physical referentiality which makes a purely spiritual or allegorical reading of the poem difficult to sustain. Herbert wants us to remember that the body is the anxious medium of the moment he describes.'[44] Schoenfeldt works convincingly to contextualize Herbert's spiritual eroticism, pointing to his poetry's ongoing ambivalent fascination with eating and sinful flesh, to theological writing on the blissfully incarnated erotics of Eucharistic eating, to the poem's shamefully marred and amorously quick eyes that evoke the sexual dimensions of vision in seventeenth-century culture, to the fairly obvious reference to impotence in 'grow slack / From my first entrance in' (3–4), to contemporary representations of an androgynous Jesus, to the bawdy referents for 'thing' (6), 'serve' (16), and 'shame' (12).[45] Helen Vendler, in response, is not amused:

Such readings 'against the grain' of Herbert's presumed intent in the poem closing *The Temple* seem to me to undo the gentle comedy of Herbert's language and plot. To psychoanalyze a poet after the fact, suggesting that he is writing about the soul's entrance into heaven in terms of a power play and an erection, seems to be a dubious form of critical assistance.[46]

In rejecting the carnal dimensions of Herbert's poem, and in reducing Schoenfeldt's historical analysis to 'psychoanalysis', Vendler misses a crucial dimension of the intimacy 'Love III' depicts. By comparing Herbert to Donne's more dramatic, explicit, and Catholic eroticism – think of

'Batter my heart, three-person'd God' – Schoenfeldt shows us what is at stake in Herbert's unique deployment of the poetics of sacred carnality:

In 'Love III' the reader experiences deep discomfort because the eroticism is at once more delicate [than Donne's] and more deeply engrained in the divine. Rather than [like Donne] apprehending the awful discrimination of heavenly and earthly love, Herbert's reader is forced to grasp their equally awe-inspiring similarity. Like the speaker, the reader is at a loss for a fit response to this figure of divine Love ... for the erotic and the religious, although never separated in the poem, work against each other even as they are expressed in precisely the same language.[47]

What Herbert demands of the speaker and the reader is 'astonishment' at a God whose ultimate 'condescension to humanity' was to take on mortal flesh. Like Vendler, who beautifully describes the poem's 'antiphony of gesture as well as of language', characterizing it as a conversation in which 'Love is merely reminding the Christian sinner of things he already knows', Schoenfeldt reads 'Love III' as a comedy (and one that ends in marriage).[48] But while Vendler's is a comedy of language, his is a 'comedy of eros', in which '"sin," in Julia Kristeva's phrase, "is turned upside down into love"', or, we might say, informed by Bray's account, into the Eucharistic celebration of true friendship affirmed through communal eating.[49] Herbert's poem thus has affinities with earlier theological writing that imagined the Eucharist as a re-enactment of Christ's assumption of flesh and thus of kinship – in early modern terms, friendship – with man. '*Deus amicitia est*', one fifteenth-century theologian wrote – 'God is friendship.'[50] We marvel at the end of 'Love III' at the humble simplicity with which faith is rendered as common flesh: 'So I did sit and eat' (18).

Paradoxically, then, Herbert's invisible listener, 'quick-eyed' inviting Love, is more real to us than Swift's Stella, sentimentalized by the nineteenth century as a 'pale beautiful shadowy form', who endures both in Swift's last poem to her and for posterity as a moving absence.[51] For the most recent and sensible authority on the relationship, Louise Barnett, 'Stella is ironically memorable for [her] erasure [Swift destroyed her letters] – for the absence of enough information about her to form an opinion or reach a conclusion, and above all, for the silence of her own voice except for its intermittent reflection in Swift's.'[52] This ghostly erasure is social as well as personal: Stella was a spinster of little means, shadowing the expected possibilities of a woman's life, 'one of those ambiguous women', as Virginia Woolf puts it, 'who live chiefly in the society of the other sex'.[53] Such ambiguity was partly the result of Swift's penchant for educating women in his own image: he first knew Stella when she was 8, and by his own account 'had some share in her education, by directing what books she should read, and perpetually instructing her in the principles of honor and virtue: from which she never swerved in any one action or moment of her life'.[54] Swift's idealized version of Stella – enforced in his poems to her and commemorated in the essay he wrote immediately after her death from which I have just quoted – is reminiscent of Pope's troublingly idealized portrait of Martha Blount, the 'lesser man' who combines the best of male and female virtues at the close of his *Epistle to a Lady.*

Swift persuaded the 19-year-old Stella to move to Ireland, close to his own home, in the company of her older friend and companion, Rebecca Dingley. This relocation, he observed, 'looked so like a frolic, the censure held, for some time, as if there were a secret history in such a removal; which, however, soon blew off by her excellent conduct'.[55] However strong the popular desire for scandal might have been – and this need for the 'secret history' of Swift's love life has persisted for centuries, inciting speculation about the possibility of a secret marriage, the possibility of incest barring the way to such a marriage, even generating the nineteenth-century French romance *Stella and Vanessa*[56] – Swift's relationship with the woman he termed 'the truest, most virtuous, and valuable friend, that I, or perhaps any other person ever was blessed with'[57] transpired, it would seem, entirely in public. Even the familiar letters now known as the *Journal to Stella,* for which Swift created a private babyish 'little language', are addressed to both Stella and Dingley; Barnett describes the intimacy of the relationship that emerges in the *Journal* as 'somewhat akin to having sex with a Siamese twin'.[58] Swift was never more alone with, never closer to Stella, than when writing poetry to her in public.

To understand this paradox we might contrast Vendler's paradigm of imaginary intimacy with an invisible listener with William Dowling's characterization of the eighteenth-century verse epistle as the 'metaphysical counterpoint' to lyric's increasing 'insubstantiality'. The verse epistle thus serves as a self-consciously material linguistic vehicle for imagined ethical community in a newly shadowy world accessible only through mental impressions and always threatened by solipsism. For Dowling, Renaissance lyric (and Herbert's 'Love III' is a classic example) 'promises a consummation in which are dissolved all distinctions between the mind and body, the spiritual and the physical ... that consummation is simultaneously a triumph over the void or absence at the heart of human consciousness'.[59] Bridging the impossible gap between perceiving minds through print standing in for writing, the eighteenth-century epistle self-consciously materializes the 'double audience' implicit in any lyric. We read over the shoulder of the friend and thus come to communal life.

Swift's last poem to Stella shares many characteristics with the verse epistle – it is an occasional poem marked by the date (headed 'March 13, 1727', the poem was initially published two months after Stella's death in 1728), privately addressed to a real historical person. But what distinguishes Swift's innovation in lyric form from the verse epistle in my view is the quality of our response: if we are moved, it is not into the future community of lovers that Pope summons at the end of the Ovidian *Eloisa to Abelard* or incites to alternative political imaginations in his Horatian epistles. Rather, we play a role not unlike that of the community who witnessed the sworn bonds of Bray's early modern friends. The difference is that we do so individually and in private, by eavesdropping on the solitary act of will with which Swift holds on to a friend who is about to elude his grasp. Swift's lyric, transpiring as does 'Love III' at the threshold of life and death – the border Bray aptly calls the 'fault line' of his history of friendship[60] – denies us secret history or heterosexual romance, creating instead an exemplary intimacy from which we are excluded but which we revive through reading.[61]

Like Herbert, Swift conceives of his union with his addressee as a kind of secular incarnation of the holy feast. Both poets contemplate the separation of the soul from the body, but while Herbert uses the language of embodiment to imagine the soul's freedom from the sins of the flesh, Swift dwells upon – we might even say redeems – the mortal, mortifying body in order to defer and compensate for his own private loss. Herbert depicts divine love in a complex, ambivalent, and remarkably colloquial erotic language; Swift's intimately conversational tetrameter domesticates and sublimates such eroticism so that his friendship with Stella might prove his faith in God and in himself. Herbert's is a poetry of belief; Swift, who wrote of Stella's death that 'I look upon this to be the greatest Event that can ever happen to me, but all my Preparations will not suffice to make me bear it like a Philosopher, nor altogether like a Christian',[62] writes against doubt. Staving off mortality's inevitable end by 'still' observing 'THIS Day, whate'er the Fates decree' (1), tenuously rooted in the present but looking forward into an indefinite future governed only by his resolution not to forget, Swift offers Stella 'serious Lines' (14) that in response to his hypothetical acceptance of the absence of an afterlife, in a conditional and questioning mode aptly characterized by Richard

Feingold as 'rational need, not rational certainty',[63] envision her virtuous
friendship as vital, nourishing, and enduring:

> Must these [Stella's virtues], like empty Shadows pass,
> Or Forms reflected from a Glass?
> Or mere Chimeras in the Mind,
> That fly and leave no Marks behind?
> Does not the Body thrive and grow
> By Food of twenty Years ago?
> And, had it not been still supply'd,
> It must a thousand Times have dy'd.
> Then, who with Reason can maintain,
> That no Effects of Food remain?
> And, is not Virtue in Mankind
> The Nutriment that feeds the Mind?
> Upheld by each good Action past,
> And still continued by the last:
> Then, who with Reason can pretend,
> That all Effects of Virtue end?   (51–66)[64]

Here the master of the excremental vision who saw the human body as
a figure for moral corruption imagines Stella's virtue as bodily nutriment,
the stuff of a secular communion that is mundane, mortal, and miraculous –
'a thousand Times have dy'd' transforms the repetitive triviality of
eating into a daily resurrection – and which nourishes communities of
friends past and present. Stella, who, Christ-like, saved 'Despairing
Wretches from the Grave' (38), and who had often ministered to Swift
himself in his sickness, as the poem's conclusion reminds us, should
preserve and fortify herself at the moment of imminent death with the
humbly invisible and sustaining effects of a life prized for no 'other
Ends / Than merely to oblige your Friends' (69–70), a line that
negatively frames a wish the poem's plaintive conclusion makes explicit.
The concrete effects of the incorporation metaphor allow Swift to
console Stella by urging her to emulate the personification of her own
virtue, a janus-faced abstraction who, taking joy in the past and courage
in the future, will stand by Stella's deathbed (a deathbed Swift himself
could not face) and 'guide you to a better State' (78).

    We don't know how Stella received this poem, but we know from
its heartfelt inconclusiveness just how much was at stake for Swift in her
response.

> Me, surely me, you ought to spare,
> Who gladly would your Suff'rings share;

> Or give my Scrap of Life to you,
> And think it far beneath your Due;
> You, to whose Care so oft I owe,
> That I'm alive to tell you so.   (83–8)[65]

Barnett – in a sentiment echoed by many – sees the poem's final lines as 'quintessentially Swiftian' in 'the unconscious egotism of his need to portray his own nobility . . . Ultimately [Stella] has not been the valuable person but someone who has sustained a valuable person.'[66] Or as Feingold puts it in a less critical and more egalitarian vein, 'This poem is as much a test of all he has written about Stella as it is of her, and it is no surprise that in its final lines it should record his sense that his moral and imaginative life is an adjunct of hers. Here he pleads for the value of his own life.'[67] Whatever we conclude, we are left with Swift, alone, importunate, willing to feed Stella with the 'scrap of life' left him, and, at the moment of our reading, very much alive in the face of impending death. She may not respond to his consolatory lesson, but we perhaps might. We become in the process Stella's double and Swift's friend, enabling him to remain present in his verse to tell us so.

In his tentative ministry and in his confrontation (in poetry if not in person) with Stella's mortal suffering, perhaps even in the vulnerability of his final plea, Swift reminds us, in Doody's words, of why, despite his misogyny as well as misanthropy, he has often been embraced as a friend to women:

Swift attracts because he does not ignore dirt . . . and because there is the insistent, unmarmoreal, perishing physicality which alone (so Swift seems to think) engages and ensures the reality of affections . . . Women are not goddesses or angels, nor inferior beasts – they are human beings living in bodies in space and undergoing like the men the ravages and opportunities of time. We always catch Swift in the flow of time, reacting to a particular situation, day or event.[68]

Doody is speaking of Swift's satiric deflations of false idealizations of women, but her remarks also apply to his anguished confrontation in this poem with the mortal limitations of the female ideal he himself created. Never has Swift been more caught in the flow of time than in his attempt to resist it here. This resistance to mortality also links the Stella poems to *Verses on the Death of Dr. Swift*, in which Swift's intimate speech to his female *alter idem* becomes at once self-colloquy and public utterance. Ronald Paulson describes the relationship between the two poems this way:

We hear Swift talking to himself as he talked to Stella a few years earlier. But perhaps because of his lack of dramatic distance, the eulogy combines with the physical frustration and decay expressed in the 'Proem' to create an image that conveys, as memorably as anything in the Stella poems, the agony of man's predicament in a physical world he cannot control.[69]

Just as Stella's mortal body serves in Swift's poems to offset and confirm her immortal virtue, so Swift's relentless depiction of a transitory world in which friends are enemies and the poet and his work will disappear without a trace allows his final self-eulogy to endure not as a gesture of ideal friendship but as that ideal's monument and tomb. In a later essay, Paulson describes *Verses on the Death of Dr. Swift* as a process of self-sacrifice and resurrection, in which the sign 'Dean Swift' is voided of its conventional iconographical meaning and placed, 'now dead and empty, in another, an existential context – and so give[n] ... a different and therefore reenlivening meaning'.[70]

In this gap between flawed mortals and dead ideals – between Swift's impartial eulogizer and his passionate words, between Stella's personified Christian virtue and Swift's desperate doubting attempt to preserve his dying friend – is the enlivening freedom of irony with which this essay began. Like Kierkegaard on Socrates, we could characterize this irony as negative; Swift thus becomes, as Traugott puts it, 'a predicateless man, in one mask or another, playing games, a philosopher *and* a comedian'. But as was the case with Socrates, Swift's elusiveness and emptiness are his golden gifts to us, icons of an ideal not yet attained; they are, in Kierkegaard's phrase parodying John 14:6, 'the way, not the truth', gesturing open-endedly against time's progression with hope and with doubt, toward an ideal friendship mourned in the present and hoped for with the reader.[71]

In their function as monuments to friendship, these poems evoke Fulke Greville's planned memorial for his intimate friend since childhood, Philip Sidney, plans elaborately detailed in a letter to John Coke, but never completed; the letter itself, cementing the friendship with its recipient, became the monument. 'I observed and loved him so much', Greville wrote in his *Life of Sidney*, 'as, with what caution soever I have passed through my days hitherto among the living, yet in him I challenge a kind of freedom even among the dead.'[72] In the symmetrical ambiguities of 'observe' – to protect and guard, but also to follow or to practice, as one would a religion, and to obey – and of 'challenge' – to demand, to claim recognition for oneself or on behalf of another and thus to call to account – and in its couplet-like balance of worldly bondage and otherworldly freedom, Greville's haunting sentence epitomizes the dyadic nature of a public intimacy that served a particular set of social interests but aspired to transcend them. 'In him I challenge a kind of freedom' – Greville lives unfettered by convention in Sidney, even among the dead, just as Swift's contingent, corporeal, decidedly un-golden world of poetry challenges us to revive him as both ironic adversary and truth-speaking friend, time-bound yet free.

I'd like in closing to speculate about how the originality of Swift's lyric raises another set of questions altogether involving the little-explored subject of male–female friendship. The queer kind of 'Conjugall love without any Conjugall act',[73] neither officially marital nor verifiably sexual, that characterized Swift's relationship with Stella was important to many of the great male Augustan writers – including Pope, Johnson, and Sterne – and has led many a critic on a wild-goose chase for evidence of 'real' sexual activity (think here of Horace Walpole's puzzling over Swift's private language of coffee-drinking in his letters to Vanessa). Doody may surprise us when she refers to Swift as 'an adventurer in human relations, and a comic hero of love',[74] but to think of him in this way is to return to the serious comedy of 'Love III', and to the complex interrelation of love and friendship that Swift's final poem to Stella illuminates. Grieving over Stella's impending death, Swift wrote with impassioned defensiveness that 'violent Friendship is much more lasting, and as much engaging, as violent Love',[75] and in his plea to Stella to take sustenance from her virtue he gives us a powerful example of what such 'violent Friendship' might mean. James Woolley has observed that '*friend* and related words appear more frequently in Swift's verse than any other noun',[76] but he does so in the context of his reading of a poem that tellingly excludes Stella altogether, *Verses on the Death of Dr. Swift*. His observation should encourage us to return to Swift's poetry to see what it can teach us about alternative, elusive, and singular modes of intimacy.

In this way Swift's passionate, personal, occasional, and didactic poems to Esther Johnson, the friend who allowed Swift to imagine constancy of spirit in a world of mutability and decay, seem distant relatives of the seventeenth-century monument to the communal tomb of two loving male friends that inspired Alan Bray to write his important history of single-sex friendship. Yet in his poems to Stella, Swift models a friendship in which he attempts, however incompletely, however one-sidedly, to break the symmetry of *amicitia*'s logic of masculine sameness, depicting instead a heterosexual bond that offers, in Derrida's phrase, 'a future for love the like of which it is not known if anyone will ever have had the experience', a bond grounded in the body but 'beyond desire and lust for possession', consisting rather in a 'shared higher thirst for an ideal above them'.[77] Carol Houlihan Flynn reminds us of the painful gap between such an ideal of mutual freedom and its asymmetrical reality, noting that in this 'serious game' of friendship Swift wrote all the rules: 'generous noble mind, through it all, she is invoked through his words made incarnate, yet only to the extent he can bear. And through it all, she remains Swift's.'[78]

Despite the fact that Stella designated funds in her will for a modest funerary monument, Swift neither attended her funeral nor honoured her wishes. His last poem to his dearest friend, clinging to her at the brink of death, offers instead, like the un-built monument to Sidney of Greville's letter, a publicly intimate mode of commemoration. The monumentalization of lyric is at least as old as Horace's boast at the end of the third book of Odes that he has built a monument more lasting than bronze. Such self-sufficiency eludes Swift, who memorializes Stella with a plea that conceives friendship as mutual dependence. 'Stella's Birthday (1727)' joins Swift and Stella – the 'true' nature of whose relationship we will never know – in a private version of a public monument that only this lyric form, immediately familiar yet of its own historical moment, can provide. Swift, so often an enforcer of the common forms (forms that over the course of the century were consolidating around strict definitions of heterosexuality), challenges us to overhear and thus to revive a friendship that eluded them.[79]

NOTES

This chapter is dedicated to my dissertation adviser, John Traugott, whose version of Swift brought me to the study of the eighteenth century, his gift to me. Thanks to Beth Goodhue, Corrinne Harol, Kathleen McHugh, Rachel Lee, Christian Thorne, Juliet Williams, and the graduate students in my friendship seminar in the spring of 2008, who helped me to think through what is new material and part of a larger project.

1 John Traugott, '"Shall Jonathan Die?" Swift, Irony, and a Failed Revolution in Ireland', in Daniel W. Conway and John E. Seery (eds.), *The Politics of Irony: Essays in Self-Betrayal* (New York: St Martin's Press, 1992), p. 45.
2 Ibid., p. 46.
3 Ibid., p. 48.
4 Ibid., p. 49.
5 Edward W. Said, 'Swift's Tory Anarchy', in *The World, the Text, and the Critic* (Cambridge, MA: Harvard University Press, 1983), p. 65.
6 Ibid., p. 63.

7 Traugott, '"Shall Jonathan Die?"', p. 32. Traugott's analysis of Socrates is indebted to Kierkegaard's *The Concept of Irony*.

8 Ibid., p. 51.

9 William K. Wimsatt describes Swift's tetrameter couplets as a sort of found art, 'composed, characteristically, of ready-made phrases, from the colloquial and stereotype repertory, pieces of stock language laid together in bundles', 'Rhetoric and Poems: The Example of Swift', in Louis L. Martz and Aubrey Williams (eds.), *The Author in His Work: Essays on a Problem in Criticism* (New Haven and London: Yale University Press), p. 235. Said describes the 'gossipy' meanness of *Verses on the Death of Dr. Swift* as conversation belonging to 'a social version of the same order that overcomes the world at the end of *The Dunciad*'. 'Swift's Tory Anarchy', p. 69.

10 Said, 'Swift's Tory Anarchy', p. 69. Following Said, David M. Veith argues for the importance of what he terms an 'affective approach' in solving the riddle of Swift's irony in *Verses on the Death of Dr. Swift*, focusing on reader response rather than inherent meaning. 'The Mystery of Personal Identity: Swift's Verses on His Own Death', in Martz and Williams, *The Author in His Work*, p. 246. His conclusion, however, undoes Said's fundamental point about the open-endedness of Swift's irony: 'The absurdly presumptuous intention of the *Verses*—more or less successful, as the poem's popularity attests—is to transform the image of Jonathan Swift into a teleological fulfillment of history' (p. 258).

11 Clive Probyn, 'Blindness and Insight: The World, the Text (of Jonathan Swift), and the Criticism of Edward Said', *Eighteenth-Century Life*, 32 (2008), 77.

12 Said, 'Swift's Tory Anarchy', p. 69.

13 Jacques Derrida, *The Politics of Friendship*, trans. George Collins (London and New York: Verso, 2005), p. 1.

14 Ibid., p. 29.

15 Swift to Alexander Pope, 29 September 1725, in *Correspondence*, II, 606–7. In a later letter to Pope he inverts this statement: 'I tell you after all that I do not hate Mankind: it is vous autr[e]s who hate them, because you would have them reasonable Animals and are angry for being disappointed' ibid., 623. This peace with mankind is the abandonment of hope, an abandonment which the '*saeva indignatio*' engraved on his tombstone shows never really occurred.

16 Clive T. Probyn, 'Realism and Raillery: Augustan Conversation and the Poetry of Swift', *The Durham University Journal*, 70 (New Series 39) (1977), 1–14. (1–2).

17 *Poems*, I, 215, 216.

18 *PW*, IV, 91.

19 Thomas Sheridan, *The Life of the Rev. Dr. Jonathan Swift, Dean of St. Patrick's*, 2nd edn (London, 1787), no page number (image 8).

20 Richard Steele, *Tatler* 225, quoted in Probyn, 'Realism and Raillery', 7; ibid. 2.

21 Swift to the Rev. Thomas Sheridan, 11 September 1725, *Correspondence*, II, 595.

22 Alan Bray, *The Friend* (University of Chicago Press, 2004), p. 24. For Bray's acknowledgement of his debt to Derrida and his effort to 'explain and find ways of transcending the ethical problems raised by friendship in a diverse world', see p. 8.

23 For the eighteenth-century shift from consanguineal to conjugal bonds as the centre of family relations, in addition to Bray see Ruth Perry, *Novel Relations: The Transformation of Kinship in English Literature and Culture 1748–1818* (Cambridge University Press, 2004).

24 Bray, *The Friend*, p. 2.

25 James Boswell, *The Life of Samuel Johnson, LL.D.*, ed. George Birkbeck Hill, rev. L. F. Powell (Oxford: Clarendon Press, 1936), vol. III, p. 289.

26 William Blake, *The Everlasting Gospel* (lines 21–2), in David Erdman (ed.), *The Complete Poetry and Prose of William Blake* (Berkeley: University of California Press, 1982), p. 519.

27 William Blake, 'To H[ayley]', in Erdman, *Complete Poetry and Prose*, p. 506.

28 *PW*, II, 551, 562.

29 Cicero, *De senectute, De amicitia, De divinatione*, trans. William Armistead Falconer (Cambridge, MA: Harvard University Press, 1938), 8.23, p. 133.

30 Lisa Jardine, 'Reading and the Technology of Textual Affect', in James Raven, Helen Small, and Naomi Tadmor (eds.), *The Practice and Representation of Reading in England* (Cambridge University Press, 1996), p. 89. On Richardson's imagination of epistolarity as a dialectic of absence and presence, see Bruce Redford, *The Converse of the Pen: Acts of Intimacy in the Eighteenth-Century Familiar Letter* (University of Chicago Press, 1986), p. 1.

31 Virginia Woolf, *Death of the Moth and Other Essays* (New York: Harcourt Brace, 1948), quoted in Redford, *Converse of the Pen*, p. 2.

32 '[I]t was a sparing speech of the ancients, to say, that "a friend is another himself"; for that a friend is far more than himself.' Francis Bacon, *The Essays or Counsels Civil and Moral*, ed. Brian Vickers (Oxford University Press, 1999), p. 64. For the friend as *alter idem*, see Cicero, *De amicitia*, 21.80.

33 Michel de Montaigne, 'Of Friendship', in Donald M. Frame (trans.), *The Complete Essays of Montaigne* (Palo Alto, CA: Stanford University Press, 1981), p. 136.

34 'You should think and deal with every man as a villain, without calling him so, or flying from him, or valuing him less. This is an old true lesson.' Swift to the Rev. Thomas Sheridan, 11 September 1725, *Correspondence*, II, 595.

35 Frame, *Complete Essays of Montaigne*, p. v. Swift is equally sceptical about the possibility of intimate exchange with himself (the kind of philosophical self-communion exemplified by Pope asking sober questions of his heart in his Horatian imitations), writing in an essay on the difficulty of self-knowledge: 'Another Reason why a Man doth not more frequently converse with himself, is, because such a Conversation with his own Heart may discover some Vice or Infirmity lurking within him, which he is very unwilling to believe himself guilty of.' *PW*, IX, 357.

36 Claude Rawson describes the near-transparency of the Stella poems well: 'Stella was the only person who drew from Swift such stark, unembarrassed sincerities.' *Order from Confusion Sprung: Studies in Eighteenth-Century Literature from Swift to Cowper* (London: George Allen & Unwin), p. 185.

37 Said, 'Swift's Tory Anarchy', p. 59. We might also note here that Swift's exchange with Stella is conversation in what he imagined as its ideal form. See Probyn, 'Realism and Raillery', 9: 'the debate in Cadenus and Vanessa stresses the intellect (e.g. lines 343–47) forcibly dramatizing Swift's complaint that the degeneration of conversation is partly due to the exclusion of women participants'. The ideal conversation is both cerebral and heterosexual.

38 Said, 'Swift's Tory Anarchy', p. 59.

39 Probyn, 'Realism and Raillery', 9.

40 Margaret Anne Doody, 'Swift and Women', in Christopher Fox (ed.), *The Cambridge Companion to Jonathan Swift* (Cambridge University Press, 2003), p. 98.

41 Helen Vendler, *Invisible Listeners: Lyric Intimacy in Herbert, Whitman, and Ashbery* (New Jersey: Princeton University Press, 2005), p. 26.

42 Ibid.

43 Michael Schoenfeldt, *Prayer and Power: George Herbert and Renaissance Courtship* (University of Chicago Press, 1991), p. 256.

44 Ibid., p. 257.

45 My text is taken from C. A. Patrides (ed.), *The English Poems of George Herbert* (London and Melbourne: J. M. Dent & Sons, Ltd, 1974).

46 Vendler, *Invisible Listeners*, p. 87.

47 Schoenfeldt, *Prayer and Power*, p. 263.

48 Vendler, *Invisible Listeners*, pp. 24, 25.

49 Schoenfeldt, *Prayer and Power*, p. 264. Here the 'power play' to which Vendler refers, the poet's hesitancy over proper deportment in the presence of a superior, resonates with Bray's analysis of male Renaissance friendship frequently taking the form of public service to a great man.

50 Bray, *The Friend*, p. 232.

51 Lady Wilde (Jane Francesca) on Stella and Vanessa, quoted in Louise Barnett, *Jonathan Swift in the Company of Women* (Oxford University Press, 2007), p. 13. I am indebted throughout this section to Barnett's sensitive and sensible analyses.

52 Ibid., p. 23.

53 Virginia Woolf, 'Swift's *Journal to Stella*', in *Collected Essays* (New York: Harcourt, Brace & World, Inc., 1967), vol. III, p. 71.

54 Jonathan Swift, 'On the Death of Mrs. Johnson', in *PW*, V, 227. Stella's rival, Vanessa, was also Swift's pupil in letters and morals, also left her mother to come to Ireland, and also had very little use for female company.

55 Ibid., p. 228.

56 Léon de Wailly, *Stella and Vanessa: A Romance from the French*, trans. Lady Duff Gordon (London, 1850).

57 Swift, 'On the Death of Mrs. Johnson', p. 227.

58 Barnett, *Swift in the Company of Women*, p. 58.

59 William Dowling, *The Epistolary Moment: The Poetics of the Eighteenth-Century Verse Epistle* (New Jersey: Princeton University Press, 1991), pp. 24, 25. From this perspective, Marvell's 'To his Coy Mistress' 'stands in relation to the verse epistles of the later seventeenth century as the last successful lyric, a great valedictory attempt to posit sexual consummation not simply as a reenactment on the physical level as spiritual communion but also as a guarantee that the lady and the world exist apart from the mind of the speaker'.

60 Bray, *The Friend*, p. 258.

61 It is worth noting in this regard that 'in every historical period since Swift's death, his reputation as a patriot and writer has been overshadowed by his reputation as a man of unconventional relations with two women' (Barnett, *Swift in the Company of Women*, citing Robert Mahony, *Jonathan Swift: The Irish Identity* (New Haven: Yale University Press, 1995), p. 31).

62 *Correspondence*, III, 2.

63 Richard Feingold, *Moralized Song: The Character of Augustan Lyricism* (New Brunswick: Rutgers University Press, 1989), p. 91. See also his claim that 'the lyric intensity toward which the poem builds is in great part created by our sense that the didactic argument is wholly shaped and tested by the private knowledge of Stella's worth that Swift brings to the occasion' (p. 90).

64 *Poems*, II, 765.

65 Ibid., 766.

66 Barnett, *Swift in the Company of Women*, p. 36.

67 Feingold, *Moralized Song*, p. 88.

68 Doody, 'Swift and Women', pp. 108–9.

69 Ronald Paulson, 'Swift, Stella, and Permanence', *English Literary History*, 27 (1960), 313.

70 Ronald Paulson, 'Suppose me Dead: Swift's *Verses on the Death of Dr. Swift*', in Frank Palmeri (ed.), *Critical Essays on Jonathan Swift* (New York: G. K. Hall, 1993), p. 243.

71 Traugott, 'Shall Jonathan Die?', p. 50.

72 Quoted in Bray, *The Friend*, p. 44.

73 A phrase used to describe the marriage of King Edward and Queen Editha, 'who observed mutual chastity over the lifetime of their marriage', in Thomas Heywood, *Gynaikeion: or Nine Bookes of Various History Concerning Women* (London, 1624), vol. VI, pp. 282–3, quoted in Barnett, *Swift in the Company of Women*, p. 39.

74 Doody, 'Swift and Women', p. 111.

75 *Correspondence*, II, 660. Barnett is less than convinced by this assertion and its attempt to blur the distinction between love and friendship. She also observes that Swift 'reserved the word *love* for "romantic love," entailing sex, and explicitly disavowed this feeling for Stella ... Swift may have been misguided in defining love as a matter of romantic superficiality and transience, and exalting friendship as a matter of nonphysical qualities and enduring

feeling, but he makes it clear that these are his definitions' (pp. 39–40). Note also Swift's claim in the earlier 'To Stella, Who Collected and Transcribed His Poems': 'With Friendship and esteem possesst / I ne'er admitted Love a Guest' (13–14).

76 James Woolley, 'Friends and Enemies in *Verses on the Death of Dr. Swift*, *Studies in Eighteenth-Century Culture*, 8 (1979), 205–25. Note also Probyn, 'Realism and Raillery', who affirms this on 9–10.

77 Derrida, following Nietzsche, in *Politics of Friendship*, pp. 70, 71 (quoting directly, his own translation).

78 Carol Houlihan Flynn, *The Body in Swift and Defoe* (Cambridge University Press, 1990), pp. 109, 130.

79 Bray's account of Anne Lister's 'marriage' to a female friend is resonant here: 'Precisely because civil society did not comprehend these customary terms of friendship, they had the power to challenge and circumvent it' (*The Friend*, p. 282).

'now deaf 1740'
Entrapment, foreboding, and exorcism in late Swift

David Womersley

To us today, there seems to be something in excess of the verifiable facts in Swift's praise of Esther Johnson, or 'Stella'. This humbly born woman of no formal education was nevertheless (according to Swift) well-versed in classical and modern history, had mastered Platonic and Epicurean philosophy, could point out the errors of Hobbes in matters of politics and religion, understood medicine and anatomy, and possessed an impeccable literary taste.[1] (Of course, the fact that Swift himself oversaw part of Stella's education during their time together at Moor Park may not be irrelevant to his later evaluation of her attainments.)

However that may be, in the birthday poem he wrote for Stella in 1725 Swift nevertheless struck a good balance between realism and affection. Indeed, the realism is the vehicle of the affection. Swift famously said that he was a man of rhymes – a claim which is at once both large and self-deprecating.[2] But in 'Stella's Birthday' Swift demonstrated his virtuosity with, not rhyme, but half-rhyme. The inescapable fact of ageing is troped in the poem as a faltering of rhyme (a word on which Swift rhymes twice in the poem):

> So, poets lose their feet by time,
> And can no longer dance in rhyme.

And in this poem of overwhelmingly simple, masculine rhymes (it contains only one feminine rhyme: 'get her / better', and none of the wildly brilliant Hudibrastic rhymes of which Swift was capable, and which so mark the verse of a poem we shall be considering in a moment, namely 'The Legion Club'), the rhyme indeed stumbles. But it does so only once, although at a most significant point in the poem:

> And if the muse deny her aid
> To have them *sung*, they may be *said*.

The fall from singing to saying, from poetry to prose, and from youth to age, is marked by this beautifully apt half-rhyme, 'aid / said'.[3]

The half-rhyme is called for here because Swift wishes to insinuate the idea that half-rhyme is the pattern followed by all our lives. What comes later inevitably cannot match the expectation of – cannot rhyme with – what went before. So the fact of ageing, and of encroaching imperfection, is not denied by Swift in this poem. Indeed, the approach of weakness is the background to the poem's final gesture of reassurance to Stella, as Swift grounds his unchanging affection and esteem for her on the decaying of his sense of sight. This is a sombrely beautiful poem, in which a measured gravity is the foundation of a measured gaiety, and in which we see Swift's agility of mind ministering to sympathy rather than to satire.

At some point in 1740 (perhaps on the anniversary of Stella's birthday, 13 March) Swift re-read this poem, and his attention was caught by its final couplet. Fifteen years before, he had imagined (and prayed to be spared) the malign mischance that old age might undermine his hearing, and so prevent him from listening to the good sense Stella spoke, while at the same time preserving his eyesight, thus allowing him to see, with undiminished clarity, how her looks were fading:

> Oh, ne'er may Fortune shew her Spight,
> To make me *deaf*, and mend my *Sight*.

Underlining the word 'deaf', in the margin he wrote: 'now deaf 1740'.[4]

If Swift did write that annotation on 13 March 1740, then it would be the last example of his handwriting that has come down to us. We have the texts of five later letters, but the holographs of none. Swift's will was dated slightly later (3 May 1740) and was apparently written in his own hand; but it has not survived.[5] So this fact in itself – if it is a fact – would bestow a certain charisma on the annotation. But what interests me most about the annotation is what it would have felt like to make it. For surely those three words crystallise the uncanny experience of feeling your life conform itself to something you have previously imagined. The normal direction of flow between experience and writing has here, for a moment, been reversed.

Looking at the annotation in that light, one realises that there were many occasions when Swift had this experience of living out something he had previously, if only playfully, imagined. For instance, the 'BOOK-SELLER's Advertisement' to the *Mechanical Operation of the Spirit* (1704) explains that:

The following Discourse came into my Hands perfect and entire. But there being several Things in it, which the present Age would not very well bear, I kept it by me some Years, resolving it should never see the Light. At length, by the Advice and

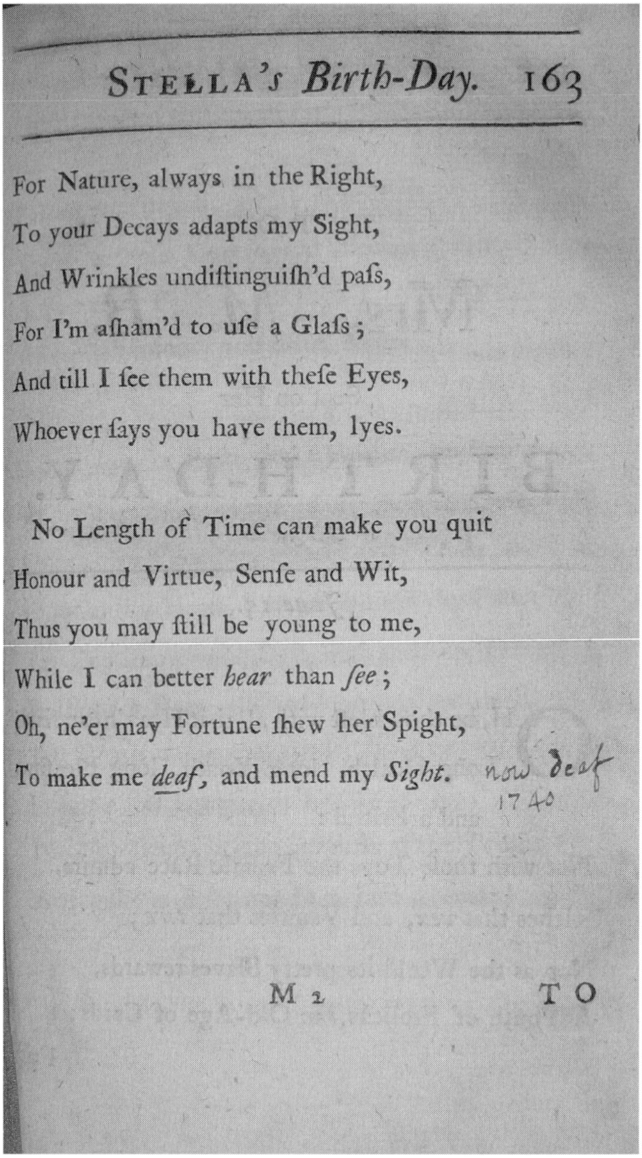

STELLA's *Birth-Day.* 163

For Nature, always in the Right,
To your Decays adapts my Sight,
And Wrinkles undiftinguifh'd pafs,
For I'm afham'd to ufe a Glafs;
And till I fee them with thefe Eyes,
Whoever fays you have them, lyes.

No Length of Time can make you quit
Honour and Virtue, Senfe and Wit,
Thus you may ftill be young to me,
While I can better *hear* than *fee*;
Oh, ne'er may Fortune fhew her Spight,
To make me *deaf,* and mend my *Sight.* now deaf
1740

M 2   T O

Figure 8. Annotated page from Swift's own copy of *Miscellanies.*

Assistance of a judicious Friend, I retrench'd those Parts that might give most Offence, and have now ventured to publish the Remainder; Concerning the Author, I am wholly ignorant; neither can I conjecture, whether it be the same with That of the two foregoing Pieces [i.e. A Tale of a Tub and The Battel of the Books], the Original having been sent me at a different Time, and in a different Hand.[6]

And a shoulder-note alongside a large lacuna in the text of the *Mechanical Operation* tells the reader that '*Here the whole Scheme of spiritual Mechanism was deduced and explained, with an Appearance of great reading and observation; but it was thought neither safe nor Convenient to Print it.*'[7] In 1704 this was all playful mystification. Just over twenty years later, however, much of it – the clandestine delivery of the manuscript to the publisher; the concealment of the identity of the author; the employment of non-authorial hands in the interests of such concealment; the decision not to publish some portions of the manuscript on the grounds that they were likely to cause offence; and the involvement of a third party or '*judicious Friend*' such as Andrew Tooke in the identification and softening of such passages – actually happened in respect of the printing and publication of Benjamin Motte's 1726 editions of *Gulliver's Travels*.[8]

Inevitably *Gulliver* is a primary focus of this anticipation of events in Swift's life by details in his literary works. Swift's correspondence shows how quickly the episodes and vocabulary of that book were imaginatively adopted by Swift and his friends – for instance, Swift writing in the character of Lemuel Gulliver or 'The Prince of Lilliput', Mrs. Howard signing herself 'sieve Yahoo'.[9] This playful admission of the literary work into the life changes character, however, and assumes less companionable forms. Swift assured Pope that he had written *Gulliver* 'to vex the world', but in preparing the text of *Gulliver* for Faulkner's 1735 edition, he found that the vexation he wished to bestow on others had rebounded on himself: 'Gulliver vexeth me more than any', he wrote to Charles Ford.[10] It is, however, the Struldbruggs which in Swift's case show the life imitating the work in the most bitter way. It is not clear that all *Gulliver*'s first readers realised quite what Swift was driving at when he created the Struldbruggs, who are condemned to feel all the increasing infirmities of age, but denied the release of death, and so offer a strong chastisement of the natural human desire for length of life. Marmaduke Phillips, writing to Swift on 2 November 1734, spectacularly missed the point when he regretted, in the context of discussing Swift's various ailments, 'that you are not like one of *Gulliver's Struldbrugs*, immortal'.[11] We don't have Swift's reply to this well-intentioned but hapless letter. Yet as Swift's health declined and life became more of a burden to him, touches of

phrasing in his letters reveal that Swift himself appreciated the justice of
the comparison between the author and his creations. Writing to Pope on
28 April 1739, Swift declared himself to be 'utterly void of what the World
calls natural Affection', a phrase recalling the fact that the Struldbruggs
are (we are told by Gulliver) 'dead to all natural Affection'.[12] ('Dead', of
course, is a vexingly unapt word to use of the Struldbruggs, who cannot
die, as is 'mortifying' when Gulliver says they were most mortifying to
look at – in both cases we have a brilliantly inappropriate choice of word
which keeps the moral significance of the Struldbruggs before us.)
So when Orrery said that Swift, in his dotage, was 'the exact image of one
of his own *Struldbruggs*, a miserable spectacle, devoid of every appearance
of human nature, except the outward form', the indignation this raised in
Deane Swift was to some extent misplaced, for in drawing the connection
Orrery was doing nothing more than making explicit something at which
Swift himself had hinted.[13] Just as when he annotated the final couplet
of Stella's birthday poem in 1740, towards the end of his life Swift was
aware that in certain respects his earlier writings had prescribed the forms
his later life would take.

Swift was given to being prophetic about himself and after 1714 was
prone to baleful reflections on futurity, as he told Bolingbroke: 'I was
47 Years old [i.e. in 1714, the year of the death of Queen Anne] when
I began to think of death; and the reflections upon it now [the letter is
dated 31 October 1729] begin when I wake in the Morning, and end when
I am going to Sleep.'[14] Edward Young relates an anecdote which drama-
tises this disposition in Swift:

I remember, as I and others were taking with him an evening's walk, about a mile
out of Dublin, he stopt short; we passed on; but perceiving that he did not follow
us, I went back; and found him fixed as a statue, and earnestly gazing upward at a
noble elm, which in its uppermost branches was much withered, and decayed.
Pointing at it, he said, 'I shall be like that tree, I shall die at top.' As in this he
seemed to prophesy like the Sybils.[15]

Swift's forebodings gave voice to his sense of entrapment in a destiny both
inexorable and unwelcome, expressed perhaps most bitterly in his prophecy to Bolingbroke: 'it is time for me to have done with the world, and so
I would if I could get into a better before I was called into the best, and
not die here in a rage, like a poison'd rat in a hole'.[16] Entrapment is also
the keynote of the annotation to 'Stella's Birthday', marking as it does the
actualising of something which, fifteen years beforehand, had been only
imagined. And social entrapment is the dominant theme of the two great

compilations of the final phase of Swift's career as a writer, *Polite Conversation* (1738) and *Directions to Servants* (first published, in an unfinished state, in 1745, the year of Swift's death). In *Polite Conversation*, conversation – which Swift thought had the potential to be 'the greatest, the most lasting, and the most innocent, as well as useful Pleasure of Life' – is transformed into the dreary drudgery of keeping up what 'Simon Wagstaff', Swift's *persona* in that work, calls 'the Ball of Discourse'.[17] In *Directions to Servants*, the master and mistress are confined in the grand rooms of the house, unable to exercise any control over the household, while the servants roam where they will, both within and without doors:

It often happens that Servants sent on Messages, are apt to stay out somewhat longer than the Message requires, perhaps two, four, six, or eight Hours, or some such Trifle; for the Temptation to be sure was great, and Flesh and Blood cannot always resist: When you return, the Master storms, the Lady scolds, stripping, cudgelling, and turning off, is the Word. But here you ought to be provided with a Set of Excuses, enough to serve on all Occasions: For Instance, your Uncle came fourscore Miles to Town this Morning, on purpose to see you, and goes back by Break of Day To-morrow: A Brother-Servant, that borrowed Money of you when he was out of Place, was running away to *Ireland:* You were taking Leave of an old Fellow-servant, who was shipping for *Barbados:* Your Father sent a Cow for you to sell, and you could not find a Chapman till Nine at Night: You were taking Leave of a dear Cousin who is to be hanged next *Saturday:* You wrencht your Foot against a Stone, and were forced to stay three Hours in a Shop, before you could stir a Step: Some Nastiness was thrown on you out of a Garret Window, and you were ashamed to come Home before you were cleaned, and the Smell went off: You were pressed for the Sea-service, and carried before a Justice of Peace, who kept you three Hours before he examined you, and you got off with much a-do: A Bailiff by Mistake seized you for a Debtor, and kept you the whole Evening in a Spunging-house: You were told your Master had gone to a Tavern, and come to some Mischance, and your Grief was so great that you inquired for his Honour in a hundred Taverns between *Pall-mall* and *Temple-bar.*[18]

Beneath Swift's exasperation and fury at the cool impertinence of these excuses, is there not also a slight but audible note of envy, an interesting inversion of that *ressentiment* which, according to Nietzsche, slaves feel towards their masters? The physical enlargement of servants, roaming from the west to the east of the city, coming to London from the country, heading off to Ireland or even the West Indies, and the exuberance of their self-serving inventions, spinning gaily away from any relation to truth or honesty, evoke a life of freedom which compares well with the impotent curses and deadening routines of their masters. In this way *Directions to*

Servants is a true companion piece to *Polite Conversation*, the former a photographic negative, the latter a photographic positive, of the stultified life of the well-to-do of Swift's own day. For Swift, there was no way out. He could only fret at the tedium to which he was exposed and fume at his vulnerability. The image of Gulliver, tied down and at the mercy of the Lilliputians, swims once more into view in these late works.

Social entrapment is one of the forms of vulnerable immobility which preoccupied Swift in his later years. Another was a foreboding of what he feared he might become, under the pressure of the unremitting provocations – as he saw them – of his surroundings. We can approach Swift's forebodings if we think about the relation between Swift and Gulliver. It is of course a cardinal principle of reading *Gulliver's Travels* that the author and the character are not to be confused (although the corollary, that neither are they at all points utterly to be put asunder, is heard less often than would be useful). The axiom of absolute separation is unhelpful, because it distracts us from an interesting feature of Swift's self-presentation after the publication of *Gulliver's Travels*, namely the existence of words and phrases which invite a perception of Swift as akin to the misanthropic Gulliver of the end of Part IV. Once his initial high-spirits at the publication of *Gulliver's Travels* wore off (as they very quickly did) Swift quickly adopted a Gulliver-like misanthropy, shunning 'Laught[e]r and ridicule, for both which my tast is gone'.[19] His later writings on Irish subjects he ascribed to 'perfect rage and resentment, and the mortifying sight of slavery, folly, and baseness about me, among which I am forc'd to live'.[20] There are echoes here, surely, of Gulliver at the end of Part IV, obliged to live with Yahoos and to be jostled on a daily basis by human depravity. 'I have no room left for new Ideas', Swift wrote to Lady Worsley on 4 November 1732.[21] Exhaustion, repetition, and repletion are the keynotes of late Swift.

These connections between Swift after 1726 and the Gulliver of Part IV, slight and fleeting as they are, should not be seen as arguing for any crude identity between the author and his creation, but rather as opening the question of the effect that the composition and publication of *Gulliver's Travels* had on Swift during the last two decades of his life. If, in his later years, Swift to some extent imitated Gulliver, that would be a tacit acknowledgement of the authoritativeness of the vision of Part IV of *Gulliver's Travels*. Certainly the idiom of Part IV resonates in, for example, *A Modest Proposal* (1729), where a bestial language is once again applied to humankind (for instance, 'a Child, *just dropt from its Dam*') in a context of ethnographical comparison (the helpful views of 'my

American Acquaintance') and fantastic voyages (the corroborative evidence supplied by 'the famous *Salmanaazor,* a Native of the Island *Formosa* – an egregious charlatan).[22] Of course, it will immediately be objected that this language is put by Swift into the mouth of the Proposer, and that one cannot draw a simple connection between the author and his persona. But again, as with Swift and Gulliver, neither can one utterly separate them. The nature of Swift's relation to the Proposer is suggested by the peroration of the pamphlet, where the separation between author and persona suddenly becomes thin and unstable. The Proposer having insisted that his remedy is calculated for Ireland alone, the tone becomes grave and the provenance of the voice uncertain: 'Therefore, let no man talk to me of other Expedients.'[23] There follows a long list of obvious and practical remedies for Ireland's economic ills, all of which had been recommended previously and in earnest by Swift himself, and then we have this bitterly complex conclusion:

Therefore I repeat, let no Man talk to me of these and the like Expedients; till he hath, at least, a Glimpse of Hope, that there will ever be some hearty and sincere Attempt to put *them in Practice.*

But, as to my self; having been wearied out for many Years with offering vain, idle, visionary Thoughts; and at length utterly despairing of Success, I fortunately fell upon this Proposal . . .[24]

As the experience of the Proposer and Swift converge, we see suddenly how they stand in relation to each other. The Proposer is both a hideous inversion of Swift, yet also a terrible imaginative projection of what Swift might become, or could be driven to become, by the bruising repetition of disappointment, exasperation, and failure.

This virtuoso manipulation of perspective and persona is one of the technical fruits bestowed on Swift by the composition of *Gulliver's Travels.* We can see Swift availing himself of it once more in the fascinating, and under-studied, late pamphlet *An Examination of Certain Abuses, Corruptions, and Enormities in the City of Dublin* (1732). Just as Part II of *Gulliver's Travels* inverts the telescope of Part I, so *An Examination* reverses the dynamic we have seen in *A Modest Proposal,* where we find a sudden convergence between Swift and his persona towards the end of the pamphlet. By contrast, *An Examination* begins with a litany of complaint about fraudulent or misleading street cries to be heard in Dublin, reminiscent of the complaints about London street cries which Swift had made to Stella in 1712; 'here is a restless dog crying Cabbages and Savoys plagues me every morning about this time, he is now at it,

I wish his largest Cabbage was sticking in his Throat'.[25] Grumbling about street cries in *An Examination* is followed by reproachful comments about the 'immense Number of human Excrements at the Doors and Steps of waste Houses, and at the sides of every dead Wall'.[26] Swift himself often claimed to hate Dublin ('the most disagreeable Place in Europe', as he said to Knightley Chetwode in 1727), and one of the things he particularly resented was its 'abundance of Dirt' and general dilapidation: 'In this great City nine tenths of the Inhabitants are beggars, the chief Streets half ruinous or desolate; It is dangerous to walk the Streets for fear of Houses falling on our heads.'[27] So far, so Swiftian. But then the pamphlet takes off without warning into the realms of Whiggish political paranoia, as street signs and cries are interpreted for seditious, Jacobite meanings, culminating in this piece of bravura deciphering:

Whoever views those Signs, may read over his Majesty's head the following Letters and Cyphers, *G.R.*II., which plainly signifies *George*, King the Second; and not King *George* the Second, or *George* the Second King; but laying the point after the letter *G.* by which the Owner of the House manifestly shews, that he renounces his Allegiance to King *George* the Second; and allows him to be only the second King, In-nuendo, that the Pretender is the first King; and looking upon King *George* to be only a Kind of second King, or Vice-roy, till the Pretender shall come over and seize the Kingdom. I appeal to all Mankind, whether this be a strained or forced Interpretation of the Inscription, as it now stands in almost every Street; whether any Decypherer would make the least Doubt or Hesitation, to explain it as I have done.[28]

To some extent Swift is here re-visiting the Academy of Lagado, with its school of political artists and decipherers. Swift deplored these dark political arts as instruments of oppression and tyranny, but – with a characteristically Swiftian reversal – it is also the case that the list of equivalences the decipherers of Lagado employ includes some equivalences which Swift himself would endorse: for instance, 'the Plague, a standing Army', or 'a Buzard, a Minister', or 'a running Sore, the Administration'.[29] So, in *An Examination*, although this deciphering of '*G.R.*II' is an example of the paranoid court Whig Jacobite hunting which, from the last four years of Queen Anne onwards, Swift had regularly mocked, nevertheless, in the volatility of his own political sentiments, and in particular given the occasional flashes of old Whig doctrine that can break out in his later letters, it was not something from which he could feel utterly immune. Merely by ventriloquising these despised voices, he has to some extent incorporated them.

Writing *Gulliver's Travels* had a double effect on Swift. It imprisoned him ethically, but released him technically. Gulliver, the Proposer, and the Examiner are all in part images of the doom which Swift foresaw for himself: a narrowed and deprived existence in a pen of misanthropy and madness, into which he would be driven by moral vexation. To that fate, Swift's prescient descriptions stand as both terrified apprehensions and attempts at placatory deflection. But that bleakness is only half the story. The facility with fantasy which Swift learned in writing *Gulliver's Travels*, the immersion of his imagination in the literally outlandish, and the array of literary resources he possessed in consequence of that, is the other part of that book's legacy to its author. It was that double inheritance, of ethical wintriness and technical invention, which set the parameters for Swift's later writings.

So much for entrapment and foreboding. I turn now to exorcism, and again I begin with that annotation to 'Stella's Birthday'. For in writing those words, surely Swift was aware, not just of pre-ordination, but also of the problematic ownership of that annotated couplet. Whose voice was speaking through those lines? Was there momentarily another voice speaking through Swift's, a voice which, unlike his, was not unaware of its predictive power? These are questions I shall pursue through 'The Legion Club', the greatest and wildest poem of Swift's old age.

In *The Mechanical Operation of the Spirit* (1704), Swift had mocked those who laid claim to inspiration and had gleefully traced their enthusiasm to earthly and material sources. Nevertheless, the idea of spirits, and in particular of the summoning of spirits and obliging them to talk, is a recurrent element in Swift's satire – most obviously in Part III of *Gulliver's Travels* when Gulliver visits the island of Glubbdubdrib, whose governor 'hath Power of calling whom he pleaseth from the Dead, and commanding their Service for twenty four Hours, but no longer; nor can he call the same Persons up again in less than three Months, except upon very extraordinary Occasions', and as a result of whose assistance Gulliver is able to 'call up whatever Persons I would chuse to name, and in whatever Numbers among all the Dead from the Beginning of the World to the present Time, and command them to answer any Questions I should think fit to ask'.[30] But, beyond this obvious example, ideas of possession, of exorcism, and of the raising of spirits surround Swift, once you start to look for them. In Pope's 'Mary Gulliver to Captain Lemuel Gulliver', Gulliver's wife puts his behaviour down to possession:

> Some say the Dev'l himself is in that *Mare*:
> If so, our *Dean* shall drive him forth by Prayer.
> Some think you mad, some think you are possest.[31]

In 1726, Peterborough described Swift as a shape-shifting raiser of the dead.[32] Much earlier in his life, Swift, commenting on a fury of composition which had overtaken him in the previous two months, said his 'mind was like a conjur'd spirit, that would doe mischief, if I woud not give it employment'.[33] So when, in *The Drapier's Letters*, Swift talks of 'that Spirit raised against' Wood, or 'that Spirit raised in the Nation . . . against this horrid Design of Mr. *Wood*', and when he encourages the Irish to 'keep up your Spirits and Resentments', these spirits are not just animal spirits: they are also the wild spirits which Swift has conjured up against Wood through the incantatory power of his language.[34] This is how Swift used the phrase in a letter to Gay, of 8 January 1723 (thus very close in date to *The Drapier's Letters*), in the course of complaining that correspondence with Gay and Pope revives in him memories of his previous English life, and makes him discontented with Ireland: 'this humdrum way of Life might be passable enough if you would let me alone [.] I shall not be able to relish my Wine, my Parsons, my Horses nor my Garden for three Months, till the Spirit you have raised shall be dispossessed.'[35]

Even Swift's most trivial writings show a strange affinity with the thread of spirit, possession, and exorcism which runs through his life. For instance, we might consider *A Discourse to Prove the Antiquity of the English Tongue* (first published 1765), the purpose of which is to prove by spoof, punning etymologies that English was the original language, along lines such as these:

Alexander the Great was very fond of eggs roasted in hot ashes. As soon as his cooks heard he was come home to dinner or supper, they called aloud to their under-officers, *All eggs under the Grate*. Which, repeated every day at noon and evening, made strangers think it was that Prince's real name, and therefore gave him no other; and posterity hath been ever since under the same delusion.[36]

The more outrageous the pun – and there is a whole series of them in that work, as Swift successively takes names and phrases from classical mythology and history and shows their 'English' origins – the more Swift seems like one who can conjure the ridiculous spirit which, we see with hindsight, was always lurking in possession of the apparently innocent word or name. It is unsurprising, then, that early editors of Swift, such as Scott, should have tried to capture the distinctiveness of his writing in terms such as these: 'Swift seems, like the Persian dervise, to have possessed the faculty of transfusing his own soul into the body of anyone whom he selected.'[37] And it is also unsurprising that Francis Jeffrey, reviewing Scott's edition and reflecting on the force of Swift's satire, should speak of the 'demoniacal inspiration with which the malison is vented'.[38] The image of Swift in his last years as a 'daemonic' figure has been dismissed by his most painstaking biographer as pieced together out of 'the crooked inventions of remote tattlers'.[39] No doubt it was a distortion. But it was a distorted response to something which is undeniably there in Swift's writing and imagination.

In using the phrase 'demoniacal inspiration' Jeffrey was speaking particularly about 'The Legion Club', whose 'force and terror' he was amongst the first to recognise. This extraordinary poem was written in response to developments in the Irish House of Commons in 1735 and 1736.[40] The point of dispute was tithe agistment, namely the tithe on pasturage, particularly pasturage grazed by dry and barren cattle. Resistance on the part of freeholders to paying this tithe had been growing and becoming better organised from the early years of the century, and had not been much discouraged by the legal establishment of the rights of the clergy in 1722. It came to a head in December 1735, when the Irish House of Commons was petitioned by a group of 'Gentlemen, in Behalf of themselves and the Rest of the Farmers, Grasiers of Ireland', asking for relief from tithe agistment on the grounds that 'according to the best Information . . . no such Tythes have ever been paid, or even demanded in this Kingdom until a few Years since'. Three months later, a second, similar petition was received. It was at this point that Swift composed and circulated in manuscript 'The Legion Club', in which he stigmatised the Irish parliamentarians who were prepared even to listen to such anticlerical arguments with the name of the Biblical unclean spirit.[41]

'The Legion Club' takes the form of an imagined visit to the magnificent new Parliament House on the north side of College Green (now the premises of the Bank of Ireland), of which the foundations had been laid in 1728 but which, in 1736, was still three years away from completion. A crowd of literary precedents contend for possession of the poem. Swift's visit to the Parliament is partly a descent into the underworld, so Book VI of the *Aeneid* is clearly invoked, and indeed is summoned up in many of the poem's details.[42] (There is no evidence that Swift ever read, or even knew of, Dante. This should cause no surprise. Even much later in the century Boswell would not know to whom the phrase 'divinus poeta' referred.)[43] But 'The Legion Club' is also a visit to a madhouse, with a keeper who points out the most important inmates, when Clio the Muse of history, and Swift's initial guide, has left, unable any longer to tolerate the smell. This summons up other literary presences: specifically, the visit to Bedlam in the 'Digression Concerning Madness' in *A Tale of A Tub*, and Gulliver's visit to the Academy of Lagado in Part III of *Gulliver's Travels* (which is itself in part a re-working of that episode from the *Tale*). Very quickly, the ghosts of other Swiftian writings throng the poem, like the moaning, flitting, shades of the dead who hurry to feed on the trench of blood dug by Odysseus at the confluence of the rivers of Flaming Fire and Lamentation.[44] When we read that —

> Such a crowd their ordure throws
> On a far less villain's nose.

— we recall the Yahoos.[45] When the Parliament is referred to as a 'harpies nest', we think of the flies in Brobdingnag, who pollute Gulliver's food in the manner of the harpies in the *Aeneid*.[46] When the keeper is urged to tie two members 'in a tether, / Let them stare and stink together', we recall the Dutch pirate who threatened to tie in pairs Gulliver and his shipmates and throw them into the sea.[47] When Swift warns Morgan that unless he reverts to being true to the precepts of his classical education —

> When you walk among your books,
> They reproach you with their looks;
> Bind them fast, or from the shelves
> They'll come down to right themselves:
> Homer, Plutarch, Virgil, Flaccus,
> All in arms prepare to back us:
> Soon repent, or put to slaughter
> Every Greek and Roman author.

— we have returned to the imaginative world of the *Battel of the Books*.[48] When Morgan is then instructed —

> to make your project pass,
> Leave them not a blade of grass.

— we are reminded by contrast of the King of Brobdingnag's criterion for worthwhile human action: 'whoever could make two Ears of Corn, or two Blades of Grass to grow upon a Spot of Ground where only one grew before; would deserve better of Mankind, and do more essential Service to his Country, than the whole Race of Politicians put together'.[49]

'The Legion Club', then, is possessed by Swift's earlier writings; and Swift himself in this poem is a man haunted by his own former work. Moreover, Swift's versification has the power to make the reader experience something like possession. Once more, it is rhyme which is the responsive instrument at Swift's command. The couplet which begins the section on Morgan —

> Bless us Morgan! Art thou there, man?
> Bless mine eyes! Art thou the chairman?

— employs a Hudibrastic rhyme ('there, man?' / 'chairman?'), of the sort which Swift often relished, but here it creates a very particular effect. In the first line, the emphasis falls heavily on 'there', so that in order to make the rhyme the reader is obliged to place an equally heavy emphasis on 'chair'. This has the effect of introducing an inescapable tone of incredulity into the verse, and so a particular judgement about Morgan is made unavoidable. It is simply not open to the reader of 'The Legion Club', I think, to withhold their subscription to Swift's own incredulous and scornful view of Morgan, because you can't read the poem without being ventriloquised by it.

However, who is exorcising whom in this poem? Initially, the possessed are clearly the Irish Members of Parliament:

> Tell us, what this pile contains?
> Many a head that holds no brains.
> These demoniacs let me dub
> With the name of 'Legion Club'.

But as the poem proceeds, its relationship to its Biblical pretexts changes. Gradually, the politicians shift from being actually possessed themselves ('demoniacs') to become the multiple unclean spirits ('for we are many') that possess and taunt Swift, who in turn becomes a version of the anonymous, tormented 'certain man' of the Biblical account, in whom the demons dwelt.

As this movement gets under way, the savage imprecations and wild intensities of the poem come to resemble a rite of self-exorcism, and this is made explicit towards the end of the poem by a significant choice of word:

> Keeper, I must now retire,
> You have done what I desire:
> But I feel my spirits spent,
> With the noise, the sight, the scent.

In this of all Swift's poems it is impossible to use the word 'spirits' without its full range of meaning being activated and available. So Swift's spirits are spent at the end of 'The Legion Club' in two respects. In the first place, the effort of poetic composition in so strident and energetic a vein has left Swift exhausted. But at the same time, the poem has allowed him to spend, or vent, the turbulent emotions of rage, indignation, and contempt by which he was initially possessed. Wholesale destruction has produced a certain 'calm of mind' in Swift. Like God's servants in *Samson Agonistes*, Swift reaches the end of the poem with 'all passion spent'.[50]

In concluding what I have to say about this poem, I want to go back to the curious feature of Swift's life with which I began, namely the frequency with which something initially written subsequently passes into experience. For 'The Legion Club' also exhibits that, but in a way which becomes visible only when we set it in the context of Swift's very first publication, *A Discourse of the Contests and Dissensions Between the Nobles and the Commons in Athens and Rome* (1701), written so many years before on behalf of the four impeached Whig lords (Portland, Somers, Halifax, and Orford).[51]

The political context of Swift's debut as an author was formed by the political turmoil in Britain which followed on from the Treaty of Ryswick (1697), and the hounding of a group of Whig peers by a rampant Tory majority in the House of Commons led by Harley (for whom, ten years later, Swift himself would work). The focus of Tory anger was the Partition Treaties, the first of which had been signed in September 1698, the second in February 1700. These treaties were attempts by William III to prevent the entirety of lands held by the Spanish crown from falling into the hands of either the Emperor Leopold I or the Dauphin, on the death of the childless and ailing Carlos II, in obedience to the fundamental maxim of English diplomacy in this period, that the balance of power in Europe would be destroyed were the territories of Spain ever to be united to the crown of either Germany or France. The first of these was a secret treaty, and neither Partition Treaty had been approved by the House of Commons, since at this time Parliament enjoyed no right to be consulted over foreign affairs, which were deemed to be matters for the monarch and the Privy Council alone.

Following the repudiation of the Second Partition Treaty by the Emperor Leopold in August 1700, Carlos II made a will leaving the Spanish empire in its entirety to the Duc d'Anjou, the grandson of Louis XIV. Carlos's death on 20 October 1700 thus put the diplomatic ball squarely in the court of Louis XIV: would the French king adhere to the provisions of the Partition Treaties, or would he recognise his grandson as king of Spain? He did the latter, and so the failure of the Partition Treaties to settle the matter of the Spanish Succession now promised to involve British forces in a European war.

Unsurprisingly, then, by March 1701 the provisions of and the manner of negotiating the Partition Treaties had become the target of Tory attacks on their Whig rivals, both within and without Parliament. On the one hand, we can see in these attacks the House of Commons as an institution flexing its muscles, on the grounds that the potential of the Partition Treaties to involve Britain in an expensive continental war made them a legitimate object of interest to that House which alone had the power to vote supplies. From the perspective of the history of Parliament, one can see here the House of Commons beginning to extend its sphere of influence into the area of foreign policy. On the other, these attacks were also instances of pure partisan opportunism, in which the Tories were joined by disaffected Whigs such as the Duke of Devonshire, and of which the purpose was simply to inflict as much damage on the Whigs as possible. In the heat of debate in the House, some of the clandestine diplomacy which had preceded the signing of the first treaty, and irregularities such as Somers's affixing of the Great Seal to a blank commission, were inadvertently disclosed. The virtually simultaneous publication on 15 March 1701 of the Tory propagandist Charles Davenant's *Essays Upon I. The Ballance of Power. II. The Right of making War, Peace, and Alliances. III. Universal Monarchy* reinforced the pressures which were building for the impeachment of the four lords most intimately implicated in the negotiation of the Partition Treaties (or the 'Lords Partitioners', as they became known): that is, Portland, Somers, Halifax, and Orford.

In this crisis, the strategy of the embattled Whigs was to appeal to the political nation over the heads of their representatives in the House of Commons, where the Tories enjoyed a majority. Petitions and libels were surreptitiously printed in London and smuggled out to the country. Petitions flowed back in their turn, most famously from Kent, signed by five electors: Thomas Colepepper, William Colepepper, David Polhill, William Hamilton, and Justin Champneys.[52] The petitions flew in the face of the anti-Partitionist line taken by the House of Commons. The petitioners encouraged William III to put the nation in a posture of defence against France, and to raise the money necessary to bring about the partition of the Spanish empire and the preservation of the balance of power in Europe by military force. As Boner, the London resident of the Elector of Brandenburg wittily remarked, never before had English subjects demanded to be taxed. The House of Commons responded by declaring the Kentish petition to be 'scandalous, insolent, and seditious' and ordering the five Kentish petitioners to be imprisoned *sine die* – a high-handed and peremptory act which would eventually return to embarrass them.

This was the feverish climate to which Swift returned from Ireland with
the Earl of Berkeley on 15 April, and (as he recalled in 1714) it immediately
set him writing:

Although I had been for many years before no stranger to the court, and had
made the nature of government a great part of my study, yet I had dealt very little
with politics, either in writing or acting, till about a year before the late King
William's death; when, returning with the Earl of Berkeley from Ireland, and
falling upon the subject of the five great Lords, who were then impeached for
high crimes and misdemeanors, by the House of Commons, I happened to say,
that the same manner of proceeding, at least as it appeared to me from the views
we received of it in Ireland, had ruined the liberties of Athens and Rome, and
that it might be easy to prove it from history. Soon after I went to London; and,
in a few weeks, drew up a discourse, under the title of *The Contests and
Dissentions of the Nobles and Commons in Athens and Rome, with the Consequences
they had upon both those States.* This discourse I sent very privately to the press,
with the strictest injunctions to conceal the author, and returned immediately to
my residence in Ireland.[53]

The *Contests and Dissensions* was thus composed in the late spring and
early summer of 1701, at the same time as Swift was preparing
Sir William Temple's *Miscellanea* for the press. In the *Contests and Dissensions*, Swift pressed ancient history into the service of the Whigs. The
keynote of the pamphlet is Swift's frank subscription to a Whiggish
location of absolute unlimited power in 'the whole Body' of a nation;
he dismisses out of hand any Filmerian patriarchalism.[54] Swift goes on to
argue that, nevertheless, the many (or, more probably, their representatives) could act as tyrannously as any monarch, and he drew particular
attention to instances of aggression towards aristocrats by the people,
while at the same time taking care to distinguish 'the Universal Bent
and Current of a People' from the petty malice of what he called 'the
bare Majority of a few Representatives'.[55] And he concluded by noting
and welcoming the 'Aversion of the People to the late Proceedings of
the Commons', by which he referred to the Tory agitation orchestrated
by Harley.[56]

The *Contests and Dissensions* was printed by John Nutt, and published
probably on 24 October, by which time Swift had returned to Ireland,
and the political crisis the pamphlet had been designed to meet had,
bathetically enough, dissolved. In June, impeachment procedures against
the four Lords had been set in motion but had quickly collapsed in
farcical circumstances when the House of Commons refused to present
its case. In the absence of any case for the prosecution, by the end of the

month all four Lords Partitioners had been acquitted. Moreover, and to complete the humiliation of the Commons, William prorogued Parliament, and so the five Kentish Petitioners were automatically released from custody.

But for a moment, exactly when Swift was busy composing the *Contests and Dissensions*, the crisis had taken a grave and dramatic turn which (in the words of Keith Feiling) 'lifted the controversy to a higher and more bitter plane'.[57] On 14 May Harley read to the House of Commons a paper which had been put in his hand that morning by a stranger on the threshold of St Stephen's Chapel. The stranger was Daniel Defoe, and the paper, said to be composed in the name of 'many Thousands of the good people of *England*', was an inflammatory warning to the House of Commons to change its stance towards the Partition Treaties. The ending of the short *Memorial* was a chilling menace, should the people's demands not be met:

Thus Gentlemen. You have your Duty laid before you, which 'tis hoped you will think of; but if you continue to neglect it, you may expect to be treated according to the Resentment of an *injured* Nation; for *Englishmen* are no more to be Slaves to *Parliament*, than to a King.

Our Name is LEGION, and we are many.

Postscript. If you require to have this Memorial sign'd with our Names, it shall be done on your first Order, and *personally presented*.[58]

Defoe's *Memorial* was certainly the most striking invocation of the Biblical text about Legion in eighteenth-century political life, and it occurred, as we have seen, at the climax of a crisis in which Swift also (albeit belatedly and ineffectively) was eager to play a part. Was that precedent at all active when Swift himself made allusion to the same Biblical text thirty-five years later in 'The Legion Club', once again in an atmosphere of intense parliamentary controversy and petitioning?

I think it was, but in order to grasp how and why, we need to trace the use of the term 'Legion' in the work of another writer who contributed to the Partition crisis, the Irish non-juror and Jacobite, Charles Leslie (1650–1722). Defoe's adoption of the group pseudonym 'Legion' for the Whigs was a gift to Leslie, the most able polemicist of the early eighteenth century ('a reasoner who was not to be reasoned against', in Johnson's famous verdict),[59] and certainly someone whose knowledge of the Bible was more profound than Defoe's. Leslie himself thought of all Whigs as devils, but even he could not have expected that they would so speak of themselves. In *The Rehearsal*, the bi-weekly political paper Leslie published from 1704 to 1709, he recalled Defoe's piece of political theatre, which he presented as an attempt

> to Assert the *Authority*, and Refer every thing to the Ultimate *Decision* of his Beloved *Legion* Anglice *Mobb*? In behalf of which he Presented a *Petition* to the *House* of *Commons*, Humbly *Praying*, That they wou'd be Pleas'd to Give up their *Authority*, and Admit of *Appeals* from them to their *Original* the *Mobb*.[60]

In pamphlet after pamphlet, and in issue after issue of *The Rehearsal*, the public were repeatedly reminded of this unguarded association of themselves by the Whigs with the Biblical 'unclean spirit'.[61] The Whigs, according to Leslie, are 'a Legion of Sectaries'.[62] Every year they hold their '*Calves-Head-Feasts*, where they *Sacrifice* to the *Legion* that *possesses* them. And not satisfied with the *Royal Blood* they have *Drank*, still *Thirst* for more.'[63] They serve 'the *Interest* of *Legion* our GOD'.[64] 'We *Bully* with our *Numbers*, and call our selves *LEGION*, *for we are many*!', Leslie makes the Whig 'Observator' say. 'Have not *WE Legion'd* and *Million'd* the *House* of *Commons*' and slavishly followed 'the Example of our *Master LEGION*'?[65] Issue five of *The Rehearsal* bore the sub-title 'Of the *Former* and *Present STATE* of *LEGION*' and repeatedly used the signature of Defoe's *Memorial* as a master-trope to unlock what Leslie painted as the diabolical heart of Whiggism.

Leslie was therefore very tenacious in his aggressive use of the term 'Legion', but he had also been very quick to seize on it. In *The New Association*, published early in 1702, he mocked the Whigs 'for all this *Out-Cry* that they have Rais'd about *Persecution*, to *Spirit* up their *Legion*' and poured scorn on their belief that 'their *Strngth* [sic] lies in their *Legion*, for *they are Many*'.[66] In *The New Association Part II* (dated 25 March 1703), Leslie concluded the pamphlet by recalling the momentous events of the spring of 1701:

> And the *Legion* which had so long *Possess'd* the Deluded *People*, with Anti-*Monarchical* and *Mob-Principles*, was, for a Time, *Driven* but not *Rooted* out. For being first *Neglected*, and then *Indulg'd*, they have had Leisure to Grow, and soon Produc'd a New *Crop* of *Devils*: Who are *Enter'd* into the *Herd* of *Swine*; We heard them lately *Grunt* from *Kent*.[67]

And earlier in the pamphlet he had also touched on those events and their pamphleteering afterlife, in terms which would have caught Swift's attention:

> And we have seen them set up *Legion* against the *Commons*, Nay, Appeal to the *Lords* from them. And they whose former *Measures of Obedience* were all

Centur'd in the *House* of *Commons*, as the only true *Representative* of the *People*,
Now, face about, and Compare them to the *Tyranny* of the *Decem-viri* at *Rome*,
of the *Ephori* at *Sparta*, of the *Council* of *Four hundred* at *Athens*, of the *Commons*
at *Carthage*, and whatever can render them *Odious* to the *People*.[68]

These remarks refer unmistakably to Swift's *Contests and Dissensions*,
which had cited just these examples from ancient Greek and Roman
history to support the stance of the Whigs against the impeachment of
the Lords Partitioners.

Swift's later comments on Leslie balance praise for his churchmanship
(particularly in respect of his detestation of the secular expropriation of
church property) with blame for his political extremism.[69] Certainly one
of Leslie's targets in *The New Association*, the modern 'virtue' of moderation, which he saw as merely a fig-leaf for lukewarmness and lack of
principle, was also eventually the object of Swift's scorn.[70] That apparent
judiciousness in balancing Leslie's failings with his strengths (so rare in
Swift's comments on his contemporaries) was perhaps really a wariness
dictated by Swift's memory of the shrewdness with which Leslie had put
his finger on the awkwardness of the position he had taken up in the
Contests and Dissensions. There is no reason to think that Leslie knew that
the *Contests and Dissensions* was by Swift (in fact he seems to think it was
written by Somers). But Leslie's acuity in seeing that the Whig strategy to
defend the Lords Partitioners entailed on the part of the Whigs a reversal
('Now, face about . . .') of their more customary positions would surely
for Swift, particularly after 1710, have prompted a painful awareness of the
particular and personal inversions this episode revealed in him: writing
against Harley, for whom he would later work; writing in alliance (albeit
unconsciously) with Defoe, whose name he would later in *A Letter
Concerning the Sacramental Test* (1709) affect not to remember;[71] most
awkwardly of all, perhaps, writing in implicit support of British involvement in the War of the Spanish Succession, which he would later unre-
lentingly portray as a fiscal, political, military, and diplomatic disaster.

So when, over thirty years later, Swift inveighed against the sacrilegious
madness of the Irish House of Commons, he drew a weapon from Leslie's
armoury. He, like Leslie before him, availed himself of the trope of
'Legion' against the Whigs, who were now Swift's enemies rather than
his allies. In so doing, he added to the general self-exorcism of the devils of
rage and indignation, which we have seen at work in the poem, a more
particular purgation and atonement for his early and embarrassing enlist-
ment in the ranks of the court Whigs. As had happened already to Swift,
and would happen again a little over four years after the composition of

this poem, what had been initially only written had subsequently to be lived. Leslie's acute thrust, that in 1701 Swift had been one of those who had 'set up *Legion* against the *Commons*', is recalled, re-enacted, but also expiated, in the complicated double exorcism of 'The Legion Club'.

NOTES

The annotated page from Swift's own copy of *Miscellanies* is reproduced (p. 164) by kind permission of the Master and Fellows of Trinity College, Cambridge, which it is a pleasure gratefully to acknowledge.

1 'On the Death of Mrs. Johnson', *PW*, V, 227 and 231.
2 'I have been only a Man of Rhimes, and that upon Trifles, never having written serious Couplets in my Life; yet never any without a moral View', *Correspondence*, III, 515. In 'To Augustus', l. 341, Pope had contrasted the 'Man of Rymes' with the true poet. But to be fully a man of rhyme might equally imply a complete identification with the poetic itself (as in, to choose a broadly contemporary example where the phrase occurs without pejorative connotation, Anon., *A Letter to a Friend in the Country* [1740], p. 17).
3 Pope would later exploit half-rhyme to point up the inconsequential sequences of human life: 'See how the World its Veterans rewards! / A Youth of frolicks, an old Age of Cards' ('Epistle to a Lady', ll. 243–4; composed 1732–4). To the argument that 'aid / said' is an Irish, and therefore perfect, rhyme, it is enough to note that it would not be heard as a perfect rhyme by its English readers; cf. Jonathan Pritchard, 'Swift's Irish Rhymes', *Studies in Philology*, 104 (2007), 123–58 – a valuable essay which, however, overlooks Swift's use of half-rhyme to enforce an apartheid of listening.
4 Swift's copy is part of the Rothschild Collection, in the Wren Library, Trinity College Cambridge, shelf mark RW. 3. 5. 1422. The annotation is to be found on p. 163 of volume IV.
5 *PW*, XIII, 147–58 and 223–4.
6 Ibid., I, 169.
7 Ibid., 181.
8 For an account of the printing of Motte's 1726 editions of *Gulliver's Travels*, see the 'Textual Introduction' to my edition of *Gulliver's Travels* (Cambridge University Press, 2011).
9 *Correspondence*, III, 58–9, 79–80, 50.
10 Ibid., II, 606; III, 708.
11 Ibid., IV, 12.
12 Ibid., 575; *PW*, XI, 212.
13 John Boyle, Earl of Orrery, *Remarks on the Life and Writings of Dr. Jonathan Swift*, 2nd edn, corrected (1752), p. 19. Deane Swift, *An Essay Upon the Life, Writings, and Character, of Dr. Jonathan Swift* (1755), pp. 216–18.
14 *Correspondence*, III, 261.
15 Edward Young, *Conjectures on Original Composition* (1759), pp. 64–5.

16 *Correspondence*, III, 295.

17 *PW*, IV, 94 and 99.

18 Ibid., XIII, 8.

19 Swift to Knightley Chetwode, 23 November 1727 (*Correspondence*, III, 139).

20 Ibid., 184.

21 Ibid., 551.

22 *PW*, XII, 110 and 113.

23 Ibid., 116.

24 Ibid., 117.

25 Jonathan Swift, *Journal to Stella*, ed. Harold Williams, 2 vols. (Oxford: Clarendon Press, 1948), p. 581.

26 *PW*, xii, 220.

27 *Correspondence*, III, 192 and 194; 139; II, 486; III, 753.

28 *PW*, XII, 232.

29 Ibid., XI, 191.

30 Ibid., 194 and 195. When Gulliver calls up 'a Dozen or two of Kings with their Ancestors in order, for eight or nine Generations' (198), this is a burlesque version of *Macbeth*, IV.i.104–24.

31 *The Twickenham Edition of the Poems of Alexander Pope*, ed. John Butt *et al.*, 11 vols. (London: Methuen, 1939–69), VI, 277, ll. 33–5.

32 *Correspondence.*, III, 61.

33 Ibid., I, 104.

34 *PW*, X, 93, 111, 22.

35 *Correspondence*, II, 441.

36 *PW*, IV, 236.

37 *The Works of Jonathan Swift*, ed. Walter Scott, 16 vols. 2nd edn (Edinburgh, 1824), I, 490.

38 *The Edinburgh Review*, 27, 53 (1816), 52.

39 Ehrenpreis, III, 919.

40 See Louis A. Landa, *Swift and the Church of Ireland* (Oxford: Clarendon Press, 1954), pp. 135–50, whose account of the political background to 'The Legion Club' I compress and paraphrase in what follows.

41 Mark 5:1–20; Luke 8:26–40.

42 For a careful account of the Virgilian presence in the poem, see Peter J. Schakel, 'Virgil and the Dean: Christian and Classical Allusion in *The Legion Club*', *Studies in Philology*, 70 (1973), pp. 427–38.

43 James Boswell, *The Life of Samuel Johnson*, ed. G. B. Hill, rev. L. F. Powell, 6 vols. (Oxford: Clarendon Press, 1934–50), III, 229 n. 4; hereafter cited as Boswell.

44 *Odyssey*, X. 503–74 and XI. 1–50.

45 *PW*, XI, 224.

46 Ibid., 109.

47 Ibid., 154.

48 Ibid., I, 137–65.

49 Ibid., XI, 135–6.

50 *Samson Agonistes*, l. 1758.
51 The following account of the context of the *Contests and Dissensions* is drawn
    from that supplied by Frank Ellis in the introduction to his edition of that
    work (Oxford: Clarendon Press, 1967); hereafter cited as Ellis.
52 This particular petition was possibly stirred up by Daniel Defoe, whose *The
    History of the Kentish Petition* [1701] is an account of the episode, on which
    see Chapter 2 above.
53 *PW*, VIII, 119. Swift confuses the *five* Kentish Petitioners with the *four* Lords
    Partitioners.
54 Ellis, p. 83.
55 Ibid., p. 114.
56 Ibid., p. 124.
57 Keith Feiling, *A History of the Tory Party 1640–1714* (Oxford: Clarendon
    Press, 1924), p. 351.
58 [Daniel Defoe], *Memorial* (1701), p. 2. Many different editions of this short
    text were printed simultaneously, with 30,000 copies said to have been
    distributed throughout the country almost immediately.
59 Boswell, iv, 286 n. 3.
60 *The Rehearsal*, no. 10 (30 September, 1704), 2.
61 Luke 8:29.
62 Charles Leslie, *The History of the Church, in respect both to its ancient and
    present condition* (1706), p. 28.
63 Charles Leslie, *A Case of Present Concern, in a letter to a Member of the House
    of Commons* (1703?), p. 3.
64 *The Rehearsal*, no. 14 (28 October, 1704), 1.
65 Ibid., no. 21 (16 December, 1704), pp. 1 and 2. Cf. also ibid., no. 23
    (30 December 1704), p. 1; ibid., no. 29 (10 February 1705), p. 1; *The Wolf
    Stript* (1704), p. 75.
66 Charles Leslie, *The New Association of those Called, Moderate Church-Men,
    with the Modern-Whigs and Fanaticks* (1702), pp. 12 and 20.
67 Charles Leslie, *The New Association* (1703), p. 38.
68 Ibid., p. 29.
69 *PW*, IV, 79–80; cf. also ibid., II, 87 (on the subject of church property) and
    III, 13–14 (praising Leslie's learning and general sense, but deploring his
    politics) and 115 (Swift carefully separating himself from the non-jurors).
70 In his sermon 'On Brotherly Love', Swift would warn his congregation that
    they should 'in a particular Manner beware of that Word, *Moderation*', which
    in its modern application he detested as a bogus virtue tending to loosen men
    from their convictions (*PW*, IX, 177; cf. also 172–3 and 178; cf. also ibid., XII,
    41 for Swift's mockery of '*moderate Men*').
71 *PW*, II, 113.

CHAPTER 8

Savage indignation revisited: Swift, Yeats, and the 'cry' of liberty

Claude Rawson

The words of Swift's famous epitaph first appeared in his will, signed on 3 May 1740, some five years before he died. The will is reprinted in the Davis edition of the *Prose Writings* from Faulkner's text of *The Last Will and Testament*, 1745, which, as Davis reports, was usually bound in with volume VIII (1745) of Faulkner's edition of the *Works*. The manuscript in Swift's own hand was 'Destroyed by fire'.[1] Except for some minor details, mostly of punctuation, the marble inscription in St Patrick's Cathedral (see Figure 9) reproduces verbatim the text of the will:

> *Hic* depositum est Corpus
> IONATHAN SWIFT S.T.D.
> Hujus Ecclesiæ Cathedralis
> Decani.
> *Ubi* sæva Indignatio
> Ulterius
> Cor lacerare nequit.
> Abi Viator
> Et imitare, si poteris,
> Strenuum pro virili
> Libertatis Vindicatorem.
>
> Obiit 19 Die Mensis Octobris
> A.D. 1745. Anno Ætatis 78.[2]

The Latin is a little eccentric, and this attempt at a literal translation is necessarily awkward: 'Here is laid the Body of JONATHAN SWIFT, S. T. D., Dean of this Cathedral, Where savage indignation can no longer lacerate his heart. Go, traveller, and imitate, if you can, this strong defender, to the utmost of his powers, of liberty. He died on the 19th day of October at the age of 78.'

This epitaph is better known than most such documents. At least two of its phrases, 'saeva Indignatio' and 'Libertatis Vindicator', have often

Figure 9. Swift's epitaph in St Patrick's Cathedral, Dublin.

been used to define the character of Swift's satire, and long usage and frequent quotation have given it something of the status of a literary work in its own right. Both W. B. Yeats and T. S. Eliot engaged with it in important poems of their own. The character of this engagement, and its relation to Swift's own poetic manner, are part of the subject of this chapter.

The epitaph, as is well known, triggered several memorable writings by Yeats. John Corbet, a character in his play *The Words upon the Window-Pane* (1934), called it 'the greatest epitaph in history', adding 'It is almost finer in English than in Latin: "He has gone where fierce indignation can lacerate his heart no more."' This version, recycled in a letter to Dorothy Wellesley (Yeats seems to have attempted several versions), differs from Yeats's own earlier translation, 'Swift's Epitaph' (1931), cited in the introduction to the play:[3]

> Swift has sailed into his rest;
> Savage indignation there
> Cannot lacerate his breast.
> Imitate him if you dare,
> World-besotted traveller; he
> Served human liberty.[4]

Neither this, nor any of Yeats's other poetic invocations of the epitaph, corresponds to the characteristic manner of Swift's own English poems, which explicitly 'decline' a lofty style and prefer a Horatian levity to the grandiloquence of Juvenal, with whom (largely because of the epitaph) Swift is often misguidedly associated.

One feature of Yeats's poem is that it raises the temperature of heroic celebration, in its way already unusually high in Swift himself. For example, Yeats's 'he / Served human liberty' has declarative vibrancy, compared with Swift's more neutral 'strong defender ... of liberty', partly because of the active verb (served), and partly because of the emotive addition of 'human', not in Swift, and possibly a creative adaptation of 'pro virili', which in the Latin means 'to the utmost of his power' (*pro virili parte*). The purely factual 'Here is laid the body of JONATHAN SWIFT S.T.D.' becomes Yeats's exotic opening line, 'Swift has sailed into his rest', which appropriates Swift into a mythologised Yeatsian ancestry of adventurous seafaring merchants, including the old skipper who 'leaped overboard / After a ragged hat in Biscay Bay', one of the forefathers who endowed the poet with 'blood / That has not passed through any huckster's loin'. Another ancestor named in the same poem, the 'Introductory Rhymes' to *Responsibilities* (1914), was 'Robert Emmet's friend', the Rev. John Yeats, rector of Drumcliff, in whose church Yeats himself was to be buried. He reappears in Yeats's own epitaph, first published (unlike Swift's) in the poet's lifetime, in 'Under Ben Bulben' (1938).

This too evokes Swift's epitaph. Both Yeats's epitaph poems offer aggrandised adaptations of the phrase 'Abi Viator', 'Go traveller'. This conventional address to wayfarers, in the words of Richmond Lattimore, is found on epitaphs from 'classical times', when 'the dead were buried, for reasons hygienic or religious or both, outside of cities, and therefore the great highways became lined with tombs'.[5] It is a variant of the injunction to stay rather than go: 'Sta', 'Siste', 'Aspice', 'Cave', 'Resta'. The purpose was to 'remind those who passed by of mortality' and to 'excite' the remembrance of 'such Great Men as were represented on those stately Tombs'.[6] The commonplace character of the formula is reflected, with comic pathos, in Homais's considering of '*sta viator*' in his feverish search for an inscription for Emma Bovary at the end of Flaubert's novel.[7]

The variant '*Abi viator*' ('Go traveller') is common, often with the injunction to imitate ('*Abi, Viator, imitari quem sequeris*').[8] One recorded form is '*Abi, viator, fac simile.*'[9] It is perhaps the most basic and recurrent adjuration to the traveller, whether he is invited to go, or stay and read, though other forms of advice, including finding 'no fault with your own wife' are found.[10] Swift's 'Abi' acquires an imperious touch, partly from the challenge, 'si poteris', 'if you can'. In his rendering of 'Swift's Epitaph', Yeats escalated this to 'if you dare'. In his own epitaph at Drumcliff, which forms the last three lines of 'Under Ben Bulben', Yeats added surplus fervour:

> Under bare Ben Bulben's head
> In Drumcliff churchyard Yeats is laid.
> An ancestor was rector there
> Long years ago, a church stands near,
> By the road an ancient cross.
> No marble, no conventional phrase;
> On limestone quarried near the spot
> By his command these words are cut:
> > *Cast a cold eye*
> > *On life, on death.*
> > *Horseman, pass by!*[11]

In 1948, the words were incised on stone, as prescribed in the poem. The ancestor was the John Yeats of 'Introductory Rhymes'.

Yeats's lines are imperious, down (or up) to the proclamation, in a published poem, that there should be 'No marble, no conventional phrase ... By his command these words are cut.' This inserts considerable pomp onto the process of renouncing pomp and constitutes much more of a flourish than the 'Just my name and dates and these lines' anticipated in a private letter about two weeks before the poem was completed.[12] By contrast, Swift had insisted that his epitaph should be cut deep in black marble, and gilded, and had specifically expressed his wish for a marble monument, though he had stipulated this posthumously public display in the strict privacy of his will. The instruction was peremptory, but perhaps more anxiously emphatic than high-handed. It is Yeats's demand for simplicity, rather than Swift's prescription for a more elaborate display, that strikes the greater note of heroic ostentation. Yeats's refusal of marble, where Swift had asked for it, palpitates with the same elated grandeur with which Yeats converted the plain 'Abi Viator' into the accents, at once 'heroic' and Romantic, of 'Horseman, pass by.' That was for Yeats's own epitaph. In his version of 'Swift's Epitaph', Yeats removed from 'Abi Viator' the imperative 'Abi' ('go'), replacing it with the bare, but perhaps even more imperious, vocative, 'World-besotted traveller'. The offbeat heroics of this phrase, incidentally, evoke a crazed tourist or pilgrim in a somewhat hyperactive drama, not unlike Pope's account of poetry groupies flocking to his villa in the *Epistle to Dr Arbuthnot*, with something of the same animated self-centredness on the part of both poet and subject. Yeats, as I noted, had also introduced the theatricality of 'if you dare' in place of Swift's 'si poteris', 'if you can'.

Yeats had a pronounced sense of the splendours and miseries of being Swift, to which Swift himself might not have returned a responsive chord:

> Swift beating on his breast in sibylline frenzy blind
> Because the heart in his blood-sodden breast had dragged
>   him down into mankind ...
> *Saeva Indignatio* and the labourer's hire,
> The strength that gives our blood and state magnanimity
>   of its own desire.   ('Blood and the Moon', 1928)

Such grandly excitable self-dramatisation was even further outside the normal range of Swift's style than the *saeva indignatio* of Swift's own Latin epitaph, or than his high claim to be *Libertatis Vindicator*. The grandiloquence of Swift's epitaph, as I shall argue, belonged to a lofty style Yeats was readier to see in Swift than Swift was disposed to display. 'Beating on his breast', however, is hardly a Swiftian gesture, and there is no 'sibylline frenzy blind' in Swift's phrase about his 'lacerated' heart. The image of Swift's heart 'dragged ... down into mankind' suggests a rapture of abasement very similar to that imagined for Yeats himself, lying down, at the end of 'The Circus Animals' Desertion' (1939), 'In the foul rag-and-bone shop of the heart'. Yeats's lines belong to an altogether different register of intensity, part of an impassioned self-image Yeats projected onto Swift along with an elated misperception of his political outlook, including the conception of liberty implied in the epitaph.[13]

Almost four years after Yeats's death, Swift's epitaph and the contemplation of rage and laceration, relinquished in old age (rather than death), reappeared, in somewhat ironic circumstances, in the tribute to Yeats in T. S. Eliot's *Little Gidding* (1942), when Eliot's 'familiar compound ghost' (95) speaks of 'the conscious impotence of rage / At human folly, and the laceration / Of laughter at what ceases to amuse' (135–7). We know on his own testimony that Eliot was thinking of Swift, in association with Yeats, who has a more extensive presence in the passage, recalling the lecture Eliot had given in 1940, soon after Yeats's death. The word 'laceration' was added late, after John Hayward had drawn attention to the Latin of Swift's epitaph and expressly suggested its adoption.[14] Eliot's 'rage / At human folly' is less exalted than Yeats's, closer to the mood of defeated world-weariness implied in Swift's epitaph but perhaps more intimately confessional. It is more inward-turning than 'savage indignation' and is without the surcharge of intensity of Yeats's use of 'Saeva Indignatio' in 'Blood and the Moon'. In the Latin of the original epitaph, Swift had himself added 'saeva' as an emotive increment to Juvenal's 'indignatio', but it is the note of elation Yeats gives the phrase which makes its intensities unSwiftian.[15]

Eliot's 'familiar compound ghost' includes other poets, but the passage is extensively concerned with Yeats. It is also a homage to Swift, for whom Eliot had a great admiration. He thought Book IV of *Gulliver's Travels* 'one of the greatest triumphs that the human soul has ever achieved'.[16] He also found, in Swift's satiric quatrains and tetrameters, and the flat couplets of 'A Description of the Morning', a powerful model for some of the poems in *Prufrock and other Observations* (1917) and *Poems* (1920). What Eliot took from Swift's poems of downbeat social observation is a side of Swift to which Yeats paid scant attention. Yeats rebuked Eliot in the *Oxford Book of Modern Verse* (1936) for a flatness that some readers might think quite closely modelled on Swift, and described Eliot as 'satirist rather than poet', who seldom found the 'great manner', and as 'an Alexander Pope, working without apparent imagination'. There is a curious disconnect between this and the fact that it is Swift who studiously avoided the 'great manner', while Pope and Yeats himself both cultivated it. It is not in Pope, but in Swift, that one finds the poet describing 'men and women that get out of bed or into it from mere habit',[17] an activity, for example, which opens Swift's 'Description of the Morning', a poem with which Eliot's 'Morning at the Window' is intriguingly in dialogue.

Yet it is Swift's epitaph, alone among his writings, that speaks explicitly of savage indignation and a lacerated breast, and it is Swift who chose the phrase *saeva indignatio* for his own marble memorial. There are few impassioned defences of freedom in the poems to match the epitaph's claim of being Libertatis Vindicator, and there is little display of indignation in the only lines of verse he ever wrote that approach the form and spirit of the epitaph, namely the impartial commentator's obituary towards the end of the *Verses on the Death of Dr Swift*:

> 'Fair LIBERTY was all his Cry;
> 'For her he stood prepared to die;
> 'For her he boldly stood alone;
> 'For her he oft expos'd his own.
> 'Two Kingdoms, just as Faction led,
> 'Had set a Price upon his Head;
> 'But, not a Traytor cou'd be found,
> 'To sell him for Six Hundred Pound.   (347–54)

The opening lines almost seem designed for a memorial tablet and are not unYeatsian. There is also no doubt that Swift thought he deserved the praise and would consider it a just tribute to his role as the Hibernian Patriot.

The somewhat less marmoreal lines about the two kingdoms refer, as is explained in the note in the Faulkner edition (1739), to the two occasions in which a price of £300 was put on the 'discovery' of the author, namely the appearance of *The Publick Spirit of the Whigs* in 1714 and '*The Drapier's Fourth Letter*' in 1724, a symmetry which establishes that the defence of 'Fair LIBERTY' was not restricted to Irish interests, as a reader of 1731 or 1739 might assume, but also extended to England, and was thus more than a matter of Irish patriotism. The earlier episode had been recalled in 1714, in another autobiographical poem, 'The Author upon Himself', where Swift spoke of 'a Proclamation spread / To fix a Price on his devoted Head' (59–60). At the time, Swift enjoyed considerable official protection and coyly acknowledges the finessing by powerful protectors of the case against him: 'thus watchful Friends preserve him by a Sleight'.[18] But the concession is also a boast of friends in high places, and this hint of deflation in any case comes only after the affirmation that 'While Innocent, he scorns ignoble Flight' (ll. 62, 61). This grandly declarative line teeters on the brink of a self-inflation through which Swift sometimes signalled intimations of self-mockery, if only as a defensive guard. Such is the status of heroic utterance at this period that straight heroic declarations can have a strutting exaggeration which seems close to parody. The words could easily find themselves at home in a declamatory heroic tragedy of the sort Fielding was to mock in the *Tragedy of Tragedies*. In any event, the poet's gestures of self-exaltation are oscillating and unwholehearted.

'The Author upon Himself' is a poem of unusually raw feeling, indignant, paying off scores, and withheld from publication until Faulkner's edition of 1735. It is unusual also in being in heroic couplets, a form Swift shrank from, as tending to the 'lofty Stile' he avoided, and also, or so one might infer from some scattered remarks, in deference to Pope's mastery of the form. The couplets, even here, are hardly Popeian, with some informalities and roughnesses of language and metre, and very little of Pope's definitional triumphalism.

The 'Liberty' Swift said he served was concerned with freeing the Anglo-Irish colonial establishment from interference by London. It had little to do with colonial emancipation in the abstract and nothing with democratic egalitarianism or universal suffrage. Yeats understood at least this when he said 'I remember his epitaph and understand that the liberty he served was that of intellect, not liberty for the masses but for those who could make it visible.'[19] It is possible, as Yeats's most authoritative biographer has suggested, that Yeats thought Swift would be sympathetic to a Mussolinian state.[20] Underlying this disconcerting perception is Torchiana's observation, chiefly borne out in the Introduction to *The Words upon the Window-Pane*, that, as Yeats understood Swift, both defended an older order they saw as giving way to a new: 'external, sentimental, logical, democratic, and optimistic Whiggery'.[21]

Whether Swift himself held such views, and whatever the ideological nuances of the epitaph's professed militancy, it is evident that even in the *Verses* he has taken care to distance himself. Unlike similar declarations by Pope or Yeats, the words are spoken not by the author but by an 'impartial' commentator, a fact of which the reader is kept unremittingly aware by the contemporary typographical practice of putting quotation marks at the beginning of every line. Although the tetrameters of 'Fair LIBERTY was all his Cry' have a declarative glow, they do not fully release their own grandeurs, as though Swift would not risk, even through the impartial obituarist, the fervour, or 'strong driving force', which Yeats was able to infuse into short metres.[22] Swift's lines stand out, in a brief but splendid isolation, in a poem whose general manner is that of a more or less light-hearted causerie. Their marmoreal affirmations share the same metre as the protracted badinage of '"the Dean is dead, (*and what is Trumps?*)"' (228), which pervades the earlier parts of the poem, and whose Hudibrastic cadences set much of its tone. The extended passage by the 'impartial' obituarist, as has often been pointed out, is itself full of coy self-undercutting and coded jokes like the couplet '"To steal a Hint was never known, / But what he writ was all his own"'

(317–18), which is itself partly lifted from Denham's poem *On Mr. Abraham Cowley* (1667, 29–30).[23]

Swift was normally and on principle not at home with high talk of any sort and made a point of leaving such things to his admired friend Pope, whose self-celebrating grandiloquence is much closer to Yeats, though Yeats (perhaps partly for this reason) had a distaste for Pope. It is Yeats who assumed a not unPopeian arrogant fervour, down to the proud sweep and cadence of a high pentameter for which Swift admired Pope and which he shied from emulating. It is not fanciful to think that a Yeatsian couplet like 'Think where man's glory most begins and ends, / And say my glory was I had such friends' is closer, in cadence and temper, to the elated self-assertiveness of Pope's *Epilogue to the Satires* than Yeats would want to admit, or than Swift, who loved and respected Pope, would consider attempting.[24]

Swift's avoidance of grand manners and Pope's predilection for them conceal a likeness between Yeats and Pope, whom Yeats 'disliked' (actually 'loathed') but was 'fascinated' by. Reading Edith Sitwell's admiring biography of Pope in April 1930, Yeats found 'in Bolingbroke the last pose and in Swift the last passion of the Renaissance, in Pope whom I dislike an imitation of both pose and passion'.[25] Arguably there is a shared allure of pose as well as passion in both Yeats and Pope, which Swift shrank from as likely to misfire. Swift could not easily assume, in his own name, in defence of that fair liberty his poem says he served, the kind of ringing statement that came easily to his friend Pope: 'Yes, the last Pen for Freedom let me draw, / When Truth stands trembling on the edge of Law' (*Epilogue to the Satires*, II. 248–9). Pope was so far from transferring his self-affirmations to an invented speaker that he would, in his Imitation of the *First Satire of the Second Book of Horace* (1733), redirect to himself compliments Horace paid to Lucilius. The fervid superbia of the couplet from Pope's *Epilogue*, a poem published the year before Swift's *Verses*, has more than a little in common with some of Yeats's impassioned affirmations, and perhaps more in common with Yeatsian exaltation than with the angry Juvenalian majesties Pope is partly emulating.

Pope's critics sometimes speak of the great Imitator of Horace as being in many ways Juvenalian, whereas the purportedly Juvenalian Swift, who spoke in the epitaph of his own 'saeva Indignatio', would side-step both the fervour and the superbia, more than once pinning his satirical flag to a Horatian mast. In refusing the addressee of *An Epistle to a Lady*, who wanted verses 'in the Heroick Stile', it is Horace whom he invoked (198–9), describing the lofty style, whether in panegyric or satire, as 'against my natural Vein' (136), likely to create for him a 'Figure scurvy' (219). Although indignation against enemies is not disavowed, and he exclaims that 'I would hang them if I cou'd' (170), his plan is not to destroy or denounce but to induce discomfiture and alarm. The *Epistle* is a poem of deceptively playful badinage, a fact which should not be allowed to obscure how important it is as a declaration of Swift's poetic principles, of his deep temperamental uneasiness with high talk, of his feeling that satirical 'bastings' were ineffective, and of the needling aggressiveness of his view that 'a little gentle Jerking / Sets the Spirits all a working'. This is represented, correctly or not, as a Horatian urbanity, not at all Juvenalian, whose lighthearted manner, in Swift's version of it, is designed to induce edginess and an undignified readerly panic (198–206).

The impartial commentator was a necessity, since Swift wanted his compliments to be paid, though even that commentator could not speak without an element of irony as long as he was scripted by Swift himself. An unironic tribute to Swift along the lines of the *Verses* was in fact provided by Pope, in his *Epistle to Augustus*, not in a mode of defiant affirmation but of respectful and affectionate sobriety:

> Let Ireland tell, how Wit upheld her cause,
> Her Trade supported, and supply'd her Laws;
> And leave on Swift this grateful verse ingrav'd,
> The Rights a Court attack'd, a Poet sav'd.
> Behold the hand that wrought a Nation's cure,
> Stretch'd to relieve the Idiot and the Poor,
> Proud Vice to brand, or injur'd Worth adorn,
> And stretch the Ray to Ages yet unborn.
>   (Pope, *First Epistle of the Second Book of Horace, Imitated*, 1737, 221–8)

These lines, a dedicated digression from the Horatian original, contain the gist of the 'impartial' obituary, down to the closing remarks about Swift's intended bequests, without any of Swift's self-mockery. A further ironic symmetry was that the Privy Council considered arresting Pope for his tribute to Swift's opposition to Wood's Halfpence.[26] They were published on 25 May 1737. Swift had remarked in a letter of 2 December 1736 that 'my Acquaintance resent that they have not seen my name at the head' of one of Pope's 'Epistles of Morality' and evidently felt a deep desire to be written about publicly in this way.

Whether or not Pope's lines were a response to this request, such solicitations seem to have been part of a reciprocal habit. Pope had asked

Swift in 1729 to record their friendship in verse, to which Swift's response was the passage beginning 'Hail! happy *Pope*, whose gen'rous Mind, / Detesting all the Statesmen kind' in the *Libel on Doctor Delany* (1730; 71–88), composed in Swift's informal tetrameters rather than stately couplets.[27] Swift characteristically described them as '18 lines relating to your self, in the most whimsical paper that ever was writ, and which was never intended for the Publick', which caused political embarrassment to Pope and therefore elicited mixed reactions.[28]

Just as in the later letter to Charles Wogan, where he professed himself 'only a Man of Rhimes', who never wrote 'serious Couplets,' he told Pope he had been hesitant to celebrate their friendship because of feeling upstaged, until he remembered Fulke Greville's epitaph, describing himself as 'friend to Sir Philip Sidney'.[29] The shadow of the feared 'Figure scurvy' hovers over both declarations. Over and above these ritual reciprocities, Swift's request for a Horatian epistle evinces an accentuated aspiration for such a tribute. Pope had previously told Swift in March 1736 of his intention, 'If ever I write more Epistles in Verse', to address one to Swift which 'would make what bears your name ... more finished than any of the rest'. That intention was not formally executed, but Pope evidently showed Swift the passage from the *Epistle to Augustus* before publication, to which Swift responded that the lines 'are to do me the greatest honour I shall ever receive from posterity, and will out-weigh the malignity of ten thousand enemies'.[30]

The obliquities of self-projection in the *Verses*, often too elusive to pin down, are compounded by the device of the disinterested obituarist who 'My Character impartial draws!', designed to uncouple Swift from lines which were after all about himself and scripted by himself. In the early years of the Ph.D. era, we, or our teachers, used to bring in 'the masks of Jonathan Swift' to cope with such situations, just as we issue wise reminders to our students that Gulliver, or the speaker of the *Tale of a Tub*, or the Modest Proposer, is not Swift. One supposes that Swift was spared any premonition of these nightmares of the classroom. But one might be justified in regarding them as a collective manifestation of a form of point-missing he rejoiced to discover in unwary readers, like the bishop in Ireland who opined that *Gulliver's Travels* 'was full of improbable lies, and for his part, he hardly believed a word of it'.[31]

The reality is, of course, that yes, the impartial obituarist is not Swift, just as *Gulliver's Travels* is not a true narrative. In this sense, of course, Gulliver and the Tale-teller and Proposer are variously not Swift, and I suppose we have to imagine that there may have been a time when some

readers had to be reminded of this. But it is even more important to
understand that they are also *not* not Swift, in the sense that in every
sentence, every rhetorical feint, every fictional speaker, there is always a
Swiftian presence insinuating itself through that speaker, which may or
may not be literally endorsing what the speaker says, but which cannot be
discounted any more than they can be taken literally or baldly attributed.
There is, behind the layers of fictional detachment, a Swiftian commitment to Gulliver's misanthropy to which Yeats responded near the end of
his life when he spoke of (and indeed associated himself with) the 'Irish
hatred and solitude, the hatred of human life that made Swift write
Gulliver and the epitaph upon his tomb', reverting perhaps for the last
time in his writings to his own obsession with Swift's *saeva indignatio.*[32]
The fact that the precise proportion of authorial commitment is seldom
the same from sentence to sentence is a characteristic Swiftian signature,
conveying truths through speakers who are excessive, or foolish, or merely
other, in a manner that dissociates the author in a formal sense while
leaving an unmistakeable authorial aura.

From what I assume to be Swift's perspective, you are equally 'bit' if
you believe literally what Gulliver says in Book IV, and if you think you
can discount it because in a formal sense he is not Swift. It is one of Swift's
ways of vexing the world rather than diverting it, doubtless capturing in
its net the explicators and persona advocates of the academy, not least
because few of them felt very vexed (I'm not sure they seem very diverted
either). The truth of masks or *personae* is that they are themselves as much
part of what is being communicated as the content of their speech, and
that the author himself created the mask as well as scripting the speech.
He bears responsibility not only for his overt statements, but for those
indirections by which we do or don't find directions out, and indeed for
the act of indirection itself. Some words of Kurt Vonnegut seem to say it
all: 'We are what we pretend to be, so we must be careful about what we
pretend to be.'[33]

The impartial obituarist of the *Verses on the Death* should not be made
to bear the weight of so much theory. It does not fit the blend of casual
earnestness and cheeky flippancy with which Swift invests the obituarist's
statement. He is, anyway, as these things go, much closer to his author
than the extravagant narrators of the great prose satires, and what he has
to say in the lines about liberty bears a close relation to how we may
assume Swift would seriously have liked to be spoken of. So the question
might be asked, why invent the obituarist, instead of speaking in his own
name? Of course, the poem imagines Swift to be dead, but he could

have scripted the obituary as a statement of how he would like to be remembered, just as he did himself compose the epitaph in the Cathedral. The substance itself of the lines is no more meant to be undercut than the epitaph is, but the lines are framed in a context of mild but distinct self-mockery, as though Swift wanted you to think he was not taking himself quite so seriously, as well as not speaking them 'himself' in the first place. The trick deceives no one, as Swift would know, but it keeps up appearances. In this, he is quite different from both Yeats and Pope, whose ways of keeping up appearances were of a different order.

This, it seems to me, defines the distance between the epitaph and the poems, as well as the intimate connection between them. It helps to explain the need for the impartial obituarist, reversing Vonnegut's phrase about being what we pretend to be, making of Swift in this instance what he pretends not to be, an overturning which, like so many such opposites, is really only a minor adjustment of its counterpart. Even the impartial obituarist, in his fit of unSwiftian grandeur, is allowed a Swiftian hint of self-undercutting, fair liberty being merely said to be 'all his Cry', as it were a routine, or a peddling of wares, though he was prepared to die for her. The OED gives a single (roughly contemporary) analogue to Swift's phrase, under the word 'crier': 'Simplicity is all their cry' (1748).[34] Swift had a lively interest in hawkers' 'cries'. He wrote with wry gusto about how they would 'cry' a 'last speech' from the gallows or a malicious 'Satyr', and his own poems include hawkers' cries for apples, asparagus, 'onyons', oysters, herrings, and oranges.[35] So it would be surprising if 'all his Cry' did not carry muted intimations of a hawker for liberty staging his show.

The zone of interplay between sublimity and performative showmanship, the panache of the circus-artist or the principled eloquence of the drunken sage, is one which Yeats explored more knowingly than Swift, not only in the beggar poems of various periods, but in the late poems 'Beautiful Lofty Things', 'High Talk', and 'The Circus Animals' Desertion', which belong to the last two years of his life.

'High Talk' (1938), which announces that 'Processions that lack high stilts have nothing that catches the eye', is not written in any of the usual forms of lofty style found in Yeats's various evocations of Swift's epitaph.

> Malachi Stilt-Jack am I, whatever I learned has run wild,
> From collar to collar, from stilt to stilt, from father to child.
> All metaphor, Malachi, stilts and all. A barnacle-goose

Far up in the stretches of night; night splits and the dawn breaks loose.
I, through the terrible novelty of light, stalk on, stalk on;
Those great sea-horses bare their teeth and laugh at the dawn.[36]

Neither the fiery epiphany nor the surreal wildness of this high talk would
be imaginable in Swift, and they are equally outside the range of Pope's
elevated speech. With the partial exception of 'Blood and the Moon', they
differ also from the high talk of Yeats's evocations of Swift's epitaph,
discussed at the beginning of this essay. The barnacle-goose is an arctic
bird which visits British coasts in winter. It is a recurrent and eruptive
high-point in Yeats's imagination as early as the *Wanderings of Oisin*
(1889) and by 1914 is part of the poetry of his beggars:

'And there I'll ...
... hear amid the garden's nightly peace,'
Beggar to beggar cried, being frenzy-struck,
'The wind-blown clamour of the barnacle-geese.'[37]

This evocation of wild natural forces is part of a Yeatsian sublime,
associated with the 'wisdom' of beggars, which is also a 'frenzy' not
unconnected with Yeats's idea of Swift's *saeva indignatio*. It is not, however,
part of the furniture of the Swiftian mind, though a secondary association
of the barnacle with confidence tricksters or swindlers, reported in
the OED and found in Greene and Dekker (1591, 1608), might not be
foreign to Swift and is germane to the figure of Malachi in 'High Talk'.[38]

The heady hint of exalted charlatanism, which Swift inserted almost as
a defensive tic in his evocation of the hawker's cry, became for Yeats a
matter of grand declarative display, not without its own diablerie of
pretended self-undermining. The high-handed self-dismissal of Yeats's
concession that 'Malachi, stilts and all' are merely 'all metaphor' shows
that what for Swift was an instinctive circumvention of the lofty style
turned for Yeats into a primary form of high expression. Swift was not
indifferent to displays of individual grandeur of the sort listed in Yeats's
'Beautiful Lofty Things' (1938), almost a companion piece to 'High Talk',
which includes among its heroic epiphanies the snapshot of 'Standish
O'Grady supporting himself between the tables / Speaking to a drunken
audience high nonsensical words'.[39] Swift compiled a prose list '*Of those
who have made great* FIGURES *in some particular Action or Circumstance
of their Lives*', though Swift did not, in Yeats's way, mythologise himself
and his friends into it, and characteristically supplied a second list
'*Of those who have made a mean contemptible Figure*'.[40] Still less did Swift
overtly take on Malachi Stilt-Jack's idiom of exalted clownerie, in which

the trickster, the jester, the itinerant confidence-man, are resublimated in a manner we don't often meet before the nineteenth century, when, for example, Baudelaire admired the high-intensity zaniness of a kleptomaniac Punch in an English farce.[41]

Yeats does not seem to have spoken much about Baudelaire, whose name (along with many others) he seemed unable to spell, though he was evidently exposed to the climate of his critical ideas, and Baudelaire is repeatedly mentioned over the years when Yeats was taking notes for *A Vision* (1925).[42] Though his interest in Baudelaire was limited, Yeats is no more likely to have escaped a generalised exposure to Baudelaire, still less to ideas to whose circulation Baudelaire contributed, than any other poet of his time. Baudelaire's famous essay 'De L'Essence du rire' (1855) is among the texts which helped to make familiar the idea that high effects of art could be generated by performances of slapstick or trickery generally regarded as demotic or louche. Baudelaire's appreciation for the way pantomime handles 'great disasters and a tumultuous destiny' with bursts of laughter and a delirium of dance opens up an imaginative terrain hospitable to the surges of enchantment of Yeats's Malachi or his beggars.[43]

Baudelaire was probing a fault-line in neoclassical taste to which Yeats was equally unsympathetic. Baudelaire thought of it as specifically French when he praised the 'monstrueuses farces' of English pantomime, a phrase Voltaire had reprovingly applied to Shakespearean tragedies.[44] Baudelaire identified Voltaire with a characteristically French shrinking from ferocity and the excessive, though in fact even Voltaire was in some degree drawn to the dimension of 'barbaric' freedom in English art, what Baudelaire described as an 'énormité britannique' seasoned with gore and blasphemous oaths.[45] Some ambivalence about Shakespearean tragedy, and the English stage in general, was also felt by English writers. Fielding parodied the multiple slaughters at the end of Shakespeare's plays, remarking on the way '*modern Tragedy ... made* Farce *with* Tragedy *unite*'.[46] The phrase echoed the not altogether unmixed contempt expressed in Pope's *Dunciad* for that poetic zone where 'Farce and Epic get a jumbled Race' (*Dunciad* I. 70; *1729*, I. 68), a region where Yeats sometimes moved with magnificent freedom. In Swift such a figure as Baudelaire's English Pierrot or Punch, with his thieving habits, would scathingly evoke the mountebank and the stage itinerant of *A Tale of a Tub*, or the incompetent poets in *On Poetry: A Rapsody* (1733), 'famed for Numbers soft and smooth, / By Lovers spoke in *Punch's* Booth' and 'lofty Lines in *Smithfield* Drols' (297–300).

The most extended treatment of Punch, or clowns or drolls, in Swift's poems is a group of satires of Irish politicians of which the best-known example is *Mad Mullinix and Timothy* (1728).[47] The principal figure is Mullinix, 'a half-crazed beggar' called Tom Molyneux, 'who went round Dublin spouting Tory sentiments', and who is possibly also Tom in the attack on Lord Allen in *Traulus*.[48] Mullinix (or Mullinex) appears in a number of poems, paired with the 'vehement Whig' Richard Tighe (alias Timothy).[49]

> In doleful Scenes, that break our heart,
> Punch comes, like you, and lets a F—t.
> There's not a Puppet made of Wood,
> But what wou'd hang him if they cou'd.   (121–4)

Swift's Punch is no Malachi Stilt-Jack stalking high on stilts. His exploit is clownish farting, not striding through 'the terrible cruelty of light' to the cry of the barnacle-goose and sea-horses laughing at the dawn. Malachi is the prophet of the last book of the Old Testament, and the name of an Irish king and a medieval saint, but it is also that of Buck Mulligan in Joyce's *Ulysses*, who thinks the name is 'absurd' but 'has a Hellenic ring'.[50] It occurs as a name in Yeats's plays. In the poem, more specifically, Stilt-Jack suggests a circus performer.[51] There is a note of haughty, inspired charlatanism in this self-caricature, well captured in Brian Farrington's centenary pamphlet on the poet, which speaks of 'his pride in his own freakish outrageousness': 'the more he mocked himself the more arrogant he became'.[52] The poem is close in date to 'The Circus Animals' Desertion', with its 'stilted boys' (published January 1939, but both poems evidently completed in August and September 1938), and the paradoxical affirmation of 'High Talk' in circus mode is the counterpart or obverse of the exalted abasement of the rag-and-bone shop, 'where all the ladders start'.[53]

Yeats's 'High Talk' is thus different from the 'lofty Stile' Swift made a point of 'declining' in the *Epistle to a Lady* (218), a poem now understood to be close in date to the Mullinix poems and sharing with them some revealing features of phrasing and satiric preoccupation. The semi-playful idea that the satiric victim ought to be hanged (*Mullinix* 124, *Epistle* 170), which bursts through the frivolities of slapstick farting and puppet-show rant, is one such feature. The idiomatic expression (as we still say someone 'ought to be shot') is subject to socially recognized indirections I have considered at greater length elsewhere. We 'mean' it, don't mean it, and don't not mean it, so that a residual element of primary aggression always attaches to the phrase and may, as much as anything in Swift's poems, be thought to approximate (in the form of Swift's many death curses on beggars, bankers, and others) to the *saeva indignatio* of the epitaph.

Mullinix's remark that Timothy's fellow politicians 'wou'd hang him if they cou'd' calls to mind Swift's declaration, in the very act of declining the lofty style in favour of a lighter Horatian mode of attack on 'the Nation's Representers', that while their madness makes him merry, and he spends his rage in a jest, 'I would hang them if I cou'd' (*Epistle to a Lady*, 155–70).[54] In *An Epistle to a Lady* (1733 but possibly composed in 1728 and thus roughly contemporary with *Mad Mullinix*), Swift seems almost pointedly to be using the same words as Mullinix for what Swift wanted to do to his enemies.[55] In the lines in which Tom says Tim is 'the *Punch* to stir up trouble in; You Wrigle, Fidge, and make a Rout ... in a perpetual Round, To Teize, Perplex, Disturb, Confound' (138–46), the behaviour of Tim and his Brother Puppets resembles or mimics what the speaker of the *Epistle* wants to achieve when he proposes to apply 'ALECTO's Whip, / Till they wriggle, howl, and skip' (*Epistle*, 179–80).

The puppets are thus doing to each other, in a perverse sense, what Swift's *Epistle* intends for the victims of his satire, as the declared result of the poet's agenda for vexing the world. The disgusting behaviour attributed to Timothy's anti-Jacobite witch-hunt, 'In every A— you run your Snout, / To find this Damn'd *Pretender* out' (25–6), bears more than a little resemblance to what the satirist proposes to do with 'the Nation's Representers': 'Let me, though the Smell be Noisom, / Strip their Bums; Let Caleb hoyse' em' (*Epistle*, 156, 177–8). The lines describe with a rare explicitness the intimacy of satirical confrontation Swift often envisages, close up and not shrinking from indignities. The rejoicing in discomfiture is a special quality of Swift's irony, in both prose and verse. In the later poems on Irish politicians, the scatological cursing, the language of farts and bums, is put to the service of a quarrelsome intimacy not dissimilar in some ways to the manner of *Gulliver's Travels*. Though the punitive activity envisaged in the *Epistle* is carried out by Caleb D'Anvers, pseudonymous author of the *Craftsman*, there is no sense of self-distancing, more a gleeful participation on the satirist's part. Such participation as there is in the impartial obituarist of the *Verses on the Death* is an altogether less open complicity.

Swift's hanging remarks in the *Epistle* are hedged with accents of flippancy or mock-flippancy, like the obituarist's discourse in the *Verses on the Death*, with its boast about fair Liberty, though in the *Epistle* Swift is speaking in his own voice rather than by proxy. In *Mad Mullinix and Timothy* the hanging wish is, as in the *Verses*, delivered by proxy, and indeed at two removes. It is spoken by the mad beggar, who is actually reporting the wishes of a collective third party, many of whom may themselves be regarded as likely targets of the satire along with Timothy/Tighe. Mullinix goes on to lecture Tim on how, as 'Philosophers suppose, / *The World consists of Puppet-shows*' (133–4), and on how political Dublin accords with the formula:

> So at this Booth, which we call *Dublin*,
> *Tim* thou'r't the *Punch* to stir up trouble in;
> You Wrigle, Fidge, and make a Rout
> Put all your brother Puppets out,
> Run on in a perpetual Round,
> To Teize, Perplex, Disturb, Confound,
> Intrude with Monkey grin, and clatter
> To interrupt all serious Matter,
> Are grown the Nuissance of your *Clan*,
> Who hate and scorn you, to a Man.   (137–46)

Swift's way of regarding the world as a fairground show is in a lower key than Yeats's circus animals, for all that they descend into the foul rag-and-bone shop, itself a low place claiming a very high talk. In some respects, they are a satirical version of Yeats's whirling drunken beggars, who 'mauled and bit the whole night through'.[56] A closer modernist counterpart to Swift's political puppet show might be Jarry's *Ubu roi*, one of the inheritors of Baudelaire's fascination with English puppet-shows, at whose tumultuous first night in 1896 Yeats was fascinated and saddened, famously remarking 'After us the Savage God'.[57]

Tighe is sometimes called Dick as well as Timothy. In 'Tom Mullinex and Dick' (not published until 1745), Tom, 'a Foot-Boy bred and born', is described as more or less literate ('*Tom* cou'd write and spell his Name'), while Dick, though of ignominious origins, 'had seen a College':[58]

> *Dick* a Coxcomb, *Tom* was mad,
>   And both alike diverting,
> *Tom* was held the merrier lad,
>   But *Dick* the best at f—rting.

In this sharp but spirited account, the mad Tom is not only merry, but 'kind and loving' and possessed of 'deep discerning'. The altogether less attractive Dick is a master of the grosser puppet-show skills. His prowess in farting is a feature of most poems about Tighe. In the companion poem 'Dick's Variety' (also published in 1745), '*Dick* can f—rt, and dance and frisk, No other Monkey half so brisk' (25–6), also the theme of the better-known 'Tim and the *Fables*', where Tighe identifies himself with the engraving of a dandified monkey in Gay's recently published *Fables* (1727).[59] Tighe-Tim-Dick is repeatedly portrayed as applying these skills, unsuccessfully, but with rather desperate merriment, to the puppet-show of Dublin politics, a recurrent image in these poems.

Mullinix and Timothy may in some ways be assimilated to the wild beggars of Yeats's imaginative pantheon. Swift has been thought to have a part in shaping Yeats's Crazy Jane and related figures at a time when Yeats was reading 'Swift for months together', almost exactly two centuries later. Swift was no secret sharer in Yeats's 'Dream of the noble and the beggar-man'.[60] Mullinix is nevertheless a truth-telling street madman, who says things Swift said or would say himself, when he exposes Timothy's political posturing and partisan zealotry as bordering on the clinically mad. This fanatically partisan Whig's alarmist ravings about Jacobite plots are ridiculed and detested by his own side and are an asset to the Tories Timothy detests. Mullinix says Timothy will only succeed in attracting attention if he joins Mullinix's crew of mad beggars, borrowing Mullinix's clothes and mimick-ing his antics (211 ff.). He is told to adopt their efforts to 'walk upright' and reform the age, lash its lewdness, and behave with political rectitude rather than partisan corruption (251 ff.). Timothy repents and agrees to join the motley fraternity, acceding to the classic scenario of the mad beggar as a model of virtue which shows up the shortcomings of the political establish-ment. Mad Mullinix here fills something of the role of Yeats's wild clear-sighted beggars, though his moral tone is hardly Yeatsian, and it would be hard to sustain in a literal sense Yeats's claim that Swift 'understood that wisdom comes of beggary'.[61] All Swift's comments on beggars, fitter to be rooted from the face of the earth than cause a tax to be levied for their upkeep in Dublin, would demonstrate this if nothing else did.[62]

Nevertheless, Mullinix has a kind of rightness, and his excoriation of Tighe is conducted in an atmosphere of at least ostensibly good-humoured geniality. If Swift is not genially disposed towards Tighe, Mullinix and Timothy seem to share an extra-parliamentary friendship, as of off-duty politicians enacting the street solidarity of a beggarly fellowship. There is none of the high-intensity truth-enforcing of Yeats's Crazy Jane and her kind, but Timothy accepts Mullinix's invitation to join the jovial crew in a harmonious discarding of partisanship which is prepared to call a plague on both their parties (284).

The poem appeared in the *Intelligencer* in June–July 1728 and was followed a few days later by 'Tim and the *Fables*'.[63] The latter poem was given an ironic introduction, written by Thomas Sheridan, also celebrating the end of party divisions and a resultant national prosperity.[64]

In the poem itself, Tim is said to identify himself with the monkey in the engraving that accompanies 'The Monkey Who Had Seen the World', No. xiv in Gay's recently published *Fables* (1727), who is portrayed as a hunch-backed but dandified Punch or Thersites, the 'hateful hideous *Grecian*' identified in the earlier poem as Timothy's blood relation (51–2).[65] Gay's monkey has learned the depraved ways of human society while serving as a pet to a fine lady. Having managed to escape, he decides 'To civilize the monkey weal' (22) by teaching them 'to copy human ways' (59). Gay's harsh parable is applied to the progress of a young human hero who, 'Studious of ev'ry coxcomb's airs', grows up in all the fashionable vices: 'He drinks, games, dresses, whores and swears' and scorns 'all virtuous arts', having, like the monkey, become vicious (63–6).[66]

The monkey achieved this through the appeal of his 'embroider'd coat', 'dapper periwig', and 'flutt'ring shoulder-knot', much admired by the 'hairy sylvans' of his own tribe (25–34). The image of this in the engraving is what, in 'Tim and the *Fables*', makes Tim recognise himself in the portrait, and he is 'smitten' with the portrait until he reads Gay's payoff. In the last four lines, written by Sheridan, the poet, or Mullinix, tries to calm Tim, in the idiom of the Caleb of the *Epistle to a Lady*:

> Dear *Tim*, no more such angry Speeches,
> Unbutton and let down your Breeches,
> Take out the Tale, and wipe your A—
> I know you love to act a *Farce*.　　　(35–8)

These last four lines were written by Sheridan, but are very much in the spirit of Swift's poem, though Swift later deprecated them as 'slovenly', and spoke of the whole poem as 'very uncorrect, but against a fellow we all hated'.[67] Before coming upon the poem's moral, Tim is delighted with his resemblance to the monkey and praises the engraver in answerable style with the usual routines of Punchinello:

> The Twist, the Squeeze, the Rump, the Fidge an' all,
> Just as they lookt in the Original.
> By — says *Tim* (and let a F—t)
> This Graver understood his Art.　　　(17–20)

The twisting, squeezing, and 'fidging' replace Gay's own more conventional list of antics, drinking, gaming, dressing, whoring, swearing. Swift's poem focuses less on Tim's moral depravity than on his frantic comportment, a dandified counterpart to that of Jack in *A Tale of a Tub*.

It is possible that in the Mullinix poems Swift had not found language to express such purposes with the *Epistle*'s tang of stinging lightheartedness, using the language used in the *Epistle*, but in a more heavy-handed idiom of strenuous clowning not altogether natural to Swift. *Mad Mullinix*, of course, is directed outwards, excoriating an enemy, not describing Swift's own satirical practices, though the teasing resemblances, as so often, show the intricacies of relationship between Swift and the objects of his satire, as well as between the styles he practices and those he disavows. It is perhaps only the protective flippancy of the *Epistle to a Lady* that permitted him to define his manner so precisely, much as in the *Verses on the Death* a frame of badinage permits the emergence of a self-celebration he would otherwise have found awkward to pass off.

This traffic between Swift and his victim, as well as his speakers, is elaborately evident in the two poems *Traulus* (1730), but in a format of invective which the *Epistle* is disavowing. In the first of these, the madman Tom, probably Mullinix again, attacks another of Swift's *bêtes noires*, Viscount Allen, who sought the prosecution of the printer and author of *A Libel on Dr. Delany*, and who had denounced in the Privy Council the award of what Swift described in his will as 'the Gold Box in which the Freedom of the City of *Dublin* was presented to me'. The name Traulus (Greek τραυλός means 'lisping') alludes to Allen's 'stut-tut-tut-er' (47), which gives a grotesque allure to his 'sputtering', 'slavering', and 'barking' against the 'Nation-saving' author of the *Drapier's Letters*.[68] Tom virulently attacks this politician, calling him worse than a Bedlamite (23 ff.), a mad dog who deserves to be shot (35 ff.), and is possessed by the Devil (70 ff.). Tom speaks with exceptional violence, and the link between Swift and his mad speaker, a righteously enraged Tory, is, even more than in the case of Gulliver's misanthropic diatribes, unsettlingly close, even as Swift can formally dissociate himself from the excessive utterance, what he called 'Timons Manner' in the famous letter to Pope of 29 September 1725.[69] But Tom's closing lines involve a comparison of Swift with Allen himself. As Swift's biographer Ehrenpreis says, the implication is that Swift himself is mad for 'wishing to free people who deserve slavery', a recurrent theme in Swift's poems. 'Thus,' Ehrenpreis adds, 'in a typical leap of self-satire, the poet merges with the madman who has been speaking for him':[70]

> Yet still the D— on Freedom raves,
> His Spirit always strives with slaves.

> 'Tis Time at last to spare his Ink,
> And let them rot, or hang, or stink.   (99–102)

These petulantly theatrical lines, like most death-dealing outbursts
(of which there are many in Swift's work), are part of a rhetoric of
obviously untenable excess, which is the enabling condition for saying the
thing at all. Thus Tom's madness is not the festive clownery of Mullinix.
Like the latter he is enraged because Traulus, instead of promoting
Jacobite scares, makes intemperate attacks on Swift, and there is a straight
man called Robin (Robert Leslie, son of the non-juror Charles Leslie) who
advocates tolerance because Traulus's 'Head is crackt' (6), like Tim's, by
party. Ehrenpreis describes the poem as 'a dialogue between a sane man and
a lunatic, with Swift's voice rising through both parts'.[71] Swift has in fact
scripted all three speakers so that the madman who attacks Swift is mirrored
by a maddened Dean, 'raving' about freedom, who offers the familiar
stereotype of the hero satirist crazed by the world's depravity.

Mad Tom is a castigator, not a seer. He expresses an old irony that in
a wicked world, only the mad are sane, even when their condition, like
Tom's or the Modest Proposer's, is pathological (in the latter case in a
moral even more than a clinical sense). I have argued that Tom's madness,
like Gulliver's, enables Swift to say certain things. The sequel to *Traulus*,
published as 'the Second Part' later the same year, continues the attack
on Lord Allen without the dialogue form.[72] It was reissued in 1732 as
'Thersites: Or, The Lordling', presumably without Swift's authority, but
in accord with Mad Mullinix's earlier comparison of Timothy with the
Homeric character who 'Was more abhor'd, and scorn'd by those / With
whom he serv'd, than by his Foes' (*Mad Mullinix*, 51–4). Similar things
had been said about Bentley in the *Battle of the Books*, which showed long
ago that it was not unSwiftian to associate a *bête noire* with the Iliadic
rogue.[73] The device of the truth-telling beggar is dropped, and the poem
speaks in the poet's presumed voice. Like Thersites, Traulus is both
ignoble and low born:

> TRAULUS of amphibious Breed,
> Motly Fruit of Mungril Seed:
> By the *Dam* from Lordlings sprung,
> By the *Sire* exhal'd from Dung . . .
>
> In him, tell me which prevail,
> Female Vices most, or Male,
> What produc'd them, can you tell?
> Human Race, or *Imps* of *Hell.*   (1–4, 53–6)

This is the idiom of several violently angry late poems on the Irish political scene of the 1730s, which include 'On Noisy Tom' (1736: not Tom Mullinix) and the most famous of all, the *Legion Club* (1736),[74] that extraordinary poem which moves from the Audenesque elan of

> As I strole the City, oft I
> Spy a Building large and lofty,
> Not a Bow-shot from the College,
> Half the Globe from Sense and Knowledge   (1–4)[75]

to much drumming invective of the *Traulus* type. The latter evokes a tradition of ritual curses and satirical magic, of the kind that rhymed rats to death and caused blisters to erupt in rival poets. It is perhaps here that the *indignatio* comes closest to being overtly *saeva*. Even here, the diablerie of the exercise, the billowing exuberance of the diatribe, the sense of outdoing the real magicians in the force of utterance, is, as in some of Rochester's imprecations, self-disarming. What Ben Jonson called the drumming rhymes he himself claimed to take from the Irish bards is exuberantly emphasised by Swift both in the hammering sequence of imprecations and the spirited metrical horseplay:

> H[arrison], and D[ilkes], and C[lements],
> Souse them in their own Ex-crements.   (185–6)[76]

The hyphen in 'Ex-crements' emphasises the ritual character of the incantation, as well as the sport of indulging it to the limit. Even in these poems, where Swift comes closest to *saeva indignatio*, there are implied quotation marks within quotation marks around every word and every cadence, so that the terms still cannot be taken at the face value claimed in the epitaph, and only there.

These reflections may shed light on some peculiarities in the Latin epitaph itself. For one thing, the word 'vindicator' is not recorded in classical Latin. *Vindico, vindicare,* means to claim (asserting one's title), rescue, absolve, punish, and avenge. The phrase *vindicare in libertatem* means, in the words of the *Oxford Latin Dictionary*, 'to claim as free (one who asserts he is wrongly held in slavery', not a champion of freedom). The noun *vindex* had the legal sense of one who assumes liability for the release of, for example, a debtor, and by extension, a defender or champion, or a punisher or avenger. *Vindicator* is ecclesiastical Latin, meaning avenger.

Swift's use of *vindicator* in Latin was immediately recognised as surprising. The usage was corrected to 'vindicem' as early as the London edition of 1746 whose title-page appears somewhat confusingly in front of the Faulkner text in the Davis edition,[77] and which astringently reports in a footnote: 'In the *Irish* Edit. it is VINDICATOREM. But not so, I imagine, from the Dean's Hand.' Davis does not accept the emendation, 'as Swift seems to have written VINDICATOREM', the evidence for his view being mainly that this 'is what has been cut on the tablet in St. Patrick's cathedral', an act Swift can, however, safely be absolved from having performed himself. Davis reports that the manuscript, in Swift's 'own hand', was 'Destroyed by fire'.[78] The *ex post facto* reasoning from the tablet cannot be conclusive. The possibility cannot be ruled out that the reading 'vindicatorem' in the '*Irish* Edit.' might be the result of a mistranscription, at any of the stages of transmission, that eventually found its way to the engraver in 1749. In any process of transferring from paper to tablet, however, it is highly unlikely that anyone would deliberately alter the correct Latin 'vindicem' to an incorrect 'vindicatorem'.[79]

A broad but not exhaustive search suggests that 'vindicem' was subsequently adopted in a majority of eighteenth-century printings of the will, as well as by such authorities as Hawkesworth, Thomas Sheridan, Craik, and Temple Scott.[80] J. V. Luce's 'Note on the composition of Swift's epitaph' castigates Maurice Johnson, who cites the 'vindicem' version, for misquotation, though Johnson was reproducing Temple Scott, then the authoritative modern edition, since the relevant volume of Davis appeared six years after Johnson's article, in 1959.[81] It is mainly, though not exclusively, in the Faulkner editions that we find the reading 'vindicatorem'. The more classical 'vindicem' tends to be adopted by non-Faulkner (including Dublin) editions.

None of this gives 'vindicem' independent, let alone conclusive, textual authority over 'vindicatorem', given the presumptive authority of the tablet and the special standing of Faulkner's edition. My non-exhaustive search suggests a correlation between the Faulkner-associated 'vindicatorem' versions of the will and the tablet, and a group of other readings for which the 'vindicem' versions share a consistent set of alternatives. Thus the initials S. T. D., for *Sacrae Theologiae Doctor*, generally occur in 'vindicatorem' versions, whereas the 'vindicem' versions generally have S. T. P., for *Sacrae Theologiae Professor*. The same is true of several variants of punctuation and numeralisation.[82] Denis Johnston remarked that 'nobody has yet managed to perform the feat of copying [the epitaph] down correctly and in full'.[83]

The tablet is likely to have been transcribed from Faulkner's edition. This, like the other published versions, supplied among other details a date of death that cannot by definition have been present in the manuscript of the will, not to mention the unlikelihood that the original will would have been handed to the engraver. As Robert Mahony has related, Faulkner's mission to create a monument to Swift in print and stone did not result in responsibility for erecting the tablet. This was assumed by the Governors of St Patrick's Hospital, who, after considering two designs on 27 February 1748, approved one of them for erection in 1749. The erection of the monument was reported in Faulkner's *Dublin Journal* for 8 August 1749.[84] Even with Faulkner apparently out of the loop, his published text of the will evidently provided that of the inscription.

I have no expectation of resolving the question, but if we assume, in the absence of further evidence, that 'vindicatorem' is what Swift wrote, a number of interesting questions invite attention. How or why would Swift stoop, for example, to non-classical Latin, and an unusual word, not only in Latin but even in English? Swift's Latin was perhaps not outstanding, though the Trinity College mark of *negligenter* recorded for his 'theme' is by no means a failing grade, perhaps something like a B in today's ideas of these things, and he received the high mark of *bene* for Greek and Latin.[85] Orrery thought Swift 'was not an elegant writer of Latin' and found the epitaph 'scarce intelligible', but the latter comment sounds obtuse, or at least captious, and doesn't in any case refer to 'vindicatorem' or any other specific example of incorrectness.[86] Swift took considerable care over the wording of his controversial epitaph for the Duke of Schomberg in 1731, consulting several advisers and commenting confidently and knowledgeably on nuances of expression.[87] Carelessness is possible, in the case of his own epitaph, in what was doubtless an emotional moment. Swift reports himself in the will to be 'of sound Mind, although weak in Body', repeating this as 'weak in Body but sound in Mind' in the Codicil two days later, an insistence which suggests an element of febrile self-concern.[88]

On the other hand, the instructions are meticulous and extremely emphatic on most matters of detail, notably the exact materials to be used and place and time of burial, 'under the Pillar next to the Monument of Primate *Narcissus Marsh*, three Days after my Decease, as privately as possible, and at Twelve o' Clock at Night: And, that a Black Marble of [ ] Feet square, and seven Feet from the Ground, fixed to the Wall, may be erected' (the one detail left unspecified is the exact size of the tablet).[89] The directions in the will of Swift's patron, Sir William Temple, had prescribed that 'a large stone of black marble may be set up against the wall', without elaborate micro-management of the location or any insistence that the inscription should be 'deeply cut' into the stone.[90] Night-burials were not uncommon in the seventeenth and first half of the eighteenth centuries, often as a means of avoiding the expense of costly daytime ceremonies.[91] But the precision of the mandate here, 'three Days after my Decease, as privately as possible, and at Twelve o' Clock at Night', is so emphatic that the plotting of privacy acquires a paradoxically theatrical quality of cloak-and-dagger drama. Two other monuments in St Patrick's which Swift orchestrated and for which he wrote epitaphs were also, as it happens, fraught with various touches of drama, though not involving privacy. The first, for his servant Alexander McGee (1722), was erected in defiance of strong opposition to bestowing such an honour on a humble servant and was written in English rather than Latin. The other, in 1731, commemorating the Duke of Schomberg, who was killed at the Boyne, proclaimed in stone what Swift saw as the shameful refusal of the Duke's descendants to contribute financially to the memorial.[92]

The case of Alexander McGee was remembered after Swift's death when Martha Whiteway, Swift's cousin and the closest friend of his last years, issued a last-minute plea for Swift's instructions not to be taken in an unduly 'literal sence'. She spoke of 'the indignation which the Town have expressed at the manner of burying their Patriot', adding that what Swift 'himself thought decency requisite at a funeral, may be known by what he did for his honest, trusty, Servant, Alexander McGee'. She said she herself was willing to contribute from her own legacy if the expense of a more fitting ceremony could not be met from Swift's 'noble' charitable bequest.[93]

The emphatic drama of secrecy in the scenario for his own funeral, and the correspondingly strenuous instructions for the inscription, may or may not suggest an unlikelihood that he got the wording wrong. If he wanted the unorthodox word at all, the preoccupation with large letters, deeply cut, and strongly gilded, might indicate that the exact wording also had an importance bordering on the obsessional. The first known use of *vindicator* in English in any sense, according to the OED, is in William Painter's *Palace of Pleasure* (1566), where Camillus is described as 'the vindicator [i.e. avenger] and deliverer' of Rome. The English use of 'vindicate' in the sense of justify, uphold, or support, as distinct from avenge, or defend in the legal sense, is first recorded in the OED in 1650, in Marvell's *Horatian Ode* ('To vindicate his helpless right' (62), itself an equivocal example). When Pope announced his intention to 'vindicate the ways of God to Man', however, he was making a claim to outdo Milton in declarative affirmation, both in the use of 'vindicate' rather than 'justify' and in the capitalised singular 'Man' (*Essay on Man*, 1733, I. 16).

It has been suggested that Swift was evoking Dryden's description of Juvenal in the 'Discourse Concerning Satire' (1693) as 'a Zealous Vindicator of *Roman* Liberty', clearly distinguishable from Painter describing the avenger Camillus. Dryden allowed a Latinate English but not Latin word of enhanced resonance into his own Latin, rather than seeking to compose classical Latin and getting it wrong.[94] An evocation of Dryden might appear surprising, in view of Swift's antipathy to this poet, his 'cousin'.[95] But the description aptly occurs in the well-known comparison between the satiric characters of Horace and Juvenal in which Dryden describes Horace as a 'Temporizing' poet.[96] This evocation would reinforce the primary object, which was to align Swift with Juvenal, rather than to invoke Dryden. But this too is unusual, since Swift professed a Horatian levity in preference to Juvenalian diatribes, cutting against the grain, notably, of the *Epistle to a Lady*.

Yet in the epitaph he used the phrase *saeva indignatio*, which picks up Juvenal's famous 'facit indignatio versum' (I. 79), but adding the adjective *saeva*, which Juvenal did not use alongside the noun, as an incremental intensive, as though bidding to be more Juvenalian than Juvenal, whom he ostentatiously avoided emulating in his own poems. Juvenal's indignation is also not often introspectively directed. He spoke of it as sometimes uncontainable (I. 30 ff.), but he did not talk about the lacerations to his heart. It is as though Swift's phrase were claiming a surplus kinship, upping the grandiloquence, as Yeats was to do with Swift himself, and adding self-torment for good measure. The resemblance to his use of 'vindicator', if he took the word from Dryden, is that it is similarly overdetermined. Swift's dislike of Dryden is overridden in order to give a vibrant evocation of Juvenal of a kind he would also be shy of making in his poems, just as the choice of the non-classical form 'vindicatorem' adds a militant ring which the more correct 'vindicem' might not have for English readers. It is of a piece with the other overdetermined features that attend the planning of the monument in the will, the choice of black marble, a hard durable stone that even Yeats was to decline, the insistence on 'large Letters, deeply cut, and strongly gilded'.

All this is surely an extraordinarily emphatic insistence on being emphatic. Could it be that Swift was here making up for all the reticences and undercuttings of the *Verses on the Death* and other poems, finally orchestrated not by a coyly surrogate figure but in his own name?

It evokes Juvenal, but Swift added the adjective for posthumous viewing, when there could be no worries about making a figure scurvy, and in the decent obscurity of a learned language, where the risks of self-exposure, or of a misfired self-exaltation, might no longer apply. The issue, to summarise, may be this: why (and how come) prefer the despised Dryden over correct Latin usage in order to achieve an honorific evocation of Juvenal, whom he usually professes *not* to be like anyway? And why add *saeva* to Juvenal, who does not have this phrase and isn't given to referring to lacerating his own heart, any more than Swift did in his published writings? Could it be that the epitaph was a declaration to posterity made precisely because it seemed to Swift unthinkable in his lifetime writings, as the lines on 'Fair LIBERTY' suggest? Those lines from the *Verses* show a compulsion simultaneously to offer and disavow grandeurs Swift would be justified to think of as his due, and which he may have felt impelled to store up for himself in the sheltered zone of a future marble memorial. In the lines from the *Verses on the Death*, hedged with coyness and jokerie, and anxieties about a lofty style and figure scurvy, the epitaph, like the thin man in the fat man's body, seems to be struggling to get out. But it took the prospect of death, not just verses upon it, to bring this about.

NOTES

1 *PW*, XIII, 149, 223–4. I am indebted to Kirk Freudenburg, Regina Janes, Roy Johnston, Stephen Karian, James McLaverty, Robert Mahony, Marjorie Perloff, and James Woolley for helpful information and suggestions.
2 See Maurice Johnson, 'Swift and "The Greatest Epitaph in History"', *Publications of the Modern Language Association of America*, 68 (1953), 818 n. 19.
3 W. B. Yeats, *The Words upon the Window-Pane* (1934), *Collected Plays*, London, Macmillan, 1960, p. 602; Introduction, *Explorations*, selected by Mrs. W. B. Yeats, London, Macmillan, 1962, pp. 345–6. On other versions, see Johnson, *The Sin of Wit: Jonathan Swift as a Poet*, Syracuse University Press, 1950, p. 133; Yeats to Dorothy Wellesley, 23 December 1936, *Letters on Poetry from W. B. Yeats to Dorothy Wellesley*, London, Oxford University Press, 1964, p. 115. For a discussion, see James Lovic Allen, '"Imitate Him If You Dare": Relationships Between the Epitaphs of Swift and Yeats', *Studies: An Irish Quarterly Review*, 70 (1981), 177–86.
4 Yeats's poems are quoted from *Yeats's Poems*, ed. A. Norman Jeffares, with an Appendix by Warwick Gould, London, Macmillan, 1989, p. 361.
5 Richmond Lattimore, *Themes in Greek and Latin Epitaphs*, Urbana, University of Illinois Press, 1942, p. 230. For another perspective on the Latin formula, see Allen, '"Imitate Him If You Dare"', 180–2.

6 Henry Ellis, *The History and Antiquities of the Parish of Saint Leonard Shoreditch*, 1798, p. 106; Thomas Greenhill, *Nekrokedeia: or the Art of Embalming*, 1705, p. 90; other examples, Elias Ashmole, *Antiquities of Berkshire*, 3 vols., 1719, I. 19; Alexander Adam, *Roman Antiquities*, Edinburgh, 1791, p. 467.

7 Gustave Flaubert, *Madame Bovary*, 1857, III. xi.

8 Browne Willis, *A Survey of the Cathedrals of York, Durham, Carlisle* etc., 1727, p. 56 (also '*Abi lector*', p. 50); *A Survey of the Cathedrals of Lincoln, Ely, Oxford, and Peterborough*, 1730, pp. 434, 458; 71 with '*imitari*'.

9 Johnson, 'Greatest Epitaph', 823.

10 Lattimore, *Themes in Greek and Latin Epitaphs*, pp. 230 ff., 236.

11 *Yeats's Poems*, pp. 451–2.

12 Yeats to Ethel Mannin, 22 August 1938 (the poem was completed 4 September), A. Norman Jeffares, *A New Commentary on the Poems of W. B. Yeats*, London, Macmillan, 1984, pp. 407, 404.

13 See R. F. Foster, *W. B. Yeats: A Life, II: The Arch-Poet (1915–1939)*, Oxford University Press, 2003, pp. 346–7 (hereafter Foster).

14 T. S. Eliot, *Complete Poems and Plays*, London, Faber and Faber, 1969, rptd 1982, pp. 193–4; for Eliot's lecture, 'Yeats' (1940), see *On Poetry and Poets*, London, Faber and Faber, 1957, pp. 252–62; for the presence of Yeats and Swift in 'Little Gidding', see Helen Gardner, *The Composition of the Four Quartets*, London, Faber and Faber, 1978, pp. 186–94 (for John Hayward's role in identifying Swift's epitaph, see p. 193); Eliot wrote to Maurice Johnson on 27 June 1947 that his 'reference … associates Swift with W. B. Yeats'. Maurice Johnson, 'The Ghost of Swift in Eliot's *Four Quartets*', *Modern Language Notes*, 64 (1949), 273; for some alternative perspectives, see Claude Rawson, *Order from Confusion Sprung: Studies in Eighteenth-Century Literature from Swift to Cowper*, London, George Allen & Unwin, 1985, pp. 155, 186 n. 5.

15 Juvenal, *Satires*, I. 79.

16 T. S. Eliot, '*Ulysses*, Order, and Myth' (1923), *Selected Prose*, ed. Frank Kermode, New York, Harcourt Brace Jovanovich and Farrar, Strauss, and Giroux, 1975, p. 176.

17 Yeats, Introduction to *Oxford Book of Modern Verse 1892–1935*, Oxford, Clarendon Press, 1936, pp. xxi–xxii.

18 *Poems*, I, 191–6, esp. 196; see Ehrenpreis, II, 711; on the whole episode, see 708–13, and the accounts by Bertrand A. Goldgar and Ian Gadd in the Cambridge Edition of the Works of Jonathan Swift, (No. 8), *English Political Writings 1711–1714: The Conduct of the Allies and Other Works*, Cambridge University Press, 2008, pp. 37–9, 449–54.

19 Yeats, 'Pages from a Diary Written in Nineteen Hundred and Thirty' (1944), p. xxxi, *Explorations*, p. 315.

20 Foster, p. 425, citing Introduction, *The Words upon the Window-Pane*, in *Explorations*, p. 354. On Yeats's brief flirtation, and disillusion, with Fascism and O'Duffy's Blue Shirts, see Donald T. Torchiana, *W. B. Yeats and*

Georgian Ireland (1966), Washington, Catholic University of America Press, 1992, pp. 154–67.

21 Torchiana, p. 132. For an excellent account of the 'undefined liberty' Yeats associated with Swift, '"something not himself that Swift served"', see ibid., pp. 140–2 [*Letters* 791]; Torchiana's chapter 4, 'Imitate Him if You Dare' (pp. 120–67), remains the most impressive account of Yeats's deep preoccupation with Swift.

22 Yeats to Dorothy Wellesley, 21 December 1935, *Letters on Poetry*, pp. 43–4; Foster, p. 620, assumes Yeats was referring to tetrameters, but the letter speaks of 'short lines', which in the play he was working on (*The Herne's Egg*) includes but is not restricted to tetrameters.

23 On these lines, see James McLaverty's comments, above, pp. 117, 119.

24 Yeats, 'The Municipal Gallery Revisited' (1937).

25 Foster, pp. 396–7, 419; Yeats to Augusta Gregory, 7 April 1930.

26 Maynard Mack, *Alexander Pope: A Life*, New York, Norton, 1985, pp. 683–4.

27 Swift to Bolingbroke and Pope, 5 April 1729, *Correspondence*, III, 231; *Poems*, II, 482–3.

28 Swift to Pope, 6 February 1730; Pope to Swift, 4 March 1730, *Correspondence*, III, 279–80 and n. 7, 288–9 and n. 6.

29 Swift to Charles Wogan, July–2 August 1732; to Pope, 5 April 1729, ibid., 231, 515.

30 Swift to Pope, 2 December 1736; Pope to Swift, 25 March 1736; Swift to Pope, 9 February 1737; Swift wrote again, on 31 May 1737, after the poem was published (ibid., IV, 366, 276, 386, 432).

31 Swift to Pope, 17 November 1726, ibid., III, 56.

32 Yeats, 'A General Introduction for my Work' (1937), *Essays and Introductions*, London, Macmillan, 1961, rptd 1980, p. 519.

33 Kurt Vonnegut, *Mother Night* (1966), Introduction; see Claude Rawson, 'Ex post facto fictions', *Times Literary Supplement*, 3 September 1982, 942.

34 The OED's only example of this phrase is under 'crier, 1' and dates from 1748: 'Simplicity is all their cry; yet hardly do these criers know what they mean by this noble word.'

35 'Clever *Tom Clinch* going to be hanged' (1726; 11); *To Dr. D – l - - - y, on the Libels Writ against Him* (1730; 75–6); 'Verses made for Women who cry Apples, &c', 'Oysters', 'Herrings' etc. (*Poems*, II, 399, 502; III, 951–3).

36 Yeats, 'High Talk' (1938), *Yeats's Poems*, p. 467.

37 Yeats, 'Beggar to Beggar Cried' (1914); *Wanderings of Oisin* (1889), iii. 155–6, 'Later a sound came ... From the grass-barnacle calling', *Yeats's Poems*, pp. 217, 31; *The Green Helmet* (1910), 270, *Collected Plays*, p. 242.

38 OED, Barnacle n. 2, 3b.

39 *Yeats's Poems*, p. 421.

40 Swift, *PW*, V, 83–6.

41 Charles Baudelaire, 'De L'Essence du rire' (1855), *Oeuvres complètes*, ed. Claude Pichois, 2 vols., Paris, Gallimard, 1975–6, II, pp. 525–43.

42 Yeats, *Autobiographies*, London, Macmillan, 1955, p. 332; Yeats to W. T. Horton, 3 September 1899, in *Collected Letters of W. B. Yeats: Volume Two 1896–1900*, ed.

Warwick Gould, John Kelly and Deirdre Toomey, Oxford, Clarendon Press, 1997, p. 447, and editorial note p. 448 n. 6; Yeats to Olivia Shakespear, 25 May 1926, *Letters of W. B. Yeats* (1955), ed. Allan Wade, rptd New York, Octagon Books, 1980, p. 715; George Mills Harper, *The Making of Yeats's A Vision: A Study of the Automatic Script*, 2 vols., London, Macmillan, 1987, I. 95, 120, 140, 246; II. 30, 140, 141, 418.

43 Baudelaire, 'De L'Essence du rire', pp. 540–1.

44 Ibid., p. 540; Voltaire, *Lettres philosophiques*, No. xviii, 'On Tragedy'.

45 Baudelaire, 'De L'Essence du rire', pp. 537, 529; Voltaire, *Essai sur la poésie épique* (1733), *Complete Works of Voltaire, 3B: The English Essays of 1727*, Oxford, Voltaire Foundation, 1996, pp. 418–19.

46 Henry Fielding, *Tom Thumb: A Tragedy* (1730), Prologue (2–3), *Plays: Volume One 1728–1731*, ed. Thomas Lockwood, Oxford, Clarendon Press, 2004, p. 381.

47 *Poems*, III, 772–82.

48 *Complete Poems*, pp. 776, 936, 816–17; *Poems*, III, 772–3, 794–5.

49 *Complete Poems*, pp. 776, 936.

50 *Yeats's Poems*, p. 467; Jeffares, *New Commentary*, p. 421; *Ulysses* (1922), ch. 1, New York, Vintage, 1990, p. 4; Don Gifford, *Ulysses Annotated*, 2nd edn, Berkeley, University of California Press, rptd 2008, pp. 14, 22, 59.

51 Jeffares, *New Commentary*, pp. 420–1. See 'Malachi's ash-pit', *Player Queen*, i.18, and 'Patrick, Malachi, Mike, John, James', *The Herne's Egg*, iv.122; Yeats, *Collected Plays*, pp. 388, 663.

52 Brian Farrington, *Malachi-Stilt-Jack: A Study of W. B. Yeats and his Work*, London, Connolly Publication's [sic], n.d. [1965?], p. 12.

53 Yeats, 'The Circus Animals' Desertion', *Yeats's Poems*, pp. 471–2; for the dates of composition of the two poems, and the circus associations connecting them, see Jeffares, *New Commentary*, pp. 420–1, 424–6.

54 *Poems*, II, 635.

55 On the date of the *Epistle*, see James Woolley, 'Swift's "Skinnibonia": A New Poem from Lady Acheson's Manuscript', *Reading Swift: Papers from the Fifth Münster Symposium on Jonathan Swift*, ed. Hermann J. Real, Munich, Wilhelm Fink, 2008, pp. 313, 317, 331–2.

56 Yeats, 'The Three Beggars' (1913), *Yeats's Poems*, p. 215.

57 Yeats, *Autobiographies*, pp. 348–9.

58 *Poems*, III, 783–5.

59 Ibid., 787–9, 782–3.

60 Jeffares, *New Commentary*, p. 307; Johnson, *The Sin of Wit*, p. 134; Foster, pp. 385–7; Yeats, Introduction to *The Words upon the Window-Pane*, in *Explorations*, p. 344; 'The Municipal Gallery Revisited' (1937), *Yeats's Poems*, p. 439. For a wide-ranging and remarkably perceptive account of the importance of Swift's poetry in Yeats's work, see D. E. S. Maxwell, 'Swift's Dark Grove: Yeats and the Anglo-Irish Tradition', in *W. B. Yeats (1865–1939): Centenary Essays on the Art of W. B. Yeats*, ed. D. E. S. Maxwell and S. B. Bushrui, Ibadan University Press, 1965, pp. 18–32. It relates the

Crazy Jane poems to Swift's 'scatological' poems about women (28–9), but leaves the beggar poems largely out of consideration.

61 'The Seven Sages', in *Yeats's Poems*, p. 357.

62 *A Proposal for Giving Badges to the Beggars* (1737), *PW*, XIII, 139.

63 *Poems*, III, 782–3; Swift and Thomas Sheridan, *The Intelligencer*, Nos. 8 and 10, 29 June–2 July and 4 July 1728, ed. James Woolley, Oxford, Clarendon Press, 1992, pp. 101–14, 130–4.

64 See *Intelligencer*, pp. 131–2; the engraving is reproduced on p. 130.

65 Ibid., pp. 130–1.

66 John Gay, *Poetry and Prose*, ed. Vinton A. Dearing and Charles E. Beckwith, 2 vols., Oxford, Clarendon Press, 1974, II. 319–21.

67 Swift to Pope, 12 June 1732, *Correspondence*, III, 489.

68 *Poems*, III, 794–9, 474–5 n.; *PW*, XIII, 155: see Ehrenpreis, III, 652–3, 656; *Complete Poems*, pp. 816–17, 907. On the possible identification of *Traulus's* Tom with Mullinix, see *Poems*, III, 795; Ehrenpreis, III, 656; and, more guardedly, Pat Rogers in *Complete Poems*, p. 817.

69 *Correspondence*, II, 607.

70 Ehrenpreis, III, 657.

71 Ibid., 656.

72 *Poems*, III, 799–801.

73 Ibid., 799; *Complete Poems*, p. 816; *PW*, I, 160–1.

74 *Poems*, III, 824–6, 827 ff.

75 *A Character, Panegyric, and Description of the Legion Club* (1736), *Poems*, III, 827–39.

76 *Poems*, III, 837; see Ben Jonson, *The Poetaster* (1601), 'To the Reader' ('Apologetical Dialogue'), 150–1, and Robert C. Elliott, *The Power of Satire: Magic, Ritual, Art*, Princeton University Press, 1960, pp. 3–48.

77 *The Last Will and Testament of Jonathan Swift, D.D.*, Dublin Printed: London Reprinted; and sold by M. Cooper, 1746, p. 3; *PW*, XIII, 147.

78 Davis's text is that of Faulkner's 'reissue of *Works*, Vol. VIII, 1745', which I have not seen. Davis adds the footnotes from London 1746 *in situ*, except for the note explaining 'vindicem', which is relegated to a general textual note at the back, where no collation is included (*PW*, XIII, 149–58, 223–4). The form 'vindicatorem' appears in Faulkner's *Volume VIII. Of the Author's Works*, 1746, as well as in *A True Copy of the Late Rev. Dr. Jonathan Swift's Will. Taken from, and compar'd with, the Original*, ?1746.

79 *Dublin Journal* (Faulkner's paper), 8 August 1749, reports the erection of the monument. Robert Mahony, *Jonathan Swift: The Irish Identity*, New Haven, Yale University Press, 1995, p. 12.

80 *The Works of Jonathan Swift*, ed. John Hawkesworth, London, Printed for C. Davis and others, 6 vols., 1755, VI. i. 209; Thomas Sheridan, *Life of the Rev. Dr. Jonathan Swift*, 1784, p. 282; Henry Craik, *The Life of Jonathan Swift*, 2 vols., London, Macmillan, 1984, 2nd edn., II. 259; *Prose Works of Jonathan Swift*, ed. Temple Scott, 12 vols., London, George Bell and Sons, 1897–1908, XI. 405.

81 Johnson, 'Greatest Epitaph', 818; J. V. Luce, 'A note on the composition of Swift's epitaph', *Hermathena: A Dublin University Review*, Swift Number, 104 (1967), 79.

82 Johnson, 'Greatest Epitaph', 818 n. 19, notes the discrepancy between the tablet and the text he reproduces, in respect of these initials. There are also minor differences of punctuation and italicisation, and in the formatting of the date of death and statement of Swift's age.

83 Denis Johnston, *In Search of Swift*, Dublin, Hodges Figgis, 1959, p. 188; even William Monck Mason, *History and Antiquities of the Collegiate and Cathedral Church of St. Patrick, near Dublin*, Dublin, 1820, p. 411, adds a comma in 'Swift, S.T.D.', in the second line, as in the Will, and reproduces 'die mensis' wholly in lower case.

84 See Mahony, *Jonathan Swift: The Irish Identity*, p. 12.

85 See Ehrenpreis, I, 57–62, 279.

86 John Boyle, Earl of Orrery, *Remarks on the Life and Writings of Dr. Jonathan Swift* (1751), Letter XXI, ed. João Fróes, Newark, University of Delaware Press, 2000, p. 270; for Orrery on Swift's undergraduate performance, see Letter I, pp. 70, 77 nn. 37–8.

87 Swift to the Rev. Philip Chamberlain, 20 May 1731, *Correspondence*, III, 397–9.

88 *PW*, XIII, 149, 157; Ehrenpreis, III, 903.

89 *PW*, XIII, 147.

90 Johnson, 'Greatest Epitaph', 819.

91 Julian Litten, *The English Way of Death: The Common Funeral since 1450*, London, Robert Hale, 1991, pp. 14, 161–4.

92 For an account of all three epitaphs, see Ann Cline Kelly, 'Written in Stone: Swift's Use of St. Patrick's Cathedral as a Text', *Swift Studies*, 21 (2006), 107–17; those for Schomberg and McGee are reported in the 'Additional Notes and Illustrations' at the end of Monck Mason's *History*, pp. l–lii, lix.

93 Martha Whiteway to an executor, 22 October 1745, *Correspondence*, IV, 671–3.

94 Luce, 'A note', 79–80.

95 For a comprehensive recent survey of Swift's treatment of Dryden, see Ian Higgins, 'Dryden and Swift', in *John Dryden (1631–1700): His Politics, His Plays, and His Poets*, ed. Claude Rawson and Aaron Santesso, Newark, University of Delaware Press, 2004, pp. 217–34.

96 Dryden, 'Discourse Concerning Satire', in *Works, Volume IV: Poems 1693–1696*, ed. A. B. Chambers and William Frost, Berkeley, University of California Press, 1974, p. 65.

PART III

The political Swift 2 (Ireland)

'Paltry underlings of state'? The character and aspirations of the 'Castle' party, 1715–1732

D. W. Hayton

In his writings, both public and private, Swift voiced a low opinion of politicians. 'I have conversed in some freedom with more Ministers of State of all Parties than usually happens to men of my level', he boasted to Pope in 1721,

and I confess, in their capacity as Ministers, I look upon them as a race of people whose acquaintance no man would court, otherwise than upon the score of Vanity or Ambition. The first quickly wears off (and is the Vice of low minds, for a man of spirit is too proud to be vain) and the other was not my case. Besides, having never receiv'd more than one small favour, I was under no necessity of being a slave to men in power, but chose my friends for their personal merit, without examining how far their notions agreed with the politicks then in vogue.[1]

Certainly he had little regard for those in power in Ireland during the long years of his Dublin exile. When they do figure in his satire, they appear as selfish and corrupt, 'paltry underlings of state': at best feeble and ineffective defenders of their country's interests, and at worst willing collaborators in its reduction to a state of slavery. Needless to say, this is not how Irish politicians saw themselves, nor how they were represented by their admirers. Clergymen preaching panegyrics, friends or family members preparing inscriptions to adorn commemorative monuments, authors offering tribute (often in the form of flattering dedications): all took a very different view, emphasising disinterested public service and genuine patriotism.[2] Not surprisingly, perhaps, posterity has tended to favour the satirist; the sharpness of Swift's wit and the power of his prose have exerted such an influence over the popular understanding of the way Ireland was governed in the early eighteenth century that his characterisation of those Irishmen who managed the Irish parliament for English viceroys and ministers – the 'undertakers' – has achieved widespread acceptance.

This chapter seeks to uncover the mentality and ideology of the Irishmen who acted as parliamentary managers and under-managers for Dublin Castle at the time when Swift was writing his *Proposal for the Universal Use of Irish Manufacture* (1720), *Drapier's Letters* (1724–5), and *Modest Proposal* (1729). It was a period which saw the affirmation of the power of the Westminster parliament to legislate for Ireland in the British Declaratory Act of 1720, the defeat of the project to establish an Irish national bank in 1721, the attempted enforcement of Wood's halfpence in 1723–5, and a serious crisis for Irish agriculture in the late 1720s, provoking a radical reassessment of strategies for economic regeneration. The intention of the chapter is not to redress the moral balance, so much as to test the prejudices of the dean against what can be discovered of the motivations and thought processes of the men who suffered at his pen. This offers a different perspective on the constitutional and political relationship of Ireland and Britain, and on the intellectual framework in which the Irish Protestant elite operated. It is also possible that, in understanding those who stood on the winning side of Irish politics, who enjoyed privilege, patronage, and a modicum of power, and felt Swift to be at best irritating, and at worst dangerously subversive, we may move closer to understanding the dean's own alienation from Dublin Castle and from the Irish parliament on College Green.

The very first task, of identifying the politicians who should be the subject of investigation, is complicated by the fact that in the period 1715–26 there were effectively two distinct '[Dublin] Castle parties' as rival magnates struggled for dominance: on the one hand the followers of Speaker (and first commissioner of the revenue) William Conolly, and on the other the faction headed in the Commons by St John Brodrick but owing ultimate allegiance to St John's father, Alan, first Viscount Midleton, who had been raised to the woolsack on the Hanoverian succession and now, as lord chancellor, acted as Speaker in the House of Lords.[3] In the party battles of Queen Anne's reign the two had fought side by side in the whig cause, but from the first Irish parliamentary session of the new reign, in 1715–16, they became bitter rivals. The demise of the tory party at the Irish general election of 1715 had left whigs in an overwhelming majority in the Commons, and a block creation of coronation peerages ensured that loyal whigs would also outnumber the surviving tory lords. Now, secure from any threat from the tories, Irish whigs were free to quarrel among themselves. Alan Brodrick, although the undisputed leader of the whig party before 1714 (and himself chosen Speaker in the short-lived 1713 parliament), found that his elevation to lord chancellor was a major political mistake, since the upper house was less important than the lower, giving Conolly the more valuable managerial role, and the patronage available to the lord chancellor was less than that available to Conolly in the revenue. Worse still, Conolly seemed to have greater access to the new lords justices, Grafton and Galway. Conolly capitalised on his advantages and tried to make himself indispensable to government by doing whatever he was asked, while the Brodricks responded to perceived slights in the 1715–16 session by joining with the rump of tories in the Commons to make trouble. This set the pattern for the next decade, with the Brodricks increasingly sidelined, though Midleton himself remained in office until the advent of Lord Carteret to the viceroyalty.

Although Midleton occasionally took a strong line in defence both of executive power and the maintenance of English constitutional supremacy, and although some of his cronies, notably the anti-clerical Cork squire Richard Bettesworth, were prime targets for Swift's scorn, the political course he charted between 1715 and 1725 was significantly different from Conolly's. In the Commons – if not in the Lords – the Brodricks joined tories in defending the sacramental test, endorsed the rights of the Irish House of Lords against English encroachment, and denounced Wood's halfpence. Conolly and his followers, by contrast, were disposed to do whatever successive lords justices and lords lieutenant wanted, except in extreme cases, where the effort would have destroyed their credibility with popular opinion. Not even after Midleton's resignation did Conolly depart publicly from the Castle's interest, although he disagreed with particular policies. And after his death in 1729 his political heir, Sir Ralph Gore, followed the same course, expressing reservations about viceregal decisions in private but remaining loyal and steering the Castle party through the potentially dangerous parliamentary sessions of 1729–32 without conceding to opposition outrage at the economic crisis gripping the country. For the purposes of the present chapter Conolly's faction clearly constituted the 'Castle party'.

Even then, the task of identifying all the members of the party would be beyond the available evidence; we have relatively few parliamentary lists for the period, and in this respect Conolly's own private papers are disappointingly uncommunicative. Moreover, one would have to accept that personal and factional allegiances shifted over time, and that those on the fringes of either of the main political 'connexions' might well have voted in different ways over different issues. What can be done, however, is to identify the leading figures through correspondence, both friendly and hostile, a few printed commentaries and satires,[4] and, to a lesser extent, through the *Journals* of the two houses of the Irish parliament, which list committees and those who reported from them, tellers in divisions, and the members responsible for introducing legislation. The parliamentary evidence has to be used carefully, but it can help to tie in particular individuals for whom other indirect evidence survives (and even more important, as we shall see, it can tell us something about the governmental priorities of those involved). It also helps to pinpoint those among Conolly's supporters who were the more active in parliament, and for the purposes of the present chapter it is the active members of the faction, not obscure or passive dependants, who are the objects of interest.

The strength of Conolly's party lay in the Commons, which in practice was the more important of the two houses, for it was there that the vital business of the session was transacted, the preparation of the 'heads' of bills granting the time-limited taxes 'additional' to the crown's 'hereditary' revenues, without which government could not function. Even though, according to Poynings' Law, bills proper could only be prepared by the Irish privy council and, after scrutiny in England, were returned for approval or rejection (but not amendment) by the Irish parliament, the two houses of the Irish parliament had developed a practice which permitted them a share in the framing of statute by drafting 'heads' that were sent to the privy council to be turned into form. Each set of 'heads' went through only one house, and drafting heads of money bills was accepted as the province of the Commons.[5] By the 1720s, in fact, most public legislation was taking its rise in the lower house, and the constitutional role of the House of Lords was being eroded.[6] Moreover, it was becoming easier for government to control the Lords: the smaller membership, the poverty of many peers, and the presence of a sizable cohort of bishops dependent on the court for preferment would create a standing ministerial majority once the remnant of High Church irreconcilables on the episcopal bench died off.[7] By the mid-1720s, therefore, Conolly could safely concentrate his energies on the management of the House in which he had himself chosen to remain. However, it was still unwise to ignore the Lords, as was evident from the heated debates in 1717 and 1719 over the vexed question of the appellate jurisdiction, and Conolly needed friends there to take care of his and the Castle's interests. Major-General Gustavus Hamilton, a veteran of the Jacobite war, who was created Lord Hamilton in 1715 and Viscount Boyne two years later, was his principal spokesman in the upper house until dying in 1723;[8] and his successor was the churchman Theophilus Bolton, successively bishop of Clonfert (1722)

and Elphin (1724), and archbishop of Cashel (1730), who, along with his
successor at Clonfert (and eventually Cashel) Arthur Price, owed his
advancement to Conolly's patronage.[9]

At the head of Conolly's troops in the Commons stood the Speaker's
henchman, Sir Ralph Gore, who served as chancellor of the exchequer and
chairman of the committees of supply and ways and means from 1717,
until he himself succeeded to the Speakership.[10] According to Alan
Brodrick, he was simply 'a creature' of Conolly, one who 'hath a spirit
low enough not to disdain being thought a dependant'.[11] Gore had not
been in the first flight of whig party politicians in Queen Anne's reign,[12]
but he was reliable and well-connected, and backed by a covey of Gore
cousins and other relations in the House. In George I's first parliament his
closest lieutenant was probably the County Down squire Henry
Maxwell,[13] who had begun his parliamentary career as a 'country whig'
(or at least the closest Irish equivalent) with a flair for political pamphleteering, but by 1715 had metamorphosed into a staunch supporter of the
Castle, or more accurately, a staunch personal adherent of Conolly,
nicknamed 'the Speaker's echo'.[14] Less prominent at the outset of the
period, but making themselves indispensable, were the portly canon
lawyer and inveterate committee-man Marmaduke Coghill, who after
Conolly's retirement succeeded to the key position of first commissioner
of the revenue;[15] Coghill's fellow civilian Thomas Trotter, who eventually
joined him in the revenue;[16] and the barristers Thomas Marlay (solicitor-
general in 1720 and eventually chief baron of the exchequer)[17] and Henry
Singleton (prime serjeant in 1726 and later master of the rolls).[18] Less
prominent in debate, but still useful politically, were 'Ben Parry', the
registrar of deeds and a regular attender at the Irish privy council;[19] his
fellow councillor Richard Tighe (the 'Dick Fitzbaker' repeatedly pilloried
by Swift);[20] Tighe's kinsman Henry Sandford, who was also brother-
in-law to the earl of Kildare;[21] Isaac Manley, the postmaster-general
notorious for prying into the mails;[22] Henry Rose from County Limerick,
another barrister and future judge, who at first enlisted with the Brodricks
but then changed sides;[23] Agmondisham Vesey, son of the former archbishop of Tuam, and ambitious for office;[24] Major- (later Lieutenant-)
General Owen Wynne, said to be one of Conolly's 'bosom friends';[25]
Brabazon Ponsonby, still a relatively junior figure, though ultimately, as
first earl of Bessborough, to become an 'undertaker' in his own right;[26]
and a cluster of minor treasury, exchequer, and customs officials, headed
by Theophilus Clements, the teller of the exchequer, and including
Clements's son, Nathaniel, and Luke Gardiner, who was to become

deputy vice-treasurer in 1733.[27] These were the men who were closest to Conolly, who attended his political house-parties, were doubtless consulted about parliamentary strategy and tactics, and formed a roster of pro-government debaters in parliament.

The first point to be made about Conolly's circle is that their party-political backgrounds were highly varied. There were dyed-in-the-wool whigs, like Conolly himself, such as Henry Maxwell, a man who enjoyed close friendships with leading members of the whig party in England,[28] Theophilus Clements, who had the reputation among fellow whigs of having been 'honest in the worst of times',[29] and Isaac Manley, whose first recorded political statement was to have joined the Monmouth rebellion in 1685.[30] But Conolly also picked up a significant number of ex-tories in the dark days for Irish toryism after 1714,[31] notably Coghill,[32] Singleton,[33] and Agmondisham Vesey.[34] Even Bishop Bolton, though a protégé of Archbishop King of Dublin, seemed more at home with the tories in the early years of the Hanoverian regime.[35] All had political pasts to live down. But with the exception of Vesey, who turned his coat sharply as soon as his father died in 1716,[36] these were all tories of a moderate hue: none could be linked with the excesses of the Irish administration headed by Lord Chancellor Phipps in 1711–14.[37] Conolly – like Walpole – liked to shine in the company of cronies and appears not to have admitted to his inner circle those who bridled at inferiority. Equally important, perhaps, is that Conolly had known a number of his recruits for some time. His association with Coghill went back at least to 1701,[38] and it was probably Coghill who had enlisted Singleton and Trotter, the latter as early as 1713.[39] Maxwell had been on terms of close friendship with Conolly by 1703, and in the 1713 election both he and Benjamin Parry had been elected to the Commons on Conolly's borough interest, with Gore also involved in campaigning.[40]

Second, Conolly's was unlike other Irish parliamentary factions in the period in that it was not primarily based on family or regional connexions, although these can be detected and in some cases were important. His party contained some substantial family groups – the much ramified Gores, for example, who at one time could boast nine representatives in the Irish House of Commons and who were attached to Conolly through Sir Ralph, and the Ponsonbys in County Kilkenny – but these groups were linked to the Speaker through friendship and patronage rather than blood ties or marriage. By contrast the Brodrick faction, which Brodrick's ultimate political successor, Speaker Henry Boyle, inherited and developed during the 1730s, was based on a network of brothers,

brothers-in-law, and cousins (the Boyles rivalling the Gores as the most extended of Irish landed families). Nor was Conolly's party in essence a regional connexion, like the St Georges in Connacht in Queen Anne's reign, or the Cork or Munster 'squadron' commanded by Brodrick, and later Boyle.[41] Because Conolly was himself from the north-west, with substantial electoral patronage deriving from his extensive land acquisitions in Counties Donegal and Londonderry, and because one or two of his key supporters, notably Gore and Maxwell, also hailed from the north (though far apart geographically), his party was sometimes identified with the province of Ulster, but this characterisation was artificial. If anything, it would be more appropriately identified with the capital and its environs. In terms of residence, rather than county of origin, men like the Clementses, Coghill, Gardiner, Manley, Marlay, Tighe, and Trotter inhabited the official world of Dublin. And when they built new country seats they often did so within easy reach of the capital: Viscount Boyne, for example, moved from his ancestral estates in the north to set himself up at Stackallan in County Meath; Henry Singleton resided across the road from Coghill in Drumcondra, just north of Dublin; Marlay at Celbridge Abbey, close to Conolly's own rural base at Castletown; Vesey down the road at Lucan (Conolly called him 'my neighbour in the country');[42] and Ponsonby at Bishop's Court, at Straffan, also in Kildare, 'so near' Castletown 'that he can be there on an hour's warning'.[43]

What, then, did distinguish them as a group and hold them together? Most obviously, Conolly's friendship and patronage. All benefited from the Speaker's ability to find jobs in government for themselves, their relations, and friends. But beyond this basic currency of political obligation were strong personal connexions to the Speaker and each other. Their presence can be traced in Conolly's correspondence, and some, though not all, appear as beneficiaries in his will.[44] They can also be traced in each other's social circles, corresponding and visiting,[45] sharing in financial transactions or the purchase of land,[46] acting together in marriage settlements,[47] and ultimately being named as executors, trustees, and beneficiaries in each other's wills.[48] Some – the lawyers – worked together in a professional capacity. Marlay, Rose, and Singleton were barristers, and eventually judges; Coghill and Trotter both held degrees in civil law and practised in the ecclesiastical courts; while Conolly himself had made his money in the humbler capacity of an attorney. Others, like Luke Gardiner, had begun their careers in the law (or, in the case of Henry Maxwell, had attended an inn of court, though never called to the bar) but now occupied places in the Castle bureaucracy. What we have, therefore, is a close-knit group of Dublin-based men of business – lawyers, government functionaries, professional politicians with well-remunerated sinecures – men from a variety of party-political backgrounds linked together by friendship and the patronage of the most powerful politician in Ireland. The backgrounds of these men are relatively easy to delineate, but what can be said about their view of themselves and of the function and purpose of government?

One possible answer comes from the American historian Reed Browning's work on the political thought of the Walpolean court whigs.[49] Browning claimed to have identified an 'ideology' of court whiggery that, as he put it, bore the 'impress' of Ciceronian ideas of law and government; that is to say, an ideology which looked for guidance to Cicero's *De officiis* and, in contrast to the 'Catonic' vision of country whiggery, demonstrated the possibility of exercising virtue in government. Whether or not one accepts these arguments, they are not automatically transferable to Conolly's clique, other than to remind us, perhaps, that there can be more to office-holding than venality, and more to the exercise of power than self-interest. The political cultures of England and Ireland in the first half of the eighteenth century, though similar in many respects, were also crucially different. Irish Protestant gentlemen studied the same classical texts as their English counterparts, their libraries included many of the same works of history and political theory, they shared many of the same assumptions and preoccupations, but with one exception: for an Irish politician the public interest that he might claim to serve was the interest of Ireland, and a common perception among diehard 'patriots' was that the principal threat to that interest came not so much from the overbalancing of the constitution or the spread of corruption in any general sense but specifically from the oppressive nature of English government. The Anglo-Irish connexion, in other words, posed a political question that Browning's 'Ciceronians' did not have to consider.

The effort to discover whether Conolly's followers possessed a shared political outlook that was anything more than a form of collective opportunism is not greatly helped by the source materials. Browning was able to concentrate on prominent individuals who had each published reflections on the nature of politics in which they attempted to rationalise and justify their own behaviour. Of the Irish Castle party headed by Conolly, only Henry Maxwell has left any published work, and all of it focused on specific rather than general issues. None of his colleagues, not even the most verbose, was given to philosophical reflection on the vocation of office-holding. Only Conolly and Coghill are represented by substantial surviving collections of private correspondence, and these discuss practical matters rather than the nature of politics – in itself, perhaps an indication of priorities. What can be traced in these letters is a prevailing impatience with what Conolly, Coghill, and their friends perceived as factious and self-advancing opposition and, in Swift's case, with the kind of indiscreet publication which made life unnecessarily difficult for government. Coghill's letters express a mild contempt for those in parliament who 'played the patriot', whether established politicians striking a pose for popularity or country gentlemen whose starry-eyed sincerity was the transient product of youth and inexperience;[50] and sometimes quite sharp irritation at the effusions of the popular press, which he regarded as ill-timed and unhelpful. On one occasion he criticised Swift for 'making that division amongst us that must do mischief ... whereas the happiness of this country must subsist by the good agreement and harmony amongst us all, whether English or Irish Protestants'.[51] He was particularly exercised by the publication in 1731 of *Some observations on the present state of Ireland* ... by the young County Cork 'patriot' Sir Richard Cox at a crucial stage in the negotiations between the 'Irish lobby' at Westminster and the Walpole administration. Just as Coghill's friend Lord Perceval was hoping to persuade English MPs of the willingness of the Irish 'political nation' to co-operate with the British parliament, Cox declaimed against the mercantilist protectionism with which Westminster had malevolently restricted Irish trading freedoms and raised again the spectre of Irish claims to legislative autonomy. Not surprisingly, Coghill described this work as a 'cursed pamphlet', whose outbursts of anti-English sentiment were 'most scandalous and wicked'.[52]

What these references perhaps indicate is a perennial sense of managerial world-weariness, rather than any explicit ideal of public service. On the positive side it could be lauded as 'moderation': a rational, and at the same time sophisticated, even cosmopolitan, awareness of what was possible in the real world; the product of experience that had broadened horizons beyond the parochialism of Dublin politics. Thus Coghill was described by one embattled supporter of the 'English interest' in the Irish House of Lords as 'a fast friend to the present government ... as moderate in the Irish interest as most who are born here', and Benjamin Parry by another as 'truly honest and steady to the English interest ... his good sense, and the advantage of seeing the world abroad have given him a right turn, and cleared him of all narrow national partialities'.[53] Negatively, it might appear as a mere reflex action of deference to the powerful and resentment at troublemakers asking awkward questions. As Midleton observed sarcastically of Henry Singleton, he displayed 'constant goodwill and affection to those in power under King George I'.[54] However, it may be possible to dig a little more deeply if we focus on the principal issues agitating Irish politics in the first decades of the eighteenth century: the nature of the Anglo-Irish constitutional relationship; and the possibilities for the economic and social 'improvement' of the kingdom.

The constitutional dependence of Ireland was determined by the essential nature of power relations between the two kingdoms, and the identification of the ruling propertied elite in Ireland with the maintenance of English rule and of the 'English interest', an identification reinforced by the events of the Glorious Revolution and its aftermath. The country was ruled by a viceroy nominated by the English crown, which in theory deprived the Irish political classes of the capacity of influencing through their parliament the choice of their own government. In practice, however, since Lord Capel's tenure of the lord deputyship in 1694–6, government had been carried on through negotiation between the viceroy and his Irish political managers, whose qualification for office lay in the support they could claim in the Irish parliament. Three significant constitutional issues remained unresolved. First, the legislative process was still determined by Poynings' Law, which gave a supervisory role to the Irish and British privy councils. Second, the British parliament had assumed a power to legislate for Ireland, on both public and private matters, a power exercised frequently in the period 1690–1707, though more sporadically thereafter, and given statutory expression in the Declaratory Act passed at Westminster in 1720. And finally, the British House of Lords had asserted an appellate jurisdiction over Irish cases above and beyond that of the Irish House of Lords, a claim also restated in the Declaratory Act.

While some political writers and a handful of the more obsessive or excitable back-benchers in the Irish parliament attacked these arrangements as contravening the political rights of Irishmen (or Englishmen living in Ireland), what is far more characteristic of Irish Protestant opinion in the so-called 'age of Molyneux and Swift' is the acceptance of constitutional restraints in pursuit of the greater good that the English connexion was assumed to bring. From time to time in the Irish House of Commons members would denounce Poynings' Law, but with a few exceptions these complaints were directed at interference by the Irish rather than by the British privy council and derived from the more immediate political motive of embarrassing either the ruling parliamentary clique or particular councillors. The admittedly frequent interventions by the British privy council were seldom directed at popular measures and only very rarely at the holiest of holies, a money bill. Amendments at Whitehall were often necessary corrections to bills which had been poorly drafted, and even when deletions were made or extra provisions inserted that had real political significance in Ireland, these were not necessarily unpopular, the best example being the Test clause added to the 1704 Popery Act, excluding Protestant dissenters from crown and municipal office, which was welcomed by a clear majority in both houses of the Irish parliament.[55] Nor, it must be said, was the Westminster parliament's power to legislate for Ireland always disputed. Such English statutes as the act of 1689 settling the crown of Ireland on William and Mary and the act of settlement of 1701 were welcomed by Irish Protestants; and even such an enthusiastic 'patriot' as Archbishop King of Dublin was prepared to avail himself of the opportunity to secure a private act at Westminster, since the more cumbersome nature of the Irish legislative process made it both easier and cheaper to do business of this kind in England.[56] Some English acts were bitterly resented, especially the Woollen Act of 1699 and the Forfeitures Resumption Act of 1700, but in each case parliamentary opposition in Ireland focused on the effects rather than the principle. Members of the Irish House of Lords were also agitated about the trumping of their appellate jurisdiction at Westminster, and the long-running controversy over the case of *Annesley* v. *Sherlock*, which focused attention on the issue, resulted in the commitment to custody of Irish judges perceived as collaborating in English encroachments on Irish judicial preserves.[57] Nevertheless, the passage of the Declaratory Act, which reaffirmed English jurisdictional authority over Ireland, produced no parliamentary response. It may well be that some of the published comment on the *Annesley* v. *Sherlock* case, and the parliamentary speeches of some of the more committed 'patriots', had come dangerously close to challenging what one peer called the '*arcana imperii*' – the constitutional connexion between Britain and Ireland.[58] Whatever the reason, Conolly's own view of the controversy was cool to the point of being dismissive. As English ministers fretted that the Declaratory Act would inflame patriotic sensibilities and discussed how to postpone the session, he wrote that:

really my humble opinion is that the House of Lords will be in a better temper, for as to the point of jurisdiction, that is over and determined, and cannot be returned or repeated, and sure no wise or thinking man will or can stir further in it, especially when they consider they may risk future parliaments and do the nation more mischief than they can ever do them good ... And further, why should this resentment reach the House of Commons, who never concerned themselves in the Lords' jurisdiction or had anything to do with that matter, but many of them to my knowledge used all their endeavours not to have the Lords commit my Lord Chief Baron and the rest.[59]

The points Conolly was making are typical of references to be found in the correspondence of his associates on such constitutional issues, that is to say, first, it was pointless to resist the fact of English constitutional domination since this was built into the nature of the relationship between the two kingdoms; second, those who agreed with him were 'wise and thinking men', and by implication those who disagreed were foolish and blindly reactive; and third, to achieve the good of the nation required a more pragmatic approach. Nothing very exciting here, intellectually, but indicative of an attempt to rationalise a position that others satirised as merely passive and self-serving.

It was not always possible to maintain this complacent attitude, however. Conolly himself, and other members of his party, occasionally found it politically necessary or convenient to make a public defence of Irish interests. As a lord justice and revenue commissioner, Conolly was placed in an extremely difficult position by the furore against Wood's halfpence and, rather than be outflanked by Midleton, was obliged to withhold the active assistance that English ministers sought from him.[60] Three years earlier, he and his closest associates had played an even more devious game in relation to the project to establish an Irish national bank, which had originally been a non-party or cross-party scheme to promote the economic welfare of the kingdom in which Viscount Boyne, Sir Ralph Gore, and Henry Sandford had been 'managers', Theophilus Clements, Gardiner, Manley, Marlay, Maxwell, Parry, Ponsonby, Rose, Vesey, and Wynne early investors, and Maxwell a public advocate, but which ran into trouble during its progress through the Irish parliament.[61] The role played by Conolly's party in the ensuing debates is difficult to explain, as he and his followers switched from supporting the Bank to opposing it on patriotic grounds, and then back to supporting it again, but it is likely that he was seeking to balance the attractions of popularity with the desirability of wrong-footing the Brodricks.[62] The same, rather desperate, opportunism gave rise in the same session to a malicious motion from Henry Maxwell against the operation of Poynings' Law, which was specifically intended as an attack on Midleton's actions in the Irish privy council.[63]

Much earlier in his career, Conolly himself had taken up a frankly confrontational position over one instance of English parliamentary interference in Irish affairs: the Forfeitures Resumption Act of 1700. Here he had a particular axe to grind, having made a fortune himself through dealing in forfeited estates, as a purchaser and manager.[64] The resumption was presented in England as an assault by the 'country party' on court corruption, but the implications in Ireland were very different, for the forfeited Jacobite estates that had been granted by King William to whig politicians and royal favourites had been sold or leased to Irish Protestants, and for parliament to rescind the grants would have resulted in serious financial consequences for a significant section of the Irish landed classes. A key element of the political crusade against the act in Ireland was the so-called 'national remonstrance', a campaign of county addresses to the King, in the organisation of which Conolly took the lead, aided by two men who were later to be closely associated with him in government, Gustavus Hamilton and Marmaduke Coghill.[65] Clearly the issue was of vital importance to Conolly personally, but it is important to note that the addresses did not challenge the right of the English parliament to legislate for Ireland (even though the signatories were caricatured by their English opponents as aiming at 'independency', a charge they vigorously denied).[66]

The only member of Conolly's faction who expressed public views on the nature of the Anglo-Irish constitutional relationship was Henry Maxwell.[67] In his younger days Maxwell had cultivated a number of interesting contacts in England, including the future chief minister James Stanhope, then an independent-minded back-bencher, and through Stanhope the circle of 'country whigs' surrounding the third earl of Shaftesbury. He wrote two political pamphlets in the early 1700s, one calling for war against the great tyrant Louis XIV and the other, in 1703, recommending a union of England and Ireland, some of the arguments of which were redolent of the 'classical republican' rhetoric in recent English tracts against a standing army.[68] Maxwell also spoke in the Irish parliament in favour of regular sessions and against the operation of Poynings' Law. It would be tempting to see the trajectory of his career in terms of the gradual evaporation of youthful principle (much as it might be possible to say the same of Stanhope), and a superficial reading of the evidence would support this interpretation. However, it is possible to trace a consistent thread in Maxwell's understanding of the Anglo-Irish political connexion. His objections to the Poynings' Law procedure were not to English conciliar superintendence but to the involvement of the Irish privy council in drafting bills of their own and amending the 'heads' sent up from the Commons in a way that made the council almost a third partner in the legislative process. Second, Maxwell's appeal for an

Anglo-Irish union in 1703 – one of the objectives of which was to defend the Irish Protestant elite from the charges that had been levelled against supporters of the remonstrance of seeking independence from England – far from releasing Ireland from the suffocating embrace of its sister kingdom would in practice have tightened English control over Irish affairs, since the English majority in a united parliament would have been empowered to legislate for Ireland without the need for a statutory instrument. Later, in the two pamphlets he wrote in 1721 in support of a national bank, Maxwell acknowledged Ireland's constitutional subordination as an unchallengeable fact of political life and argued that English supervision was a guarantee of Ireland's freedom from the machinations of its own vested interests.[69] He explained publicly the virtues of a pragmatic constitutionalism in the same terms as Conolly had done privately:[70]

the circumstances of Ireland, by reason of her dependence, are such, that she cannot always obtain the advantages she aims at, when she would, nor in the manner she desires; yet I have constantly observ'd, that we have thought it our wisdom, rather to take a part, than refuse the whole, and, in favours granted, rather to accept them in the manner they would be granted in, than refuse them, because we could not have them in the manner we desired.

A cynic might well have said, of course, that the advantages arising from the English connexion to Maxwell himself, his political chieftain, and their friends were considerable, in the shape of jobs, pensions, and opportunities to turn political power into profit. None the less, it is clear from the correspondence of other members of the Conolly connexion, notably Coghill, writing in the early 1730s, that there was genuine belief in the constructive possibilities of the existing constitutional system. Between 1729 and 1731 Coghill, now a revenue commissioner, worked in close co-operation with Viscount Perceval (the future Lord Egmont) to persuade the English parliament to remove the duty on imported Irish yarn, open more ports to receive Irish wool and woollen products, and remove some of the restrictions on colonial trade in the earlier Navigation Acts, in return for a pledge from the Irish parliament to restrain the illicit trade to France.[71] Coghill relied not only on Perceval's friendship with Sir Robert Walpole and on his own contacts among English politicians, but also on his belief that English MPs would accept that the English and Irish economies could and should be mutually supportive. Sadly for him, few of them did.

Economic issues figured prominently in Coghill's correspondence from the late 1720s onwards, and not only while he held office as a revenue commissioner, when he might have been expected to take an official interest in the promotion of trade. Although not himself possessed of large estates and thus of the opportunity for direct participation in economic enterprise, he took a particular interest in the 'improvement of Ireland', reading and disseminating the literature on the subject, collecting information on trade patterns and communicating these to friends in England whom he thought able to shape policy.[72] His circle of correspondents included many of the leading figures involved in promoting agricultural and technical innovation and settling new industries: Thomas Prior (whom he was said to have employed)[73] and James Hamilton, Lord Limerick, both stalwarts of the Dublin Society; the pamphleteer David Bindon; and two absentee landowners who, despite residing in England, took a great interest in the 'improvement' of their estates, Viscount Perceval and Edward Southwell.[74] Coghill himself served for many years on the Linen Board, which had been established by act of parliament in 1711 for the promotion of the linen manufacture, and from 1729 on the Navigation Board, a similar statutory body that granted public money for developing economic infrastructure. He was also closely involved in the management of a number of charitable enterprises, including schools, hospitals, and the Dublin workhouse, which took the notion of 'improvement' beyond economic progress to encompass broader social objectives, alleviating poverty and inculcating in the Irish population a form of English civility which in the minds of many enthusiasts was also intimately connected with the promotion of Protestant piety.[75]

Almost all the other prominent members of Conolly's party were involved in schemes for the 'improvement' of Ireland, through their own efforts, through belonging to voluntary organisations or government bodies, or through promoting legislative initiatives. Archbishop Bolton, as his private papers make clear, was exercised both by what we might term macro-economic issues – the imbalance of Anglo-Irish trade and the weakness of the Irish coinage, on both of which he wrote at some length – and micro-economic issues – investment in building and the promotion of manufacturing in his dioceses.[76] At one point his economic 'patriotism' extended to endorsing the idea of a tax on absentees.[77] Henry Maxwell – whose writings had recommended increased Protestant settlement in Ireland for just this purpose[78] – was included by Bishop Francis Hutchinson among a small number of exemplary 'improvers'.[79] Together with Richard Tighe, Maxwell was among the subscribers to John Laurence's *A new system of agriculture* (1727).[80] He may also be linked (as may Henry

Rose), through tellerships and committees in the House of Commons, with Arthur Dobbs, author of the *Essay on the trade and improvement of Ireland* (1729), someone who was also a favourite of William Conolly,[81] and through Dobbs with the circle of public advocates of improvement that included Coghill's friends Prior and Bindon. These were the men who provided the ideas and energy behind the foundation in June 1731 of the Dublin Society, itself both a symbol and instrument of the cause of improvement,[82] and several members of the Castle party were among the members admitted in its first year. Archbishop Bolton and Bishop Price joined in September 1731, Luke Gardiner, Isaac Manley, and Henry Rose in November, Richard Tighe in December, and Benjamin Parry in the following March. Others may also have been admitted, but their membership was not formally recorded in the minutes.[83] Of course, not everyone joined such societies for entirely serious purposes, and elements of sociability and snobbery presumably became even more pronounced when the new viceroy, Dorset, gave the society his patronage in December 1731, but the records of meetings exude an earnestness in the cause of national improvement, and occasionally we encounter specific evidence of agricultural or industrial activity, as in March 1732, when barrels of a new compost were distributed to members, including Marmaduke Coghill.[84]

Membership of the various statutory bodies charged with supervising schemes for the economic and social 'improvement' of Ireland provides less clear proof of commitment to the cause, since the overall number of nominees in each case was high, and prominent dignitaries, clerical and lay, could expect to be named. But the cumulative evidence is suggestive. The Linen Board established by the Linen Act of 1711 (9 Anne, c. 3 [I]) to oversee the development of the linen manufacture included Conolly, Coghill, Gustavus Hamilton, and Henry Sandford among its more than seventy original members. They were later joined by Bolton, Gardiner, Gore, Marlay, Ponsonby, Rose, Singleton, and Trotter.[85] The Dublin workhouse, when reorganised by statute in 1727–8 (1 Geo. II, c. 27 [I]), included Conolly, Gore, Marlay, and Singleton *ex officio*, and among the eighty or so named trustees were Bolton, Nathaniel and Theophilus Clements, Coghill, Manley, Maxwell, Parry, Ponsonby, Rose, Tighe, Vesey, and Wynne.[86] And finally the Navigation Board, established to administer the funding raised by the Navigation or Tillage Act of 1729–30 (3 Geo. II, c. 3 [I]), a portmanteau measure pushed forward by the ministry as of vital importance to the regeneration of the Irish economy, which comprehended the draining of bogs, the promotion of tillage, and the building of canals,[87] included among its over ninety nominated members a squadron of familiar faces: Bolton, Coghill, Gardiner, Gore, Marlay, Maxwell, Parry, Ponsonby, Rose, Sandford, Singleton, Tighe, Trotter, Vesey, and Wynne.[88] How many of these individuals attended meetings of the respective boards is unknown, but we do know from Coghill's own correspondence that he, for one, did involve himself in the work of the Navigation Board,[89] while a signed order of the workhouse governors in 1729 bears the names of Manley, Sandford, and Tighe;[90] and the records of the Linen Board show that Bolton, Coghill, Gardiner, Gore, Marlay, Ponsonby, Rose, Sandford, Singleton, and Trotter were all at one time or another active members.[91]

In parliament Henry Maxwell had a particularly strong record of sponsoring legislation to foster economic development. Between 1715 and his death in 1730 he was involved in the preparation, introduction, and progress of bills for harbour construction, the improvement of tillage, the reduction of interest charged on loans (a nostrum advanced by various apostles of economic improvement),[92] the safeguarding of fisheries, the employment of the poor, the facilitation of export sales of beef and dairy products, the protection of the woollen industry, the encouragement of tanning and of the manufacture of 'Bologna crape', and, almost on an annual basis, measures to improve the quality of linen.[93] But he was far from unusual in this regard among the leading lights of the Castle party. Agmondisham Vesey and Henry Rose were particularly active. They helped Maxwell draft tillage bills, bills for reducing interest, and for regulating the sale of butter, and were also prominent in the legislative campaign for improving Ireland's roads. Vesey took a leading role in the promotion of measures for the development of mining, and Rose in preparing bills setting the poor to work.[94] Thomas Marlay, too, was frequently given responsibility for such legislation, as might only have been expected from someone who was a senior law officer for ten years, as solicitor-general 1720–7 and attorney-general 1727–30. From 1717, when he was named to a drafting committee on heads of a bill for the employment of the poor, he was involved in the preparation and discussion of legislation on improving roads, planting and preserving timber, encouraging tillage, and regulating the Dublin workhouse.[95] Coghill worked on bills for the planting of timber, the manufacture and sale of dairy products, the leather industry, and the repair of highways.[96] Trotter chaired the committee appointed to examine the petition of a paper-maker for, in effect, financial sponsorship by parliament, and was also involved in a timber planting bill, and in various legislative attempts to deal with poverty.[97] Richard Tighe led a Commons inquiry into the possibility of manufacturing gunpowder in Ireland and worked on bills for tillage, timber, roads, and the problem of the idle poor.[98] Sir Ralph Gore chaired the committee in 1715–16 preparing heads of a bill to preserve the salmon fishery and was involved in measures to regulate the linen industry and the improvement of Dublin harbour.[99] Henry Singleton took prime responsibility in 1729 for the legislation establishing the Navigation Board and also participated in the drafting of heads of bills for the regulation of the Dublin workhouse and the construction of roads.[100] Benjamin Parry was involved in managing several linen bills and the Dublin harbour bill;[101] Isaac Manley bills for reducing the interest of money and employing the poor;[102] and Henry Sandford bills for the employment of the poor and establishing the Dublin–Kinnegad turnpike.[103] The 'Castle party' was also identified with the parliamentary campaign to improve the education of poor children – in both the Protestant religion and the 'habits of industry'. When leave was granted in 1723 for heads for a bill to amend the act relating to free schools, the MPs named were Trotter, Marlay, Coghill, and Singleton; and a similar bill in 1725 included Trotter, Coghill, and Maxwell on the drafting committee, with Maxwell in the chair.[104]

It is worth pointing out that Conolly himself, though singled out for praise by Thomas Prior in his *List of absentees . . .*, published in 1729, as a landlord who lived in Ireland and kept his wealth in the country,[105] did not have a reputation for the energetic exploitation of the economic resources of his landed empire and for most of his career left the management of his property to stewards and agents, his eyes turned to rental income rather than agricultural productivity.[106] However, he did engage more directly in the last years of his life, when a series of bad harvests across Ireland plunged the economy into crisis. The effects were felt most keenly in north-west Ulster, where Conolly owned large tracts of land, and where miserable economic conditions had resulted in a mass emigration, mainly of Presbyterians, to North America. His agent, Robert McCausland, kept him informed of the condition of the tenantry, and although he did not take McCausland's advice and recommend the introduction of a law to prevent emigration, he did what he could to advance charitable efforts for the relief of distress.[107]

If it existed at all, Conolly's public commitment to 'improvement' took a more personal form. While he did not pay particular attention to the economic progress of his estates, he was prepared to pay, and on a lavish scale, for the building of a new house, in the latest architectural fashion, at Castletown in County Kildare. Conolly's Palladian mansion, probably designed in part by the young Edward Lovett Pearce, decorated with plaster ceilings by visiting Italian craftsmen, decked out with fine furnishings, and surrounded by formal gardens, staged the house parties which were his, and Ireland's, equivalent of the congresses held by Walpole at Houghton.[108] Clearly the building of Castletown was meant in part as a political statement. It has been linked with the building of the new Parliament House in Dublin between 1729 and 1731, designed by Pearce, much more obviously an assertion of patriotic self-respect.[109] But whether the kind of conspicuous consumption that Castletown represented can properly be classified with more constructive investment in agricultural or industrial development is an open question. Some historians think it should be, and discussions of the vogue for 'improvement' in eighteenth-century Ireland have included under this general heading the construction of new houses, importation of English and continental luxuries, emparking of demesnes, and horticultural experimentation.[110] In this respect it is worth noting that Conolly's example was followed, or perhaps in some case anticipated, by most of his close friends: Marmaduke Coghill left the house outside Dublin that he had inherited, Belvedere House, in the hands of his friend Henry Singleton and built a new mansion across the road, Drumcondra House, which may also have been the work of Pearce, with gardens and pleasure grounds and a sumptuous interior.[111] Singleton in turn began to remodel Belvedere in his retirement. He was 'very busy adding to his house and altering his gardens', as Mrs. Delany observed, 'like a conceited connoisseur … doing strange things, building an absurd room, turning fine wild evergreens out of his garden, and planting twigs'.[112] Elsewhere Theophilus Bolton may have engaged Edward Lovett Pearce to build the new episcopal palace at Cashel, on which he is alleged to have spent £3,600; Arthur Price, while rector of Celbridge, possibly employed the surveyor-general Thomas Burgh (architect of the new library at Trinity College) to build Oakly Park nearby; Lord Boyne erected a new house at Stackallan, while, in the same county, Thomas Trotter had the renowned Irish architect Richard Castle create for him a mansion on his ancestral estate at Duleek, and Brabazon Ponsonby employed another rising star, Francis Bindon, to produce plans for Bessborough House in County Kilkenny.[113] Luke Gardiner, the vice-treasurer, developed several squares and streets on the north side of Dublin city, a process which his protégé and successor, Nathaniel Clements, a very junior member of the Castle faction under Conolly and his immediate successors, carried forward, before reconstructing the house in Phoenix Park which he occupied by virtue of holding the office of ranger of the park.[114]

Of course, none of this effectively distinguishes the members of the Castle party from the general run of eighteenth-century Irish country gentlemen. Conolly's and Coghill's new houses and gardens could be matched by the embellishments to architecture and landscape undertaken by political opponents, such as Viscount Molesworth.[115] Nor was a concern for economic 'improvement' only to be found in the ranks of the Castle party. There were opposition 'patriots' as well as government officials in the Dublin Society, and, to give only one example, the support given by Maxwell in his published writings to the further settlement in Ireland of colonies of foreign Protestants with manufacturing expertise were echoes of Molesworth.[116] But what is significant about the commitment to improvement to be found in Conolly's party is that it was presented as an expression of their 'patriotism' and used to distinguish this more conservative brand from what they saw as the factiousness of their opponents.

The elaborate arrangements for Conolly's funeral in 1729, organised by his widow, included the distribution of 700 Irish linen scarves among the mourners, an ostentatious gesture intended to emphasise the Speaker's commitment to Irish industry.[117] In making these arrangements Mrs. Conolly was not only expressing her own well-known concern for the encouragement of Irish manufacture,[118] but also staking a claim for her deceased husband's credentials as a representative of Irish 'patriotism' in what was contested ground between government and opposition. Each side claimed a commitment to the interests of Ireland, but went about proving their sincerity in different ways. 'Country' members put forward votes and resolutions aimed at preserving the rights and privileges of the Irish parliament, exposing corruption and incompetence in government, or, in some cases, seeking to embarrass the viceroy by engineering a crisis in Anglo-Irish relations.[119] This was what Bishop Bolton called 'peevish patriotism', espoused by those who 'set up for popularity', as opposed to the genuine 'patriotism' he perceived in his ministerial colleagues.[120] For the Castle party, on the other hand, patriotic pretensions could be established by supporting constructive measures for the development of the Irish economy, and for the improvement of Irish society, within the existing constitutional framework.

The obvious question is whether this kind of pragmatic, economic-oriented patriotism constituted a genuine aspiration or merely a posture. The evident concern shown by ministerialist whigs for fostering improvement on their own property, for passing legislation to nurture Irish manufactures and improve infrastructure, and their connexion with bodies like the Dublin Society and the Linen and Navigation Boards provides one answer.[121] Another is suggested by the complexities of the relationships within government, between Irish politicians and English appointees. When Conolly fell seriously ill in 1728, and the end of his political career was in sight, he was lauded by one of his lieutenants for the way in which he had been able to represent the native-born political elite on the commission of lords justices; it was vital, the argument ran, that his replacement be an Irishman, and one similarly committed to advancing national interests.[122] Gore, his successor, was said to have run into difficulties with his English colleagues on the commission, who neither knew nor cared for Ireland as he did.[123] Admittedly, the sharpest differences occurred between lords justices, and indeed more generally between men like Conolly and Gore, and agents of the 'English interest' like Primate Boulter and Lord Chancellor Wyndham, concerning recommendations to office. When responding to vacancies in the judiciary, or the Church of Ireland episcopate, Conolly invariably pushed forward Irishmen – and invariably his own loyal supporters – while Boulter at first argued the advantages of reminding the Irish of their subordinate status by bringing in Englishmen, who would be more likely to stand loyal to government in any crisis in Anglo-Irish relations, such as had occurred over Wood's patent.[124] This was indeed 'patriotism' of a sort, even if it was in Conolly's personal interest to recommend his friends and dependants. In the revenue commission he took a similar line, appointing Irishmen to posts in the customs and excise ostensibly on grounds of knowledge and experience, and with an explicit objective of increasing the professionalism and efficiency of collection, though with the additional benefit to himself of expanding the reserves of obligation among Irish political families.[125] But not all the battles fought by Conolly and Gore with their English colleagues were over patronage. Others concerned matters of policy, often economic policy – whether to revalue the currency, for example, or to prevent the export of corn in times of distress.[126] Over the course of their careers in government the two Speakers could claim a number of successes in struggles which were hidden from the public gaze and from which they derived no political capital. It would probably have surprised back-bench 'patriots' that staunch courtiers like Bolton and Coghill should be accused by Archbishop Boulter, the prime spokesman for the 'English interest' in the Dublin government, of being unreasonably 'patriotic' and thus unreliable.[127]

No amount of searching will reveal a clearly and expressly articulated 'ideology' among the governing elite in early Hanoverian Ireland. Unlike Browning's selection of court whigs, Conolly and his friends were not given to public reflection on the moral difficulties of reconciling virtue

with the exercise of power. One obvious place to look for evidence of the
way in which the concept of public duty was understood, epitaphs on
funerary monuments, also yields a poor return, except for the tributes
paid by Mrs. Conolly to the memory of the Speaker, and Marmaduke
Coghill's sister to her deceased brother, to which I shall return. What can
be identified, however, is the social context which the Castle party
inhabited, and the mentality which they seem to have shared and which
shaped their political attitudes. Much of this is perfectly unexceptional
for men of their class and time: acceptance of the constitutional arrangements under which Irish government operated – given the absence of a
practicable alternative – and a concern for the social and economic
improvement of the kingdom. But for those charged with the business
of administration and the making of law, such commonplaces might
easily be elevated into points of principle, especially when contrasted with
the more extreme rhetoric of 'patriots' within parliament and popular
pamphleteers outside it.

It was an attitude that Swift professed to regard as bogus. In a memorable passage in the Drapier's *Letter to the whole people of Ireland*, he
parodied ministerial patriotism in describing how the myrmidons of
the Castle would in all likelihood seek to persuade Irish MPs to accept
the ruinous coinage minted by the rascal Wood:

Depending persons would have been told, in plain terms, that it was a service
expected from them, under the pain of public business being put into more
complying hands. Others would be allured by promises ... It would perhaps
have been hinted ... that gentlemen ought to consider whether it were prudent
or safe to disgust England. They would be desired to think of some good bills
for encouraging of trade, and setting the poor to work; some further acts
against popery ... Perhaps a seasonable report of some invasion would have been
spread ... and we should have been told, that this was no time to create
differences, when the kingdom was in danger.[128]

The stinging force of this passage comes from the wicked accuracy with
which it imitated the case usually made by parliamentary 'undertakers'
and their assistants in order to convince MPs of the necessity of accepting
unpopular measures. When in due course such arguments were put
forward, readers would infer what the dean wished them to infer, namely
that the Castle spokesmen were hacks serving a turn rather than patriots
serving their country. This does not, of course, mean that we should take
Swift's public denunciations at face value; indeed, he may not himself
have taken an entirely negative view of Conolly's 'Castle' party. While
Tighe, Clements, and Vesey were roundly condemned in print, Luke

Gardiner reprimanded in public as a sham patriot, and Speaker Conolly himself sneered at in private correspondence,[129] Swift enjoyed good relations with Coghill, eventually appreciated the merits of Bolton, regarded Price as 'honest and good natured', and held a high opinion of Henry Singleton, whom he described as 'one of the first among the worthiest persons in this kingdom' and named an executor of his will.[130]

Some at least of Conolly's followers may indeed have conformed to the caricature of Dublin lawyers and officials on the make, second-rate political figures who were emulating their patron in making fortunes from a privileged access to power. But amidst the flaunting of wealth they do seem to have prided themselves on the possession of a genuine concern for the improvement of their country, and a coherent and realistic strategy for achieving it. This self-belief is expressed in the words of the monument to Speaker Conolly, in Kildraught church near Castletown, which eulogised his devotion both to crown and kingdom: 'as a subject he was loyal; as a citizen, patriotic' – 'he served his country without forgetting his duty to his king, and served his king without forgetting what was due to his country'.[131] It appears even more floridly in the inscription placed by Hester Coghill under the oversized statue of her brother, Marmaduke, in the church built from the ample profits accrued from his two decades in high office.[132] Whether or not it accurately represents his character is immaterial; what is important is the terms in which Hester couched her eulogy, and which may stand as an epitome of the political pretensions of her brother and his friends:

his experience of the true interest of his prince and of his country, and his strict attention and invincible regard to both, qualified him equally to discharge his trust as a counsellor and servant of the crown and a representative of the subject ... his universal benevolence, endeared by the most engaging and affable behaviour, and associated with the greatest zeal and abilities, distinguished him in every scene and period of life as the friend of mankind, and caused his death to be lamented as a national loss.

NOTES

I am much obliged to my colleague, Professor S. J. Connolly, for a penetrating commentary on a draft of this chapter.

1 Swift to Pope, 10 Jan. 1721, *Correspondence*, II, 370.
2 See, for example, the dedications to Speaker Conolly in James Sterling, *The rival generals: a tragedy. As it was acted at the Theatre Royal, in Dublin ...* (London, 1722), p. iv, and John Browne, *An essay on trade in general; and, on*

that of Ireland in particular (Dublin, 1728); James Sterling, *A funeral poem on the death of the right honourable William Conolly* ... (Dublin, 1729); the brief ode to Conolly's memory included in *Tunbrigalia: Or, Tunbridge miscellanies, for the year 1730* (London, 1730), p. 12; the dedication to Lord Chancellor Midleton in [David Bindon,] *Some reasons, shewing the necessity the people of Ireland are under, for continuing to refuse Mr. Wood's coinage* (Dublin, 1724), p. 4; and the monumental inscriptions to Coghill and Conolly, quoted at p. 243.

3 For what follows, see Patrick McNally, *Parties, patriots and undertakers: parliamentary politics in early Hanoverian Ireland* (Dublin, 1997), pp. 120–36; D. W. Hayton, *Ruling Ireland, 1685–1742: politics, politicians and parties* (Woodbridge, 2004), pp. 217–35.

4 For example, D. W. Hayton, 'Two ballads on the County Westmeath election of 1723', *Eighteenth-Century Ireland*, 4 (1989), 7–30, esp. 17–18, 28–9.

5 See in particular Charles Ivar McGrath, *The making of the eighteenth-century Irish constitution: government, parliament and the revenue, 1692–1714* (Dublin, 2000), ch. 3; and McGrath, 'English ministers, Irish politicians and the making of a parliamentary settlement in Ireland, 1692–5', *English Historical Review*, 119 (2004), 585–613; and more generally John Bergin, 'Irish legislative procedure after the Williamite revolution: the operation of Poynings' Law, 1692–1705' (University College Dublin PhD thesis, 2005); and James Kelly, *Poynings' Law and the making of law in Ireland, 1660–1800* (Dublin, 2007), ch. 2.

6 Hayton, *Ruling Ireland*, pp. 108–9; Kelly, *Poynings' Law*, pp. 134, 204. Cf. F. G. James, *Lords of the ascendancy: the Irish House of Lords and its members, 1600–1800* (Blackrock, Co. Dublin, 1995), pp. 75–8, 83–6.

7 F. G. James, *Ireland in the empire, 1688–1770: a history of Ireland from the Williamite wars to the eve of the American Revolution* (Cambridge, Mass., 1973), pp. 95–7; James, *Lords of the ascendancy*, pp. 78–9; R. E. Burns, *Irish parliamentary politics in the eighteenth century* (2 vols., Washington DC, 1989–90), I, 18: McNally, *Parties, patriots and undertakers*, pp. 52–4.

8 See the biographical entries in Edith Mary Johnston-Liik, *History of the Irish parliament, 1692–1800* (6 vols., Belfast, 2002 (henceforth *Hist. Ir. parl.*)), IV, 333–4, and *ODNB*, XXIV, 809–10.

9 Abp Boulter of Armagh to Ld Carteret, 7 Mar. 1726[/7] (*Letters written by his excellency Hugh Boulter,* ... (2 vols., Oxford, 1769–70), I, 146); Conolly to Thomas Clutterbuck, 2 Jan., 17/18 Feb. 1726[/7] (Irish Architectural Archive (henceforth IAA), Conolly papers, A/3/43, 46); Francis Burton to Jane Bonnell, 19 Jan. 1729/30 (National Library of Ireland (henceforth NLI), Smythe of Barbavilla papers, MS 41,579/10). For Bolton see *ODNB*, VI, 495–6; for Price, ibid., XLV, 281–2.

10 For Gore's importance, see Henry Rose to Maurice Crosbie, 25 June 1720 (NLI, Talbot-Crosbie papers, PC 188).

11 [Ld Brodrick] to [Thomas Brodrick], 14 June 1717 (Surrey History Centre (henceforth SHC), Brodrick papers, 1248/4/35–6). For Gore, see *Hist. Ir. parl.*, IV, 284–6; *ODNB*, XXII, 985.

12 He was not included among the whig leaders invited to Dublin Castle in January 1714 by the viceroy, Shrewsbury, to explore the opportunities for a compromise settlement of political differences that would permit a resumption of the parliamentary session: Ld Abercorn to [Edward Southwell], 5 Jan. 1713/14 (Public Record Office of Northern Ireland (henceforth PRONI), Abercorn papers, D/623/A/3/12).

13 During the parliamentary session of 1715–16 Lord Chancellor Brodrick referred to Gore and Maxwell as 'the Speaker's two confidants' (Ld Brodrick to Thomas Brodrick, 5 Apr. 1716 (SHC, 1248/3/352–5).

14 D. W. Hayton, 'Henry Maxwell, M.P., author of *An essay upon an union of Ireland with England* (1703)', *Eighteenth-Century Ireland*, 22 (2007), 35–7. On Maxwell in general, see ibid., 28–63; Caroline Robbins, *The eighteenth-century commonwealthman* (Cambridge, Mass., 1959), pp. 147–8; *Hist. Ir. parl.*, V, 222–3; *ODNB*, XXXVII, 500–1.

15 *Letters of Marmaduke Coghill, 1722–1738*, ed. D. W. Hayton (Irish Manuscripts Commission, Dublin, 2005), pp. xi–xxii. See also *Hist. Ir. parl.*, III, 442–5; *ODNB*, XII, 411–12.

16 *Hist. Ir. parl.*, VI, 443–4.

17 Ibid., V, 191–3. Marlay was recommended by Conolly for a place on the judicial bench in 1720: rough note by Conolly on legal promotions (IAA, Conolly papers, A/3/15A–B).

18 *Hist. Ir parl.*, VI, 276–7; *ODNB*, I, 787–8.

19 *Hist. Ir. parl.* VI, 21–2. See also Sir Richard Levinge to Edward Southwell, 17 Oct. 1721 (Sir Richard G. A. Levinge, *Jottings for early history of the Levinge family* (privately printed, Dublin, 1873), p. 65).

20 *Hist. Ir. parl.*, VI, 395–7; *Swift: poetical works*, ed. Herbert Davis (London, 1967), pp. 339–46, 247–51, 605–6; Jonathan Swift and Thomas Sheridan, *The Intelligencer*, ed. James Woolley (Oxford, 1992), pp. 100–14, 130–4.

21 *Hist. Ir. parl.*, VI, 233–4; Hayton, 'Co. Westmeath election ballads', 29; [Ld Midleton] to [Thomas Brodrick], 21 Oct. 1723 (SHC, 1248/5/323–4).

22 *Hist. Ir. parl.*, V, 190–1; Swift to Charles Ford, 27 Nov., 31 Dec. 1724, *Correspondence*, II, 531, 539–40; St John Brodrick to [Ld Midleton], 11, 21 Jan. 1723[/4] (SHC, 1248/5/358–9, 368–9).

23 *Hist. Ir. parl.*, VI, 188–90; Charles Delafaye to ——, 4 May 1716 (The National Archives [of the United Kingdom], Public Record Office (henceforth TNA, PRO), SP 63/374/219); rough note by Conolly on legal promotions (IAA, Conolly papers, A/3/15A–B).

24 *Hist. Ir. parl.*, VI, 468–9; [Midleton] to Thomas Brodrick, 30 Sept. 1717, 11 Nov. 1721 (SHC, 12548/4/73–4, 1248/5/136–7).

25 *Hist. Ir. parl.*, VI, 562–3; [Midleton] to Thomas Brodrick, 11 Nov. 1721, 21 Oct. 1723 (SHC, 1248/5/136–7, 323–4).

26 *Hist. Ir. parl.*, VI, 79–81.

27 Ibid., II, 433–4, 425–30; IV, 257–60; A. P. W. Malcomson, *Nathaniel Clements: government and the governing elite in Ireland, 1725–75* (Dublin, 2005), chs. 1–2, 5; Theophilus Clements to Conolly, 29 July 1727 (IAA, Conolly papers, A/3/49).

28 Hayton, 'Henry Maxwell', pp. 29–30.

29 Charles Delafaye to Lord Sunderland, 24 Jan. 1715/16 (British Library (henceforth BL), Blenheim papers, Add. MS 61640, f. 80).

30 George Roberts, *The life, progresses and rebellion of James, duke of Monmouth* (2 vols., London, 1844), I, 262; II, 51, 260; Bp Godwin of Kilmore to [Abp Wake of Canterbury], 9 June 1716 (Christ Church, Oxford, Wake papers, Arch. W. Epist. xii); Hayton, 'Co. Westmeath election ballads', 28; Jane Bulkeley to Jane Bonnell, 9 Dec. [?1721] (NLI, Smythe of Barbavilla papers, MS 41580/3), referring to Manley as one of Conolly's 'creatures', and 'is said to be one of them that is a cat's claw, to do things that he has no mind to appear in himself'.

31 The flexibility of Conolly's attitude to former political enemies may also be visible in his admission as a freeman of Galway in 1722, alongside the ex-tory George Staunton, as part of a resurgence of the Staunton-led tory interest in the city (Galway corporation minute, 28 Aug. 1722 (National University of Ireland, Galway, Hardiman Library, Galway corporation records, minute book F, p. 103)).

32 Bp Godwin to [Abp Wake], 27 Feb. 1715/16 (Christ Church, Arch. W. Epist. xii) described Coghill as 'a tory more by dependence than principle', and a supporter of Henry Boyle in 1729 referred to him as a 'moderate' (Arthur Hill to Boyle, 15 Apr. 1729 (PRONI, D/2707/A/1/2/39)).

33 In 1729 he was said to stand at the head of 'a brigade of tories' (Arthur Hill to Henry Boyle, 15 Apr. 1729 (PRONI, D/2707/A/1/2/39)), and as late as 1738 he was still being 'represented as a warm tory' by those who wished to prejudice the English ministry against his claims to preferment (William Richardson to Bp Howard of Elphin, 4 Jan. 1738 (NLI, Wicklow papers).

34 Thomas Trotter, as a civil lawyer and consistory court judge, and the son-in-law of a former tory MP, Abel Ram, may also have been a tory by political inclination, but he had not sat in the Irish parliament before 1715, and it is impossible to confirm this supposition.

35 Bp Godwin to [Abp Wake], 31 Oct. 1716 (Christ Church, Arch W. Epist. xii).

36 Ld Brodrick to Thomas Brodrick, 5 Apr. 1716 (SHC, 1248/4/352–5) ranked Vesey with the tories in the 1716 parliament, but during 1717 Conolly described him as having acted the part of an 'honest man' in the Commons then and in the preceding sessions (Conolly to Charles Delafaye, 8 Aug. 1717 (TNA, PRO, SP 63/375/152)).

37 Coghill, Singleton, and Vesey may still have been reckoned as sympathetic to the tory interest on the questions relating to the established church, as all three were included early in the 1719 session on what appears to be a lobbying list of MPs – the vast majority recognisable tories from Queen Anne's reign – in relation to the proposed repeal of the Test: IAA, Conolly papers, A/3/9B.

38 Coghill had been involved with Conolly in organising the so-called 'National Remonstrance' against the English Forfeitures Resumption Act (*Commons' Journals*, XIII, 718; Patrick Walsh, 'The career of William Conolly, 1689–1729' (Trinity College Dublin (henceforth TCD) PhD thesis, 2007, p. 108).

39 Memorandum by Trotter about election matters [1713] (PRONI, Conolly papers T/2825/A/1A–B).

40 Hayton, 'Henry Maxwell', pp. 56, 49–56, 58–63; Thomas Knox to Conolly, [?22] Nov. 1713 (PRONI, Conolly papers, T/2825/C/5/20).

41 Robert Johnson to duke of Ormond, 2 Aug. 1707 (HMC, *Ormond MSS*, new ser., VIII, 307); Richard Stewart to [Edward Southwell], 18 Nov. 1707 (BL, Southwell papers, Add. MS 9712, f. 82); Charles Delafaye to [earl of Sunderland], 24 Jan. 1715/16 (BL, Add. MS 61640, f. 81); Thomas Carter to Henry Boyle, 7 Oct. 1727 (PRONI, Shannon papers, D/2707/A/1/2/25); Marmaduke Coghill to Edward Southwell, jr, 4 Dec. 1733 (*Letters of Coghill*, ed. Hayton, p. 120).

42 Conolly to Delafaye, 8 Aug. 1717 (TNA, PRO, SP 63/375/172).

43 [Midleton], Dublin, to [Thomas Brodrick], 9 Mar. 1723[/4] (SHC, 1248/5/384–5).

44 TNA, PRO, Prob. 11/636, ff. 90–2: there are bequests to his 'good friends' Bps Theophilus Bolton and Arthur Price, and to Coghill, Marlay, and Trotter (the first two also executors (cf. Thomas Pearson to Jane Bonnell, 16 Mar. 1729[/30] (NLI, MS 41,580/24)).

45 See e.g. Agmondisham Vesey to Sir Thomas Vesey, bp of Ossory, 11 Apr. 1727 (NLI, De Vesci papers, MS 38,876/2).

46 See, for example, deed relating to mortgage on lands in Denbighshire, held by Marmaduke Coghill and Agmondisham Vesey, 1705 (NLI, De Vesci papers, MS 38,745/5); mortgage between Thomas Carter *et al.* and Thomas Meredith, Marmaduke Coghill, Thomas Marlay *et al.*, 8 Aug. 1720 (NLI, Wicklow papers, MS 38,369/19); assignment of lands to Brabazon Ponsonby and Luke Gardiner, 24 Aug. 1728 (NLI, Gardiner papers, MS 36,502/8); exemplification of common recovery, 28 Nov. 1729 (again involving Gardiner and Ponsonby) (Nottinghamshire Archives, Staunton papers, DD/5/9/20); Registry of Deeds, Dublin, 10/318/3759; 16/395/7803; 27/493/17899; 47/441/31372; 53/196/35056; 61/521/42288; 63/160/43049; 71/215/50168; 89/38/61972; 94/542/67599; 114/16/79251.

47 For example, marriage settlement of Thomas Carter, jr, and Mary Claxton, 10 Oct. 1719 (NLI, Wicklow papers, MS 38,613/14).

48 Coghill's, with a bequest to Henry Singleton is at TNA, PRO, Prob. 11/695, ff. 223–30; Singleton's, with a bequest to Thomas Marlay, is at National Archives of Ireland, 999/431, and abstracted in P. B. Eustace and Eilish Ellis (eds.), *Registry of Deeds, Dublin: abstracts of wills* (3 vols., Irish Manuscripts Commission, Dublin, 1954–84), II, 124; the wills of Gore's widow and General Wynne, witnessed by Nathaniel Clements, are at ibid., I, 282, 240. See also ibid., 217 (the will of James Topham, for which Coghill and Marlay were trustees), and 238 (the will of Thomas Pearson, MP, Conolly's

brother-in-law, who named Marlay and Trotter among the beneficiaries, together with 'my niece Coghill').

49 Reed Browning, *Political and constitutional ideas of the court whigs* (Baton Rouge, La. and London, 1982).

50 Coghill to Edward Southwell, 8 Dec. 1727 (*Letters of Coghill*, ed. Hayton, pp. 40–1).

51 Coghill to Southwell, 18 June 1728 (ibid., p. 55).

52 Coghill to Ld Perceval, 14 Apr. 1731 (ibid., pp. 111–12).

53 Bp Godwin to [Abp Wake], 6 July 1720 (Christ Church, Arch. W. Epist. xiii, no. 184); Bp Evans of Meath to [same], 24 Dec. [1716] (ibid., Arch. W. Epist. xii).

54 [Ld Midleton], Dublin, to [Thomas Brodrick], 10 Jan. 1721[/2] (SHC, 1248/5/170–3).

55 J.G. Simms, 'The making of a penal law (2 Anne, c. 6), 1703–4', *Irish Historical Studies*, XII (1960–1), 105–18; Edward Southwell to earl of Nottingham, 26 Feb. 1703–4 (*C.S.P., Dom.*, 1703–4, pp. 542–4).

56 Philip O'Regan, *Archbishop William King of Dublin (1650–1729) and the constitution in church and state* (Dublin, 2000), pp. 150–1; King to Robert King, 22 Nov. 1705 (TCD, Lyons (King) papers, MS 1995–2008/1181).

57 Isolde Victory, 'The making of the 1720 Declaratory Act' in Gerard O'Brien (ed.), *Parliament, politics and people: essays in eighteenth-century Irish history* (Blackrock, Co. Dublin, 1989), pp. 14–19; O'Regan, *Abp King*, pp. 263–74; D.W. Hayton, 'The Stanhope–Sunderland ministry and the repudiation of Irish parliamentary independence', *English Historical Review.*, 113 (1998), 612–13.

58 Ld Perceval to Charles Dering, 5 Mar. 1719/20 (BL, Egmont papers, Add. MS 47029, ff. 22–5). See also [John Toland,] *Reasons most humbly offer'd to the hon[ourable] House of Commons, why the bill sent down to them from the most hon[ourable] House of Lords, entituled, An act for the better securing the dependency of the kingdom of Ireland, upon the crown of Great Britain, should not pass into a law* (London, 1720), pp. 12–13. The debates are discussed in Victory, 'Making of the Declaratory Act', pp. 17–22, 26–8, and Hayton, 'Repudiation of Irish parliamentary independence', pp. 615–20.

59 Conolly to duke of Grafton, 29 Aug. 1720 (IAA, Conolly papers, A/3/15A–B).

60 Albert Goodwin, 'Wood's halfpence', repr. in Rosalind Mitchison (arr.), *Essays in eighteenth-century history* (London, 1966), pp. 122–3; Hayton, *Ruling Ireland*, pp. 233–4.

61 James Macartney *et al.* to Ld Perceval, 2 June 1720 (BL, Add. MS 47029, ff. 32–3); list of subscribers to the Bank (Marsh's Library, Dublin, MS Z.1.1.13); Henry Maxwell, *Reasons offer'd for erecting a bank in Ireland; in a letter to Hercules Rowley, esq.* (1st and 2nd edns, Dublin, 1721); Maxwell, *Mr. Maxwell's second letter to Mr. Rowley; wherein the objections against the bank are answer'd* (Dublin, 1721). On the controversy over the Bank, see in general Michael Ryder, 'The Bank of Ireland, 1721: land, credit and dependency', *Historical Journal*, 25 (1982), 557–82.

62 Hayton, 'Henry Maxwell', pp. 39–40.

63 [Midleton] to [Thomas Brodrick], 5, 10 Jan. 1721[/2] (SHC, 1248/5, ff. 165–6, 171–3).

64 Walsh, 'Career of Conolly', ch. 3.

65 J. G. Simms, *The Williamite confiscation in Ireland, 1690–1703* (London, 1956), pp. 125–6; Hayton, *Ruling Ireland*, pp. 82–3; Walsh, 'Career of Conolly', pp. 107–8.

66 Hayton, *Ruling Ireland*, p. 80; Hayton, 'Ideas of union in Anglo-Irish political discourse: meaning and use' in D. G. Boyce *et al.*, *Political discourse in seventeenth- and eighteenth-century Ireland* (Basingstoke, 2001), pp. 150–1.

67 For what follows, see Hayton, 'Henry Maxwell'.

68 *Anguis in herba: or the fatal consequences of a treaty with France . . .* (London, 1702); *An essay towards an union of Ireland with England* (London, repr. Dublin, 1703).

69 Maxwell, *Reasons offer'd for erecting a bank . . .* (1st edn), p. 4; Maxwell, *Mr. Maxwell's second letter . . .*, pp. 9, 17, 18, 19, 20.

70 Maxwell, *Reasons offer'd for erecting a bank . . .* (1st edn), p. 4.

71 Coghill to Perceval, 5 Apr. 1729, 14 Feb., 5 Mar. 1729/30, 25 Jan., 23 Feb., 4, 12, 23 Mar. 1730/1, 30 Mar., 14 Apr., 4 May 1731 (*Letters of Coghill*, ed. Hayton, pp. 65–7, 90, 92–4, 104–12, 114–15); Perceval to Coghill, 19 Apr. 1729, 6 May 1730 (BL, Add. MS 47032, ff. 110, 178–9). HMC, *Egmont diary*, I, 31, 48–9, 156, 159, 161–6; James, *Ireland in the empire*, pp. 156–7.

72 *Letters of Coghill*, ed. Hayton, pp. xvii–xviii.

73 James Smyth to William Smyth, 23 Dec. 1729 (NLI, MS 41,582/7).

74 For Prior, see Desmond Clarke, *Thomas Prior, 1681–1751, founder of the Royal Dublin Society* (Dublin, 1951); Robbins, *Eighteenth-century commonwealthman*, p. 159; *ODNB*, XLV, 423; for Hamilton, *Hist. Ir. parl.*, IV, 342–4; for Bindon, ibid., III, 180. For Coghill's connexions with Bindon, Hamilton, and Prior, see Coghill to Edward Southwell, 4 Feb. 1728[/9], to Ld Perceval, 4, 12 Mar. 1730/1, 14 Apr. 1731 (*Letters of Coghill*, ed. Hayton, pp. 60, 106, 108, 112); for his correspondence with Perceval and Edward Southwell, see ibid., passim.

75 *Letters of Coghill*, ed. Hayton, p. xix.

76 'A view of the trade of Ireland for the year ending the 25th day of March 1729', annotated by Bolton (PRONI, Foster-Massereene papers, D/207/3/11); draft of pamphlet by Bolton on the coinage of Ireland, n.d. (ibid., D/207/3/13); commentary by Bolton on Irish imports and exports, n.d. (ibid., D/207/3/15); Bolton to ——, [c.1730] (ibid., D/562/937).

77 Commentary by Bolton on Irish imports and exports, n.d. (ibid., D/207/3/15).

78 See p. 240.

79 Francis Hutchinson, *A letter to a Member of Parliament, concerning the imploying and providing for the poor* (Dublin, 1723), p. 6.

80 John Laurence, *A new system of agriculture, being a complete body of husbandry and gardening . . .* (Dublin, 1727), subscription list.

81 *Commons' Journals, Ireland* (henceforth *CJI*) (4th edn), II, 613; IV, 34; James Smyth to William Smyth, 11 Dec. 1727 (NLI, MS 41,582/5); Dobbs to Alexander McAuley, 2 June 1732 (PRONI, Dobbs papers, D/162/26). On Dobbs, see Desmond Clarke, *Arthur Dobbs esquire 1689–1765* (Chapel Hill, N.C., 1957); Robbins, *Eighteenth-century commonwealthman*, pp. 149–52; *ODNB*, XVI, 340–2. Note that Dobbs's *An essay on the trade and improvement of Ireland* (Dublin, 1729), pp. 69–72, echoes Maxwell's earlier pamphlet in arguing for the advantage to England of a British–Irish union (Robbins, *Eighteenth-century commonwealthman*, p. 149).

82 On the establishment and early history of the society, see Terence de Vere White, *The story of the Royal Dublin Society* (Tralee, [1955]), chs. 1–3; Clarke, *Arthur Dobbs*, ch. 4; Toby Barnard, *Making the grand figure: lives and possessions in Ireland, 1641–1770* (New Haven and London, 2004), p. 198.

83 Dublin Society minutes, 16 Sept., 11, 18, 25 Nov., 4 Dec. 1731, 2 Mar. 1731[/2] (Royal Dublin Society (henceforth RDS), society minute book 1, ff. 4, 16–18, 23, 48). *Hist. Ir. parl.* also records 'information taken from the *Almanacs*' to the effect that Coghill, Marlay, Singleton, and Trotter were 'foundation members' of the society, while noting that this evidence is 'not necessarily reliable' (I, 11; III, 445; V, 192; VI, 277, 443).

84 Dublin Soc. min., 23 Mar. 1731[/2] (RDS, soc. min. bk 1, f. 51). One of the means suggested by Bolton for the development of Irish agriculture was the establishment of a board, on the lines of the Linen Board, to distribute to farmers seed for crops such as grass or barley (draft by Bolton for a pamphlet entitled 'A brief enquiry into the use of premiums in respect to trade' (PRONI, D/207/3/15)).

85 *Precedents and abstracts from the journals of the trustees of the linen and hempen manufactures of Ireland* (Dublin, 1784), pp. 2, 60, 67, 101, 117, 131.

86 *The statutes at large, passed in the parliaments held in Ireland ...* (20 vols. Dublin, 1786–1801), V, 314–15.

87 See Ld Carteret to Edward Southwell, 8 Jan., 9 Feb. 1729/30 (BL, Southwell papers, Add. 38016, ff. 19, 23); and also the covering letter with the 'transmiss' of the bill sent by Carteret and Irish privy council (the signatories including Bolton, Coghill, and Maxwell) to the British privy council, 3 Jan. 1729 (BL, Hardwicke papers, Add. MS 361348, ff. 116–17).

88 *Statutes at large ... Ireland ...*, V, 342–3. For Bolton's particular practical interest in schemes to drain bogland, see Edward McParland, *Public architecture in Ireland, 1680–1760* (New Haven and London, 2002), p. 25.

89 Coghill to Edward Southwell, 7 May 1730 (*Letters of Coghill*, ed. Hayton, pp. 101–2). The charter establishing the Incorporated Society for Promoting English Protestant Working Schools in Ireland, in 1733, the 'charter schools', included, besides the great officers in church and state, Coghill, Manley, Sandford, Tighe, Trotter, and Wynne (*A copy of his majesty's royal charter, for erecting English Protestant schools in the kingdom of Ireland ...* (Dublin, 1733)), but I am inclined to put little weight on this, since, although Conolly himself left money in his will to establish a charity school, none of Conolly's

close supporters had previously been involved with the foundation or maintenance of such institutions: see D. W. Hayton, 'Did Protestantism fail in early eighteenth-century Ireland? Charity schools and the enterprise of religious and social reformation, *c.* 1690–1730' in Alan Ford, James McGuire, and Kenneth Milne (eds.), *As by law established: the Church of Ireland since the Reformation* (Dublin, 1995), pp. 166–86; Edward Synge, *Methods of erecting, supporting and governing charity-schools: with an account of the charity-schools in Ireland; and some observations thereon . . .* (3rd edn, Dublin, 1721).

90 *By-laws, rules and orders, for the better regulating of hackney-coaches . . . within the city of Dublin . . . made by the governors of the workhouse of the city of Dublin* (Dublin, 1729), p. 18.

91 *Precedents and abstracts*, pp. 23, 55, 77, 83, 97, 101, 117, 131, 139. Ponsonby applied for a grant from the board in 1725 to set up a bleach yard; Theophilus Clements in 1726 for encouragement for a spinning school (ibid., pp. 73, 79). Other evidence shows Vesey dispensing largess under the aegis of the Linen Board (James Hamilton Maxwell to Vesey, 13 Jan. 1721/2 (PRONI, T/2524/12), a reference I owe to my research student, Robert Whan), and Bolton, while bishop of Elphin, seeking to introduce linen manufacture into the town (Bolton to ——, [c.1730] (ibid., D/562/937)).

92 See, e.g. John Browne, *Seasonable remarks on trade. With some reflections on the advantages that might accrue to Great Britain . . .* (Dublin, 1728), p. 63; Browne, *A reply to the observer on Seasonable remarks* (Dublin, 1728), p. 18; David Bindon, *A scheme for supplying industrious men with money to carry on their trades, and for better providing for the poor of Ireland* (Dublin, 1729), pp. 6–7, 9, 12–14, 21–2; Thomas Prior, *A list of the absentees of Ireland, and the yearly value of their estates and incomes spent abroad . . .* (Dublin, 1729), p. 19; Arthur Dobbs, *An essay on the trade and improvement of Ireland, part II* (Dublin, 1731), pp. 19–20.

93 *CJI* (4th edn), III, 14, 38, 130, 133, 252, 253, 296–7, 317, 332, 348, 349, 350–1, 400, 407, 418, 426, 434, 480, 484, 523, 545; drafts of heads of bill to regulate the weighing and packing of butter [c.1723] (PRONI, Perceval–Maxwell papers, D/1556/16/4/9–10); Hayton, 'Henry Maxwell', pp. 41–2.

94 *CJI* (4th edn), III, 14, 127, 328, 407, 416, 434, 612, 616–17; IV, 12, 15, 34. In Rose's case, we have direct confirmation of his interest in spreading tillage and protecting Irish industry. In 1731, looking forward to the new parliamentary session, he informed a correspondent in County Kerry (where his own parliamentary seat lay) that he favoured a prohibition on the importing of French brandy, since 'our own spirits, extracted from malt etc., will bring in a much greater revenue, and at the same time consume our corn, and increase the tillage, and, as the French trade is grown very pernicious I could also wish that a further duty might be laid on claret, and white wine. This would hinder it from being so common as it is, and such whose purses could not come at it would be contented with their own manufacture' (Henry Rose to Sir Maurice Crosbie, 23 Sept. 1731 (NLI, Talbot–Crosbie papers, PC 188)).

95 *CJI* (4th edn), III, 133, 206, 252, 315, 480, 519.

96 Ibid., 252, 337–8, 449–50, 484.

97 Ibid., 227, 315, 406, 434, 437, 519.

98 Ibid., 185, 252, 315, 326, 327, 348.

99 Ibid., 38, 144, 525.

100 Ibid., 490, 599, 613.

101 Ibid., 39, 92–4, 144, 525.

102 Ibid., 268, 407, 434.

103 Ibid., 315; IV, 12.

104 Ibid., III, 349, 425.

105 Prior, *List of absentees*, p. 19 He was of course a multiple internal absentee.

106 Walsh, 'Career of Conolly', chs. 1, 8.

107 Ibid., pp. 285–6.

108 Maurice Craig and the Knight of Glin, 'Castletown. Co. Kildare', *Country Life*, 165 (1969), 722–6, 798–802; the Knight of Glin and John Cornforth, 'Castletown. Co. Kildare', ibid., 882–5; Barnard, *Making the grand figure*, pp. 91–3; Finola O'Kane, *Landscape design in eighteenth-century Ireland: mixing foreign trees with the natives* (Cork, 2004), pp. 48–55; Mary Jones to Jane Bonnell, 13 Jan. [?1727] (NLI, Smythe of Barbavilla papers, MS 41,577/1).

109 Edward McParland, 'Building the Parliament House in Dublin', *Parliamentary History*, XXI (2002), 131–40; McParland, *Public architecture in Ireland*, ch. 7.

110 L. J. Proudfoot, 'Landownership and improvement, c.1700 to 1845' in Proudfoot and William Nolan (eds.), *Down: history and society. Interdisciplinary essays on the history of an Irish county* (Dublin, 1997), pp. 214–18; Andrew Sneddon, 'Bishop Francis Hutchinson (1660–1739): a case study in the eighteenth-century culture of improvement', *Irish Historical Studies*, 35 (2006–7), 308–9; Sneddon, *Witchcraft and whigs: the life of Bishop Francis Hutchinson, 1660–1739* (Manchester, 2008), ch. 8.

111 F. E. Ball, *A history of the County Dublin* (6 parts, Dublin, 1902–20), pt 6, p. 171; T. U. Sadleir and P. L. Dickinson, *Georgian mansions in Ireland …* (Dublin 1915), pp. 65, 67; Rolf Loeber, *A biographical dictionary of architects in Ireland 1600–1720* (London, 1981), p. 54; McParland, *Public architecture in Ireland*, p. 12; Barnard, *Making the grand figure*, p. 174.

112 *Letters from Georgian Ireland: the correspondence of Mary Delany, 1731–68*, ed. Angélique Day (Belfast, 1991), p. 44.

113 Barnard, *Making the grand figure*, pp. 54, 173, 182, 202–3; Mark Bence-Jones, *Burke's guide to country houses*, vol. I: *Ireland* (London, 1978), pp. 41, 113, 226, 264. For a more sceptical view of Bolton's responsibility for building at Cashel, see A. P. W. Malcomson, *Archbishop Charles Agar: churchmanship and politics in Ireland, 1760–1810* (Dublin, 2002), pp. 334–8, 340, 342–50.

114 Malcomson, *Nathaniel Clements*, pp. 202–4; McParland, *Public architecture in Ireland*, pp. 145–59.

115 O'Kane, *Landscape design in eighteenth-century Ireland*, ch. 1.

116 Maxwell, *Reasons offer'd for erecting a bank in Ireland . . .* (1st edn), pp. 14, 21, 23, 40, 48.

117 Francis Burton to Jane Bonnell, 19 Nov. 1729 (NLI, MS 41,579/9).

118 In 1721 she had bought 'seven stuff suits of clothes' to give away 'for the encouragement of the poor weavers' (Jane Bulkeley to Jane Bonnell, 4 Apr. 1721 (ibid., MS 41,580/3).

119 McNally, *Parties, patriots and undertakers*, pp. 185–91.

120 Bolton to [Ld Carteret], 16 July 1728 (PRONI, D/562/92); Bolton to ——, [c.1730] (ibid., D/207/3/14). Cf. Philip Perceval to Ld Perceval, 1 Feb. 1725/6 (BL, Add. MS 47031, ff. 93–4); Abp Boulter to [duke of Newcastle], 23 Oct. 1729 (TNA, PRO, SP 63/391/184–5); Carteret to Edward Southwell, 26 Feb. 1729/30 (BL, Add. MS 38016, ff. 25–6).

121 In this connexion it is instructive to note the thesis proposed in James Livesey, 'The Dublin Society in eighteenth-century Irish political thought', *Historical Journal*, 47 (2004), pp. 615–40, that the intellectual principles underlying the establishment of the Dublin Society (with which Conolly's faction had close links) represented a new departure in Irish 'patriotism', away from the old obsession with the Anglo-Irish constitutional nexus and towards a programme of social reformation.

122 Coghill to Edward Southwell, 13 June 1728 (*Letters of Coghill*, ed. Hayton, p. 53). See also Coghill to Edward Southwell, jr, 22 Feb. 1732[/3] (ibid., p. 120).

123 Coghill to Edward Southwell, jr, 31 Mar. 1733 (ibid., p. 124).

124 McNally, *Parties, patriots and undertakers*, pp. 168–73; Hayton, *Ruling Ireland*, p. 249; Walsh, 'Career of Conolly', ch. 7.

125 See Walsh, 'Career of Conolly', chs. 6–7.

126 Abp Boulter to Carteret, 14 Dec. 1728, 25 Apr. 1730 (*Boulter letters*, I, 268; II, 3–4); Boulter to duke of Dorset, 22 July 1732 (ibid., II, 78–80).

127 Boulter to Bp Gibson of London, 25 Apr. 1727 (ibid., I 157); Boulter to Newcastle, 20 Feb. 1728[/9] (ibid., 283).

128 Swift, *The Drapier's Letters . . .*, ed. Herbert Davis (Oxford, 1935), p. 76. See also the *Humble address to both Houses of Parliament . . .* with its reference to 'certain bold undertakers of weak judgment, and strong ambition, who seek to find their accounts in the ruin of the nation, by securing or advancing themselves' (ibid., pp. 145–6) and its further condemnation of corrupt office-holders (ibid., p. 147). I am grateful to Professor S. J. Connolly for reminding me of the passage in the *Letter to the whole people of Ireland*, which is quoted at greater length in his *Divided kingdom: Ireland 1630–1800* (Oxford, 2008), p. 238.

129 Swift to John Gay and the duchess of Queensberry, 28 Aug. 1731, *Correspondence*, III, 428. See also Swift, *Drapier's letters*, p. 8. The exchange with Gardiner occurred in 1735 when, according to Sir Arthur Acheson, he and the dean met at a grand occasion in Dublin Castle: 'Luke Gardiner was there, talking like a great patriot, and said no gentleman of this country should be forgiven that wore anything but the manufactures of it. The dean answered

him thus: "I am told you have got into employments worth two thousand pounds, and possibly you lay out ten pounds a year for a suit of clothes; for this you would be esteemed a great friend to the country, though in an affair of any importance you gave it up" (Acheson to George Dodington, 23 Oct. 1735 (HMC, *Various collections*, VI, 64–5), a reference I owe to Professor Connolly).

130 Swift to Abp King of Dublin, 2 Mar. 1716/17, *Correspondence*, II, 229; Swift to Knightley Chetwode, [Dec. 1723], ibid., 482; Swift to Charles Ford, 2 Apr. 1724, ibid., 493; Swift to Carteret, [17 Apr. 1725], ibid., 552; Swift to John Barber, 1 Mar. 1734/5, ibid., IV, 61–2; Thomas Sheridan to Swift, 23 June 1735, ibid., 131–2.

131 Quoted in C. I. Graham, 'The right honourable William Conolly, Speaker of the Irish House of Commons', *Journal of the County Kildare Archaeological Society*, 3 (1899–1902), 113–14.

132 Homan Potterton, *Irish church monuments 1570–1880* (Ulster Architectural Heritage Society, Belfast, 1975), pp. 76–7; Ball, *History of the County Dublin*, pt 6, pp. 173–4.

CHAPTER 10

Old English, New English and ancient Irish: Swift and the Irish past

S. J. Connolly

In 1693 Jonathan Swift paid a visit to the English court. According to his own account, written some three decades later, he had been sent there by his patron, Sir William Temple, to brief King William III and his chief adviser, the earl of Portland, on an episode in English constitutional history. The occasion was a proposed Triennial Bill, intended to limit the life of future parliaments to three years. Opponents of the bill had informed William that Charles I, half a century earlier, had lost his throne and his life by consenting to a similar measure. Swift's mission was to refute this claim by demonstrating that Charles's mistake had not been his acceptance of the triennial bill. Instead, it was a separate concession, the surrender of his right to dissolve a parliament without the consent of its members, that had placed him at the mercy of his enemies. Although 'under twenty-one years old', Swift recalled, he was 'well versed in English history'. He provided the king with a short briefing on the issue, and Portland with a fuller account. That both men ignored his intervention, and persisted in their opposition to the bill, became in his recollection an early experience of the untrustworthy character of royal courts and 'the first incident that helped to cure him of vanity'.[1]

This account by Swift of his own first appearance on the stage of national politics, included in an unfinished autobiography apparently written in the late 1720s, is unencumbered by modesty, or even by chronological accuracy. In 1693 he was not in fact 20 years old, but rather 25.[2] Even with that adjustment, the image of the young secretary to a retired diplomat correcting the king's understanding of history remains improbable. Swift's revelation that Temple had sent him to Kensington 'with the whole account of the matter in writing' is almost certainly a more accurate indication of his role. But the episode itself remains revealing. It serves as a reminder of the importance that Swift and others continued to attach to the political events of the 1640s and 1650s, and to the lessons and warnings they provided. This sense of the continuing relevance of the Civil War and Interregnum had not been undermined by the more recent constitutional upheaval of 1688. The agreed version of the Revolution settlement drew a very clear distinction between the abdication or providential removal from the throne of James II and the overthrow and execution of his father. After 1688, as before, the anniversary of 30 January continued to be observed as a day of national penance for the regicide perpetrated in 1649. Tory propagandists denounced dissenters as still harbouring the principles of the Solemn League and Covenant, and offered lurid fantasies of their Whig opponents secretly gathering to celebrate the memory of Oliver Cromwell.[3] Whigs might on occasion have responded by comparing politically assertive high churchmen to Archbishop Laud.[4] More commonly, however, debate on the Civil War or its aftermath put them on the defensive. A Whig clergyman in Dublin who used his sermon on 30 January 1709 to suggest that the execution of Charles I was the justified removal of a tyrant found himself repudiated by his own party, horrified at the gift he had made to their Tory opponents.[5]

As well as providing ammunition for the party conflict of the post-Revolution era, the events of the 1640s remained central to the continuing, and closely related, debate on the rights of Protestant dissenters. In 1709, at a time when the Whig government was clearly contemplating an attempt to repeal the sacramental test, William Tisdall, vicar of Belfast and Swift's one-time rival in love, responded to claims of Presbyterian loyalty with a furious frontal assault, using detailed citations from contemporary records to show that the Presbyterians of Ireland had been 'equally deep in the plots, associations and factions against the king, not only in the period ... between [16]41 and 60, but generally in every turn of government since the Reformation'.[6] Ten years later Archbishop Synge of Tuam, arguing against the minimal concessions to dissenters contained in the Toleration Bill, likewise appealed to the terrifying precedent of the Interregnum, when 'every man set up for what religion he pleased, and placed his meeting where he thought fit', with disastrous consequences for not only the ecclesiastical but also the political order.[7]

Whatever the truth of his intervention in the matter of the Triennial Bill, there is no doubt that Swift shared fully in this continuing preoccupation with the events of the Civil War. In 1741 he noted that he had just completed his fourth reading of the great royalist statesman Clarendon's massive *True Historical Narrative of the Rebellion and Civil Wars in England*. His copy, which survives, is extensively annotated. Swift also read closely, if in a more hostile spirit, in the works of other writers on the period, such as Gilbert Burnet and Edmund Ludlow.[8] His unfinished autobiography, meanwhile, included a lively account of his grandfather, Thomas Swift, vicar of Goodrich in Herefordshire, a staunch royalist whose sufferings through his loyalty to Charles I had been 'more than any person of his condition in England', and who had supposedly once brought about the death of no fewer than 200 Cromwellian troopers by an ingenious act of sabotage at a river crossing.[9]

Swift's loyalties in relation to the Civil War, as these details make clear, were unambiguous. Like his favourite author, Clarendon, he was willing to accept that some of the devices that Charles I had resorted to during his years of personal rule had been unacceptable. However, he insisted that the king had acted as he had only because parliament had refused his reasonable requests for taxation. And in relation to the war that followed, his sympathies were wholly with the crown. The long-term origins of the crisis, in Swift's view, lay in two developments. The first was the massive secularisation of church lands that had taken place in the reign of Henry VIII, upsetting the natural balance between the crown and its subjects. 'Power, which always follows property, grew to lean to the side of the people, by whom even the just rights of the crown were often disputed.'[10] The second development was the persecutions in the reign of Mary Tudor that had driven English Protestants overseas to Geneva and elsewhere, from where they had returned as militant Puritans hostile to both religious and political authority. In 1641 an unholy alliance of ambitious politicians and Puritan fanatics had joined forces against Charles I, spurning his offer to redress legitimate grievances and eventually forcing him to take up arms in defence of his just prerogatives. Defeated, the king had died 'a real martyr for the true religion and liberty of his people', while his opponents went on to create 'a government of the people, and a new religion, both after the manner of Geneva, without a king, a bishop, or a nobleman'.[11]

Like most of his contemporaries, Whig as well as Tory, Swift thus regarded the events of 1641 and after with abhorrence. This did not necessarily make him a royalist in the conventional sense. More than once, in his comments on the Civil War era and elsewhere, he made clear his view that monarchs were inherently untrustworthy and prone to seek arbitrary power, and he flatly rejected Clarendon's suggestion that a people who were denied their rights were not entitled to assert them by force.[12] These were part of the contradictions that have allowed historians to continue to debate whether Swift should be categorised as a Whig or as a Tory. More fruitfully, perhaps, they can be seen as the response of a man torn between contradictory impulses: a deep suspicion of political power and of those who held it, combined with an equally deep antipathy towards those who sought to upset the established order. Perhaps it was precisely these conflicts within his own mind that gave the period such a fascination for Swift. Certainly it helps to explain his attachment to the classical model of the balanced constitution, where monarchy, aristocracy and commons each helped to keep in check the tendency of the other two to degenerate towards the alternative triad of tyranny, oligarchy and mob rule. In this sense, to adopt the distinction proposed by Ian Higgins, Swift's views on the disasters of the Civil War can be seen as reflecting the Harringtonian rather than the moral strand within his political thought.[13]

The political crisis of the 1640s was not of course confined to England. In Ireland too this was a decade of civil war: indeed, it was the outbreak of revolt in Ireland in October 1641 that provided the occasion for the final breakdown in relations between Charles I and his opponents. Swift's view of these conflicts was for the most part clear cut. Where Clarendon had written that 40–50,000 English settlers had been massacred in the insurrection, Swift noted in the margin 'at least'.[14] Elsewhere he blamed the English parliament both for encouraging by their example 'the Irish Popish massacre' and for their subsequent refusal to allow Charles I an army to suppress the revolt: 'we may truly say that the English parliament held the king's hands, while the Irish Papists here were cutting our grandfathers' throats'.[15] Swift did not have a great deal to say about the complex alignments and oppositions, or the long-drawn-out military struggle, of the next ten years. But it is notable that his scattered comments on Cromwell, generally hostile, contain just two positive remarks. Among Swift's memoranda is a list of 'those who have made great figures in some particular action or circumstance of their lives'. Here he included 'King Charles the Martyr during his whole trial and at his death'. But in addition, in a reminder of his commitment to order and discipline, he listed 'Cromwell, when he quelled a mutiny in Hyde Park'.[16] Secondly, in 'Thoughts on Religion' he quoted approvingly from Cromwell's reply to the governor of the Irish town of New Ross, who had sought to have a promise of liberty of conscience included in his articles of surrender. 'I meddle not with any man's conscience. But if by liberty of conscience you mean a liberty to exercise the mass, I judge it best to use plain dealing, and to let you know, where the parliament of England have power that will not be allowed of.' This reply, Swift noted, 'was natural and right'.[17]

For the most part, then, Swift accepted without question the story of an unprovoked massacre of tens of thousands of Protestant settlers by a Catholic population driven by religious fanaticism. This was the version of events first developed for propaganda purposes during the Civil War and kept alive in subsequent decades by the designation of 23 October, anniversary of the rising, as an official day of commemoration, as well as by regular reprintings of Sir John Temple's classic history, first published in 1646. Two pamphlets setting out the Catholic side of the story had appeared in the early 1660s, as part of the debate over the Restoration settlement. Thereafter, however, it was not until the late 1740s that the first Catholic spokesmen were again bold enough to challenge the dominant Protestant narrative.[18] Swift's casual acceptance of the fact of wholesale massacre is thus hardly surprising. There was, however, one occasion when he departed strikingly from the conventional Protestant narrative of his day, in a way that suggests a wholly different level of engagement with the Irish dimension of the wars of the 1640s.

The occasion for this intervention was the attempt in 1733 by the Dublin executive, on orders from London, to push through the Irish parliament a repeal of the sacramental test. Supporters of Presbyterian claims had emphasised their contribution to the restoration of the monarchy in 1660 and to the replacement of James II by William III in 1688–9. Swift's initial response, *The Presbyterian's Plea of Merit*, set out to refute both claims. Presbyterians, he insisted, had initially supported James's regime, transferring their support to William only when his victory became certain. In the 1640s, likewise, they had taken a leading part in the overthrow of Charles I. In this latter case Swift was following in the footsteps of Tisdall a quarter of a century earlier. Yet his historical analysis was, in comparison, both coarse and tendentious. Tisdall had based his argument on a close analysis of the official pronouncements both of the Scottish kirk and of the Presbyterian ecclesiastical structure that took shape in Ulster as the crisis of the 1640s unfolded, taking particular pains to demonstrate how closely the Ulster Scots had aligned themselves with their fellow countrymen. Swift, by contrast, offered a crude genealogy. Already before 1641 the term 'puritan' had signified the presence of disruptive sectaries. Soon after the outbreak of the Civil War, however, 'the term "puritan" gradually dropped, and that of Presbyterian succeeded'.

There remained the problem that the actual execution of the king had become possible only after what contemporaries described as the Presbyterian party, supporters of a centralised (though non-episcopal) church and a negotiated settlement with the crown, had been displaced by the more radical Independents. Swift acknowledged that the king's trial had come only after the army had excluded from parliament 'moderate members' willing to reach a settlement with the crown. However, he noted that the purge had been overseen by Fairfax, 'a rigid Presbyterian', and went on to argue that there had been no real difference in principle between Presbyterian and Independent. 'The design of utterly extirpating monarchy and episcopacy was equally the same in both.' If some Presbyterians had condemned the king's murder, it was 'from perfect spite, rage and envy to find themselves wormed out of all power by a new infant spawn of Independents, sprung from their own bowels'. And in any case the Independents, the actual murderers of the king, had since the Restoration gradually 'mingled with the mass of Presbyterians, lying ever since undistinguished in the herd of dissenters'.[19]

The Presbyterian's Plea of Merit is thus an unimpressive piece of work, wilfully downplaying the real ideological divisions between different parties on the parliamentary side, and oversimplifying the historical links between the dissenters of his own day and their seventeenth-century predecessors.[20] But Swift also produced a second pamphlet, whose focus was on Ireland rather than England, and whose approach and arguments were considerably more startling. This was *Reasons Humbly Offered to the Parliament of Ireland for Repealing the Sacramental Test*, also dating from 1733 but not published – possibly for reasons of prudence – until five years later. The reasons in question were supposedly offered by a member of a group not normally represented in the pamphlet literature of the day, an Irish Catholic, and their thrust was to argue that he and his co-religionists had in fact a stronger claim to be readmitted to full political rights than the Presbyterians whose case was currently being considered. Ireland, the pamphlet pointed out, had been first won for England by 'English Catholics, subjects to English Catholic kings ... to which merit our brethren the Dissenters of any denomination whatsoever, have not the least pretensions'. Although the descendants of these English Catholic conquerors had subsequently been driven to revolt, this had been in response to misgovernment and the threatened loss of their lands. By contrast, the repeated rebellions of Puritans and other sectaries had rested on no real grievance, 'except that they were not suffered to change the government in Church and State and seize both into their own hands'. In the Civil War the Catholics, still loyal supporters of monarchy, had fought for Charles I against his parliamentary enemies, for which they had been punished by the confiscation of their estates, while the 'schismatics' who had overthrown and murdered a king had been allowed to flourish.[21]

Reasons Humbly Offered must of course be read in its polemical context. The main purpose is to strike out at the Presbyterians in the most offensive manner possible. But in developing his argument Swift showed an awareness of the ethnic distinctions of seventeenth-century Ireland that is out of line both with his own usual practice and with the conventions of his day. In the late sixteenth and early seventeenth centuries the Catholic descendants of the medieval English settlers in Ireland had continued to insist on their separate identity as the Old English, separate from the native or Gaelic Irish, and, despite their refusal to adopt the religion of the state, unswervingly loyal to the crown of England.[22] Already by the reign of James I, however, the position of this long-established middle nation was being eroded. The defeat of the last major challenge from Gaelic Ireland in the war of 1595–1603 meant that their political loyalty was now of less consequence, while the rising population of more recent Protestant settlers, the New English, provided an alternative administrative elite. As early as 1614 the veteran soldier and administrator Sir George Carew warned that shared interest and grievances united Old English and Gaelic Irish in hostility to the state.[23] After 1641, despite some evidence of continued mutual hostility, the two groups did in fact come together as the Confederate Catholics of Ireland, and went on to share in military defeat and the loss of the greater part of their lands.[24] By 1672 Sir William Petty believed that 'the differences between the Old Irish and Old English papists is asleep now, because they have a common enemy'.[25] A generation later Sir Richard Cox, a conservative in these matters, still argued that if the Catholics should ever triumph, the Irish would turn on their Old English allies, 'upon the old indelible national antipathy'. But he nevertheless conceded that 'at this day we know no difference of nation, but what is expressed by papist and Protestant'.[26]

In the Ireland in which Swift came to adulthood, then, the tripartite division of Old English, New English and native Irish had largely given way to a simpler distinction between Catholic and Protestant. Indeed, the terms 'Irish' and 'English' were themselves coming to be reinterpreted in these terms. A government proclamation of May 1692 could still call for the seizure of arms held by 'the Irish and other Roman Catholics'.[27] But much more commonly 'Irish' was used to refer to Catholics, irrespective of ethnic origin, and 'English' to refer to Protestants.[28] This was also the usage Swift generally favoured. Responding to claims that the opposition to Wood's Halfpence came from Papists and Jacobites, for example, the Drapier responded indignantly that it was 'the true English people' of Ireland who rejected the coin, before adding dismissively that 'we take it for granted that the Irish will do so too whenever they are asked'.[29]

Reasons Humbly Offered, however, returned to an older set of distinctions. It unambiguously condemned the revolt of the Ulster Gaelic Irish in 1641, 'the rebellious riot committed by that brutal ruffian, Sir Phelim O Neal, with his tumultuous crew of rabble'. But it drew a clear line between this episode and 'the force raised afterwards by the Catholic lords and gentlemen of the English Pale, in defence of the king, after the English rebellion began'. This was a gross oversimplification. There was a case for the view that the Old English had been pushed into rebellion by the suspicion and hostility of the Dublin government.[30] But they had quite clearly taken up arms, in defiance of the king's government, before hostilities broke out in England. However, Swift was on safer historical, if not political, ground in the remainder of his argument. The Catholics had, after tortuous negotiations, allied with the royalist forces commanded by Ormond[31] and had fought under his leadership against the king's parliamentary opponents. For this they had been stripped of their estates. Yet at the Restoration their loyalty had been ignored, while the schismatics and republicans who had executed Charles I 'obtained grants of those very estates which the Catholics lost in defence of the ancient constitution'.

From where did Swift derive this reading of the ethnic divisions within the Catholic population? Sir Richard Cox had shown more sensitivity than other Protestant writers to the historical divide between Old English and native Irish. But his account of the 1640s made no distinction between the two. Indeed, Cox poured scorn on the claim that the Old English had been forced into rebellion by the actions of the Dublin government. The clearest statement of a separate Old English pathway to the taking-up of arms in 1641 was by Richard Bellings, but this was not printed until 1882.[32] Another Catholic history, *Ireland's Case Briefly Stated* by Hugh Reilly, was available in Swift's lifetime, being published in 1695 and again in 1720. Reilly distinguished between two groups: a party of royalists who had plotted with the earl of Ormond to seize power in the king's name in Ireland, and a group in Ulster, 'those they call the Old Irish', who were not part of Ormond's plan but had learned of its existence and had responded by launching their own pre-emptive coup, in the hope of securing both religious toleration and the restoration of lands lost in the plantation thirty years before. However, there is nothing to indicate that Swift had ever encountered Reilly's work. Moreover, Reilly did not identify the royalists specifically as Old English; he noted simply that they included both Catholics and Protestants. And where Swift had denounced Sir Phelim O'Neill, commander of the Ulster insurgents, as a 'brutal ruffian', Reilly specifically absolved the 'Old Irish' leaders of responsibility for the massacre of Protestants, which he presented as initiated by the rank and file in retaliation for the indiscriminate killing of Catholics by government forces.[33]

Two possible sources for Swift's treatment of the Old English remain, one intriguing, the other less dramatic but perhaps more likely. Some time before 1711 an unknown author of Old English ancestry and firmly Jacobite views produced a history of the war of 1688–91 under the title 'A Light to the Blind'. This began in terms fairly similar to Swift's pamphlet, by arguing that the real representatives of 'the English interest' in Ireland were not the Cromwellian upstarts who had annexed the term to serve their own vested interests. Instead, 'the true conquerors of that kingdom, who by their blood annexed the Irish crown to the English diadem' had been 'Catholics landed from England in Ireland under the happy fortunes of Henry the second', and it was their descendants, the Old English, who had since remained the most loyal supporters of the crown.[34] 'A Light to the Blind' was published only in 1892. However, one of the two surviving manuscripts was found among the papers of the historian Thomas Carte. Carte first appears in Swift's correspondence in 1729, when he is dismissively referred to as 'a Jacobite parson'. But he later became an acquaintance and in 1736 sent Swift a copy of his biography of the duke of Ormond, with a letter acknowledging his assistance.[35] Did Swift, perhaps directed by Carte, read at least the opening part of the manuscript and put some of its sentiments in the mouth of his fictional Catholic author? If so, *Reasons Humbly Offered* becomes an even more audacious assault on Irish Protestant sensibilities. But the parallels between the two texts remain too loose to be conclusive, and it is open to question whether Swift would in fact have regarded an Old English Catholic history of the war of 1688–91 as worthy of his attention.

An alternative source for Swift's treatment of the Old English was his favourite historian, Clarendon. Clarendon's account of 1641 itself is brief, referring simply to a rebellion among the Irish. But much later, in Book XI, in the context of an account of negotiations between Ormond and the Confederate Catholics in 1648, he offered his readers a fuller analysis of Catholic politics. Here he distinguished between the descendants of the first English plantation, who had 'performed the duty of good subjects during all those rebellions which the whole reign of Queen Elizabeth was seldom without', and the Old Irish, O'Neills, Maguires and MacMahons, among whom 'the rebellion was first contrived, cherished and entered upon with that horrid barbarity'. Even after the two groups had come

together in the Catholic Confederation, a distinction remained between
'the more moderate party . . . whose main end was to obtain liberty for the
exercise of their religion without any thought of declining their subjection
to the king' and 'the fiercer and more savage party', which had no
intention of returning to obedience under the crown.[36] If this was Swift's
source, however, he drew on it selectively. Clarendon's account of the
Old English was markedly less favourable than his own. They had
'degenerated into the manners and barbarous customs of the Irish', and
were 'stupidly transported' with the superstitions of Rome. In the same
way, Clarendon's qualified acceptance that the 'undistinguishing severity'
of the Dublin government had led 'many persons of honour and quality'
among the Catholics to join in the revolt 'for their own security, as they
pretended' was some distance from Swift's account of 'the Catholic lords
and gentlemen of the English Pale' mobilising 'in defence of the king'.
But then Swift had already made clear, in his treatment of the Civil War
Presbyterians, that fidelity to his sources took second place to his own
polemical purposes.

In all this, it is important to remember, Swift was adopting the persona
of a Catholic petitioner. But this novel approach to Ireland's complex
ethnic past allowed him not only to attack the Presbyterians but to
develop certain other themes close to his heart. *Reasons Humbly Offered*
revived the distinction between the Old English and the native Irish, and
also, implicitly, between the Old English and the Protestant New English
who had displaced them. But it also gave this latter distinction a new
twist. What had happened, according to Swift's fictional petitioner, was
that the descendants of the first conquerors had been forced to rise in their
own defence against 'new colonies from England, who treated them like
mere native Irish, with innumerable oppressions . . . until in the next
generation the children of these tyrants were used in the same manner
by the new English adventurers, which practice continued for many
centuries'.[37] The picture, in other words, was of successive waves of
English settlers arriving in Ireland, each enjoying a brief period of unmer-
ited ascendancy over those who had preceded them, before they too found
themselves not only shouldered aside by newcomers but subjected to the
humiliation of being categorised as Irish rather than English.

Swift's account of these defensive risings that had preceded the wars of
the 1640s is vague, and it is hard to know exactly to what he is referring.
His reading in Irish history may have made him aware of the major revolts
of the Old English in Tudor Ireland: the Kildare rebellion of 1534, and the
Desmond rebellions of 1569–73 and 1579–83. But it is unlikely that he

would have wanted to justify such recent outbreaks, especially since all of them had in part been Catholic revolts against a Protestant crown. It is more probable that he was simply aware, in general terms, of the numerous internal conflicts, chronicled by Cox and others, that had taken place in the medieval colony, and of the frequent complaints that had been made regarding the supposed cultural and political degeneracy of the English settlers. By recasting this behaviour as a series of risings against oppressive governors, Swift buttressed his ostensible case for the superior merits of Catholic as opposed to Protestant religious dissidents. In addition, and perhaps more important, he gave a historical pedigree to two of his most common complaints about the Ireland of his own day. The first was that its Protestant inhabitants, faithful defenders of the English interest, found themselves shouldered aside by carpetbaggers more recently arrived from England, who monopolised the best positions in the church, the law and elsewhere. The second was the refusal of the government and people of England to acknowledge what was for Swift the all-important distinction between the English Protestant inhabitants of Ireland and the uncouth natives: 'they look upon us as a sort of savage Irish, whom our ancestors conquered several hundred years ago'.[38] An imaginative identification with the Old English allowed Swift to present both grievances as just the latest in a series of examples of England's wilful blindness to the real character of Irish society and of its ingratitude towards those who had served its interests there.

A further effect of Swift's presentation of the injustices suffered by the Old English was to show the origins of the Protestant landed class of his own day in a distinctly unflattering light. The lands that the Catholics had lost had been seized by the fanatic regicides, 'many of which estates are at this day possessed by the posterity of those schismatics'.[39] This negative characterisation of the Cromwellian grantees put Swift at odds with the generally accepted Protestant narrative of Irish history, in which the process of English conquest and settlement had been an unmixed good, bringing political order, civility and prosperity to a violent and under-developed society. It was also a significant misrepresentation. In reality, as modern studies have confirmed, the main beneficiaries of the Cromwellian and Restoration land settlements had been Protestant families established in Ireland before 1641.[40] And as for the new arrivals, Swift's own father, neither mechanic nor sectary, had been one of the many drawn to the opportunities opening up in a newly pacified Ireland. But then Swift had his own reasons to dislike the Protestant propertied society in which he lived. The lack of metropolitan sophistication was a constant reminder of the provincial exile to which a twist of political fate had consigned him; the boisterous, drink-fuelled Whiggery that characterised Irish social gatherings can only have grated; and there was also the frequent anti-clericalism of a landed class that competed with the Church of Ireland for the modest profits to be extracted from an underdeveloped agrarian system.[41] To exaggerate the mean and politically disreputable origins of what he repeatedly depicted as a boorish and rapacious landed class thus made perfect sense. In 1733, preoccupied with the Presbyterians, Swift did not labour the point. But the connection was one that he had already made explicit. Writing to Pope in 1721, he attributed the 'whiggish or fanatical Genius so prevalent among the English of this kingdom' to 'that number of Cromwell's soldiers, adventurers establish'd here, who were all of the sourest Leven, and the meanest birth, and whose posterity are now in possession of their lands and their principles'.[42]

Does all this mean that we should open a new chapter in Swift studies, by crediting him with a more sophisticated and historically informed sense of ethnic identity than his Protestant contemporaries? The answer is fairly clearly no. His acknowledgement of the separate history of the Old English in *Reasons Humbly Offered* is an isolated excursion. Elsewhere he slipped naturally into the more conventional pattern of equating Irish with Catholic and Protestant with English. Even on the one other occasion when Swift demonstrates a degree of sympathy for the misfortunes of Irish Catholics, his exchange of letters with the exiled Jacobite soldier Charles Wogan in 1732, the Old English have disappeared. Wogan's family claimed descent from a late thirteenth-century English chief governor. But for Swift the highest compliment he could pay him was to claim that the success enjoyed by himself and other members of the Jacobite diaspora was proof that English observers were wrong to cast aspersions on the intellect or spirit of 'the Irish Natives'. As further evidence, Swift cited the 'good Sense, Humour and Raillery' he had encountered among those of 'the poor Cottagers here, who could speak our Language', whose depressed condition he saw as due only to the tyranny of their landlords and the superstitious zeal of their priests. For Swift, in other words, Wogan's Catholicism meant that he shared the ethnic identity and national character of the native Irish peasantry.[43]

What then do we learn from Swift's brief venture into the detail of what had happened in Ireland in the 1640s? By the time he wrote, the distinction between Old and New English, long central to political debate, had been buried beneath a simple equation of Irish with Catholic and English with Protestant. Hence his invocation of the Old English case in 1733 is testimony both to the depth of his interest in the history of the mid-century civil wars and to his detached and critical view of the assumptions and prejudices of his own society. At the same time it was an invocation for a purpose. On other occasions Swift, along with most of his contemporaries, was happy to work with the simplistic model of Irish Catholic native and English Protestant conqueror. The difference is that we know, from this brief excursion, that he was quite capable, when it suited him, of a more accurate analysis. The conclusion must be that he was simply not very interested. Events in England up to and after the fateful year of 1641 were clearly of intense personal concern to him: he studied them with close partisan attention and used them as a yardstick to judge developments in his own day. The parallel, and closely related, happenings in Ireland clearly had nothing like the same fascination. Swift was passionately concerned to establish that the mere fact of residence in Ireland did not make one Irish. But how he developed that point, with greater or lesser attention to the real, and quite complex, ethnic history of the island, depended on circumstances and on what suited his rhetorical purposes. In retrospect, Swift's often tortured arguments can be seen as a step towards the creation of a distinctively Irish Protestant identity. But that, it is clear, is something to which he himself attached little importance.

NOTES

1 'Family of Swift', *PW*, V, 193–4.
2 Swift had originally written that he was under 'three and twenty', then altered the manuscript. J. A. Downie charitably suggests that he confused his mission of 1693 with an earlier visit to court in 1690 (*Jonathan Swift: Political Writer* (London: Routledge and Kegan Paul, 1985), pp. 34–5). But since this would still mean that Swift shaved two years off his real age, it only adds carelessness to the charge of self-glorification.
3 See for example Joseph Trapp, *Her Majesty's Prerogative in Ireland Asserted and Maintained* (Dublin, 1712), pp. 4–5, 45. For the Solemn League and Covenant, see 'A representation of the present state of religion with regard to infidelity, heresy, impiety and popery', drawn up by the Irish Convocation in 1711, The National Archives, Public Record Office (hereafter TNA, PRO), SP63/368/22.
4 George Dodington to John Hopkins, 28 Aug. 1707, TNA, PRO SP63/366/241.
5 For a full discussion see S. J. Connolly, 'The Church of Ireland and the royal martyr: regicide and revolution in Anglican political thought c.1660–1745', *Journal of Ecclesiastical History*, 44 (2003), 484–506.
6 William Tisdall, *A Sample of True-Blew Presbyterian Loyalty, in all Changes and Turns of Government* (Dublin, 1709), p. 5.

7 Edward Synge, Speech before a committee of the whole House of Lords, Gilbert Mss, Dublin Municipal Library 28, pp. 125–6.

8 D. F. Passmann and Heinz Vieken, *The Library and Reading of Jonathan Swift* (4 vols., Frankfurt-on-Main: Peter Lang, 2003), vol. I, p. 12; vol. II, p. 957, 1134–5.

9 'Family of Swift', *PW*, V, 188–90. For a fuller discussion of the points made in this and the two succeeding paragraphs see S. J. Connolly, 'Swift and History', in H. J. Real (ed.), *Reading Swift: Papers from the Fifth Münster Symposium on Jonathan Swift* (Munich: Wilhelm Fink, 2008), pp. 187–202.

10 Swift's fullest account of the origins of the English Civil War is in his 'Sermon upon the martyrdom of King Charles I' (1726), *PW*, IX, 219–31.

11 Ibid., p. 223.

12 Passmann and Vieken, *Library and Reading*, vol. II, p. 940.

13 Ian Higgins, 'Swift and Sparta: the nostalgia of *Gulliver's Travels*', *The Modern Language Review*, 78:3 (1983), 518.

14 Passmann and Vieken, *Library and Reading*, vol. II, p. 942.

15 'Sermon on the Martyrdom of King Charles I', *PW*, IX, 223.

16 'Of Mean and Great Figures', ibid., V, 84.

17 Ibid., IX, 263. Cromwell's reply was published in *A Letter from the Right Honorable, the Lord Lieutenant of Ireland, Concerning the Surrender of the Town of Ross, and the Artillery, Arms and Ammunition there* (London, 1649), pp. 8–9. However, neither I nor his most recent Irish biographer, Dr. Micheál Ó Siochrú, have been able to find it reprinted in any of the subsequent histories that would have been available to Swift. If he did in fact rely on this contemporary dispatch, Swift clearly took a closer interest in the course of events in Ireland after 1641 than is apparent from his few comments on the subject.

18 T. C. Barnard, '1641: a bibliographical essay', in Brian MacCuarta (ed.), *Ulster 1641: Aspects of the Rising* (Belfast: Institute of Irish Studies, 1993), pp. 173–86.

19 *The Presbyterian's Plea of Merit* (1733), *PW*, XII, 263–79.

20 See, for example, Tisdall's considerably more sophisticated treatment of the Presbyterian/Independent issue. The Independents, he conceded, had carried out the king's execution, but it was the Presbyterians who had 'first murdered him in his political capacity' by stripping him of all power (*A Sample of True-Blew Presbyterian Loyalty*, p. 18).

21 *Reasons Humbly Offered to the Parliament of Ireland for Repealing the Sacramental Test, In Favour of the Catholicks, Otherwise Called Roman Catholicks, and by their Ill-Willers, Papists … Written in the Year 1733*, in *PW*, XII, 285–95.

22 Aidan Clarke, *The Old English in Ireland 1625–42* (London: MacGibbon and Kee, 1966).

23 J. S. Brewer and William Bullen (eds.), *The Carew Manuscripts Preserved in the Archiepiscopal Library at Lambeth* (6 vols., London, 1867–73), vol. VI, pp. 305–7.

24 For the most recent assessment of the internal politics of the Confederate Catholics see Micheál Ó Siochrú, *Confederate Ireland 1642–1649: A Constitutional and Political Analysis* (Dublin: Four Courts Press, 1999).

25 Sir William Petty, *The Political Anatomy of Ireland* (London, 1691), p. 43.

26 Sir Richard Cox, *Hibernia Anglicana, or the History of Ireland, Part One* (London, 1689), 'Address to the Reader'.

27 *Calendar of State Papers, Domestic Series, 1691–1704* (11 vols. London, 1900–24), vol. VI: *1695*, p. 187.

28 For examples see David Hayton, 'Anglo-Irish attitudes: changing perceptions of national identity among the Protestant ascendancy in Ireland c. 1690–1750'. *Studies in Eighteenth-Century Culture*, 17 (1987), 145–57. See also S. J. Connolly, *Religion, Law and Power: The Making of Protestant Ireland 1660–1760* (Oxford, 1992), pp. 114–20.

29 *To the Whole People of Ireland*, in *PW*, X, 67.

30 For a brief discussion see S. J. Connolly, *Divided Kingdom: Ireland 1630–1800* (Oxford, 1998), pp. 54–8.

31 James Butler, 11th earl of Ormond, was created marquis in 1642 and duke in 1661.

32 Raymond Gillespie, 'The social thought of Richard Bellings', in Micheál Ó Siochrú (ed.), *Kingdoms in Crisis: Ireland in the 1640s* (Dublin: Four Courts Press, 2001), pp. 212–28.

33 Hugh Reilly, *Ireland's Case Briefly Stated; or, a Summary Account of the Most Remarkable Transactions in that Kingdom since the Reformation* (n.p. 1720), pp. 27–8, 38–40. Reilly also denounced at length the injustice of the Restoration land settlement, where Charles II was 'strangely imposed upon to reward his inveterate enemies, who now became great by being thorough-paced rebels', while 'hundreds of ancient and loyal gentlemen were stripped of their birthright' (ibid., pp. 98, 104).

34 *A Jacobite Narrative of the War in Ireland 1688–1691*, J. T. Gilbert ed. (Dublin, 1892), pp. 5–6. For a modern analysis see Patrick Kelly, '"A Light to the Blind": The Voice of the Dispossessed Elite in the Generation after the Defeat at Limerick', *Irish Historical Studies*, 24 (1984–5), 431–62.

35 Swift to Gay, 20 Nov. 1729 (*Correspondence*, III, 268); Carte to Swift, 11 Aug. 1736 (ibid., IV, 337–9).

36 Edward Hyde, earl of Clarendon, *The History of the Rebellion and Civil Wars in England, Begun in the Year 1641* (Oxford, 1702), pp. 156–7.

37 *PW*, XII, 285.

38 *To the Whole People of Ireland*, ibid., X, 64.

39 Ibid., XII, 288.

40 T. C. Barnard, 'Planters and policies in Cromwellian Ireland', *Past and Present*, 61 (1973), 31–69.

41 For upper-class manners see Connolly, *Religion, Law and Power*, pp. 65–73, and for anti-clericalism ibid., p. 191. For toasting see ibid., p. 262; M. J. Powell, 'Political toasting in eighteenth-century Ireland', *History*, 91 (2006), 508–29.

42 Swift to Pope, 10 Jan. 1721 (*Correspondence*, II, 359).

43 Swift to Charles Wogan, July–2 Aug. 1732 (*Correspondence*, III, 514–15).

CHAPTER 11

Jonathan Swift and the Irish colonial project

Robert Mahony

The Irish colonial project – the attempt over centuries to render Ireland peacefully submissive to English dominion – had two phases, one mediaeval and the other early modern. The mediaeval phase saw the establishment of the English 'Pale', the enclave along Ireland's eastern coast settled by the Anglo-Normans who arrived in the twelfth century. Ireland had sustained earlier incursions, but the native Gaelic population had arrived at a *modus vivendi* with these other invaders – Danes and Vikings especially – and by the twelfth century was gradually absorbing them. The Anglo-Normans, later to be known as the 'Old English', tended instead to segregate themselves from the Gaelic natives and resisted absorption by maintaining close social and educational links with England as well; they were concerned more to preserve a colony of their own people in Ireland than to expand it beyond the Pale. But there were signs even before the Reformation that the Pale colony was in danger of succumbing gradually to the assimilative pressures of Gaelic culture, and with the Reformation it actually did succumb, much less gradually, to pressures from England. The cultural differences between the Old English and the Gaels were glaring. Politically the Old English were much more consistently and vocally loyal to the English Crown, while ecclesiastically the practice of Catholicism among them was far less demotic. The Gaelic Irish often mixed prayers in Gaelic with the Latin Mass, for instance, while the Old English rarely included even local devotions; and among the latter also clerics were proudly more rigorous about celibacy. The English Reformation threatened to erode these distinctions between natives and colonials, which had been preserved by the *de facto* segregation of the pre-Reformation Irish church. Neither group welcomed the prospect of comprehension with the other in a single national church, and to the Old English some features of Protestantism, like a non-celibate clergy and vernacular devotions, resembled the native laxities they had long avoided. The resistance of the Old English to the new religious arrangements prompted the government in London to the second, early modern or

Protestant phase of the colonial project, facilitating a large-scale immigration of Protestants from Britain in the later sixteenth century and throughout the seventeenth. These settlers, known as the 'New English', displaced the Old English from their accustomed governance and spread Protestant dominion throughout Ireland.

Jonathan Swift was well aware of the pre-Reformation phase of the Irish colonial project, but its second, Protestant phase was of vastly greater moment to him. The segregation that characterized the Old English colony was replaced by a system of domination including a frequent and eventually constant English military presence underpinning three sets of relationships. The first relationship was country-to-country, as Ireland became tied to the English government in London much more closely than in the earlier phase of the colonial project. The second was the relationship between the government in London and the Protestant 'New English' settlers, whose migration to and survival in Ireland that government had fostered. The third was the relationship between the settlers and the natives, the Gaelic Irish majority of the population. This Protestant phase of the colonial project was much more complicated than the Pale colony in terms of the various parties involved in these relationships, politically, socially and historically. It had the straightforward goal of pacifying the Irish by securing their allegiance, and the means was to Anglicize the country thoroughly; but that Anglicizing process was not consistently or even frequently a matter of schooling the natives in the language and culture of England. Indeed, maintaining a pattern of social and political subordinations was far more important to that process than educating the natives or the colonists. Thus in terms of the relationships of the two islands, Ireland was to be subordinated to England; in terms of the relationships between the settlers and the London government, the former were subordinate to the latter, and in terms of the relationship between the settlers and the Gaelic natives, the latter were subordinate to the former. In practice, it would seem that Anglicization meant that whatever was the more proximately English interest was to prevail in any comparison or clash, and this produced some apparent anomalies, not least that by restricting Ireland's external trade, England impeded prosperity for her Protestant settlers there. The settlers, the New English, viewed these impediments as oppressive, and the landed proprietors among them sometimes responded by oppressing the natives in turn, rack-renting their Gaelic Catholic tenants. Compensating in this way for the unfairness they felt the London government was inflicting upon them lost the settlers whatever moral advantage their own suffering might have allowed them among the English, while hardly assuaging their own resentment against England, and it further impoverished the natives. Lording it over the natives may have offered the settlers fleeting pleasure, but in the longer term it inflicted real economic damage, since increasing poverty kept poor tenants from taking active part in a market that English legislation had already restricted by excluding Irish exports. Thus the New English or Irish Protestant colonial who rack-rented his tenants to purchase a few imports was doing his country no good at all, nor, ultimately, himself, beyond projecting the appearance of prosperity that such a level of consumption can facilitate.

On a general scale, such consumption can make a whole class or country seem prosperous, and one of the targets of Swift's *Short View of the State of Ireland* (1728) is the notion that a country in which there is so much consumption has to be prosperous. A bountiful Ireland would surely vindicate the colonial project. But in each of its phases the official motivation for the colonial project was less the desire specifically to render Ireland prosperous than to make the country England's submissive, peaceful neighbour, a process that involved 'civilizing' Ireland, 'improving' its morals and religion particularly upon the Christian model prevailing in England. Even before some of his knights embarked upon the Anglo-Norman invasion of Ireland, King Henry II had received a papal license to rectify the practice of Irish Christianity by invading that country; and the second phase of the colonial project was explicitly designed to supplant the ascendancy of the Old English Catholics with that of the New English Protestants. Both of these religious motivations were couched as attempts to refine Irish native culture along English lines, which at first meant becoming more properly Catholic than that native culture, and much later, more properly Protestant. As a moralistic clergyman of the established Church who considered English culture far superior to Gaelic, Swift supported the colonial project in the general sense that he advocated the cultivation of good manners, honesty and thrift, and not just for the native Irish, for such 'civilizing' is a theme in various sermons, as is the discouragement of backbiting, false witness and slackness of behaviour in general. He was in favour of making Ireland more prosperous, evidently enough in his complaints about the economic disadvantages under which Ireland laboured in its unequal relationship with England. But he took issue with some of the preferences of the colonial Irish, the Protestants of British ancestry, such as a desire to display prosperity even if the means for it are lacking. His remedy was to promote self-reliance, which would make the colonial wealthier, as well as disciplining his appetites and reducing dependence upon Britain, both in the direct sense that Ireland would import much less from Britain and indirectly by lessening the oppression of the natives that made it necessary to maintain a large garrison in Ireland. Self-reliance, and hence self-discipline, have the effect of cultivating or civilizing oneself and, if generally practised, of civilizing one's country. In this 'civilizing' sense of the colonial project, Swift's Irish writings exhibit a moralism verging on (and frequently falling into) the puritan, as his distaste for colonial vanities of dress typifies; he seems as much drawn to the idea of disciplining appetites as reforming the Irish economy.

To emphasize Swift's stress upon moral discipline in his concern with Ireland is to run athwart of two opposing narratives that have predominated in discussions of Swift and Ireland over the last couple of centuries. The first derives from Whiggish perceptions of Swift as a Tory of so deep a dye that, in the famous words of Sir Francis Jeffrey in the *Edinburgh Review* of September 1816, his 'Irish politics may all be referred to one principle – a desire to insult and embarrass the government by which he was neglected, and with which he despaired of being reconciled'. Swift couldn't really have been concerned with Irish interests for their own sake, for throughout his career 'we hear nothing of [Ireland's] radical grievance, the oppression of its Catholic population. His object was, not to do good, but to vex and annoy the English ministry.'[1] Jeffrey's assertion that Swift's interests were exclusively English, even when he was writing about Irish issues, because he expressed little concern for the plight of Irish Catholics, demonstrates that Jeffrey equates Ireland's interests with those of its Catholics alone, exhibiting a cast of mind that became far too common among Irish nationalists later in the nineteenth century. The other narrative counters the first by presenting Swift as a precursor of Irish nationalism, a notion that rests securely in the Irish popular imagination, though the evidence for it is less determinative. The perception of Swift as sympathetic to what was to become Irish nationalism draws upon a comparatively small number of works, like the *Drapier's Letters*, that breathe defiance in their advocacy of Irish interests against misgovernment from London. Although Theobald Wolfe Tone, the late eighteenth-century Irish revolutionary, argued that Swift would have agreed with his 'discovery' that 'the connection with England' had to be sundered if Ireland was to become 'free, prosperous or happy',[2] Swift never actually advocated breaking the link with England; he considered the exercise of authority over Ireland by the English Parliament illegitimate, of course, but he was enthusiastic about Ireland's sharing the same monarch with England. Moreover, certain works and especially *A Modest Proposal*, resonant with antipathy for the oppressions visited upon the Catholic native Irish poor, have been inter- preted as thereby sympathetic to the poor or to Catholics, though it is hard to read that work without sensing that Swift, however he hates oppression, has no affection for the poor he describes; and his treatment of Catholicism in *A Tale of a Tub*, his describing it as 'a false religion' in his sermon commemorating Charles I,[3] and his approbation of the Penal legislation curtailing the political and religious rights of Catholics[4] should indicate sufficiently his lack of regard for the Roman church.

Jeffrey was in fact closer to the mark, since Swift was no Irish separatist, much less what we would now recognize as a nationalist, and showed vastly more concern for the interests of the settler, the colonial, than for those of the native Irish. As a clergyman and preacher, he had a congregation of colonials, and they comprised the main readership for his pamphlets on Irish matters. Their Ireland was what mattered to him, and just as he ridiculed them when their speech grew barbarous, too 'Irish' in flavour,[5] so he also chastened them for their habits of consumption and criticized their falling short of Christian moral standards in other respects; they were failing, in the context of the colonial project, as agents of civilization. Inasmuch as he had himself failed to curtail their lust to consume, he satirized these Irish Protestants in *A Modest Proposal* but included himself as well. He wasn't ridiculing the poor in that work, but their betters, nor defending the Catholic Irish more generally, so much as warning the Protestants. *A Modest Proposal* has a number of objectives, but its irony certainly implies to his Protestant readership that oppressing the native Irish hurts the interests of the colonial Irish, just as eating human flesh makes one a cannibal – thus by definition uncivilized – and thereby erodes the distinctions between them. The colonial Irish might gain some brief pleasure from feeling replete at table or buying silken fabrics, but this provided no genuine economic benefit and moreover depleted their moral credit, rendering them little superior to the barbaric natives. That near-equation of natives and settlers is more important to Swift's understanding of the colonial project, I would argue, than the colonists' political relationship with England, or indeed than the plight of the natives. By way of example, we can look at a passage in *Gulliver's Travels* that would seem to be promoting compassion for victims of colonial oppression and consider it in a larger context.

In Chapter 5 of Part IV of *Gulliver's Travels*, Gulliver famously recounts to his Houyhnhnm master some of 'the usual Causes or Motives that made one Country go to War with another'.[6] He includes among these that 'If a Prince send Forces into a Nation, where the People are poor and ignorant, he may lawfully put half of them to Death, and make Slaves of the rest, in order to civilize and reduce them from their barbarous Way of Living.'[7] In our own day we tend to interpret this passage as ironical because we view as immoral the very idea of invading another country to extend civilization. Indeed, even before civilizing is mentioned as the goal, Gulliver's statement moves from a description of a people being invaded, to their vulnerability owing to poverty and ignorance, to taking lawful advantage of just that vulnerability to kill half of them and enslave the rest. Most modern readers would consider that civilization as an end cannot justify such dreadful actions as its means and so would wince at the description of that means as 'lawful'. Such excess makes us challenge the credibility of the literal statement: it must be taken ironically, and it is to Gulliver's detriment that we become aware of his own deafness to the moral vacuity of his literal sense, his seeming demand that he be taken literally by his master. The wider context ratifies our insistence upon irony in this specific passage: as a *casus belli* it is, after all, to be found between 'It is justifiable to enter into a War against our nearest Ally, when one of his Towns lies convenient for us' and 'It is a very kingly, honourable, and frequent Practice, when one Prince desires the Assistance of another to secure him against an Invasion' that the assisting king should first drive out the invader and then seize his ally's country himself.[8] This passage would seem to most modern readers almost trans-parently easy to interpret, since the absence, almost the denial, of a moral focus in Gulliver's words functions as signposting: we perceive that the way of extending civilization that Gulliver describes makes the would-be civilizers uncivilized themselves, and that seems to us nonsense. Hence, presented with literal positives that we find morally repellent, we determine Swift's meaning by reading the positives as negatives: we dispute that a prince might lawfully invade a country, massacre half the population and enslave the rest so that they may be civilized. The meaning so easily perceived is quite obviously not the 'literal' meaning: it instances what Wayne Booth termed stable irony – the meaning intended by the author is perceptible, but it differs from the literal meaning, even if the literal meaning is intended by the speaker of a particular passage or statement.[9] And since *Gulliver's Travels* is a satire, the irony seems the more intended in certain key locutions in this passage, especially 'lawful' and 'civilize': that is, the lawfulness anywhere in the world of invading, massacring and enslaving is disputable indeed, and at any rate incompatible with a civilizing purpose. So, reading this passage as satire facilitated by stable irony, we would tend to take it as a satirical denunciation of the very idea that civilization could be extended by violence and coercion, finding Swift anticipating an anti-interventionist ideology which has advanced since his death in 1745, unsteadily for a long while but becoming prominent – if not dominant – in Western thinking during the last two or three generations.

But disparaging imperialism in this fashion is strikingly modern. In our own day the law of force is both distasteful and, we would like to think, ineffective: imposing a particular standard of civilization by force upon people of a very different culture is at once wrong and unworkable. But force has established facts on the ground for many centuries; coercion has often and very effectively made people accommodate themselves to a different culture. Rather than anticipating a twentieth-century liberalism by inducing an inverted or negative reading of 'lawful' and 'civilize' in this passage from *Gulliver's Travels*, Swift offers an irony that complicates the stability Booth's category describes. The literal expression should be taken not as a literal positive we turn upside down, but as a simple literal positive: such action is indeed lawful when the objective is to civilize a savage people. Swift was not trying to appeal beyond the sensibilities of his contemporaries, and Gulliver is not being foolish here (as we would tend to see him), so much as representing with some accuracy his own fairly advanced European country, which had already engaged in colonialism on a major scale and would expand that enterprise. The secular morality of modern times, less concerned with individual salvation than with collective well-being, would suggest that Swift is satirizing colonialism by pointing to its deleterious effects on the population being colonized. A more traditional Christian morality, while deploring those effects on the victims, is concerned also to awaken the conscience of the perpetrator to his sin: the violent colonizer, far from forwarding civilization, discovers his own lack of civilization, his lust to control and consume disguised by an ideology of advancement and improvement. That ideology has been deemed 'lawful' and as improvement ought to be moral as well; that its consequences are disastrous offers a bitter irony, but while we might see the disaster as mocking 'lawfulness' because of its impact upon the victims, for Swift it mocks more broadly the human tendency to find a moral disguise for immoral action. The ironic potential in the fact that immoral behaviour is often acceptable in legal terms is the more enhanced if we perceive the issue as the law's actually enabling and accommodating sin rather than countering it. Swift is passionately attached to the notion that secular law does not necessarily counter sin;

this informs his opinion of himself, as inscribed upon the memorial over his grave, as a defender of liberty, since promoting freedom from sin can mean acting even counter to the law. The immediate object of Swift's satire in this passage from *Gulliver's Travels* is not, thus, Gulliver, nor indeed the imperial impulse – even granting that Swift is satirically derogatory about both – but a widespread, even characteristic, human moral flexibility in the face of temptation.

The colonial project in Ireland offered Swift ample opportunity to develop and exercise this moral concern. Indeed, his irony at this point in *Gulliver's Travels* has some Irish rhetorical particularity, since Gulliver's statement echoes a contention made early and maintained throughout Sir John Davies's *Discoverie of the State of Ireland* (1613):

a barbarous Country must first be broken by a warre, before it will be capable of good Government, and when it is fully subdued and conquered, if it bee not well planted and governed after the Conquest, it wil eft-soones return to the former Barbarisme.[10]

Davies, Solicitor-General and then Attorney-General for Ireland in the reign of James I, was writing after the defeat of the Earl of Tyrone's long rebellion against England, which enabled major colonization from England and Scotland in the estates confiscated from Tyrone and his allies in what is now Northern Ireland. Anticipating that at last Ireland might be 'thoroughly subdued and reduced to Obedience of the Crowne of *England*,'[11] Davies repeated this verbal formula within a few sentences to condemn 'a vulgar error . . . namely, *That Ireland long since might have been subdued and reduced to* Civility, *if some Statesmen in policy had not thoght* [sic] *it more fit to continue that Realme in Barbarisme*'.[12] Davies's locution 'reduced' here would seem to make Davies a target of the mockery in *Gulliver's Travels*, where Swift uses the phrase 'reduced them from their barbarous Way of Living'; but the locution dates before Davies well into the sixteenth century, when 'reducing' was often used as a term for breaking subject peoples of their bad cultural habits. Davies may be more closely indebted for 'reducing' to Edmund Spenser's *View of the Present State of Ireland*, written about 1596 but not published until 1633. Spenser actually devotes the *View*, a lengthy dialogue, to the question of 'reducing' the Irish so that they might become civilized, beginning the work with a question put by Eudoxus, a representatively well-meaning Englishman:

Eudox: But if that country of Ireland whence you late came be so goodly and commodious a soil as you report, I wonder that no course is taken for the turning thereof to good uses, and reducing that savage nation to better government and civility.[13]

Because of the delay in publishing Spenser's *View*, his application of 'reducing' in this sense to Ireland reached print later than that in Samuel Daniel's *Collection of the History of England* (1621), which recounts the invasion of Ireland by King Henry II of England. Henry had applied to the Pope in 1155 for permission to conquer Ireland, which was granted by the Pope at the time – Nicholas Brekespere, an English Augustinian monk who reigned as Adrian IV – in a bull titled, from the initial word in the Latin text, *Laudabiliter*. Daniel describes the Pope licensing Henry's '*reducing rude and vnlettered people from their vicious manners, to the veritie of the Christian faith, and ciuilitie*'.[14] This phrasing is not, interestingly, that of the Latin text, which is preserved in the Irish history of Giraldus Cambrensis, produced in the generation after the invasion. There, Henry is given leave 'ad declarandum indoctis et rudibus populis Christiane fidei veritatem'[15] (to proclaim the truth of the Christian faith to untaught and barbarous people): no equivalent of 'reducing' appears in the Latin. But Daniel's *Collection* was a major source for Sir William Temple's *Introduction to the History of England*,[16] which Swift prepared for the press; Swift would have been familiar with Daniel's *Collection*, the 1626 edition of which he owned. For his usage of 'reducing' a people from savagery, then, he was as probably indebted to Samuel Daniel as to Spenser or Davies.

There is, however, a precedent for this usage in Swift's own writing about Ireland. He undertook about 1703 a project for an *Abstract of the History of England*, greatly indebted to Temple's introductory English history, and supplemented this *Abstract* with a more fragmentary sketch of the reigns of a few kings who followed William the Conqueror on the English throne. He broke off this latter project just after he described King Henry II's decision to invade Ireland with the objective of 'reducing the savage people of Ireland from their brutish way of living, and subjecting them to the crown of England'. If here in his account of Henry II Swift echoes Daniel's term 'reducing' fairly straightforwardly, the context in which he uses the phrase offers an irony very different from that of the passage in which he repeats the phrase in *Gulliver's Travels*, Part IV. It is of course not possible to determine if Swift when writing *Gulliver's Travels* knowingly echoed Spenser, Davies, Daniel or indeed himself, but while the verbal formula of 'reducing' was standard in a context of invading to civilize, his echo of his own phrase of twenty years earlier is arresting. It isn't common at all for Swift to echo a locution he had used decades before. This echo in particular, inadvertent or not, allows us to gauge a definite shift in Swift's attitude toward the colonial project over the span of twenty years. Our measure is the difference in the ironic freight between the passage quoted from the sketch of Henry II and that from *Gulliver's Travels*: this calls not so much for our discerning gradations of irony among Swift's various comments on Ireland during this period as for noticing a shift in Swift's moral focus. His account of Henry II registers approval for the colonial project, since whatever the moral deficiencies of the putative civilizers, about which Swift can be ironically caustic, Irish barbarism is a greater moral deformity. But by the time Swift was writing *Gulliver's Travels*, his irony applies to this very idea he had formerly embraced, that barbarism justifies invasion; that is, the determination on the part of the putative civilizers to invade a country and otherwise act with violence to advance a project to civilize is itself a moral deformity that outweighs the moral deformity of barbarism.

In his sketch of Henry II, Swift provides a context for the king's interest in Ireland. He describes how Henry manoeuvred his advance to the throne in the first place, swearing an oath that he would respect his younger brother's inheritance of the earldom of Anjou from their father:

But after he [Henry] was in possession of *England*, whether it were that his ambition enlarged with his dominions, or that from the beginning he had never intended to observe what he had sworn, he prevailed with pope *Adrian* (of *English* birth) to dispense with his oath, and in the second year of his reign went over into *Normandy*, drove his brother intirely out of *Anjou*, and forced him to accept a pension for his maintenance. But the young prince, through the resentment of his unnatural dealing, in short time died of grief.

Nor was his treatment more favourable to the king of *Scots*, whom, upon a slight pretence, he took occasion to dispossess of *Carlisle, Newcastle,* and other places granted by the empress to that prince's father, for his services and assistance in her quarrel against *Stephen.*

Having thus recovered whatever he had any title to demand, he began to look for new acquisitions. Ireland was in that age a country little known in the World. The legates sent thither from the Court of *Rome*, for urging the payment of annats, or directing other Church affairs, represented the inhabitants as a savage people, overrun with barbarism and superstition: for indeed no nation of Europe, where the Christian religion received so early and universal admittance, was ever so late or slow in feeling its effects upon their manners and civility. Instead of refining their manners by their faith, they had suffered their faith to be corrupted by their manners; true religion being almost defaced, both in doctrine and discipline, after a long course of time, among a people wholly sunk in ignorance and barbarity. There seem to have been two reasons why the inhabitants of that island continued so long uncultivated; first, their subjection or vassalage to so many petty kings, where of a great number is mentioned by authors, besides those four or five usually assigned to the several provinces. These princes were engaged in perpetual quarrels, in doing or revenging injuries of violence, or lust, or treachery, or injustice, which kept them all in a continual state of war. And indeed, there is hardly any country, how renowned soever in ancient or modern story, which may not be traced from the like original. Neither can a nation come out from this state of confusion, until it is either reduced under one head at home, or by force or conquest becomes subject to a foreign administration.

The other reason why civility made such late entrances into that island, may be imputed to its natural situation, lying more out of the road of commerce or conquest than any other part of the known world. All the intercourse the inhabitants had, was only with the western coasts of Wales and Scotland, from whence, at least in those ages, they were not like to learn very much politeness.

The King, about the second year of his reign, sent ambassadors to Pope *Adrian*, with injunctions to desire his licence for reducing the savage people of *Ireland* from their brutish way of living, and subjecting them to the crown of *England*.

The king proceeded thus, in order to set up a title to the island, wherein the pope himself pretended to be lord of the see; for in his letter, which is an answer and grant to the king's requests, he insists upon it, that all islands, upon their admitting the Christian faith, become subject to the see of *Rome*; and the *Irish* themselves avowed the same thing to some of the first conquerors. In that forementioned letter, the pope praises the king's generous design, and recommends to him the civilizing the natives, the protection of the Church, and the payment of *Peter-pence*. The ill success of all past endeavours to procure from a people so miserable and irreligious this revenue to the holy see, was a main inducement with the pope to be easy and liberal in his grant; for the king professed a design of securing its regular payment. However, this expedition was not undertaken until some years after, when there happened an incident to set it forward, as we shall relate in its place.[17]

The account of Henry II as a whole breaks off at this point. Unfinished as it stands, the passage here offers an emergent irony, as Swift's distaste for Henry and the collusive cupidity of Rome competes with his conviction that Ireland was barbarous and needed civilizing, and the implication that England was the obvious agent of civility. The irony here is languorous, relaxed by comparison with the successive, morally awkward juxtapositions in the 'reducing' passage quoted earlier from *Gulliver's Travels*. At first reading the passage seems to imply that the barbarism reputed of the Irish was merely the pretext for the territorial expansion that was Henry's only real interest. After all, it follows directly upon a description of Henry as a trickster, colluding with the Pope to cheat his brother out of a minor, second son's inheritance. The savage nature of the Irish is described initially here not as a matter of fact, but as something reported merely, and reported moreover to the 'Court of Rome', which in Swift's preceding paragraph was complicit in Henry's injustice toward his younger brother. If this passage were taken from a finished rather than abandoned work of Swift's, we would very probably see Henry's treatment of his younger brother as prelude to his treatment of Ireland, constructed for a clearly satiric aim, more sardonic than the 'reducing' passage quoted earlier from *Gulliver's Travels* but broadly similar in purpose. But there is a serious difference between the passages, not merely one of rhythm, for as we consider the account of Henry II and Ireland there emerges a dialectic about power and the civilizing mission: the irony is a product of Swift's ambivalence about England's relationship with Ireland in its references to the king Swift clearly dislikes, and the Irish reputation for savagery, which he even more clearly accepts as sound. Swift is thus at some pains, with such ambivalence, to disclose his reluctance about the civilizing mission, but as he dwells upon Irish barbarism, he all but explicitly condones Henry's aggression. His historical analysis, presenting a country in a state of unimproved nature, justifies the invasion as necessary to advance the Irish from their barbarous way of living, even regardless of Henry's venality and the Pope's complicity. The ironic element functions to sustain our sense of Henry II's moral repugnance to Swift, even as the gravity of this recognition must concede to the understanding that the condition of savagery is a social defect so profound as to validate the actions even of a deceitful king.

Hence for Swift in 1703, the immorality of Irish barbarism outweighs the immoral character and motives of the king. By 1726, in Part IV of *Gulliver's Travels*, he has shifted from this position to imply instead that the goal of civilizing the Irish has had the effect of accommodating immorality, perverting law and masking the all-too-human lust for consumption and power. Swift's writing 'reduce' in 1726 draws attention to this shift by echoing 'reducing' in 1703; but this could be a rhetorical inadvertency,[18] especially if we could show that Swift continued to regard Irish barbarism an overwhelming moral defect. Certainly he would have remained part of a larger body of opinion historically, for in a broad European historical context, Ireland by the time of Henry II was in need of conquest by a Christian civilizer. Imperium had long been understood as the antidote to barbarism; Christianity in particular had been understood as a counter to savagery even before Europe began founding colonies in the Americas during the sixteenth and seventeenth centuries. It was a commonplace in Swift's time, as it had been for centuries, for northern and western Europeans to consider that conquest and absorption into the Roman Empire had been the remedy for their own ancestors' wild incivility. A pioneering colonist in Ulster in 1572 wrote of his learning 'from histories how England was as uncivil as Ireland until colonies of Romans brought their laws and orders, whose moulds no nation, not even the Italians and Romans, have more straitly and truly kept'.[19] By never having been part of the Roman Empire, Ireland was effectively denied a chance to become civilized. Now, hundreds of years after the demise of Rome, such an opportunity became available with Ireland's incorporation into the English crown's dominions. Yet there remained a second, geographical, reason for Irish barbarism: Ireland will always lie far from the centre of events in Europe, closer to Wales and Scotland than anywhere else, countries, as Swift puts it, 'from whence, at least in those ages, they were not like to learn very much politeness'. This wry witticism at the expense of the Celtic fringe seems a tentative pointer that Swift anticipates the futility of overcoming Irish savagery, however seriously it ought to be perceived.

Those involved with the colonial project from its inception in the later twelfth century had tended to take Irish savagery very seriously indeed. What Patricia Coughlan has termed Ireland's 'radical alterity' or 'challenging otherness' in relation to attempts at Anglicization in the sixteenth century is not only a reference to the considerable differences between English and Gaelic civilizations, but alludes as well to the stout resistance of the latter to English culture.[20] As Patricia Palmer has shown, by the early years of the sixteenth century that Gaelic resistance had developed into encroachment, compromising the English culture of the Pale, and without that integrity the English colonial elites were hard pressed to maintain their civilizing reach, much less extend it.[21] As against the persistence and even aggressiveness of Gaelic culture, still associated in the English mind with the evil of barbarism,[22] the Old English unwillingness to adopt the new religion could seem the culmination of their cultural exhaustion. To John Hooker in 1586, it was the 'want of a generall Reformation'[23] among the Old English that accounted for Gaelic rebelliousness and cultural tenacity, and so the colonial project entered a new phase, supplanting the Old English as agents of civilization among the native Gaelic population by new infusions of English Protestants, cohorts which included Edmund Spenser. To assist this renewed effort to civilize the country Ireland was shired and political control much more centralized, but the settlements were only indifferently successful until the plantation of Ulster with British Protestant settlers was made possible early in the seventeenth century upon the forfeiture of much of present-day Northern Ireland to the crown.

Beyond Ulster the Protestant settlement pattern was much less effective; gradually in the seventeenth century Ireland's towns became Protestant, while the countryside remained overwhelmingly Catholic. The shift in polarities from Gaelic and Old English to Protestant and Catholic meant that the influence of the Old English grew markedly dominant within Catholic Ireland, and that of Gaelic culture lessened; certainly the knowledge of English increased very considerably among the Gaelic population, though their primary language remained Irish. The weight of persecution against Catholics increased overall as well, especially in the wake of their militancy in the 1640s and 1689–91, which brought military defeat and large-scale civil disabilities, and most notably a major shift in land ownership. As Toby Barnard puts it succinctly, 'in 1641 they had owned an estimated 59 per cent of the profitable acreage; by 1688, only 22 per cent. Further seizures following a fresh war and further defeats for the Catholics between 1689 and 1691 reduced their total to about 14 per cent.'[24] The speed of the revolution in land ownership made it a deceptive gauge of cultural penetration, but there was nonetheless discernible progress in Anglicization, and as Richard Cox, an ardent Protestant recorder of Catholic enormities, looked forward to William III's defeat of James II in the early 1690s, he could anticipate the earnest pursuit of the reformation of Irish society:

the English have heartily endeavoured to Reform that People, and to bring that Noble Country into a general Practice of True Religion and Civility, and though we do not boast much of our Success hitherto, yet now that it is likely better and more effectual Methods will be used than heretofore, we do not doubt but that they will produce suitable Effects.[25]

The suitable effects were long delayed, however, since, as history had shown, English culture was at risk where there was no demographic preponderance. An observer in 1697 noted:

'Twas the misfortune of the *English* that they were but few in number in respect of the *Irish*: they came into the Land by single Families, or but a few at a time; therefore instead of Reforming them, they fell into the Manners and Religion of the People of the Land.[26]

This commentator anticipated a recurrence of the same, since Protestant veterans were so commonly awarded land distant from Protestant settlements:

how many there are of the Children of *Oliver's* Souldiers in this Kingdom, who cannot speak one word of English. And, which is stranger, the same may be said of some of the Children of King *Williams's* Souldiers, who came but t'other day into the Country.[27]

By contrast with such observers, Swift's concern with the colonial project is moral to a greater extent than social or political. If in his 1703 account of the background to Henry II's invasion he is able only reluctantly to overcome his ambivalence about the king's character and motives, it is because he understands Gaelic culture as barbaric, even a moral deformity. His insinuation, further, of the futility of the civilizing mission owing to Ireland's geography implies all the more strongly the necessity to keep moral rectification as its goal. But instead of a morally focussed policy, Gaelic cultural predominance had been addressed since the Reformation mainly by depriving the Catholic gentry of property, political power and social influence. That tactic forestalled any resurgence of Catholicism as a political threat but hardly weakened the extensive hold of Gaelic culture upon the native Irish population at large.[28] Swift persisted in regarding Irish native culture as barbarous, yet after alluding to its moral defectiveness in the account of Henry II generally refrained from linking barbarity and moral deficiency. The strongest such link is the putative metaphor of Yahoos for the 'savage old Irish', while 'O'Rourke's Feast' offers condescension, and he considered that civilizing the Irish could make little headway while the Irish language continued in widespread use.[29] On the other hand, his concern with the mentality and morality of his own Protestant Irish people increased steadily. He had broken off his account of Henry II without noticing the psychology of the Old English settlers, but four years later he spoke directly to the colonial cast of mind, negotiating their Irish space in the shadow of England. His allegory of 1707, 'The Story of the Injur'd Lady', examines England's preference for a legislative union with Scotland, notwithstanding Ireland's longer history of loyalty. The Scottish union was contrived to bind Scotland fast to England, against the impending shift to a Hanoverian royal family, since Scotland had shared a crown with England only for a century, and then only under a Scots royal family. Because Ireland was in no danger of shaking off English royal dominion, there was no such union in prospect there. The 'injur'd Lady' of Swift's title is Ireland, who many years since had allowed a neighbouring gentleman, England, to manage her estate, and remained loyal to him, but now finds that he has married another neighbour lady, Scotland, despite a history of friction between them. Presented only from the Irish Lady's perspective, the 'Story' rehearses an allegory of English perfidy capped at last by romantic betrayal, in which the rival is at fault as much as the gentleman. Half a century ago Ricardo Quintana all but dismissed the 'Story of the Injur'd Lady': 'Its interest for us lies in its showing at how early a period Swift's resentment at England's treatment of Ireland had become articulate.'[30] There is more to the allegory that that, however, for included with the Lady's letter is the 'Answer' from her friend, which dwells more upon the blame the Lady herself deserves than on that either of the gentleman or her rival; for she has been credulous to the point of gullibility, short-sighted and in general politically inept. These are political failings, to be sure; but the Lady's inability to see her own part in her predicament, to account adequately for her own actions, is a very decidedly moral shortcoming – she must acknowledge her own responsibility before she can do anything to remedy the situation. And that remedy involves seeing to her own interests rather than expecting fair dealing from her neighbour; experience has taught her that her interests and those of the gentleman who betrayed her are not identical, and she should look to her own.

The 'Story of the Injur'd Lady' is remarkable for Swift's concentration upon the Protestant Irish, rather than upon England or the natives, which underscores the moral necessity to acknowledge personal responsibility and cultivate prudence. However greater the gentleman's fault, the lady is not without moral faults either, so while the lady's friend can offer her no redress for the gentleman's faults, he does propose steps that she can take to avoid repeating her own mistakes. The politics of the Scottish union Swift has converted into terms of personal prudential morality, which veils a pro-Irish stance from seeming anti-English, foreshadowing a procedure he follows years later in the pamphlet on *Irish Manufacture*. This advice to remedy distress by cultivating your own resources is also evident in the sermon 'Causes of the Wretched Condition of Ireland'. Though here England is again seen as most responsible for Irish poverty, Swift concentrates upon what individuals and groups in Ireland can do. As legislators, for instance, the Irish Parliament could without interference from London 'found a School in every Parish' for the poor, which would eventually 'abolish that Part of Barbarity and Ignorance, for which our Natives are so despised'; shopkeepers for their part could refrain from stocking imported fabrics, and their customers from buying imports.[31] Fittingly for a clergyman, the sermon proceeds morally and follows the 'Story of the Injur'd Lady' by considering the condition of Ireland in terms of personal behaviour.

The pattern continues with Swift's response to the Declaratory Act of 1720, which subordinated the Dublin Parliament explicitly to Westminster and sparked a torrent of outraged pamphleteering in Ireland. The year before, in 1719, Swift had dismissed the Protestant Irish as a 'most profligate and abandoned People',[32] but the passage of the Declaratory Act gave him an opportunity to pose a moral challenge to his people: instead of making constitutional arguments, *A Proposal for the Universal Use of Irish Manufacture* (1720) recommends cultivating self-reliance to reform Irish habits of consumption and contain the disabilities the Act imposed on Irish trade. Four years later, when Swift entered the controversy over William Wood's patent with the *Drapier's Letters*, it becomes clear that he sees reclaiming self-respect and (thereby) economic and political leverage with England as further benefits from economic self-reliance. The emphasis has shifted from economics to politics: the *Irish Manufacture* pamphlet exhorts the (Protestant) Irish to act as though they control their own internal economy, implicitly to mature beyond their lust to consume according to English fashion; the *Drapier's Letters* confirms that declining to consume – specifically, to use Wood's coins – is an exercise of political power, an assertion of political maturity. And the balance of blame has shifted as well: in 1720 Swift admonishes Irish colonials to look to themselves, to correct their bad habits, but in 1724 they are to notice the political defects of misgovernment from London with its attendant, indeed arrogant, corruption. The stress upon rights issues from Swift's characteristic moral foundation: refusing English fashions, or Wood's coins, is resistance to temptation, with the difference here that he is not concerned with how the Irish might alter patterns or habits of consumption. Rather, he is recommending that by refusing Wood's coinage they forestall a new vehicle for consumption: resistance to change becomes an exercise in asserting rights. It isn't hard to understand why, though the *Irish Manufacture* pamphlet gave the impetus to Swift's patriotic reputation as an Irish patriot, that reputation was subsequently informed by the *Drapier's Letters*. For not only did the agitation against Wood's coinage succeed in forcing the revocation of his patent (however handsomely he was compensated) and thereby provide Irish patriotism with a rare occasion to celebrate, but resistance, especially to something novel, is generally more attractive than reforming customary behaviour.

Satire, moreover, is conducive to emboldening resistance, which offers a link between the theme of the *Drapier's Letters* and a number of moments in *Gulliver's Travels*, one of them the passage quoted earlier in this essay. The ironic tone might seem to enhance mainly an emphasis upon rights, implying that the natives in question have a right not to be 'civilized' by a process of invasion, murder and enslavement. But the stress in that passage, seen as an element in a pattern of concern for Swift's own people, is as much upon the behaviour of the colonizers, the Protestant Irish, as upon the natives. The Irish colonial project had become valuable to Swift ultimately less for the native Irish that it was originally intended to civilize – something he could endorse in 1703 – than as a means of moral guidance for his own people. Swift could define oppression in terms of England's choking Irish commerce, but by the time he wrote *Gulliver's Travels* his hatred of oppression included prominently mistreatment of native peoples. Most in our day would oppose oppression for the sake of the victims, but for Swift, certainly regarding the relationship of Irish Protestants to native Catholics, oppression was also bad behaviour that eroded any moral position the dominant Protestants might foster and degraded their self-respect as agents of civilization. Indeed, putative civilizers who invade, murder and enslave – like Henry II – are no less barbarous than the barbarians they want to reform; the motivation of morality merely disguises their bad intentions. To extend the moral focus beyond Ireland, as Ricardo Quintana put it late in his career, Gulliver's failure in Part IV 'is a failure of determination to act in the way that human beings, neither impossibly perfect nor utterly abhorrent, are capable of acting. The message is not different from what Swift gives us in his epitaph: assert your strength to the utmost, act in the cause of freedom.'[33] Ireland has claimed Swift as a patriot, but that patriotism reflected a broader moral sense, for the liberty he fostered, and of which he boasted in his epitaph, is the liberty of humans to act morally, to resist evil.

NOTES

1 Sir Francis Jeffrey, 'Jonathan Swift' [review of Walter Scott's edition of Swift], *Edinburgh Review*, 27 September 1816, 22.
2 Theobald Wolfe Tone, *The Life of Theobald Wolfe Tone ... Edited by his Son*, 2 vols. (Washington: Gales & Seaton, 1826), vol. I, p. 32.
3 Swift, 'A Sermon upon the Martyrdom of K. Charles I', (1726), *PW*, IX, 229.
4 Swift's comment in his sermon 'On Brotherly Love' is typical: 'The Papists, GOD be praised, are, by the Wisdom of our Laws, and their own Want of Power, put out of all visible Possibility of hurting us ...', ibid., 172.
5 E.g. Swift, 'A Dialogue in Hibernian Style', ibid., IV, 277–8.
6 Swift, *Gulliver's Travels*, ibid., XI, 245.
7 Ibid., 246.
8 Ibid.
9 Wayne Booth, *A Rhetoric of Irony* (University of Chicago Press, 1975), pp. 5–7.
10 Sir John Davies, *A Discoverie of the State of Ireland, With the true Causes why that Kingdom was never entirely Subdued ...* (London: Iohn Haggard, 1613), p. 5.
11 Ibid., p. 2.

12 Ibid., pp. 3–4.

13 Edmund Spenser, *A view of the Present State of Ireland*, ed. W. L. Renwick (Oxford: Clarendon Press 1970), p. 1.

14 Samuel Daniel, *The Collection of the History of England* (London, 1621), p. 80.

15 Giraldus Cambrensis, *Expugnatio Hibernica The Conquest of Ireland*, ed. A. B. Scott and F. X. Martin (Dublin: Royal Irish Academy, 1978), p. 144. Annotating this text (p. 323), the editors survey the controversial history of the text of *Laudabiliter*, concluding that while Giraldus's text may not be completely accurate, he himself believed in its authenticity. His is also the version that was known to scholars in the early modern period. The translation following the Latin is my own.

16 Homer E. Woodbridge comments that 'it is clear that he wrote with Daniel's book before him, or close at hand', *Sir William Temple* (New York: Modern Language Association, 1940), p. 257.

17 Swift, 'A Fragment of the History from William Rufus', *PW*, V, 75–7.

18 Such a rhetorical inadvertency can be seen in Swift's repetition of 'reduce', also within the context of civilizing, in his pamphlet 'An Answer to several letters sent me from unknown Hands. Written in the year 1729': abolishing the Irish language would 'in great measure, civilize the most barbarous among them, reconcile them to our customs and manner of living, and reduce great numbers to the national religion', and it would be gratifying if 'some public thoughts were employed to reduce this uncultivated people from that idle, savage, beastly, thievish manner of life in which they continue sunk', *PW*, XII, 89. 'Reduce' was utterly conventional in the context of advancing civilization among those supposed barbarous, though it remains remarkable that in *Gulliver's Travels*, Part IV Swift should have echoed so exactly his usage from 1703, in the fragmentary history of Henry II.

19 Sir Thomas Smith to Lord Deputy Fitzwilliam, 8 Nov. 1572, Carte MS 57, f. 435, quoted in D. B. Quinn, 'Sir Thomas Smith (1513–1577) and the Beginnings of English Colonial Theory', *Proceedings of the American Philosophical Society*, 89 no. 4 (1945), 546.

20 Patricia Coughlan, 'Some secret scourge which shall by her come into England: Ireland and Incivility in Spenser', in Coughlan, ed., *Spenser and Ireland: An Interdisciplinary Perspective* (Cork University Press, 1979), p. 46.

21 Patricia Palmer, *Language and Conquest in Early Modern Ireland* (Cambridge University Press, 2001), pp. 40–4.

22 Assessing Edmund Spenser's first-hand observation of the native Gaelic culture of Ireland, Clare Carroll finds that 'the moral qualities attributed to the Irish constitute a taxonomy of vice'. *Circe's Cup: Cultural Transformations in Early Modern Writing about Ireland* (Cork University Press, 2001), p. 40. I am indebted to Professor Carroll for providing this reference to me.

23 Hooker, commenting upon his own translation of the *Expugnatio Hibernica* of Giraldus Cambrensis in Raphael Holinshed, *The First and Second volumes of Chronicles*, 2 vols. ([London], 1586), vol. II, p. 53 [second pagination].

24 Toby Barnard, *The Kingdom of Ireland, 1641–1760* (London: Palgrave Macmillan, 2004), p. 4.

25 Richard Cox, *Hibernia Anglicana* (London: H. Clark for Joseph Watts, 1689), pp. 7–8.

26 Anon., *The True Way to Render Ireland Happy and Secure* ... (Dublin: A. Crook & E. Dobson, 1697), pp. 9–10.

27 Ibid., p. 17.

28 Máirtín Ó Murchú contends that throughout the seventeenth and most of the eighteenth centuries, Gaelic culture, especially as measured by attachment to the Gaelic language, remained widespread, and that a pronounced shift toward English among the mass of the Irish people got its first impulse, ironically, 'by the relaxation of the Penal Laws' against Catholicism starting in the 1770s. See Ó Murchú, *Language and Community: Comhairle na Gaeilge Occasional Paper No. 1* (Dublin: Stationery Office, 1971), p. 27.

29 Swift, 'An Answer to several letters sent me from unknown Hands', *PW*, XII, 89.

30 Ricardo Quintana, *Swift: An Introduction* (Oxford: Clarendon Press, 1962), p. 90.

31 Swift, 'Causes of the Wretched Condition of Ireland', *PW*, IX, 202.

32 [Draft dedication] 'To the Count de Gyllenborg', Swift, ibid., V, 11.

33 Ricardo Quintana, '*Gulliver's Travels*: Some Structural Properties and Certain Questions of Critical Approach and Interpretation', in Claude Rawson, ed., *The Character of Swift's Satire: A Revised Focus* (Newark, Del.: University of Delaware Press, 1983), p. 296.

Index

'Account how far the Peace is complete between her Majesty's Allies and France and Spain ...', (anonymous), 54
Account of the Earl of Galway's Conduct in Spain and Portugal (anonymous), 134
Act of Union (1707), 17, 93, 94, 95, 284, 285
Addison, Joseph, 106
  Spectator, 109
Adrian IV, Pope (Nicholas Brekespere), *Laudabiliter*, 278, 279, 280, 281
Aislabie, John, 54
Allen, Joshua, second Viscount, 10, 200, 205
Alliance of Hanover, 70
Alliance of Vienna, 70
American Constitution, First Amendment to, 34
Ames, Joseph, *Typographical Antiquities*, 123
Anjou, Duc d', 176
Anne, Queen, 7, 10, 32, 42, 45, 55, 56, 59, 63, 64, 65, 67, 93–4, 96–7, 99, 103, 105, 116, 124, 166, 170, 222, 225, 227, 236
Annesley v. *Sherlock*, 231
Answer to Bickerstaff (anonymous), 97, 99
Arbuthnot, John, 6, 66
Aristotle, 142
Athens, 35, 37–8, 40, 42, 43, 46
Atterbury, Francis, 9, 20, 41, 58, 70
Auden, W. H., *Oxford Book of Modern Verse* (1936), 190

Bacon, Francis, 146
Barber, John, 62, 123, 127
Barnard, Toby, 283
Barnett, Louise, 149, 150, 153
Barrier Treaty, 133
Bathurst, Allen, 1st Earl, 68
Baudelaire, Charles, 199, 202
  'De L'Essence du rire', 199
Bellings, Richard, 262
Bentley, Richard, 206
Berkeley, Earl of, 8, 178
Berkenhead, John, 19

Bettesworth, Richard, 223
Bindon, David, 235, 236
Bindon, Francis, 239
Blackall, Ofspring, 14
Blake, William, 145
Blount, Martha, 150
Bolingbroke, Henry St John, Viscount, 7, 36–7, 53, 56, 59–60, 62, 63, 64, 65, 67, 68, 69, 70, 103, 119, 166, 193
  Occasional Writer, 59
Bolton, Theophilus, Bishop, later Archbishop, 224, 226, 235, 236, 237, 239, 240, 241, 243
Booth, Wayne, 275, 276
Boswell, James, 173
  Life of Johnson, 117
Boulter, Hugh, Primate, 241 (at 241, Archbishop)
Boyer, Abel, 7
Boyle, Henry, 226, 227
Boyne, Viscount. *See* Hamilton, Gustavus
Bray, Alan, *The Friend*, 144, 149, 151, 155
Brodrick, Alan, first Viscount Midleton, 6, 222–3, 225, 226–7, 230, 232
Brodrick, St John, 222
Brown, Tom, 20
  'Comical View of the Transactions ... in ... London and Westminster', 85
Browning, Reed, 228, 241
Burgh, Thomas, 239
Burke, Edmund, 36, 39–41, 53
  Annual Register, 55
Burnet, Gilbert, Bishop, 20, 42, 257
  History of his own Time, 12
Burns, William, 81
Butler, James, *see* first and second Dukes of Ormond, 10

Cambrensis, Giraldus, 278
Capel, Henry, Baron, Lord Deputy of Ireland, 8, 230
Carew, Sir George, 261
Carlos II, 176

Carte, Thomas, 263
Carteret, John, Lord, Viceroy of Ireland,
    69, 140, 223
Case, Arthur E., 58
'Castle' party, 221–43 *passim*
Castle, Richard, 239
Catalans, 54
Cattle Acts, 14
Chamberlayne, Edward, *Angliae Notitiae*, 36–7
Charles I, 4–5, 9, 13, 18, 40, 96, 255, 256, 257, 258,
    259–60, 262, 274
    Answer to the Nineteen Propositions, 40, 41
    Swift, 'Sermon upon the Martyrdom
        of King Charles I', 9
Charles II, 14, 37–8
Charleton, Arthur, 10
Chetwode, Knightley, 170
Church of England, 8, 68, 83, 98, 105, 272
Church of Ireland, 4, 8, 16, 83, 241, 266
Churchill, Sarah, 64
Cicero
    De Amicitia, 145–6
    De Officiis, 228
Civil Wars, 13, 33, 40, 47, 64, 256–7,
    258–9, 260, 264, 267
Clarendon, Edward Hyde, Earl of, 256, 257,
    258, 263, 264
    *History of the Rebellion and Civil Wars in
        England*, 4, 5–6, 256
Clements, Nathaniel, 225, 227, 236, 239
Clements, Theophilus, 225, 226, 227, 232, 236, 242
Coghill, Hester, 243
Coghill, Marmaduke, 225, 226, 227, 228,
    229, 233, 234–5, 236, 237, 238, 239,
    240, 241, 242, 243
Coke, John, 154
Collins, Anthony, 3, 17–18, 20, 21
    *Discourse Concerning Ridicule and Irony in
        Writing*, 17–18
    Discourse of Free-Thinking, 18, 21
Commonwealth, 13
Confederate Catholics of Ireland, 261, 263, 264
Conolly, William, 222–43 *passim*
Coughlan, Patricia, 282
Covenanters, Scottish, 4, 10, 17 *See also* Solemn
    League and Covenant
Cowper, William, first Earl, 55
Cox, Sir Richard, 261, 262, 265, 283
    *Some observations on the present state
        of Ireland . . .*, 229
Craftsman, 60, 61, 201
Craik, Sir Henry, 208
Cromwell, Oliver, 13, 20, 69, 256, 257, 258, 263,
    265, 266, 283
Curll, Edmund, 58

Daniel, Samuel, *Collection of the History of
    England*, 278
Dante Alighieri, 173
Darlington, Countess of, 57
Davenant, Charles
    'Danger of Appealing to the People from their
        Representatives in Parliament', 41
    Essays, 177
Davies, Sir John, 278
    Discoverie of the State of Ireland, 277
Davis, Herbert, 55, 87, 185, 208
Declaratory Act (1720), 222, 230, 231, 285
Defoe, Daniel, 31, 33, 34, 35, 38, 42, 44, 47, 181
    Hymn to the Pillory, 21
    Jure Divino, 38
    Legion's Memorial, 38, 44, 45, 179, 180
    *Original Power of the Collective Body of the
        People of England*, 38
    Review, 39
    Shortest-Way with the Dissenters, 12, 21
    True-Born Englishman, 38
Delany, Mary, 239
Denham, Sir John,
    Coopers Hill, 5
    'On Mr Abraham Cowley', 119, 146, 193
Derrida, Jacques, *The Politics of Friendship*,
    140, 142, 144–5, 155
Devonshire, Duke of, 177
Dingley, Rebecca, 150
Dissenters, Dissent, 8, 9, 12, 18, 20, 45,
    231, 256, 260
Dobbs, Arthur, *Essay on the trade and
        improvement of Ireland*, 236
Dodwell, Henry, *An Epistolary Discourse*, 106–9
Donne, John, 148, 149
Doody, Margaret Anne, 147, 153, 155
Dorset, viceroy, 236
Dowling, William, 150
Drake, James,
    *Memorial of the Church of England, Humbly
        Offer'd to the Consideration of all True
        Lovers of Our Church and Constitution*, 12
Dryden, John, 19, 20, 211, 212
    'Discourse Concerning Satire', 211
Dublin Society, 235, 236, 240, 241
Dublin workhouse, 236, 237
Dundee, John Graham, Viscount, 12, 13
Dunkirk, 121, 124–5, 132

Eachard, John, 21
    *Grounds and Occasions of the Contempt
        of the Clergy and Religion Enquired
        into*, 20
East India Company, 16, 71
Eddy, William Alfred, 83

Edinburgh Review, 273
Ehrenpreis, Irvin, 205, 206
Elector's Right Asserted, The, 36–7
Eliot, T. S., 186, 189
    Little Gidding, 189
    'Morning at the Window', 190
    Poems, 190
    Prufrock and other Observations, 190
Elizabeth I, 263
Emmet, Robert, 187
English Pale, 262, 264, 270, 271, 282
    See also Old English
Erasmus, Desiderius, 145
Eton, 52
Exchequer Bills, 72–4

Fairfax, Sir Thomas, third Lord, 260
Farrington, Brian, 200
Faulkner, George, 60, 165, 185, 191, 192, 208, 209
    Dublin Journal, 209
Feiling, Keith, 179
Feingold, Richard, 151, 153
Fielding, Henry, 199
    Tragedy of Tragedies, 191
Fielding, Isaac, 129
Filmer, Sir Robert, 13, 34, 178
Firth, Sir Charles, 58
Flaubert, Gustave, *Madame Bovary*, 188
Flynn, Carol Houlihan, 156
Ford, Charles, 64, 69, 165
Forfeitures Resumption Act (1700), 231, 232
Fox, Christopher, 5
*Foxes and Firebrands, or, A Specimen of the
    Danger and Harmony of Popery and
    Separation*, 20
Friend, John, *Account of the Earl of Peterborow's
    Conduct in Spain*, 134

Gadbury, Job, 85, 96, 104
    *Ephemeris: Or, A Diary Astronomical,
    Astrological, Meteorological, for the Year of
    our Lord, 1708*, 96, 98
Gadd, Ian, 120, 121
Gaelic (native, 'Old') Irish, 261, 262, 263, 264,
    270, 271, 272, 274, 282–4
Galway, Henri de Massue de Ruvigny,
    Earl of, 223
Gardiner, Luke, 225, 227, 232, 236, 237, 239, 243
Gaskell, Philip, 120
Gay, John, 61, 62, 66, 68, 172
    Beggar's Opera, 118
    Fables, 203, 204
George I, 3, 60, 63, 64, 103, 225, 230
George II, 4, 60, 61, 64, 170, 236
Glencoe massacre, 13

Godolphin, Sidney, 12, 53, 55, 56, 62
Goldgar, Bertrand A., 120, 129, 132
Gore, Sir Ralph, 223, 225, 226, 227, 232, 236, 237,
    238, 241
Governors of St Patrick's Hospital, 209
Grafton (lord justice), 223
Greville, Fulke, 154–5, 195
    Life of Sidney, 154
Grub Street, 118, 121, 125, 127
Guardian, 132. *See also* Swift, Jonathan, *Importance
    of the Guardian Considered . . .*

Halifax, Charles Montagu, Lord, 42, 177
Halley, Edmund, 88
Hamilton, Gustavus, Major-General, later
    Lord Hamilton and Viscount Boyne,
    224, 227, 232, 233, 236, 239
Hamilton, James, Lord Limerick, 235
Harding (printer), 127
Harley, Edward, second Earl of Oxford, 15, 71
Harley, Robert, first Earl of Oxford and
    Earl Mortimer, 9, 53, 55, 56, 57, 63,
    64, 65, 66, 67, 68, 69, 72, 73, 103, 129,
    176, 179, 181
Harrison, William, 119
Hawkesworth, John, 208
Hayward, John, 190
Henry II, 263, 272, 278, 279–81, 284, 287
Henry VIII, 257
Herbert, George, *The Temple*, 'Love III', 147–9,
    150, 151
Hervey, John, Lord, 74
    Answer to the Occasional Writer, 59
Heylyn, Peter, *Aërius Redevivus: or The History of
    the Presbyterians*, 18
Higden, William, 14
Higgins, Francis, 8
Higgins, Ian, 258
Hill, Jack, General, 121
Hobbes, Thomas, 40
Homer, *Odyssey*, 174
Hooker, John, 282
Howard, Henrietta, Countess of Suffolk, 57, 61,
    64, 165
Hue and Cry after Daniel Foe, 123
Hue and Cry after Dr. Swift, 123
Huguenots, 18–19
Hume, David, 36–7
Hutchinson, Francis, bishop, 235
Hyde, Edward, Earl of Clarendon.
    See Clarendon, Edward Hyde, Earl of

Interregnum, 256
Irish national bank, 232, 234
Irish Catholics, 261

Irish Protestants, 261
Irish Test, 62

Jacobite Rebellion, Jacobitism, 3, 8, 10, 11, 12, 13,
    45, 170, 233, 261, 263, 266
James I, 261, 277
James II, 8, 9, 11, 12, 20, 87, 88, 105, 256, 259, 283
Jarry, Alfred, *Ubu roi*, 202
Jeffrey, Sir Francis, 172, 173, 273, 274
Jerome, Saint, 145
Johnson, Esther ('Stella'), 7, 10, 121, 124, 128, 131,
    146–7, 149–50, 151–4, 155, 156, 162–3
    Journal to Stella, 117, 118–19, 121, 128–9,
        134, 150
    'Stella's Birthday', 143, 162–3, 166, 171
Johnson, Maurice, 208
Johnson, Samuel, 117, 134, 144–5, 155, 179
    Lives of the Poets, 116–17, 137
Johnston, Denis, 208
Jonson, Ben, 207
Joyce, James, *Ulysses*, 200
Juvenal, 211, 212

Kendal, Ermengarde Melusina, Duchess of,
    57, 58, 63
Kennet, White, Bishop, 15, 16
Kentish Petition, ch. 2 *passim*, 32, 33–5, 38, 45,
    177–9, 180
Kierkegaard, Søren, 154
King, Sir Peter, 54
King, William, Archbishop of Dublin, 8, 9,
    226, 231
    State of the Protestants of Ireland, 12
King's College, Cambridge, 52
Knowles, Mary, 144–5
Kristeva, Julia, 149

Ladies Diary: or, The Womens Almanack, 94–5
La Rochefoucauld, François, duc de, 119, 145
Lattimore, Richmond, 187
Laud, William, Archbishop of Canterbury,
    4, 20, 22, 256
Laurence, John, *A new system of agriculture*, 235
Lechmere, Nicholas, 54
Lecky, W. E. H., 141
Leopold I, 176
Leslie, Charles, 12, 13, 17, 20, 179–82
    *New Association of the Modern Whigs
        and Fanatics*, 44–7, 180–1
    Rehearsal, 17, 45, 179–80
Leslie, John, Bishop of Raphoe, 20
Leslie, Robert, 206
L'Estrange, Roger, 19–20, 123
    Dissenters Sayings, 19–20
    Observator, 20

Lewis, Erasmus, 73
'Light to the Blind' (anonymous), 263
Lilburne, John, 36
Lindsay, Thomas, Bishop, 6, 9
Linen Act (1711), 236
Linen Board, 235, 236, 237, 241
Locke, John, 11, 14, 31, 33, 35, 36–7,
    38, 39, 44, 47
    Two Treatises of Government, 31, 33, 34, 37,
        39, 44, 45
Louis XIV, 32, 176, 233
Lowe, N. F., 87
Luce, J. V., 208
Ludlow, Edmund, 257

Macaulay, Catherine, 34
McCausland, Robert, 238
McGee, Alexander, 210
Mackworth, Sir Humphrey, 35, 41, 45
    *Vindication of the Rights of the Commons of
        England*, 39–41
Mahony, Robert, 209
Manley, Delarivier, 119
    Comment on Hare's Sermon, 119
Manley, Isaac, 91, 99, 225, 226, 227, 232,
    236, 237, 238
Marlay, Thomas, 225, 227, 232, 236, 237, 238
Marlborough, John Churchill, Duke of, 53, 55,
    56, 62, 69, 102, 125, 127
Marvell, *Horatian Ode*, 210
Mary I, 257
Mary II, 11, 231
Masham, Abigail, Lady, 64, 121
Maxwell, Henry, 225, 226, 227, 228, 232, 233–4,
    235, 236, 237, 238, 240
Mayhew, George, 81, 97, 98, 99
Mercurius Aulicus, 19
*Mercurius Rusticus: or, The Countries Complaint
    of The Barbarous Outrages Begun in the
    Year 1642, by the Sectaries of this late
    flourishing Kingdom*, 19
Memoirs of Captain John Creichton
    (Swift 'ghost writer'), 13
Midleton, Viscount. *See* Brodrick, Alan
Milbourne, Luke, 7
Milton, John, 106, 211
    Samson Agonistes, 176
Molesworth, Robert, Viscount, 14, 127, 240
Molineux, William, 14
Molyneux, Tom, 200, 230
Monmouth rebellion, 226
Montaigne, Michel de, 145, 146
Montrose, James Graham, Marquess of, 6
Morgan, Henry, Captain, 15
Morphew, John, 123

Motte, Benjamin, 58, 72, 73, 165
Moxon, Joseph, *Mechanick Exercises*, 123
Mr Partridge's Answer to Esquire Bickerstaff's
    Strange and Wonderful Predictions for the
    Year 1708 (anonymous), 90, 91–2, 99

Nalson, John, 20
Native Irish. *See* Gaelic Irish
Navigation Acts, 234
Navigation Board, 235, 236, 237, 238, 241
Nelson, Robert, *A Companion for the Festivals*
    and Fasts of the Church of England, 98, 99
New English, 261, 264, 266, 271, 272, 282–4
    See also English Pale; Old English
Neynoe, the Reverend Philip, 58
Nietzsche, Friedrich, 167
Nottingham, Daniel Finch, Earl of ('Dismal'),
    53, 55, 62, 124–5, 127
Nutt, John, 178

O Neal or O'Neill, Sir Phelim, 262
Oates, Titus, 123
Old English, 262, 263, 264, 265, 266,
    270–2, 282–4. *See also* English Pale
Old Irish. *See* Gaelic Irish
Oldisworth, William, 20
Ormond, James Butler, first Duke of, 262, 263
Ormond, James Butler, second Duke of, 10, 16
Orrery, Roger Boyle, first Earl of, 14, 166, 209
Oxford, Earl of. *See* Harley, Robert, first Earl of
    Oxford and Earl Mortimer

Painter, William, *Palace of Pleasure*, 210, 211
Pale. *See* English Pale
Palmer, Patricia, 282
Pancier, Andrew, 58
Parker, George, 83, 96
    Parker's Ephemeris, 96, 98
Parker, Sir Thomas, 54
Parnell, Charles Stewart, 141
Parry, Benjamin, 225, 226, 229, 232, 236,
    237, 238
Partition Treaties, 176–7, 179–82
Partridge, John, 81 *passim*
    Almanac for ... 1715, 103
    Almanac for ... 1716, 104
    'Answer to an Horary Question ...', 107
    Mene Tekel, 87–8
    Merlinus Liberatus, 83, 84, 87, 93–4, 95, 96–7,
        100–1, 104–5, 105–6
    Merlinus Redivivus, 101–3
    Squire Bickerstaff Detected, 109
Paul II, Pope, 3
Paulson, Ronald, 153–4
Pearce, Edward Lovett, 239

Perceval, John, Viscount, later Earl of Egmont,
    229, 234, 235
Peterborough, Charles Mordaunt, Earl of, 14, 172
Petty, Sir William, 261
Phillips, Marmaduke, 165
Phipps, Sir Constantine, Lord Chancellor, 226
Pilkington, Matthew, 62
Pitt, William, the elder, 68
Pittis, William, 91
Platina, Bartolomeo, *Vitae Pontificum*, 3
Plato, *Symposium*, 142–3
Police Gazette, 123
Ponsonby, Brabazon, first Earl of Bessborough,
    225, 227, 232, 236, 237, 239
Pope, Alexander, 52, 61, 117, 120, 143, 155, 165,
    166, 172, 190, 192, 193, 194–5, 197, 198,
    205, 210, 221, 266
    Dunciad, 118, 199
    Eloisa to Abelard, 151
    Epilogue to the Satires, 193
    Epistle to a Lady, 150
    Epistle to Augustus, 194, 195
    Epistle to Dr Arbuthnot, 117, 189
    'Epistles of Morality', 194
    Imitation of the *First Satire of the Second*
        Book of Horace, 193
    'Mary Gulliver to Captain Lemuel
        Gulliver', 171
    Translation of *Iliad*, 119
Popery Act (1704), 231
Portland, Earl of, 255
Poynings' Law, 224, 230, 232, 233
Presbyterianism, 8, 18, 20, 22, 95, 238, 256, 259,
    260, 264, 266
    Scots, 3, 4, 5–6, 7, 9–10, 11, 12, 13, 16, 17,
        20, 21, 256
Pretender, the. *See* Stuart, James Francis Edward
Price, Arthur, Bishop, later Archbishop, 225, 236,
    239, 243
Printing Act, 93
Prior, Matthew, 103
Prior, Thomas, 235, 236
    List of absentees ..., 238
Probyn, Clive, 142, 143, 144, 146
Pulteney, William, later Earl of Bath, 59, 62,
    68, 69, 74
Punch, 199, 200, 204
Puritans, 257, 259, 260

Quakers, 20, 45
Quintana, Ricardo, 284, 287

Reilly, Hugh, *Ireland's Case Briefly Stated*,
    262–3
Restoration, 20, 40, 259, 260, 262, 265

Revolution of 1688, 8, 9, 11, 12, 13, 14, 32, 33, 34, 42, 230, 256
Richardson, Samuel, 145
Rochester, John Wilmot, Earl of, 207
Rome, 42, 43, 44, 46
Rose, Henry, 225, 227, 232, 235, 236, 237
Roundheads, 17
Rousseau, Jean-Jacques, 37
Russell, William, Lord, 103
Ryswick, Treaty of, 32, 176
Ryves, Bruno, Dean of Windsor, 19

Sacheverell, Henry, 8, 14, 53, 54
Sacramental Test, 6, 8, 9–10, 14, 16, 19, 223, 256, 259
Said, Edward, 141, 142, 146
St John, Henry. *See* Bolingbroke, Henry St John, Viscount
St Patrick's Cathedral, Dublin, 10, 185, 208, 210
Sandford, Henry, 225, 232, 236, 237, 238
Sawbridge, Dr Thomas, 15, 16
Schoenfeldt, Michael, 148, 149
Schomberg, Duke of, 209
Scott, Temple, 208
Scott, Walter, 172
Scriblerians, 118
Scythians, 17
Shaftesbury, third Earl of, 233
Shakespeare, William, 199
Shelburne, Lord, *Some Free Thoughts upon the present State of Affairs*, 65
Sheridan, Thomas, 61, 144, 203, 204, 208
Intelligencer, 203
Shippen, William, 71, 74
Sidney, Algernon, 14, 38, 39
Sidney, Sir Philip, 147, 155, 156, 195
See also Greville, Fulke
Singleton, Henry, 225, 226, 227, 230, 236, 237, 238, 239, 243
Sitwell, Edith, 193
Socinians, 20, 45
Socrates, 141, 142, 154
Solemn League and Covenant, 4, 10, 17, 256
Somers, John, Lord, 31–2, 33, 39, 42, 44, 45, 47, 70, 177
Jura Populi Anglicani, 34, 35, 36–7, 41, 44
Somerset, Elizabeth Seymour, Duchess of, 64
South, Robert, 20
South Sea Bubble, 57, 70, 71
South Sea Company, 66, 71
Southwell, Edward, 235
Spanish Succession, War of the, 72, 85–6, 93, 176–7, 181
Sparta, 42, 46

Spencer, Charles. *See* Sunderland, Charles Spencer, third Earl of
Spenser, Edmund, 17, 278, 282
Epithalamion, 148
View of the Present State of Ireland, 277–8
Stamp Act, 121
Stanhope, James, 54, 68, 233
Stationers' Company, 93
Steele, Sir Richard, 53, 54, 83, 117, 120, 132–3, 144
Importance of Dunkirk Consider'd . . . , 132–3
Spectator, 109, 119
Tatler, 83, 101, 106–9, 118–19
Stella and Vanessa, 150
Sterne, Laurence, 155
Stratford, William, 71
Stuart, James Francis Edward, 'James III' or 'the Pretender', 10
Stuart, House of, 39, 40, 94, 96
Sunderland, Charles Spencer, third Earl of, 42, 55, 68
Swift, Jonathan
    Colonialism, 15–17, 270 *passim*
    Dean of St Patrick's Cathedral, Dublin, 10
    Dissenters, 5, 7, 8, 21, 22
    'dominatio plebis', 43
    Epitaph, 185, 287 *passim*,
    Family, 19, 53, 257, 265
    in Antrim, 7, 8
    in London, 3
    Irish nationalism, 273–4, 286, 287
    Johnson, Esther ('Stella'), 7, 10, 117, 118–19, 121, 124, 128, 131, 146–7, 151–4, 155, 156, 162–3, 169
    Last Will and Testament, 163, 185, 208–12, 243
    Ordination, 53
    Reformation, 22
    Return to Dublin, 56
    Revolution of 1688, 8, 41
    'Scotophobia', 5–6
    Temple, Sir William, 8, 32, 53, 178, 209, 255, 278
    Trinity College, 53, 209
    Vanhomrigh, Esther ('Vanessa'), 155
    'Vengeance Ecclesiastique', 3–4, 7, 22
    Vicar of Laracor, 33
    Visits court of William III, 255–6
    Walpole, Sir Robert, 3–4, 14 Ch 3 *passim*
    Wogan, Charles, Chevalier, 22, 195, 266
    Wood, William, 56–7, 172, 194, 222, 242, 261, 286
    Abstract of the History of England, 278–81
    Accomplishment of the First of Mr. Bickerstaff's Predictions, 89
    'Account of the Court and Empire of Japan', 3, 60

Swift, Jonathan (cont.)
  'Author upon Himself', 54, 191, 192
  Autobiography, unfinished, 255, 257
  Bickerstaff Papers, 81–109 *passim*,
  'Causes of the wretched Condition
    of Ireland', 285
  'Character of Sir Robert Walpole', 61
  Conduct of the Allies, 53, 54, 63, 66, 67, 68,
    116–17, 134–6
  'Description of the Morning', 190
  Dialogue upon Dunkirk, 121, 125–7
  'Directions for a Birthday Song', 61
  Directions to Servants, 167
  *Discourse of the Contests and Dissensions
    between the Nobles and the Commons in
    Athens and Rome*, 31–2, 33, 35, 39, 41–4,
    46, 47, 68, 176, 178–9, 181
  *Discourse to Prove the Antiquity of the English
    Tongue*, 172
  Drapier's Letters, 14, 16, 32, 56, 57, 62, 63, 127,
    136, 140, 141, 172, 191, 205, 222, 242–3,
    261, 273, 286
  Dunkirk Still in the Hands of the French, 121
  Elegy on Mr. Partridge, 90
  *Enquiry into the Behaviour of the Queen's Last
    Ministry*, 65–6, 70
  Epistle to a Lady, 62, 193–4, 200, 201, 204,
    205, 211
  *Examination of Certain Abuses, Corruptions,
    and Enormities in the City of Dublin*,
    169–71
  Examiner, 17, 19, 20, 32, 53, 119, 134–6, 171
  'Famous Prediction of Merlin', 123
  'Further Thoughts on Religion', 32
  Gulliver's Travels, 10, 15–17, 32, 58–9, 64, 66,
    70, 71, 72, 73, 74, 141, 165–6, 168–9,
    170–1, 173, 174, 190, 195, 196, 201, 205,
    206, 274–7, 278–9, 280, 281, 284, 286–7
  History of the Four Last Years of the Queen,
    54–5, 55–6, 67, 68
  Hue and Cry after Dismal, , 121–3, 124, 127, 136
  'Humble Petition of Frances Harris', 90
  Importance of the Guardian Considered . . .,
    127, 132–4
  Intelligencer, 61
  It's Out at Last, 121, 125
  Journal to Stella, 117, 118–19, 121, 128–9, 134, 150
  Last Will and Testament, 185
  Legion Club, 162, 171, 173–6, 179, 182, 207
  Letter Concerning the Sacramental Test, 10,
    21, 181
  *Letter from a Member of the House of Commons
    in Ireland to a Member of the House of
    Commons in England Concerning the
    Sacramental Test*, 6, 14

  Letter from the Pretender to a Whig-Lord, 121, 127
  Letter to Bishop Thomas Lindsay (lost), 9
  Libel on Dr Delany, and a Certain Great Lord,
    61, 195, 205
  Mad Mullinix and Timothy, 200, 201–2,
    203, 205
  Memoirs of Captain John Creichton
    ('ghost writer'), 13
  *Mr Collins's Discourse of Freethinking Put
    into plain English, by way of Abstract
    for the Use of the Poor*, 18, 21
  Modest Proposal, 136, 168–9, 171, 195, 206,
    222, 274
  New Way of Selling Places at Court . . ., 127, 129
  'Ode to the Athenian Society', 123
  'Of Mean and Great Figures', 4
  '*Of those who have made a mean contemptible
    Figure*', 198
  '*Of those who have made great* Figures . . .',
    198, 258
  On False Witness, 89
  'On Mr. Pulteney being Put Out of the
    Council', 60
  'On Noisy Tom', 207
  On Poesy: A Rapsody, 62, 199
  'Peace and Dunkirk', 124
  Polite Conversation, 81, 167, 168
  Predictions for the Year 1708, 81, 86, 88, 89,
    97, 98, 99
  *Preface to the B[isho]p of S[a]r[u]m's
    Introduction To the Third Volume of the
    History of the Reformation of the Church
    of England*, 20
  Presbyterian's Plea of Merit, 259, 260
  'Progress of Patriotism: A Tale', 61
  *Proposal for the Universal Use of Irish
    manufacture*, 222, 285, 286
  Public Spirit of the Whigs, 32, 54, 120, 191
  *Reasons Humbly Offered to the Parliament of
    Ireland for Repealing the Sacramental
    Test*, 260, 262, 263, 264, 266
  Sentiments of a Church-of-England Man, 10–11,
    12, 13, 32
  Serious Poem upon William Wood, 57
  'Sermon upon the Martyrdom of King
    Charles I', 9, 82
  Short View of the State of Ireland, 5, 272
  *Some Advice Humbly Offer'd to the Members of
    the October Club . . .*, 127–9
  *Some Reasons to Prove That No Person is
    obliged . . .*, 127, 129–32
  'Stella's Birthday', 143, 162–3, 166, 171
  'Story of the Injured Lady', 95, 284–5
  Tale of a Tub, 17, 19, 20, 32, 83, 97, 98, 124,
    134, 165, 173, 195, 199, 204, 274

Battle of the Books, 19, 165, 174, 206
Mechanical Operation of the Spirit, 163–5, 171
'Thoughts on Religion', 258
'Thoughts on Various Subjects', 22
'Tim and the *Fables*', 203, 204
'Toland's Invitation to Dismal', 124
'Tom Mullinex and Dick', 202–3
'To Mr. Delaney', 143–4
'To Mr. Gay', 61
Traulus, 200, 205–6, 207
Verses on the Death of Dr. Swift., 4, 5, 117, 119, 142, 143, 145, 146, 153, 154, 155, 191, 192–3, 194, 195, 196–7, 201, 205, 211, 212
Verses said to be Written on the Union, 95
Vindication of Isaac Bickerstaff, Esq., 90, 92, 99, 104
'Virtues of Sid Hamet the Magician's Rod', 123
'W—ds—r Prophecy', 123
Swift, Thomas (grandfather), 257
Synge, Archbishop of Tuam, 256

Temple, Sir Richard, 56
Temple, Sir William, 8, 32, 209, 255, 259
Introduction to the History of England, 278
Letters, 32
Miscellanea, 32, 178
'Of Popular Discontents', 32
Test Act, 69, 83
Theobald, Lewis, 118
Tighe, Richard, 200, 202–3, 225, 227, 235, 236, 237, 238, 242
Tisdall, William, 256, 259
Tithe agistment, 173
Toleration Bill, 256
Tone, Theobald Wolfe, 273
Tonson, Jacob, 118
Tooke, Andrew, 165
Tooke, Benjamin, 20
Townshend, Charles, Viscount, 58
Traugott, John, 140–1, 141–2, 154
Trinity College, 53, 239
Trotter, Thomas, 225, 226, 227, 236, 237, 238, 239
Tutchin, John, 45
Tyrone, Earl of, 277

Ulster,
Linen industry, 14
Scots Presbyterians, 4, 16, 17, 259
Utrecht, Treaty of, 55, 64, 66, 70, 84, 86

Vanhomrigh, Esther ('Vanessa'), 155
Vendler, Helen, 147–8, 149, 150
Vesey, Agmondisham, 225, 226, 227, 232, 236, 237, 242

Vesey, John, Archbishop of Tuam, 11
Virgil, *Aeneid*, 173, 174
Voltaire (François-Marie Arouet), 199
Vonnegut, Kurt, 196, 197

Wales, Caroline, Princess of, 57
Walpole, Horace, 68, 155
Walpole, Sir Robert, 3–4, 14, 228, 229, 234, 239, Ch 3 *passim*, 226
Short History of the Late Parliament, 54, 66
Wellesley, Dorothy, 186
Wentworth, Peter, 54
Wentworth, Thomas, first Earl of Strafford, 4–5, 17, 20, 22
Wettenhall, Edward, Bishop, 11
Wharton, Thomas, Earl of, 53, 55, 62, 124, 127
Whiteway, Martha, 210
William the Conqueror, 278
William III, 8, 11, 12, 13, 31, 32, 64, 82, 103, 176, 177, 178, 231, 233, 255, 259, 283
Williams, Sir Harold, 55
Wilkes, John, 36
Winder, John, 11
Wogan, Charles, Chevalier, 22, 195
Wood, William, 56–7, 141, 172, 194, 222, 223, 232, 241, 242, 261, 286
Woolf, Virginia, 145, 149
Woollen Act, 14, 231
Woolley, James, 155
Worsley, Frances, Lady, 168
Wotton, William, 124
Observations on *Tale of a Tub*, 134
Reflections upon Ancient and Modern Learning, 124
Wyndham, Thomas, Baron, Lord Chancellor, 241
Wynne, Owen, Major, later Lieutenant-General, 225, 232, 236, 237

Yeats, John, the Reverend, 187
Yeats, W. B., 186–9, 190, 192, 193, 197–9, 202, 203, 211
'Blood and the Moon', 189, 190, 198
'Beautiful Lofty Things', 197, 198
'Circus Animals' Desertion', 189, 197, 200
'High Talk', 197–8, 200
'Introductory Rhymes', 187
'Swift's Epitaph', 187, 189
'Under Ben Bulben', 187, 188
Vision, A, 199
Wanderings of Oisin, 198
Words upon the Window-Pane, 186–7, 192
Young, Edward, 166